The Catholic Church
and Antisemitism
Poland, 1933–1939

Studies in Antisemitism

Series Editor Yehuda Bauer
Chairman, Vidal Sassoon International Center for the Study of Antisemitism
The Hebrew University of Jerusalem

Studies in Antisemitism brings together in one series major worldwide research on this complex phenomenon from which the student and decision-maker as well as the general public may learn. The studies cover antisemitism, ancient and modern, from a broad range of perspectives: historical, religious, political, cultural, social, psychological and economic.

Volume 1

The Catholic Church and Antisemitism
Poland, 1933–1939
Ronald Modras

This book is part of a series. The publisher will accept continuation orders which may be cancelled at any time, and which provide for automatic billing and shipping of each title in the series upon publication. Please write for details.

Ronald Modras

The Catholic Church and Antisemitism Poland, 1933–1939

Published for the
Vidal Sassoon International Center
for the Study of Antisemitism (SICSA)
The Hebrew University of Jerusalem

by

harwood academic publishers
Australia • Canada • France • Germany • India
Japan • Luxembourg • Malaysia • The Netherlands
Russia • Singapore • Switzerland

First published 1994
Second printing 2000

Amsteldijk 166
1st Floor
1079 LH Amsterdam
The Netherlands

LIBRARY OF CONGRESS CATALOGING-IN-PUBLICATION DATA

Modras, Ronald E.
    The Catholic church and antisemitism Poland, 1933–1939 / Ronald Modras.
       p.   cm. -- (Studies in antisemitism)
    Includes index.
    ISBN 90-5823-129-1
    1. Antisemitism--Poland--History--20th century. 2. Catholic Church--Poland--History--20th century. 3. Catholic Church--Relations--Judaism--History--20th century. 4. Judaism--Relations--Catholic Church--History--20th century. 5. Christianity and antisemitism. 6. Poland--Ethnic relations. I. Title. II. Series.
DS146.P6M63   1994
261.2'6'09438--dc20   94-4488
                                    CIP

COVER DESIGN BY
Louise Burston

For Mary Elizabeth

Contents

Preface

More Catholics and more Jews lived side by side for more years in Poland than anywhere else in their histories. Before the frontiers of the First Polish Republic began to recede in 1772, an estimated four-fifths of the world's Jews lived within them. This was hardly surprising, since Jews had earlier been expelled from England (1290), France (1394), Spain (1492), Portugal (1497), and Hungary (1526). Blamed for epidemics like the Black Death (1347–1351), regularly harassed and persecuted in Germany and Bohemia, Jews came to Poland as a place of refuge. The climates of Western European might have been milder and the economies more diversified, but, in the opinion of Rabbi Moses Isserles in seventeenth century Kraków, it was "preferable to live on dry bread and in peace in Poland."

One of the most influential sages in all of Jewish history, Isserles interpreted the Hebrew word for Poland, *Polin,* to mean "here" (*poh*) there is "rest" (*lin*). Poland in the late middle ages had become what first Babylonia and then Spain had been earlier, the spiritual center of world Jewry and principal wellspring of its learning. Needless to say, the idea of a haven and spiritual center for Jews was hardly congruous with what would be a dominant Roman Catholic perspective on Poland, namely a bulwark of Western Christianity vis-à-vis Muslim infidels, Eastern Orthodox schismatics, and in this century Soviet atheists.

I have written this book to fill a gap and draw attention to the activity of the Catholic church at a critically sensitive time and place. The topic is controversial. Selective traditions of writing the history of Polish-Jewish relations have developed over the last several decades. Some Polish historians have tended to focus on the centuries when Poland was a haven for Jews. Jewish historians generally give much more attention to the twentieth century, when Nazi Germany transformed Poland into what is now for many Jews simply a cemetery. Of course, Poland is much more than that, especially now after the collapse of the communist empire which it helped to engineer. But even for those for whom the events of 1933 to 1945 are a source of profound personal loss, for Jews and Christians both, cemeteries are places that command respectful attention.

No nation suffered more under German occupation than Poland did. Three million Polish Jews and three million ethnic Poles died under the Nazi terror. Although World War II was fought conventionally on the western front, it was anything but conventional in Poland. Under ordinary rules of warfare, the killing of non-combatants ends with surrender. In Poland the killing of unarmed civilians increased with pacification. Poland was filled, in Richard L. Rubenstein's apt and insightful phrase, with "surplus populations."

In the Nazi hierarchy of races, the Poles, like all Slavic peoples, were classified as *Untermenschen* (sub-humans), fit only to be slaves (*Slaven* = *Sklaven*) for the *Herrenvolk*. Obviously the Reich did not need more than twenty million slaves to work its factories, mines, and quarries. The surplus Polish population was marked for programmatic reduction by way of overwork, starvation, and, beginning with potential leaders of a resistance, more systematic measures. Poland's more than three million Jews, the largest Jewish community in Europe, were even less than sub-human according to the Nazi taxonomy. Designated as inhuman, disease-ridden vermin, they were not only "not worthy of life" but a mortal danger to the rest of Europe, fit only for extermination.

Auschwitz was the ultimate outcome not only of engineering and modern bureaucratic routine, but of a racist ideology that saw state-sponsored genocide as an *Endlösung* or "Final Solution." The phrase is often used today without advertence to the fact that solutions are answers to problems or questions. Before there was a "Final Solution," there was—not only for Nazis but for Christians throughout Europe, especially for conservative Catholics, and even for Jews who succumbed to the prevailing ideology—a "Jewish question."

This book is largely an exercise in retrieval. It seeks to recover an era made distant not only by the passage of over fifty years but by the horrific events of World War II, the Holocaust, and the Cold War. Substantial historical research and reflection has been brought to bear on the *Shoah,* the destruction of Europe's six million Jews. Less attention has been given to the years immediately prior to it. This book attempts to recall that period in European, specifically Polish history, when Jews constituted a "question." It also reappraises and rejects the commonplace assumption that the church's traditional "teaching of contempt" (Jules Isaac's term) was of peculiar significance for the Polish church. There was more to the "Jewish question"for traditionalist Catholics than seeing Jews as rejected by God for their supposedly singular responsibility for the death of Jesus.

In interwar Poland as elsewhere in Catholic Europe, the "Jewish question" was seen as largely originating in 1717. Catholic theologians found it striking that Providence seemed to unleash Satan at two-hundred year intervals: first 1517, then 1717, and most recently 1917. Readers with a sense of history will recognize 1517 as the onset of the Protestant Reformation, and 1917 as the year of the Bolshevik revolution. But 1717? Most reflection on the 1930s and the "Jewish question" ignores or gives short shrift to the founding of the Grand Lodge in London and the organization of modern Freemasonry in 1717.

The notion of a sinister alliance between Freemasons and Jews to subvert traditional European society originated in Germany but first flourished in France, where it played a conspicuous role in the turn-of-the-century Dreyfus Affair. *"Juden und Freimauer"* was a battle-cry for the German right wing, as it was for Hitler in his rise to power. Although a staple of the antisemitic arsenal of the 1930s and closely connected with the notorious *Protocols of the Elders of Zion,* the idea of a Masonic-Jewish alliance has been largely forgotten today, neglected even by writers on Christian-Jewish relations and the Holocaust.

The enormously important book by Jacob Katz, *Jews and Freemasons* (1970), has not had the impact on scholarship that, in my opinion, it deserves. Hans Küng, in his imposing and virtually encyclopedic work on Judaism and Jewish-Christian relations, *Judaism: Between Yesterday and Tomorrow* (1992), appears unaware of Katz's work on the significant role played by the mythic alliance. Even in its revised, updated edition, Edward Flannery's excellent history of Christian antisemitism, *The Anguish of the Jews* (1985), gives the alliance only brief notice. No author, to my knowledge, has expounded with any detail the connection of the supposed alliance with the Catholic church's century-long struggle against political liberalism. And yet this, my research reveals, was not only present but central to the efforts of the Polish hierarchy and clergy to create or preserve what they conceived of as a "Catholic Poland." Far from singular, their efforts, the literature also indicates, were merely one component in the broader Catholic polemic that saw Jews as agents of liberalism, associated with Masons to disestablish the church.

This is not a book about Poland. I am not a student of Polish history. My training has been that of a theologian, and, as an American Roman Catholic, I have spent much of my professional life studying and reflecting on the history and theology of the Roman Catholic church. Three of my grandparents came from Poland, however, and I have expended considerable time and effort toward understanding the historical stance of my church toward Jews. This is a book about one aspect of the Catholic church—in the 1930s, when Jews throughout Europe constituted a "question"; in Poland, where no other institution could claim an even comparable moral authority in forming popular attitudes and opinions.

I have limited my research almost exclusively to published works and to the years circumscribed by the Nazi rise to power and the German invasion of Poland. I have concentrated on Polish Catholic periodical literature to create a window on the public Catholic consciousness of that most Catholic nation. My research is based on some two-thousand pages of material, photocopied from virtually every important periodical published during those years under Catholic auspices. They were gleaned from thousands of pages more, perused for any significant reference to Jews, Judaism, or antisemitism. No one, of course, read all those periodicals. (In some instances I found myself opening journals previously uncut.) And it is methodologically impossible to determine the precise influence they had on their readers, let alone the broader Polish Catholic consciousness. But taken collectively they tell us not only what individual Catholic writers thought about Jews but what their readers, especially priests, were wont to think. They are indicative of the clerical mind-set at the time. How much influence the church's pulpit exerted on Catholics at the time is even more indeterminate, but it was hardly negligible.

In the analysis and presentation of my research, I allow my sources to speak for themselves, saving any extended moral assessment until the end. I have found it necessary, however, to place it in an historical context. No church in the Roman Catholic communion is an island. The church in Poland was the recipient of a tradition and part of a network, very much in union with the Holy See. I will also leave to the end any judgment whether or not it was out of step with the other Catholic churches of Europe when it came to antisemitism and the "Jewish question."

I came to this study inspired by the dedicated example of Dr. Joseph Lichten of the Anti-Defamation League of B'nai B'rith, a professional in Catholic-Jewish relations, a pioneer in Polish-Jewish relations. I came to it too after many years on the Advisory Committee to the U.S. National Council of Catholic Bishops' Secretariat for Catholic-Jewish Relations. It was, however, my participation in the Polish-American Jewish-American Council that most convinced me of the need for such a work. When I first approached the Jewish Community Council of Detroit to enter into dialogue with Polish-American representatives, I never imagined that the American Jewish Committee and Polish American Congress would raise that local interchange to the level of a national coalition. I am obliged to those who made it possible: Harold Gales, George Szabad, Leonard Chrobot, and David Roth.

More immediately my research was made possible by an initial grant from the Vidal Sassoon International Center for the Study of Antisemitism (SICSA) of the Hebrew University of Jerusalem, and a sabbatical granted by Saint Louis University, both of which allowed me to travel to libraries in Poland and Rome. Subsequent grants for research travel came from the National Endowment for the Humanities, the American Philosophical Association, and the Mellon Faculty Development Fund of Saint Louis University. A fellowship awarded by the Annenberg Research Institute (Philadelphia) allowed me to begin the analysis of my research, freed from my university teaching responsibilities.

I wish to acknowledge the helpful courtesy of the staffs of at the following institutions: in Rome the Polish Institute, the Polish College, and the Pontifical Center for Ecclesiastical Research; the Secret Vatican Archives; in Kraków the Jagiellonian University and the Jesuit College; the University of Warsaw; Yad Vashem in Jerusalem; Catholic University of America, Washington, D.C.; Saint Hyacinth Seminary-College (Granby, MA), home of the Maximilian Kolbe Archives; the Library of Congress; the New York City Library; the YIVO Institute (New York); and the library of Saint Louis University.

I wish to thank those colleagues and friends who read parts of this manuscript and offered their helpful and constructive criticism: Rabbi David Berger (Brooklyn); Dr. John Klier (London); Dr. Anthony Kosnik (Detroit); Dr. Francis Nichols (St. Louis); Dr. Harry Offenbach (St.

Louis); Dr. Kenneth Parker (St. Louis); Dr. Neal Pease (Milwaukee); Dr. Jose M. Sanchez (St. Louis); Mr. and Mrs. George and Shirley Szabad (Haverford), and Rabbi Sherwin Wine (Detroit). They are, of course, not responsible for its shortcomings. I am indebted to Mrs. Janice Harbaugh for her invaluable expertise and technical assistance in bringing this manuscript to completion, and to Ms. Alifa Saadya of the Vidal Sasson International Center for the Study of Antisemitism of the Hebrew University of Jerusalem for her skill and solicitude in editing it. Singular thanks go to my wife, Mary Elizabeth Hogan, for sitting with me in under-heated libraries and lending this enterprise her long-suffering support.

Ronald Modras
Saint Louis University

Chapter 1

Poland, Jews, and the Catholic Church: History and Context

Poland was already a state in 965/966, when Ibrahim Ibn-Jakub, a Moorish Jew, accompanied a Spanish embassy from Cordoba to Central Europe and described the dominions of Prince Mieszko, the warlord of the Polanie. It was the same year that Mieszko, with a wary eye on German ambitions, married the Czech princess Dubravka and embraced the Christian faith in its Roman rather than Byzantine expression. With that one, politically astute action, Mieszko aligned Poland's future with that of Western Europe, making it (with Hungary) the most eastern outpost of Western Christendom.

Prehistoric migrations had brought a series of tribal peoples to transverse and sometimes settle the fields between the Odra and Nysa rivers on the west and the Bug and later Dnieper rivers on the east: Scythians, Celts, Goths, and Slavs. One of those Slavic tribes, the Polanie ("field-dwellers" from the Slavic word for field, *pole*), settled the lands between the Odra and Vistula rivers by the seventh and eighth centuries C.E. From a union of tribes there evolved a national identity and culture that in 1634 made Poland the largest kingdom in all Europe. Written history tells of both immigrants and invaders coming to reside among the Poles and eventually making the Polish language and culture their own: not only other Slavic peoples but Armenians, Germans, Italians, Scots, Tartars, and Turks. It is not without irony that the writing of that history begins with the travel record of a Jew and the advent in Poland of the

Catholic church.[1]

From its very beginning, Poland's written history has been intertwined with that of the Catholic church in Poland. No less integral to that history, however, is the story of Poland's Jews, brought to a horrific end in this century by Nazi Germany and the Holocaust. While scholars have addressed these histories individually, more serious research is required into the relationship of the Catholic church and the Jewish community in Poland. This present study examines the last years of that relationship before the invasion of Poland and Hitler's war of extermination against the Jews. It demonstrates that Poland's Catholic leaders, in the 1930s as in previous centuries, shared the traditional thinking and attitudes of the church elsewhere in Europe and in the Catholic world. Loyalty to tradition and a habit of looking to the West were traits that had long characterized Poles. For the leaders of the Catholic church in Poland, that meant looking to Rome.

A History of Ambivalence

1. Jewish origins and autonomy

Judaism, like Christianity, came to Poland from the west.[2] Jewish

---

[1] For a general history of Poland in the English language, see: Oscar Halecki, *A History of Poland,* (New York: Roy, 1943); A. Gieysztor, S. Kieniewicz, E. Rostworowski, J. Tazbir, H. Wereszycki, *History of Poland,* 2nd ed., (Warszawa: PWN, 1979); Norman Davies, *God's Playground: A History of Poland,* 2 vols. New York: Columbia Press, 1982. Adam Zamoyski, *The Polish Way: A Thousand-Year History of the Poles and their Culture,* (New York/Toronto: Franklin Watts, 1988).

[2] For a succinct presentation of the most recent scholarship on the beginnings of Jewish settlement on Polish lands, see Aleksander Gieysztor in Chimen Abramsky, Maciej Jachimczyk and Antony Polonsky (eds.), *The Jews in Poland* (Oxford: Blackwell, 1984), 15–21. The bibliography on the millennial history of Jews in Poland is not unexpectedly immense. An overview is provided by Gershon David Hundert and Gershon C. Bacon, *The Jews in Poland and Russia: Bibliographical Essays,* (Bloomington, Indiana University, 1984. Convenient summaries are to be found by Haim Hillel Ben-Sasson, Ezra Mendelsohn, Stefan Krakowski, Isaiah Trunk, Sara Neshamith, and David Sfard in the *Encyclopedia Judaica* (New York: Macmillan, 1971). Among other notable works in English are: S.M. Dubnow, *History of the Jews in Russia and Poland,* Trans. by I. Friedlander (Philadelphia: Jewish Publication Society, 1946); Salo Wittmayer Baron, *A Social And Religious History of the Jews,* 2nd rev. ed., 18 vols. (New York: Columbia,

merchants may well have traveled across what would become Poland as early as the ninth century, thus antedating the advent of Christianity. Portentous of the future, the first written record we have of Jewish immigration relates to the first crusade, when anti-Jewish violence erupted across Western Europe. A Bohemian chronicle tells of Jews fleeing Prague for Poland in 1097/98. In an effort to escape persecution in the regions of the Rhine and Danube, Jews settled in Silesia, then as now in western Poland. According to a Polish chronicler of that period, Wincenty Kadłubek, bishop of Kraków, Prince Mieszko III (1173–1209) imposed heavy fines on Christians molesting Jews.[3]

The cities of Poland attracted not only Jews but large numbers of other foreigners, especially Germans who brought with them the so-called Magdeburg Laws. Adopted first in Silesia in 1211 and then elsewhere in Poland, they granted cities a large measure of autonomy, so that the burghers or city-dwellers evolved into a special class. The same became true for Poland's Jewish immigrants. By 1264 enough Jews had migrated to Poland to warrant legal provisions guaranteeing their rights and responsibilities to the Polish crown. Prince Bolesław V (the Pious) promulgated the celebrated Statute of Kalisz. Although modeled after similar charters issued a few years earlier in Austria, Hungary, and Bohemia, the Statute of Kalisz was far more comprehensive. It freed Jews from the jurisdiction of local magistrates or overlords. By conferring upon Jews the status of *servi camerae* (literally servants of the treasury or more simply tax-payers to the crown), it made them answerable only to the king or his deputy, with full protection of life and property.[4]

The Statute of Kalisz set no restriction on the amount of property Jews

---

1976), particularly vol. 16; Bernard D. Weinryb, *The Jews of Poland, A Social and Economic History of the Jewish Community in Poland from 1100 to 1800*, (Philadelphia: Jewish Publication Society, 1973); Thaddeus C. Radziałowski, "The Jews in Poland," *Perspectives* (1978/1979). Marian Fuks, Zygmunt Hoffman, Maurycy Horn, and Jerzy Tomaszewski, *Polish Jewry, History and Culture*, (Warsaw: Interpress, 1982); Isaac Lewin, *The Jewish Community in Poland, Historical Essays*, (New York, Philosophical Library, 1985); Harold B. Segal (ed.), *Poles and Jews: Myth and Reality*, (New York: Columbia University, 1986).

[3] Weinryb, *Jews of Poland*, 23.

[4] Lewin, *Jewish Community*, 38–53.

could acquire and no limits on their choice of occupation. It guaranteed them the right to travel, to keep what they had inherited, and to conduct business activities, specifically money-lending. In both civil and criminal proceedings, Jews were exempted from municipal jurisdiction, subject rather to the crown and its representatives, to whom any Christian accused of physically injuring a Jew was also answerable. Jewish oaths were recognized as evidence in these legal proceedings, and any testimony of a Christian against a Jew was recognized as evidence only if corroborated by a Jewish witness. The Statute furthermore forbade anyone to attack synagogues, Jewish cemeteries, or schools. Similarly outlawed was the harassment of Jewish merchants on the road or exaction of higher duties from Jews than from other merchants. Jewish children could not be forcibly baptized, and Jews who deserted their religion were bound to relinquish their inheritances. In addition to privileges guaranteed by earlier charters, the Statute made additional provisions, two of them particularly striking. Consistent with papal decrees, no Jew was to be accused of using Christian blood (the "blood libel") because, in the words of the Statute, "their law prohibits the use of any blood." And just as Christian townspeople were bound to help each other, if attacked at night, a Christian neighbor was required to help a Jew or else pay a fine.[5]

Originally promulgated in 1264 for the province of Great Poland (*Wielkopolska*), the Statute of Kalisz was confirmed four times for all the Polish kingdom by King Casimir the Great and expanded in 1453 by King Casimir IV. Jewish elders were invested with the authority to judge cases between Jews, and permission was granted for Jews to slaughter cattle according to ritual prescriptions (*shehita*). Polish Jews, in short, enjoyed the status of freemen. According to a 1457 document in Mazovia, they enjoyed the rights of the nobility (*jus nobilium*).[6] It was a condition obviously far superior to the masses of Poles who were enthralled to serfdom, and arguably the most humanitarian regulation of their status anywhere in late medieval Europe.

While exceptional for its liberality, the Statute of Kalisz was not singular to Poland. Utterly original and unique to Poland, however, was the Council of the Four Lands (*Vaad Arba Artzot*) which afforded Poland's Jews more autonomy than anywhere else in the entire history

---

[5] Lewin, *Jewish Community,* 49–50; Zamoyski, "Jews in Poland," 74.

[6] Weinryb, *Jews of Poland,* 35, 38.

of its diaspora. After a number of conflicts between the Jewish community and the Jewish tax-collectors appointed by the crown, King Zygmunt August II in 1551 granted Jews first in one province and then in others the right to elect their own leaders. Each Jewish community was entitled to elect their own rabbis and "lawful judges" to take charge of their spiritual and social affairs. This led to the creation in each Jewish community of a *kahal,* a body of elders (forty in large centers, ten in smaller towns) who governed the affairs of the local community. Entrusted to the *kahal* were such duties as administration of the synagogue, schools, and cemeteries, provision of kosher meat, and the settling of disputes within the community.

Out of these local bodies there grew conferences or assemblies of rabbis and *kahal* leaders, generally one a year in Lublin. Institutionalized by King Stefan Batory in 1581, the name of the annual assembly came to be fixed as the Council of the Four Lands, drawing as it did the Jewish leadership from all over Poland. Its primary task, from the crown's point of view, was to collect and deliver taxes from the Jewish communities to the royal treasury. But once the right to be governed by elected leaders was established, the cornerstone was laid for autonomy in other spheres of life as well. Functioning as a parliament, it not only allocated taxes for the king but regulated the entire economic life of the Jewish community, issuing regulations on matters ranging from bankruptcy to the allocation of rabbinical positions. It served as the official representative of all Jews in Poland through the *stadlan,* a special delegate who alone was authorized to intervene for Jews before the parliament or other offices. The authority of the Council was enforced by the crown. A Jew who ignored its commands faced not only excommunication by the Council (*herem*) but confiscation of property by the state. The autonomy afforded by the Council was enjoyed by Polish Jews for nearly two hundred years, until 1764 when, on the eve of its partitions, Poland became no more than a Russian protectorate.[7]

Throughout the medieval period Jews proved to be a valuable resource to the Polish kings and nobility, developing both crafts (fur-making, tailoring, tanning) and trade, local and long-distance (with Hungary, Turkey, the Baltic and Black Seas). The fourteenth and fifteenth centuries saw Jews prosper as merchants and middlemen. Wealthy Jews leased the

---

[7] See Maurycy Horn in Fuks et al., *Polish Jewry,* 15.

royal mint, salt mines, and the collection of customs and tolls. Jews from Grodno, for example, owned villages, manors, fish ponds and mills.[8] The most conspicuous success story was undoubtedly that of Abraham Esofowicz, who was elected to the nobility (*szlachta*) and made treasurer of Lithuania by King Zygmunt I. Before his elevation, he converted to Christianity, but his brother Michał remained a practicing Jew when he was elevated to the nobility (1525), a case without parallel anywhere in Christian Europe.[9]

2. Opposition: the church and the guilds

In stark contrast to Poland's secular princes in their treatment of Jews, were the princes of the church. Three years after the Statute of Kalisz, Guido, the papal legate to Poland, convened the Council of Wrocław (1267) to deal, among other things, with the issue of Jews. The resolutions of the Council simply affirmed and applied the canons of the Fourth Lateran Council, legislated earlier (1215) in Rome. Jews were ordered to live apart from Christians in separate sections of the city or village. The reason given for the segregation was that "Poland is a new plantation on the soil of Christianity," and there was reason to fear that its Christian population would "fall an easy prey to the influence of the superstitions and evil habits of the Jews living among them."[10] Other resolutions by the Council of Wrocław stipulated that Jews were to wear the peculiarly shaped hat *(cornutum pileum)* that distinguished them from Christians. Each town was to possess no more than one synagogue, and Jews were barred from collecting customs or duties or holding offices where Christians would be subordinate to them. Christians were forbidden to invite Jews to a meal, to eat or drink with them, or to serve Jewish households as servants, wet-nurses, or nursery-maids.[11]

The canons of Wrocław were reiterated at subsequent councils like that at Buda in Hungary (1279), attended by Polish ecclesiastics, and Łęczyca (1285). The Council of Buda decreed that Jews of both sexes were obliged to wear a ring of red cloth sewed to the upper left side of their

---

[8] Horn, in Fuks et al., *Polish Jewry,* 10.

[9] Zamoyski, *Polish Way,* 79.

[10] Dubnow, *History of the Jews,* 48.

[11] Dubnow, *History of the Jews,* 48–49.

garments and Muslims a similar, saffron-colored sign. In practice, none of these regulations was enforced by the secular authorities in Poland. The kings continued to encourage Jewish immigration, and by the end of the fifteenth century there were more than sixty Jewish communities in the united kingdom of Poland-Lithuania. In 1534 King Zygmunt I explicitly decreed that Jews need not carry any distinguishing mark on their clothing.

Life was not without its perils and difficulties for Polish Jews in the fourteenth and fifteenth centuries. There were anti-Jewish riots in Poznań (1390) and Kraków (1407), instigated principally by members of German guilds against their competition or by debtors eager to be free of their creditors.[12] Jews were also caught up in the church's campaign against the Hussite movement. The Council of Kalisz (1420), convened to counteract the Hussites, also reaffirmed the earlier anti-Jewish canons of Wrocław and Buda. When King Casimir IV ignored the canons and confirmed all the privileges and rights conferred on Polish Jews by his predecessors, Cardinal Zbigniew Oleśnicki of Kraków denounced the king's actions (1454). He urged the king to revoke the Jewish privileges and liberties as constituting "insult and injury" to the Christian faith.[13]

Cardinal Oleśnicki was also responsible for inviting to Kraków the Franciscan Friar, John of Capistrano, later canonized by the Roman Catholic church as a saint. Though his primary aim was to instigate popular rebellion against Hussites, Capistrano also preached incendiary sermons against Jews. After succeeding in having Jews banished from lower Silesia, ruled at that time by the Hapsburgs, he provoked similar anti-Jewish hostilities in Kraków and demanded that the king revoke the "godless" Jewish privileges. The king was finally forced to relent; initial defeats suffered by Polish forces against the Teutonic Knights were being interpreted by churchmen as divine punishment for favoring Jews. The king revoked the privileges but only for a time. Two years later he confirmed most of the Jewish charters, in his words, because of "the principle of tolerance, which is in conformity with God's laws."[14]

The traditional Roman Catholic attitude toward Jews was an ambiguous

---

[12] Harry M. Rabinowicz, *The Legacy of Polish Jewry* (London: Yoseloff, 1965), 19.

[13] Dubnow, *History of the Jews*, 62.

[14] Weinryb, *Jews of Poland*, 50.

mix of toleration and contempt. Unlike pagans and heretics (for whom conversion or extirpation was the choice, if there was a choice), Jews could be allowed to practice their religion. But, as formulated in the theology of Saint Augustine, they could be tolerated precisely as witnesses of the validity and superiority of Christianity. They were a people marked with the sign of Cain, forced to wander without a homeland, punished for their part in the death of Jesus and their refusal to accept him as the Messiah. This was the theological thinking behind the decree of the Polish church Synod of Piotrków (1542): "While the Jews are tolerated by the church in memory of the passion of our Savior, their numbers should be allowed to increase in but a very limited way." The Synod went on to allow Polish Jews to repair old synagogues but not build new ones. The prohibition itself was unremarkable, dating back to Roman times. More noteworthy is the fact that the sixteenth century Polish bishops did not harp on it in its synods and pronouncements. In general, beset by difficulties arising from the Protestant reformation, the Polish church at this time apparently considered the issue of Jews to be of relatively minor importance.[15]

The more forceful opposition to Jewish immigration at this time came not from the church but from the burghers who feared and resented the competition that was being generated by an influx of Jewish artisans and merchants. As a result, Jews in 1495 were ordered out of the center of Kraków but allowed to settle on the outskirts, in their own district of Kazimierz. By the sixteenth century more than twenty towns had obtained the *privilegia de non tolerandis Judaeis*. In practice the ban on Jewish residency was observed only inconsistently or altogether ignored. As in Kraków, separate suburbs or towns were formed and in some instances accorded analogous *privilegia de non tolerandis Christianis,* prohibiting Christian settlement.[16]

3. A haven for dissent

Even during the Counter-Reformation, when Jews in Germany often found themselves caught in the cross-fire between Catholics and Protestants, viewed by both sides as aligned with the enemy, Poland was

---

[15] Baron, *Social and Religious History,* 16:9-10.

[16] Horn, in Fuks et al., *Polish Jewry,* 12.

notable for its lack of internecine blood-letting. Between 1550 and 1650, when religious dissenters in England and Holland were being executed and when France underwent the Saint Bartholomew's Day massacre, Poland became a haven for more than Jews. For over a century, radical Protestants (unitarian Socinian Arians), who were tolerated no where else in Europe, were allowed to live in peace in Poland. When a papal envoy demanded that Poland's heretics be arrested and executed, King Zygmunt the Old (1506–48) responded: "Permit me to rule over the goats as well as the sheep." When his successor King Zygmunt August was asked to take sides between Catholics and Protestants, his equally celebrated response was: "I am not king of your consciences." Even the leader of the Counter-Reformation in Poland, Cardinal Stanisław Hosius, was fundamentally opposed to violence in dealing with religious dissent. Referring to Queen Mary I of England ("Bloody Mary"), he warned in 1571, "Let Poland never become like England."[17]

In the wake of the bloodletting in Western Europe, specifically the St. Bartholomew's Day massacre, the nobility were intent on preventing any such occurrences in Poland. In 1573 the Warsaw confederation of the electoral diet passed the so-called *pacta conventa*. Making explicit reference to Jews as well as other religious observances, it required that Poland's future kings safeguard religious freedom:

Since Turks, Armenians, Tartars, Greeks, and Jews not only sojourn in Poland but also reside there and (freely) move from place to place, they ought (undisturbed) to press their faiths, enjoy their liberties, and benefit, so to say, from the same rights of citizenship.[18]

This lack of fanaticism among the Polish nobility was not without its affect upon the Polish bishops as well. From time to time synods demanded implementation of the old canons regarding segregation, occasionally even complete exclusion from certain areas. But these resolutions carried little conviction and were not vigorously pursued. So half-hearted was the enforcement of the canons that a sizeable Jewish community was established even in Gniezno, the metropolitan see of the

---

[17] Zamoyski, *Polish Way*, 84, 89.

[18] Baron, *Social and Religious History*, 16:35.

primatial archbishops of Poland.[19]   The fact of the matter is that the
bishops came from precisely that segment of Polish society for whom the
Jews proved themselves most useful, the nobility.

Thanks to the special albeit self-interested protection of the nobility and
crown, Jews in Poland enjoyed more security than anywhere else in
medieval Europe. Rabbi Solomon Luria (1510–1573) praised the Polish
kings "who many times are kind to Jews and postpone for them the time
of tax payment." A contemporary who had studied in Poland and then
became a rabbi in Germany, Hayim ben Bezalel (1530–1588) wrote: "It
is known that, thank God, His people is in this land [Poland] not despised
and despoiled. Therefore a non-Jew coming to the Jewish street has
respect for the public and is afraid to behave like a villain against Jews,
while in Germany every Jew is wronged and oppressed the day long."
The celebrated Rabbi Moses Isserles (1520–1572) wrote: "Had not the
Lord left us this land as a refuge, the fate of Israel would have been
indeed unbearable. But by the grace of God, the king and his nobles are
favorably disposed toward us." In another context Isserles wrote to a
former student of his: "In this country there is no fierce hatred of us as
in Germany. May it continue until the advent of the Messiah."[20] Late
medieval Poland had become, in the words of a contemporary Jewish
scholar from Holland, a "second Palestine."[21]

The security described above was relative, of course, to the rest of
Europe. Jews as well as Protestants were often the victims of unruly
Catholic students being trained in Poland's Jesuit colleges. During the
sixteenth century increasing numbers of students were coming from
foreign lands to study at the Jagiellonian University in Kraków, one of
Europe's oldest. There and elsewhere, student attacks on Jewish districts
had led to major disturbances. When the Jews took defensive measures
against the students, their clerical teachers protested that the Jews were
beating up "innocent youngsters." Such accusations were dangerous,
especially in the case of students from noble families. Jewish
communities found it more prudent to buy off their would-be assailants
with a special tax (the *kozubalec*), the Polish equivalent of the

---

[19] Baron, *Social and Religious History*, 16:32, 90.

[20] Weinryb, *Jews of Poland*, 166.

[21] Rabinowicz, *Legacy*, 22.

Schülergeld collected from Jews in certain areas of Germany. This tax, paid to the rectors of local Catholic schools by several Jewish communities in Poland, did not, however, altogether preclude further harassment. The primary culprits appears to have been the Jesuits, frequently alluded to in the sixteenth and seventeenth century Jewish chronicles as "the black Jew-baiters."[22]

4. 1648: the Ukrainian uprising and Polish decline

There is no comparison, however, between student harassment and the devastation suffered by Polish Jews in 1648. Poland in the sixteenth century had become the granary of Europe. Fortunes were being made, especially by the magnates, nobles who owned vast tracts of land. Poland's monarchy had become elective and its Jews had passed from the jurisdiction of the crown to the nobles. These nobles made Jews their active and valued partners in their many economic enterprises, among them the colonization of the Ukraine. The interests of the magnates and Jews complemented each other. Glad to leave western Poland, Jews settled on huge estates in the east, where they could become the majority, even the whole population of a town or hamlet (*shtetl*). By 1648 there were 114 Jewish communities in the east.

Serving in the position of economic adviser and factotum to the nobility, Jews became the middlemen in the *arenda* system, leasing fixed assets (land, mills, inns, breweries, distilleries) and special rights (collecting taxes, duties). So far as the Byzantine orthodox Ukrainian peasants were concerned, Jews were the agents of the Roman Catholic nobles who were exploiting them, and it was the Jews, not the distant nobles,with whom the Ukrainians dealt directly. The situation exploded in 1648 when Jews especially were singled out for revenge in the uprising of Ukrainian peasants and cossacks commonly referred to as the Chmielnicki massacres.

The year which ended the Thirty Years' War for Germany was for Poland the beginning of almost uninterrupted wars, from 1648 to 1717, against Ukrainians, Russians, Swedes, Tartars, and Turks. Bohdan Chmielnicki led the 1648/49 revolt of cossacks and peasants against Poland with the intention of creating an autonomous Ukraine, whether

---

[22] See Weinryb, *Jews of Poland,* 130; Baron, *Social and Religious History,* 16:85; Dubnow, *History of the Jews,* 161.

under the Ottomans, Moscow, or Sweden, but in any case *Judenrein*. Both Jewish and Polish sources tell of cruel deaths and atrocities being inflicted on Jews and Catholics, men, women, and children alike. According to the most recent scholarly estimates, forty to fifty thousand Jews perished in the uprising, some twenty to twenty-five percent of Poland's total Jewish population.[23] Thousands more were forced to convert to Christianity to save their lives; still others surrendered to the Ukrainians' Tartar allies to possibly survive by being sold into slavery. Some of the Jews who escaped joined the Polish forces and fought against the cossacks as Jews had fought earlier (1610 and 1632) with the Poles against Moscow.[24] Jewish chroniclers described the Polish commanders sympathetically. Particularly singled out as a "friend of Israel" was Count Jeremy Wiśniowiecki to whom campaigns were ascribed solely for the purpose of avenging Jews. A case in which Poles surrendered Jews to the cossacks in order to save themselves is regarded as an aberration. Both the Jewish chroniclers of the 1660s and those of a hundred years later clearly identified with Poland and the Polish cause.[25]

Despite the destruction and loss of tens of thousands of lives, the recovery of the Jewish community from the uprising appears to have been surprisingly rapid. Survivors were numerous. Contrary to traditional Catholic practice, Jews who had embraced Christianity to save their lives were allowed by the king to revert to their practice of Judaism. Jews also appear to have rescued a considerable amount of their worldly possessions, entrusted to non-Jewish neighbors and friends.[26] Jewish resources were obviously strained, however, and records tell of individual Jews and Jewish communities borrowing money not only from individual Christians but from churches and monasteries.

The almost unremitting series of wars after 1648 left Jews and Poles alike the victims of spreading lawlessness and violence. The epidemic of witch-hunting that was sweeping western Europe at the time also infected Poland, resulting, it has been contended, in the deaths of thousands of

---

[23] Weinryb, *Jews of Poland,* 318.

[24] Horn, in Fuks et al., *Polish Jewry,* 16.

[25] Weinryb, *Jews of Poland,* 172-73, 200.

[26] Weinryb, *Jews of Poland,* 197.

innocent women.[27] For Jews the environment was ripe for a wave of accusations not so much of witchcraft as of host desecrations and ritual murder. Ever since the Protestant criticism of Catholic teaching and piety with respect to the Mass, Protestants and Jews alike had become likely game for allegations of profaning the blessed sacrament. As mentioned previously, the Polish kings had prohibited accusations of ritual murder as far back as the 1264 Statute of Kalisz, and in 1556 King Zygmunt August issued a sharp decree requiring that all such allegations be tried exclusively in the presence of the king or his delegate (hence not in an ecclesiastical court). Furthermore, no Jews could be convicted without the testimony of four reliable Christian witnesses and three Jewish witnesses. But the Pope at that time was Paul IV (1555–1559), the notorious anti-Jewish, former Grand Inquisitor, Gian Pietro Caraffa, who strongly supported prosecution of ritual murder accusations. The papal nuncios to Poland berated the Polish crown for moral laxity in obstructing their prosecution.

In the mid-eighteenth century, with a far different Pope in power, a spate of ritual murder accusations and an appeal to Rome by Polish Jews resulted in a critical censure of the Polish church. Clearly Poland was not quite deserving of the designation a recent Polish historian gave it of being a "state without stakes." But in contrast to western Europe, blood accusations in Poland rarely endangered entire communities, and only a "comparatively small" number if individuals were cited before the courts."[28]

The development of printing and concomitant increase of literacy witnessed a rise of anti-Jewish literature as well. Caricatures and satires were imported from Germany and translated into Polish. In imitation of the German models, Polish clerics began writing their own tracts, no longer in Latin but in Polish for popular consumption. Two of the most notorious pamphleteers, Sebastjan Mieczyński and Przesław Mojecki, accused Jews of murder, cruelty, and exploitation. They did not go without criticism of their demagoguery, however, and, despite the turbulence and sometimes anarchy of the times, records indicate that crimes against Jews did not go unpunished. Court documents also report cases in which nobles and even clergy-landowners appeared in court on

---

[27] A. Gieysztor, et al., *History of Poland,* 229.

[28] Baron, *Social and Religious History,* 16:88. See also 16:101.

behalf of "their" Jews.[29]

Contrary to the situation elsewhere in Europe, Christians in Poland, including higher ecclesiastics and monasteries, were often the creditors of Jews, especially after the Chmielnicki uprising. Church dignitaries were often nobles who owned their own private estates. Like other nobles they would lease lands to Jews, rent them houses, and sell them produce. Monasteries since the seventeenth century had also leased lands or lent money to Jews as long-term investments that would reap annual returns. With Jews as tenants, lease-holders, and guarantors of investment, Polish bishops and monasteries were more than interested in the well-being not only of "their" Jews but often of Jews generally. Despite the anti-Jewish tradition of Catholicism, these churchmen often intervened in court on behalf of Jews and sought to mitigate violent attacks on them.[30]

Along with general laxity in enforcing the ancient canons regarding Jews, this peculiar situation became widespread enough to attract the attention of the Holy See. In one of the earliest encyclicals to be written (1751), Pope Benedict XIV wrote to the Polish bishops on the subject of Jews and Christians living in the same places. He expressed concern that Jews in some cities and towns outnumbered Catholics. Among his bill of particulars: Jews had gained control of inns, bankrupt estates, villages, and public lands. They controlled the collection of public revenues and the sale of liquor and wine. As superintendents for the wealthy, Jews were "cruel taskmasters" who subjected poor Christian farmers to harsh labor and punishment. Jews were also employing Christians as their domestics. It was common for Christians and Jews to intermingle anywhere, the pope complained. And if Jews borrowed money from Christians using their synagogues as collateral, "they gain as many defenders of their synagogues and themselves as they have creditors." The pope reminded the bishops that the church had long forbidden these practices. He promised his energetic cooperation to help the Poles remove this "stain of shame." The bishops and clergy must themselves give good example to the rest of the nation by not hiring Jews or doing business

---

[29] Weinryb, *Jews of Poland,* 154.

[30] Weinryb, *Jews of Poland,* 131.

with them.[31]

Not without reason the turbulence of the era made its impact on the inner life of Polish Jews. The southeast in particular, Podole, where large numbers of Jews resettled after leaving the Ukraine, became a fertile breeding ground for sectarian movements. Besides the Hasidic movement in the person of the Baal Shem Tov (1700–1760), the region also gave rise to Jacob Frank (c. 1726–1791) and his following. Notorious among Poles as a charlatan, and among Jews as an apostate, Frank and his "conversion" became an excuse for antisemites in interwar Poland to cast doubts on the sincerity of all Jewish conversions to Christianity. Among the bizarre twists of Frank's career, the only point germane to consideration here is his rejection of the Talmud. Accusations against the Talmud by Frank and his followers led to a debate (1757) before Bishop Jan Dembowski of Kamieniec. The rabbinic defenders of the Talmud could not dissuade the bishop's court from finding the Talmud to be harmful. An ensuing book-burning of certain tractates was cut short only by the sudden death of the bishop, widely regarded by more traditionalist Jews as a miracle of retribution.[32] This traditionalist majority also produced a leading figure in the person of Elijah ben Solomon Zalmon (1720–1797). An inveterate opponent of Hasidic sectarianism, he mastered the Talmudic literature with an erudition that earned him the honorific title *Gaon* ("exalted") of Wilno (Vilna, Vilnius).

5. *Finis Poloniae?*

After entering into a constitutional union with Lithuania and becoming a republic with an elected monarchy (1572), Poland came with good reason to be called a commonwealth of nobles. Land, wealth and political power were concentrated in the hands of an oligarchy of magnates. They dominated the Sejm, Poland's parliament, and dealt with the Polish kings as with equals, each ruling over his estates like a princeling with his own "state within a state." Political life was effectively reduced to the ambitions and antagonisms of a few dozen families. Identifying the good of the nation with their own personal and class interests, they were assiduous in preserving their privileges, including the notorious *liberum*

---

[31] Claudia Carlen, I.H.M., *The Papal Encyclicals, 1740–1981*, 5 vols. (1981; reprint, Ann Arbor, MI: Pierien Press, 1990), 1:41–44.

[32] Weinryb, *Jews of Poland,* 256.

veto, whereby any single member of the Sejm had a right to obstruct passage of any piece of legislation.

From the very beginning of the elected monarchy, the nobles had been predisposed toward electing foreigners who could be more easily controlled. In 1697 they chose Friedrich-August of Saxony, and Poland entered into what is generally regarded as the most humiliating period of its history. A decline begun fifty years earlier with the cossack uprisings became a virtual free-fall.[33] Aristocratic self-interest and foreign opposition successfully frustrated all attempts at social and political reform. Precisely at a time when its neighbors had begun massive military build-ups, the Polish army, under the control of the magnates, began disarming. By promising to uphold the privileges of the nobility, Russia's Peter the Great had been able to bring sufficient numbers of magnates under his sway, so that by 1717 Poland became little more than a Russian protectorate. Both in Saint Petersburg and Berlin there began a systematic campaign of propaganda to the effect that the Poles were endemically anarchic and unable to govern themselves.

The last decades before the partitions saw genuine efforts by some of the nobility to bring about reform. Efforts were made in the Polish parliament to address the situation of both peasants and Jews after the massacres of Humań, another uprising of Ukrainian peasants (1768) in which Jews once again bore the especial brunt of the violence. Reformers urged the integration of Jews into Polish society by making them citizens.[34] The Sejm in 1775 granted tax exemptions to Jews who settled on uncultivated land and in 1792 accorded Jews the right of habeas corpus against illegal imprisonment. A year earlier the Sejm passed a liberal bill of rights enshrined in the Third of May Constitution; its first anniversary was celebrated by synagogues with services of thanksgiving.[35] But the more Poles tried to correct their situation, the more their powerful neighbors determined that nothing would change.

---

[33] The conservative gentry idealized economic decline with the principle that "Poland stands by lack of order." By serving the gentry in the *arenda* system, Jewish middlemen allowed them to live comfortably without giving up their principled condemnation of trade. See Hillel Levine, *Economic Origins of Antisemitism: Poland and its Jews in the Early Modern Period,* (New Haven: Yale, 1991).

[34] Gieysztor, *History of Poland,* 312.

[35] Horn, in Fuks et al, *Polish Jewry,* 18.

Their efforts at liberal reform simply became the excuses for Poland's dismemberment in the unprecedented partitions of 1773, 1793, and 1795 by Russia, Prussia, and Austria.

In reaction to the second partition, General Thaddeus Kościuszko led four thousand regulars and two thousand peasants in an insurrection against Russia. Among them were enough Jews to form a special Jewish regiment under the command of Colonel Berek Joselewicz, the first Jewish military unit in over 1,600 years. Kościuszko pointed to the Jewish participation as proof of the justice of the insurrection. But most magnates did not join in the effort, and Polish resistance found itself too heavily outnumbered. The failed insurrection resulted in the final and complete annihilation of Poland as a political entity. Prussia annexed the western regions, Austria annexed Galicia, and the core of Poland became a province of the Russian empire. Though it proved to be the end only of the First Republic, for anyone with reasonable expectations it certainly appeared to be *finis Poloniae*.

According to a sixteenth century Italian rhyme, pre-partitioned Poland was "heaven for the nobility, purgatory for city-dwellers, hell for the peasants, and paradise for the Jews." Despite its obvious exaggeration, there was a kernel of truth to the saying.[36] As much as any other nation, pre-partitioned Poland belied what has been described as "that lachrymose view of Jewish history which sees the fate of Jews in the Diaspora as a sheer succession of misery and persecution."[37] Poland was no paradise, but Jews were allowed to lead a tolerable, human existence, freer and, until the onslaught of uprising and invasion, more secure than anywhere else in Europe. But it was a precarious existence with Jews caught between sympathetic nobles and unsympathetic clergy, oppressive landowners and oppressed peasants. Even the attitude of the Polish church was ambiguous, a mix of exclusion and toleration, hostility and benign neglect. By mutual agreement of religious leaders on both sides, the two communities could meet for business dealings but not otherwise. Jews and Poles lived side by side, but not together, contiguous but divided by religion, culture, and often enough language. Jews in Poland

---

[36] Harry M. Rabinowicz, *The Legacy of Polish Jewry: A History of Polish Jews in the Inter-war Years 1919–1939,* (New York: Yoseloff, 1965), 22.

[37] Baron, *Social and Religious History,* 2:31.

became a separate "caste."[38] While this fundamentally medieval arrangement had long proved satisfactory to bishops and rabbis alike, it was already crumbling under Enlightenment criticism when Jews and Poles had to face the social, political, and industrial revolutions of the ninteenth century as part of three different empires.

Interwar Poland: A Context for Conflict

1. The partitions and the church

It is no little thing that Poles in general (not just religious Catholics) commonly referred to Poland's reappearance as an independent state in 1918 as a resurrection. Polish nationalists in the nineteenth century had borrowed from the stock of Christian symbolism to sacralize Poland's fate into a martyrdom of religious proportions. Once crucified between thieves and buried, the Christ among nations was now risen. Polish messianism had been censured by church authorities, but the Vatican could not control language or the perceptions words generate. The systematic attempts by the partitioners to russify and germanize the Poles, together with punitive measures meted out after failed uprisings against Russia in 1830 and 1863, served only to inculcate into the Polish consciousness a high sense of unwarranted suffering. Not without reason Poles came to see themselves as quintessential victims.

Except for certain members of the nobility, the onset of the partitions meant deteriorating fortunes for Poles and Jews alike. Jews in Austria were required to pay increased taxes and apply (at a high price) for permission to marry. Jews in Russia were confined to an area called the Pale of Settlement, their young men eventually made subject to draconian draft laws. Prussia after the first partition ousted all Jews beneath a certain level of wealth, and after the second partition, when there was no place to send them, discouraged their existence with heavy taxation.[39] The governments of all three empires regularly intervened in the internal affairs of the Catholic church. None of the partitioning powers saw fit to

---

[38] For an important sociological study of Jews as a "caste" in nineteenth and twentieth century Poland, see Aleksander Hertz, *The Jews in Polish Culture* (Evanston, IL: Northwestern University, 1988).

[39] Zamoyski, "The Jews in Poland," *History Today* (1976): 195.

grant the church unrestricted control over its property or the education of Catholic youth. In all three partitions government policy called for more or less aggressive measures to stamp out anything like a Polish national consciousness.

For 123 years Poland was no more than an idea, but it was an idea that would not go away. "If you cannot prevent your enemies from swallowing you whole," Rousseau had written in 1772, "at least you must do what you can to prevent them from digesting you."[40] Poles rebelled against Russia in 1830/31 (the November Uprising) and again in 1863/64 (the January Uprising). Jews participated in both these insurrections: several hundred in the first uprising, in the second several thousand, some rising to high-ranking office.[41] Thousands of Jews were tortured, hanged, or sent to Siberia with the Poles, among them members of the lower clergy who were sympathetic to these efforts for independence. Over a thousand Polish priests were exiled to Siberia between 1864 and 1914. The same, however, cannot be said of the Polish bishops.

While the priests had experienced first hand the sufferings of the common people, the bishops were often bound by ties of family or class to the ruling elites of the partitioning empires. Even more to the point, the bishops followed the course set down by the Vatican which, in the wake of the French Revolution, was anything but sympathetic to Polish revolutionary ideals. Pope Clement XIV had openly welcomed the first partition on the grounds that Maria Theresa, Austria's "apostolic empress," could protect the church more effectively. After rejecting the Polish ambassador's appeals for aid against Russia, Pope Pius VI ordered the Polish hierarchy in 1795 to cooperate fully with the partitioners.[42] Pope Gregory XVI condemned (1832) the November Uprising with an encyclical that enjoined Poles to submit to the czar's "legitimate authority," because obedience to divinely established authorities was an "absolute precept."[43] Pope Pius IX spoke out in sympathy for the Poles and in criticism of Russia only when the Polish forces were all but defeated in the 1863/64 January uprising. A wave of terror by the

---

[40] Davies, *God's Playground,* 1:369.

[41] Rabinowicz, *Legacy of Polish Jewry,* 26.

[42] Davies, *God's Playground,* 2:213.

[43] Carlen, *Papal Encyclicals,* 1:233–34.

Russians finally prompted a remarkable acknowledgement of papal error: *"Vae mihi quia tacui,"* the response began, (Woe is me that I kept silent.)[44]

As late as 1894, Pope Leo XIII enjoined the Poles to trust and obey the imperial authorities. The czar was viewed as the chief guarantor of social order. Even if it meant that Roman Catholic Poland would be subject to schismatic, orthodox Russia, maintaining the ancient order restored by the Congress of Vienna was a priority for the popes. In response to those who criticized the Vatican's lack of sympathy to the Polish cause, Pope Leo simply asserted that the Holy See was ever solicitous of Poland's welfare.[45] Polish nationalists were bitter at what appeared as the popes' indifference if not outright hostility toward their aspirations. They felt misunderstood and betrayed. Schism, however, was out of the question, for in the absence of a Polish state they needed to draw upon Roman Catholicism as well as the Polish language and history as sources of national identity.

The Roman Catholic church had never enjoyed a monopoly in the religious affairs of the former commonwealth. Poland had always been a multi-ethnic, multi-religious society first with pagans then Jews, Orthodox Ukrainians and Uniate Ruthenians, Hussites, Lutherans, Calvinists, Socinian Unitarians, and even Muslim descendants of the Tartars.[46] There were Polish nationalists who during the partitions rejected their earlier Catholicism on account of the church's conservative political stance. Many nationalists, especially liberal intelligentsia, entered into the ranks of the Polish Freemasons.[47] But the last decades of the old republic had seen a rise in the influence of the Roman Catholic church, in reaction to the incursions of Orthodox Russians and Protestant Prussians and Swedes. In the heavily Orthodox and Uniate eastern provinces, Roman Catholicism had long been known as "the Polish religion." Polish nationalists, not necessarily religious, began to draw

---

[44] Davies, *God's Playground,* 2:213.

[45] Carlen, *Papal Encyclicals,* 2:341–46.

[46] See Davies, *God's Playground,* 1:166. According to Zamoyski, *Polish Way,* 73, there were nearly a hundred mosques in the Polish-Lithuanian commonwealth during the mid-16th century.

[47] Davies, God's Playground, 2:58–59.

from the store of Christian symbolism to idealize Poland as the Christ among nations. In this vein Poland's foremost romantic poet, Adam Mickiewicz, viewed the sufferings of Poland as part of a divinely-ordained messianic mission similar to that of Israel. Jews and Poles for him were two "brotherly peoples" involved in the fulfillment of great supranational tasks.[48]

"A nation," wrote Ernest Renan, "is a community united by a common error with regard to its origins and a common aversion with regard to its neighbors."[49] Already united by an aversion to their imperial neighbors, Poles increasingly succumbed to the erroneous identification of Poland's origins with the Roman church. Even though Catholicism had never been a touchstone of Polish national identity, by the late nineteenth century mounting numbers of Polish clerics and popular demagogues were happy to make it so.

2. Acculturation and antisemitism

The social, political, and industrial revolutions of the nineteenth century affected Poles and Jews at varied times and to disparate degrees, depending on which empire to which they were attached. The ideals of the French Revolution, despite the restorationist efforts of Metternich, eventually made their impact on the absolutist partitioning powers, in the west earlier than in the east. In the wake of emancipation and enfranchisement, the Jews of Western Europe embraced its laws and culture with enthusiasm. They became French, Austrian, or German citizens of the Mosaic faith. But unlike the situation elsewhere, coming out of the ghetto in the former Polish lands did not mean becoming Polish citizens. The links Jews had to a land had been for centuries their loyalty to the monarch. In the nineteenth century, in what had been Poland, that traditional principle meant looking to Moscow, Vienna, and Berlin.

Jewish acculturation in Prussian Poland was almost exclusively a move toward German culture; anything else would have been met with reprisals. In former Lithuania, simply incorporated into Russia, Jews (the so-called Litvaks) adopted Russian culture. In Galicia, where widespread

---

[48] Baron, *Social and Religious History,* 16:88.

[49] Quoted in Davies, *God's Playground,* 2:10.

poverty led to massive emigration to the west, the direction of inculturation was either Polish or Austrian (never Ukrainian). In the central Congress Kingdom of Poland, Jews who left the ghetto embraced Polish culture. Given the abovementioned tradition of loyalty to the monarch, it is hardly remarkable that there were considerable numbers of Jews who under the partitions had become germanized or russophile. Far more notable were the not insignificant numbers of Jews who chose to identify with the language and culture of the Poles, a defeated and subject people. If it was a tribute to the vitality and attractiveness of the culture, most antisemitic nationalists at the time did not see it as such.[50]

When German pamphleteer Wilhelm Marr coined the term "antisemitism" in 1879, he did it to make "Jew-hatred" (*Judenhass*) sound more respectable and "scientific."[51] His doing so marked a decisive transformation: hostility toward Jews was no longer exclusively or even primarily motivated by religion but—in line with the social Darwinist spirit of the times—given a racial and biological basis. In Germany the racist theories of Arthur Gobineau and Houston Stewart Chamberlain gave rise during the 1880s to an anti-democratic nationalism that exalted the German spirit and *Volk* at the expense of the inherently unequal Jews. The popularity of Eduard Drumont's *La France Juive* (1886), followed by the Dreyfus Affair, laid bare the extent that antisemitism was still to be found in France. The Poles were obviously not untouched by what was transpiring in the rest of Europe, especially when the czarist government pursued a policy of using propaganda to set Poles against Jews as a means of suppressing revolutionary movements.

3. *Endecja*

When the assassination of Czar Alexander II unleashed a wave of pogroms in 1881, threats of something similar appeared in Warsaw. Bishop Sotkiewicz issued a pastoral letter appealing for calm, however, and the Polish press decried anti-Jewish violence as inconsistent with the Polish tradition of tolerance. Despite their efforts, an anti-Jewish riot did take place toward the end of that year but was decried by both the church

---

[50] See Roman Zimand, "Wormwood and Ashes: Do Jews and Poles Hate Each Other?" in *Polin*, 4:337.

[51] See Moshe Zimmermann, *Wilhelm Marr: The Patriarch of Anti-Semitism,* (New York: Oxford University Press, 1986).

and the Polish press. With the exception of that event, the relationship between Poles and Jews throughout the period of partitions can be described as "relatively good." At least, that is, until 1912. It was in that year that the National Democratic Movement of Roman Dmowski made antisemitism and the boycott of Jewish business part of its program for Polish emancipation.[52]

Aside from Marshal Józef Piłsudski, no one had more impact on early twentieth century Polish history and politics than Roman Dmowski (1864–1939). The principal ideologue and co-founder of the National Democratic Movement (*Endecja*), he has been called the father of Polish nationalist antisemitism.[53] The profound hostility Piłsudski and Dmowski had for each other was not merely a matter of personal rivalry. They each embodied mutually contradictory solutions to the question of Polish identity. The controversy over the "Jewish question" in interwar Poland was a debate about Poland itself. Should Poland be a pluralist federation of peoples led by the Polish majority, a modern version of its earlier form, as Piłsudski advocated? Or should it be, as Dmowski maintained, a unitary national state in which all minorities were either polonized or forced to emigrate? The Jews were obviously a key to the debate. Official policy would eventually incorporate elements from both solutions, but in an age drunk on the heady wine of nationalism the pluralist solution was clearly not the more popular. It was Dmowski's rather than Piłsudski's thinking that dominated Polish politics in the interwar period.[54]

When he helped create the National League in 1893 and then Endecja in 1897, Dmowski's aim was to win the widest possible concessions from Russia so as to eventually achieve Polish autonomy. With his movement active in all three partitioning empires, Dmowski was critical of the conservative landowning nobility, who, to safeguard their standing and

---

[52] For the most thorough study of this period see Frank Golczewski, *Polnische-Jüdische Beziehungen 1881–1822* (Wiesbaden: Franz-Steiner, 1981). For the most detailed study of Polish antisemitism between the wars, see Paweł Korzec, *Juifs en Pologne: La question juive pendant l'entre-deux-guerres* (Paris: Fondation Nationale des Sciences Politiques, 1980).

[53] Korzec, *Juifs en Pologne,* 33.

[54] For an excellent survey of the interwar period, see M. K. Dziewanowski, *Poland in the Twentieth Century,* (New York, Columbia University, 1977).

estates, had embraced the same policy of tri-loyalism that the Vatican had imposed upon the Polish bishops. Even without the support of the bishops, Dmowski's movement proved attractive to the younger Polish clergy.[55] But the principal recruits to the movement, came from the rapidly growing professional and commercial middle class. Dmowski followed the pattern established in thirteenth century England and repeated in nineteenth century France. He convinced the nouveau urban Polish middle class that Jews were the major hindrance to their social and economic ambitions.

The Jews of Warsaw saw no reason to elect a National Democrat to be their representative to the Duma in 1912. Their solidarity resulted in the Endek candidate losing to a member of the Polish Socialist Party (PPS). It was then that a boycott of Jewish businesses became a central part of Endek policies. Endecja became not only programmatically antisemitic but obsessed. Convinced that Polish and Jewish interests were irreconcilable, Dmowski viewed Poland's Jewish population as its primary social problem. Whereas Piłsudski saw the danger to Poland being the enemies without, Dmowski focused on Jews as the enemy within. Although he headed the Polish delegation to the Peace Conference at Versailles, Dmowski never grasped the reins of power. He did succeed, though, in transforming smoldering resentment over cultural and religious differences into a political program and by the mid-1930s into a national force.[56]

4. 1918: Frontier wars and Polish pogroms

On the eve of World War I, the partition of Poland was generally regarded as permanent. The re-emergence of an independent Poland was hardly expected, except by visionaries like Piłsudski who, foreseeing the collapse of the partitioning empires, prepared for it. Sentenced to Siberia for underground terrorist activity, later a leader in the Polish Socialist party, he moved to Galicia where the Austrian government was not unsympathetic to his anti-Russian aims. There he founded his legions and a confederation of parties demanding independence. Interred by the Germans for refusing allegiance to the Reich, he returned to Poland in

---

[55] William W. Hagen, *Germans, Poles, and Jews: The Nationality Conflict in the Prussian East, 1772-1914* (Chicago: University of Chicago, 1980), 233.

[56] Davies, *God's Playground*, 2:52–53.

November 1918, with the mantle of a martyr. His reputation as an indomitable fighter for independence allowed him to assume leadership.

The collapse of Germany and Austria and Poland's proclamation of independence did not bring peace to Poland. Another three years of warfare ensued until the boundaries of the new states were fixed. Throughout this period the predicament of Jews was acutely dangerous, especially in disputed border areas. With no vested interest in the victory of one side or another, Jews were blamed for disloyalty by all sides, Polish, Russian, and Ukrainian. Poorly disciplined armies inflamed by revolutionary or nationalist fervor committed atrocities not only against each other but noncombatants as well. Of all groups, Jews suffered the most. Hostile mobs and undisciplined soldiers, brutalized by long years of war, gave vent to their basest instincts and plundered Jewish stores and homes under the pretext of national ideals.

According to the best modern estimates, between one and two thousand Jews were killed by Poles during this period, virtually all within the war zone.[57] Some were clear and deliberate pogroms, while others were part of the terror inflicted on civilian populations regardless of nationality or religion. Among the most notorious atrocities were those in eastern Galicia, particularly that amid the battle between Poles and Ukrainians for the city of Lwów. Shortly before the battle, Austrian authorities had released and armed virtually all prisoners for the defense of the city against the Ukrainians. Caught between belligerent forces, the Jews of Lwów proclaimed strict neutrality but formed a military unit for self-defence. The Polish military saw this as a hostile act and accused the Jews of siding with the Ukrainians. First uniformed soldiers attacked the Jewish quarter, then a mob. Rioting, plunder, and arson resulted in three synagogues being destroyed and seventy-two Jews killed (though the number was later inflated to three thousand). The government denied that the disorder was a pogrom and attributed the violence to the wholesale release of prisoners. Other Poles, like the Polish Socialists, condemned the violence and accepted the term.[58]

During the fighting over the Polish-Soviet frontier, thousands more (perhaps as many as 75,000) Jews, stereotyped as bolsheviks, perished at

---

[57] Radziałowski, "Jews in Poland," *Perspectives* (1979): 482.

[58] Golczewski, *Beziehungen,* 182–208; Korzec, *Juifs,* 74–77.

the hands of Ukrainian nationalists.[59] But world attention focused on the Poles, and the Western press published sensational accounts of Polish atrocities against Jews. Outraged Jewish communities in western Europe and the United States organized protest demonstrations and questioned the political maturity of the Poles. Jewish-American newspapers, which had earlier published articles questioning whether the Poles deserved independence, could now claim their criticisms confirmed. Biased accounts in the newspapers of both communities merely convinced the other of inveterate hostility. International Jewish concern resulted eventually in the drafting of the "minorities treaty" at the 1919 Versailles Peace Conference, imposed by the victorious Allies on all the Central European states except Germany. The "minorities treaty" was deeply resented in Poland as an affront to its autonomy. For Polish nationalists like Dmowski, it also served to prove that Jews were an international force to be reckoned with, powerful and endemically anti-Polish.

5. A multi-national state

When the Polish-Soviet frontier was finally settled, Poland was once again a multi-national state; over one-third of its population was non-Polish. The Ukrainians formed the largest minority (5 million), concentrated in the east along with some one million Byelorussians. In the western regions were over one million, mostly Protestant, Germans. The Jews, numbering some three million, were dispersed throughout Poland, (though least in the west), concentrated, in small towns and cities. In accord with Piłsudski's vision, it was his government's stated and apparently sincere intentions to reconcile and integrate these minorities into the new Poland, founded on the multi-ethnic, federalist traditions of the old commonwealth. However sincere those intentions, they were thwarted by political and economic problems that seemed more pressing.

The Polish constitution of 1921 established a democratic republic (modeled after that of France), with universal suffrage and a bicameral legislature consisting of a Senate and a vastly more powerful House of Deputies, the Sejm. Executive power was exercised by a cabinet, chaired by the Prime Minister. On the issue of church and state, the constitution guaranteed equal rights to all religions, but among them the Roman

---

[59] Radziałowski, "Jews in Poland," *Perspectives* (1979): 482.

Catholic church occupied "a leading position" inasmuch as it was the religion of "the overwhelming majority of the nation." The rights of all citizens were guaranteed without regard for nationality, language, or religion. Minorities were to enjoy "full and free development" of their national character and allowed to establish schools and religious and social organizations.[60] Notwithstanding these constitutional principles, patterns of thinking developed under years of foreign rule obscured for many Poles, both in and outside the government, the need to accord fair treatment to minorities. While the Polish Socialist Party identified itself with Piłsudski's vision, Endecja rejected it out of hand, insisting that Poles alone should be masters in their own house. Endek policies called for excluding all ethnic minorities from political power; the Slavic minorities were to be polonized, the Germans and Jews expatriated as incapable of assimilation.[61]

Despite the liberality and sophistication of the constitution, the new Polish government did not function well. The principle of proportional representation allowed the proliferation of small parties. By 1926 there were twenty-six Polish parties: chief among them the National Democrats and the much smaller *Chadecja* (Christian Democratic party) on the right; on the left the Polish Socialist Party and several peasants' parties. The ethnic minorities had an additional 33 parties, among them the similarly splintered Jewish Parties: Agudat Israel, representing religious orthodoxy, hostile to Jewish radicalism and friendly to the Polish state; the General Jewish Workers' Alliance (the Bund), which was the largest Jewish socialist party; Zionist parties and assimilationist parties opposed to Zionism.[62]

---

[60] Polonsky, *Politics,* 48–49.

[61] Antony Polonsky, *Politics in Independent Poland, 1921–1939: The Crisis of Constitutional Government* (Oxford: Clarendon, 1972), 139; Joseph Rothschild, *East Central Europe between the Two World Wars* (Seattle/London: University of Washington, 1974), 31.

[62] On Jewish politics in interwar Poland see Ezra Mendelsohn, *The Jews of East Central Europe between the World Wars* (Bloomington: Indiana University, 1983), 43–63; Polonsky, *Politics,* 84–95. See also Mendelsohn's essay in John Micgiel, Robert Scott, and H.B. Segel (eds.), *Poles and Jews: Myth and Reality in the Historical Context* (New York: Columbia University, 1986), 203–22. Other notable works on Jewish life in interwar Poland are Simon Segal, *The New Poland and the Jews* (Furman, 1938); Harry M. Rabinowicz, *The Legacy of Polish Jewry* (New York: Yoseloff, 1965); Celia Heller,

The unfortunate effects of this fragmentation on interwar Poland were intensified by lack of political experience. The multiple parties and interests found it difficult to form a stable majority, especially in the face of Poland's intractable problems. Among the challenges facing them were integrating disparate parts of the country into a single economic unit, overcoming the effects of wartime destruction, and contending with an increasingly rampant inflation. Unable to cope with Poland's economic problems, governments rose and fell with rapidity, intensifying the economic crises and discrediting the parliamentary system.

One of the first questions the Sejm was made to face was mandatory Sunday rest. Despite the millions of Jews, Protestants, and Orthodox Christian citizens, the National Democrats wanted to present Poland as a "Catholic state." Such legislation obviously posed an economic hardship on orthodox Jewish merchants who observed the Sabbath and thus would have to refrain from work for two days, while their Christian competitors needed to observe only one. Belying the myth of Jewish-Socialist solidarity, Polish Socialists voted for the legislation for the sake of the social benefits it offered workers. Some few assimilationist Jews saw it as an opportunity to reduce Sabbath observance and force orthodox Jews out of their religious ghettos.[63]

Piłsudski had determined not to stand for the office of president in the new Republic. As tailored by the Endeks with him in mind, the 1921 constitution deprived the office of any real power. In 1922, the National Democrats ran the nation's largest landowner as their candidate for president. A coalition of the socialist, peasant, and minority parties defeated them and elected Gabriel Narutowicz to be Poland's first president. Claiming they were cheated of an electoral victory, Endecja blamed the minority, especially the Jewish, parties. Writing in a National Democratic newspaper, Father Kazimierz Lutoslawski, an Endek deputy, asked: "How could the Jews dare to impose their president on us?" Several days after being sworn in, Narutowicz was assassinated by a nationalist fanatic. The assassination created popular revulsion and a widespread reaction against the political right. Piłsudski never forgave

---

On the Edge of Destruction (New York: Columbia University, 1977).

[63] Golczewski, *Beziehungen,* 275–80.

Endecja for creating the climate that led to it.[64]

6. *Sanacja*

The regular rise and fall of governments together with scandals involving the bribery of deputies served to produce widespread disillusionment with parliamentary institutions. Criticism of the constitution was rife from both the right and left. Pointing to financial irregularities and governmental corruption, Piłsudski came out of retirement and in May 1926, and successfully executed a coup. He declared himself against dictatorship but demanded that the parliament reform itself: the Sejm was too powerful, the presidency too weak. Although elected to the presidency, Piłsudski preferred to serve as minister of war with a rubber-stamp president subservient to him. The coup signaled a break with his political allies on the left; the Jewish parties were for the most part sympathetic. They regarded Piłsudski as a lesser evil than the Endeks. Piłsudski governed with the aid of the "colonels," as they were called, a small clique of military advisers from the his legionary days. His government styled itself *Sanacja*, a term connoting reform and the desire to clear away the negative features of the former political system.[65]

The Piłsudski government embarked on an open and liberal policy vis-à-vis Poland's minorities. By extending and reorganizing Jewish communal organizations, it won support among the orthodox. It took steps to aid Jewish trade, which was benefitting from the economic revival that stability in government engendered. In 1927, the Minister of Religious Cults and Education declared himself against the quota system that limited the number of non-Poles at universities (*numerus clausus*) and forbade its application in institutions of higher learning. The government could do little against the National Democrats' economic boycott, and it did not provide funds for Jewish schools. In practice the *numerus clausus* was still widely practiced.[66]

As a means of fostering national consolidation, the Sanacja government was also intent on improving relations with the church. Several leading members of the hierarchy had long been known for their opposition to

---

[64] Polonsky, *Politics,* 111; Rothschild, *East Central Europe,* 50.

[65] Polonsky, *Politics,* 147–85; Rothschild, *East Central Europe,* 33.

[66] Polonsky, *Politics,* 213–16.

Piłsudski, just as several in Piłsudski's entourage were known for their anti-clericalism. In 1914 Archbishop Sapieha of Kraków had complained that Piłsudski wanted to create a "socialist and Jewish" Poland. Identified along with Sapieha as endorsing Endecja were Archbishops Bilczewski and Teodorowicz, Bishops Pelczar, Łosiński, and Łukomski. In the primatial see of Gniezno, Edmund Cardinal Dalbor was also an enthusiastic supporter of the National Democrats, but his successor as of 1926, August Cardinal Hlond was not closely associated with any political party.[67]

In 1926 Dmowski published a tract in which he explicitly renounced Endecja's earlier anticlerical tradition and openly called for an alliance with the church. The National Democrats, together with other nationalist groups, promised the church "complete independence and an appropriate position in the state" in virtue of it being the "director" of the nation's moral life. Newspapers supportive of Piłsudski, on the other hand, had criticized the proposed concordat between Poland and the Vatican as too favorable to the church. The conference of Polish Bishops complained about the slow implementation of the concordat and protested attacks in the "anti-Catholic press" which was "considered to have the support of official circles." In the end the government implemented the concordat, and Cardinal Hlond, who had quickly become the most powerful churchman in the country, pursued a policy of cultivating good relations with the Sanacja government.[68]

Not all Catholic clergy and thinkers were sympathetic to the Endeks' divisive policies. There were outspoken critics like F. Kujawiński, Father Jan Piwowarczyk, and Professor Władysław Jaworski, who attacked the use of religion and love for country as a mask to spread hatred among citizens.[69] It is safe to say, however, that most parish priests were emotionally tied to National Democratic principles. In December 1927, with an upcoming election, the bishops issued a pastoral letter urging action for the sake of the "Catholic and national camp." Cardinal Kakowski denied that the bishops' letter had any anti-government intention, but its use of National Democratic catchwords made it seem so,

---

[67] Polonsky, *Politics*, 83, 209; Golczewski, *Beziehungen*, 281.

[68] Polonsky, *Politics*, 59, 209–12.

[69] Golczewski, *Beziehungen*, 281; Polonsky, *Politics*, 212.

and the Endeks exploited it as such. If the letter was a veiled endorsement of the right, it backfired seriously. The parties of the right and center suffered serious losses. Endecja in particular experienced a crushing defeat, mustering only little more than 8% of the vote and winning back only 37 of its previous 98 seats.[70] The political influence of the church was obviously limited by more than what has been called "the markedly anti-clerical temper of the ruling elite."[71]

7. World depression

With the onset of the world depression, the calm Piłsudski had been able to impose on daily life shattered. Fragile truces with minorities fell apart, and Poland became the scene of agricultural and industrial strikes, riots, and mass protests by non-Poles. Irrespective of political viewpoints or religious affiliations, by 1933 many segments of Polish society became alienated from the government and were ready to challenge Sanacja claims to total control. The impact of the depression on Poland was especially severe. Between 1929 and 1933, the Polish national income fell by 25% (compared to a 4% drop in Great Britain). Efforts at land reform were paralyzed. No one in the government was prepared to embark on any sort of radical solution. Peasant farmers were especially hard hit by a fall in prices for agricultural produce and a rise in prices for manufactured goods. They found it virtually impossible to purchase agricultural machinery or fertilizer. The deteriorating economic situation served only to radicalize politics further on both the right and the left. Nonetheless, Endecja made only modest gains in the 1930 election, winning less than 13% of the vote.[72]

The depression affected the Jewish community with particular severity. As elsewhere in eastern Europe, Jewish poverty had been widespread in Poland since before World War I. Emigration and industrialization had alleviated the problem somewhat, but most Jews were concentrated in less modernized industries and by the early 1930s restrictions had cut emigration by half. The majority of Polish Jews, still devoutly orthodox,

---

[70] Polonsky, *Politics,* 250.

[71] Davies, *God's Playground,* 2:224.

[72] Edward Wynot, Jr., *Warsaw between the Wars: Profile of the Capital City in a Developing Land* (New York: Columbia, 1983), 51–52; Polonsky, *Politics,* 280, 323.

avoided working in heavy industry because of Sabbath observance. Many were poorly paid cottage workers in the textile industry. Although there were Jewish professionals (law and medicine), small factory owners, and some few capitalists (in banking, sugar, and textiles), the largest percentage of Polish Jews worked in retail trade (most typically as self-employed shopkeepers, shoemakers, tailors, and bakers).[73] Obviously this group could not help but be affected by the Endek campaign to boycott Jewish businesses. But the Poles' disregard of the Endek campaign was both common and widespread. More than the boycott, it was pauperization among the general population, especially among the peasants, that impacted harshly upon the small Jewish traders.[74]

To speak of the Jewish community or Jewry in interwar Poland is something of a misnomer. The Jews of Poland after the partitions were as divided and divergent as the Poles, if not more so. In the formerly German provinces of Poznań, Pomerania and Silesia, Jews were few but westernized. In former Galicia Jews were almost ten percent of the local population and conspicuously traditional. Religious reform had made little headway; Yiddish-speaking, Hasidic Jews with black coats and sideburns personified foreignness and peculiarity to the Poles. The largest number of Jews lived in central, formerly Congress Poland, concentrated in large cities like Warsaw and Łódź. There alongside the dominant world of separatist (including Hasidic) orthodoxy, were a smaller but important group of Jews who under the impact of Jewish Enlightenment (*Haskala*) had embraced Polish culture. In the multi-national eastern provinces (Lithuania, Byelorussia) Jewish enlightenment tended not toward polonization but religious Zionism and socialism.[75]

Taken altogether, the majority of Polish Jews were still strongly orthodox (anti-socialist and anti-revolutionary), with a small but growing sector of polonized Jews embarrassed by the dress and outlandish ways of the various Hasidic sects. These divergences, however, did not prevent the nationalists in Endecja from holding on to their conviction of international Jewish solidarity. Neither did the orthodox majority and differences between socialism and communism prevent them from

---

[73] Mendelsohn, *East Central Europe,* 25–28.

[74] See chapter nine on the Polish economy.

[75] Mendelsohn, *East Central Europe,* 17–23.

identifying Jews with communism. The polonized Jews were accused of trying to take over Polish culture. Inner divergences among Jews paled in comparison with their deviation from the majority culture. Jews were an urban element in a largely peasant country, a distinct economic group whose faith, language, and customs differed sharply from those outside it.

The rise of Nazism to power in Germany had its impact on Poland. It encouraged younger nationalists to split off from Dmowski's party and form in 1934 the National Radical Camp (ONR), clearly based on the Nazi model. Since 1928 Endecja had dropped the word democratic from its name, and the National Party had already moved further to the right. Despite the dangers to Poland inherent in a resurgent Germany, nationalists could not help but be impressed by the impunity with which Hitler was able to deprive Europe's wealthiest Jewish community of its political rights.[76] As elsewhere in East Central Europe, universities became centers of anti-Jewish riots, much of it in imitation of the Nazis. After only a few months the government disbanded the ONR because of its violent antisemitic agitation, but its former members continued their efforts under guise of different youth organizations.

8. Antisemitism under the Colonels

The effects of the world depression lasted in Poland until early 1936, far longer than in most countries. But as long as Piłsudski lived, his semi-mythical figure allowed his Sanacja government to maintain control. His opponents were unable to muster any serious challenge. All this changed when Piłsudski died on May 12, 1935. It was one of his Jewish comrades in arms, General Bernard Mond, who was charged with the responsibility of arranging his funeral, and Poland's Jewish community sincerely mourned his passing.[77] They had good reason to do so. Piłsudski had clearly been a restraining influence on the nationalist right. Although illness had already forced Piłsudski to relinquish much of the day-to-day management of the government to his small coterie of associates, none

---

[76] Polonsky, *Politics,* 370.

[77] Rabinowicz, *Legacy,* 56. In 1928 there were some sixty Jewish officers in the Polish army. See Franciszek Kusiak, *Życie codzienne oficerów Drugiej Rzeczypospolitej* (Warszawa: Państwowy Instytut Wydawniczy, 1992), 13–17; Zbigniew Mierzwiński, *Generałowie II Rzeczypospolitej* (Warszawa: Polonia, 1990).

of the "Colonels" was named his successor, and none enjoyed his charisma or popular support. With Piłsudski out of the way, nationalists and radical right youth groups were now able to make the "Jewish question" the center of Polish political life.

In 1936 Piłsudski's "Colonels" attempted to resolve the disunity in their own ranks as well as in the government with a new political organization, the so-called National Unity Camp (OZON). While not totalitarian, it succumbed to the right as Piłsudski had never done, and sought to engender popular support by refusing to allow Jews to join their ruling coalition. In a 1937 policy statement, the National Unity Camp declared that, while it disapproved of antisemitic violence, it was understandable for the country to defend its culture, and it was natural for Polish society to "seek economic self-sufficiency." The reference to "economic self-sufficiency" meant governmental sanction of the nationalist boycott, first formulated by a Polish prime minister in 1936: "Economic struggle by all means—but without force."[78] The separation of economic considerations from violence was easier to articulate than accomplish, however, particularly when the unity camp's youth movement was given over for a time to nationalist extremists. Young Poles especially now saw themselves as pitted against Jews in a struggle for jobs and survival.

The years 1936 to 1939 were among the darkest in modern Polish history. No racial laws were passed. No Jewish newspapers or cultural institution were suppressed. None of the thousands of Jews who held political positions, local or national, was driven from office. But a significant if not overwhelming majority of the nation now appeared to accept the nationalists' narrowed definition of a Pole as a Slavic Roman Catholic who was a product of Polish culture. Jews were explicitly excluded. Ironically, many nationalists who were accepted as "Poles" under this new definition were descendants of families that had come to Poland as foreigners at a time when Jews had already been living there for centuries.[79]

Although official state violence was never used against Jews in Poland as it was in Germany, the government did not act forcefully in combatting the unofficial but organized violence of the nationalists. University authorities claimed to be powerless to quell the organized

---

[78] Mendelsohn, *East Central Europe,* 71.

[79] Radziałowski, "Jews in Poland," *Perspectives,* (1979), 482.

attacks Endek youth were making against Jewish students. Claiming it was for the sake of peace, university rectors caved into Endek demands for segregated seating for Jews, the "ghetto benches." Not satisfied with merely calling for the boycott of Jewish merchants, more radical nationalists devised methods to enforce it, especially in the countryside. Incidents erupted into full-scale anti-Jewish riots with the police often looking away. For the radical right, any means that encouraged Jews to leave Poland was justified.

Jews in those fateful last years were not totally without Polish friends and allies. Opposition from the left was vocal, and even within the government there was conflict between more authoritarian and more liberal elements. In 1937 the mayor of Warsaw, Stefan Starzyński, made a national speech in defense of Jewish rights. Thousands of Polish workers joined sympathy strikes. There were Polish students who joined their Jewish colleagues and suffered beatings for defending Jewish rights. Scholars and intellectuals condemned the violence and governmental discrimination. Some of the most prominent professors in Poland refused to honor the ghetto benches. The rector of the University of Lwów resigned over the issue. By the eve of the invasion by Germany in 1939, the antisemitic wave began to recede. Foreign observers noted a growing revulsion to violence and propaganda, and in the municipal elections of 1938, extreme nationalists suffered a stunning defeat. Victory went to parties like the Polish Socialists which opposed antisemitism.

The reaction of the Catholic church in Poland to the antisemitic wave of the 1930s constitutes the chief focus of this book. It is conventionally identified with a celebrated statement of Cardinal Hlond which condemned violence but approved of the economic boycott. As such, it corresponded to the position of the government. Distinctly different was a criticism of the Catholic church by one of its own leading lay members. Count Antoni Sobański complained about priests tolerating the distribution of anti-Jewish pamphlets at the doors of their churches. Preachers, he wrote, were more concerned about the influence of erotic movies on young people than that of antisemitic propaganda. "Does not the boycott of Jewish goods always terminate with attacks of Jewish stores and finally with assaults on the Jews themselves?" Concern for one's co-religionists was becoming an excuse for hatred.[80]

---

[80] Segal, *The New Poland,* 80–81.

Count Sobański was not the only Pole to criticize the church for its response, or apparent lack of response, toward antisemitism. The attitude of Catholic church leaders toward Jews, however, involved more than concern for their co-religionists. And it involved more than toleration of anti-Jewish propaganda.

Poland's Jews and the Catholic church were necessarily at odds over a fundamental question of church-state relations: Was Poland to be a Catholic or a secular state? Disagreement over that issue could not help but affect others as well.

The Catholic Church in Interwar Poland

The Catholic church was by far the largest religious body in interwar Poland.[81] The nineteen-and-one-half million Latin rite Catholics and well over three million Byzantine and Armenian Catholics in union with Rome constituted some two-thirds of the Polish population. All together they were organized into 7,054 parishes in twenty-five dioceses, under the leadership of nearly 13,000 parish and religious order priests. In 1935 there were fifty-one bishops, seven of whom were archbishops with the duty of surveillance over the other bishops in their provinces: August Cardinal Hlond, the Primate (Gniezno-Poznań); Aleksander Kakowski (Warsaw); Bolesław Twardowski (Lwów); Adam Sapieha (Kraków); Romuald Jałbrzydowski (Wilno); Andrzej Szeptycki (Byzantine Catholics); and Józef Teodorowicz (Armenian Catholics). No one in this complex network was independent of the others, and all were under the authority of a man who knew many, if not most, of them personally, since he had been the former papal nuncio to Poland, Archbishop Achille Ratti, elected in 1922 Pope Pius XI.

At the behest of Pope Benedict XV, Ratti had come to Poland in 1918 when it was still under German occupation, the first diplomatic representative in 126 years. At first he was only an "apostolic visitor,"

---

[81] The most authoritative historical survey of the church in interwar Poland is that of Bishop Wincenty Urban, *Ostatni etap dziejów w Polsce przed nowym tysiącleciem, 1815-1965* (Rome: Hosianum, 1966). Covering the same period from a Marxist perspective is Wiesław Mysłek, *Kościół katolicki w Polsce w latach 1918–1939* (Warsaw: Książka i Wiedza, 1966).

but the next year he was named papal nuncio and consecrated an archbishop by Cardinal Kakowski. The Polish church had to face the same task as the nation at large, to integrate differing and disparate territories, and as nuncio Ratti took an active part in the reorganization of church life. In 1920 he experienced personally the threat of Soviet invasion and the battle of Warsaw Poles came to call the "miracle at the Vistula." In 1921 he left Poland to become the Archbishop of Milan and a year later the Bishop of Rome. As Pope he concluded what he had begun as nuncio, the regulation of church-state relations with the 1925 concordat.

1. Church-state relations

The concordat guaranteed the church complete freedom in its internal affairs and the disposition of its property. It mandated that religion be taught in public schools at the elementary and intermediate levels. Teachers of Catholic religion classes had to be approved by the local bishops, as were professors of Catholic theology in the state universities. The concordat also obligated the state to pay the salaries of clergy in those areas where church lands had been confiscated during the partitions. As mentioned above, the 1921 constitution guaranteed equal rights to all religions, and simply stated that the Roman Catholic church occupied "a leading position" in the nation as the religion of the majority. For many Catholics this was not enough. In 1936 a congress sponsored by the Jesuits in honor of the sixteenth century Polish patriot priest, Piotr Skarga, issued a call for formal recognition of the Catholic church as the state religion. Jesuit Jan Pawelski criticized the constitutional separation of church and state as contrary to papal teaching and an "echo of confused liberalism and secularism."[82]

While in accord with official church teaching, such views were not typical of all Catholics; not even perhaps the majority. Complaints were frequent that, although Catholics had superior numbers, they had little impact on Polish political life.[83] The fact of the matter is that considerable numbers of Poles, including practicing Catholics, belonged to the Polish Socialist Party (PPS) and the *Wyzwolenie* (PSL, Polish Peasants

---

[82] *Przegląd Powszechny*, 213 (1937): 69–85.

[83] Dr. Andrzej Niesiołowski lamented the weakness of the Christian democrats in *Przegląd Powszechny*, 216 (1937): 277–94.

Party) which favored separation of church and state and opposed the concordat with its payment of clergy salaries. *Wici,* a peasant youth organization, not only stood for separation of church and state but for a land reform that would confiscate church property without indemnification. Wici's numbers posed a great enough threat to elicit alarmed pastoral letters from several bishops. Various church institutions owned considerable tracts of land, which were coveted by the peasantry. The bishops in their first joint pastoral letter expressed a willingness to relinquish property but only so long as land reform would not constitute an impairment to the church or the clergy. It was not without reason that the 1936 Plenary Synod of Polish Bishops had to declare: "Catholics may not support or cooperate with sects, masonry, socialists or other organizations which openly or secretly are hostile to the church."[84]

2. Catholic Action

The clergy did not shy away from being actively involved in partisan politics at the onset of Poland's independence. There were priests and even bishops who had been elected to public office in the Senate and the Sejm. But by 1935, with some few exceptions, the clergy were forbidden to run for office. The Vatican came to deem the laity rather than the clergy as the more appropriate agents of Catholic influence on social and political life. The new approach was to be Catholic Action. Although the term had been used by earlier popes, it was Pius XI who gave Catholic Action its classical definition: "the participation of the laity in the apostolate of the church's hierarchy." Pius XI also gave Catholic Action its charter and a sense of apocalyptic urgency. Purely religious organizations for laity had existed earlier in the church, in Poland as elsewhere in Europe. But Catholic Action gathered them under one umbrella and gave them a this-worldly as well as spiritual mission. Catholic Action was to be above partisan politics, but its aim was the renewal of Catholic life in society as well as in the family. That meant that its concerns also extended to socio-economic and therefore political issues.

In 1929 the Vatican Secretary of State sent a letter to Cardinal Hlond informing him that, in the mind of Pope Pius XI, it was necessary to organize Catholic Action in Poland. In accord with the Pope's wishes,

---

[84] Urban, *Ostatni etap,* 499. See also Mysłek, *Kościół,* 78–79, 565.

priests were sent abroad to study Catholic Action in other countries, and a process of reorganization began. Catholic Action was to represent Catholic interests by becoming the bishops' lay arm. In Poland that meant countering efforts at secularizing social and political life. It meant lobbying aggressively against left-wing critics for maintaining religion in the public schools. When a project arose in 1932 for reforming Poland's marriage laws by allowing for civil marriage and divorce, Catholic Action marshalled signatures protesting the proposed changes. It was credited with defeating the measure even before it came before the Sejm. The bishops explicitly linked the aims of Catholic Action to their own at their 1936 Plenary Synod: the purpose of the Synod was the garnering of "influence upon the ethics of public and private life with the help of Catholic Action."[85]

3. The Catholic Press

Along with Catholic Action and, of course, the pulpit, one of the most important means for the church's leaders to influence and inform the faithful was the Catholic press.[86] Although complaints could be lodged regarding its quality, there was no gainsaying the quantitative significance of the interwar Polish Catholic press.[87] In 1927 there were at least 131 Catholic periodicals being published in Poland; ten years later there were 228, most of them were weeklies or monthlies, publishing on the average of five to ten thousand copies per issue. The most popular was the *Rycerz Niepokalanej* (Knight of the Immaculata); founded by Maximilian Kolbe, it eventually enjoyed a press run of two-hundred thousand copies a month. The most popular weekly was the *Przewodnik Katolicki* (Catholic Guide), published by the Archdiocese of Poznań with a press run averaging 150 thousand copies each issue. Other dioceses published weeklies (Kraków, Lwów, Łuck, Częstochowa), as well as regular news and informational bulletins for priests (e.g. Warsaw's *Wiadomości* and Kraków's *Notationes*). Also published for the clergy were the *Ateneum*

---

[85] Urban, *Ostatni etap,* 497; Mysłek, *Kościół,* 287–93.

[86] For an overview of the interwar Catholic press, see Urban, *Ostatni etap,* 485–90; Mysłek, *Kościół,* 198–217; and Czesław Lechicki, "Prasa katolicka Drugiej Rzeczypospolitej," *Kwartalnik Historii Prasy Polskiej,* 23, 2 (1984): 46–69.

[87] Urban, *Ostatni etap,* 485.

Kapłańskie (Priests' Atheneum), *Przegląd Homiletyczny* (Homiletic Review) and *Homo Dei* (Man of God), published by the Redemptorists. Most of the Catholic periodicals were published by religious orders for men. The Jesuits alone published eleven periodicals, ranging from the high-level *Przegląd Powszechny* (Universal Review), which treated current events as well as theological issues, to the popular *Głosy Katolickie* (Catholic Voices), which also treated contemporary issues but for a mass audience. The Pallotine priests also published several periodicals, including the weekly *Przegląd Katolicki* (Catholic Review) aimed at intellectuals. The Marianists in Warsaw published *Pro Christo—Wiara i Czyn* (For Christ—Faith and Action), an unabashedly right-wing monthly aimed at Catholic youth, especially university students. Catholic Action published *Ruch Katolicki* (Catholic Movement) for socially active laity and *Kultura,* a literary journal. *Prąd* (Current) had earlier been a partisan nationalist monthly, but in 1929 it was taken over by Father Antoni Szymański and the faculty of the Catholic University of Lublin (KUL). It became the organ for *Odrodzenie* (Renaissance), a nationwide student organization integrated into Catholic Action.

In addition to the foregoing, there were specialized publications like *Oriens,* concerned with union with Eastern churches; *Verbum,* a literary journal; and periodicals devoted to purely biblical, theological, or devotional topics. All of them, whether published by religious orders or not, were at least indirectly under the control of the hierarchy, since no periodical could describe itself as Catholic without the permission of the local bishop. Unique in that it was directly under the Polish Bishops' Conference as a whole was the *Katolicka Agencja Prasowa* or KAP (Catholic Press Agency). It was founded in 1927 by Archbishop Józef Gawlina, who first investigated Catholic press agencies in other European countries. From 1929 to 1939 it was directed by Fr. Zygmunt Kaczyński and sent out almost daily press releases and opinion pieces to newspapers throughout Poland and abroad. Operating out of the offices of the Archdiocese of Warsaw, the Press Agency enjoyed the particular support of Cardinal Kakowski.[88]

Despite this quantitatively imposing array of titles, the Vatican was not satisfied with the Catholic press in Poland, because it lacked a daily

---

[88] Urban, *Ostatni etap,* 490; Lechicki, "Prasa katolicka," 53–54.

newspaper. Attempts to initiate a Catholic daily had been made for some years in Poland but were consistently hindered by popular indifference. Cardinal Hlond had announced plans in 1928 for a non-partisan Catholic daily, and the Pallotine Fathers attempted to realize his promise, but poor sales brought all efforts to nought. By 1934 the Vatican was tired of waiting. Pope Pius XI sent a letter to the Polish bishops in which he demanded that they promote Catholic Action by promptly establishing a Catholic daily newspaper. Publication of the Pope's letter brought a swift response. Within two months the monastery of Conventual Franciscan Friars at Niepokalanów, founded by Maximilian Kolbe, informed the bishops that they intended to publish an inexpensive daily newspaper out of their own resources.

Canonized a saint and a martyr of charity in 1982, Maximilian Kolbe gave his life for another prisoner at Auschwitz in 1941. Even without that heroic act of self-giving, he might well have been canonized as one of the church's outstanding evangelists.[89] With a single-minded faith and zeal that were by any definition extraordinary, he organized the largest publishing center in all of Poland. The impetus behind that achievement was an experience in 1917, while he was studying for the priesthood in Rome. It was the 200th anniversary of modern Freemasonry, and in the streets of Rome he witnessed anti-clerical Masonic demonstrations that shocked him deeply. Though only a 23-year-old student, he founded the "Militia of the Immaculata," an organization dedicated to the conversion of sinners, non-Catholics (including Jews), and "especially Freemasons."

When the young priest returned to Poland, he determined to fight the influence of Freemasonry by means of a popular Catholic press. In 1922 he began publishing the *Rycerz Niepokalanej,* an inexpensive monthly that by the end of the next decade enjoyed the largest circulation of any periodical in Poland. In 1927 he founded a monastery of Conventual Franciscans not far from Warsaw which he named Niepokalanów (City of the Immaculata). By 1939 it numbered nearly eight hundred members and was one of the largest monasteries in the world. It was Kolbe's intention to make it a publication center, and he succeeded phenomenally,

---

[89] For biographical information on Kolbe, see Antonio Ricciardi, *Maximilien Kolbe, prêtre et martyr: sources historiques* (Paris: Mediaspaul, 1987); Maria Winowska, *Szaleniec Niepokalanej, Ojciec Maksymilian Kolbe* (London: Veritas, 1959); Francesco Panchieri, *Massimiliano Kolbe, Santo del Secolo* (Padua: EMP, 1982).

despite the fact that he left Poland in 1930. For six years he labored as a missionary in Japan, establishing a similar monastery in Nagasaki.

It was in May 1935, while Kolbe was in Japan, that the Conventual Franciscans at Niepokalanów began publishing the *Mały Dziennik* (Little Daily). They succeeded where the bishops could not by producing the paper cheaply and selling it for only five *groszy,* half the price or less of other Polish dailies. Father Marian Wójcik was the editor-in-chief; a layman, Jerzy Rutkowski, was responsible for political affairs. Kolbe never edited the *Mały Dziennik* and wrote only a few articles for it of a purely religious nature. But in 1936 he returned from Japan to become the superior of Niepokalanów and its vast publishing enterprise. He had general indirect supervision over the *Mały Dziennik* and saw its circulation grow from a hundred thousand copies an issue in 1935 to three hundred thousand copies at the end of 1938. By that time eleven publications were emanating from the Franciscan monastery, employing a work force of some 577 men, most of them members of the order.

Kolbe's was a militant Catholicism. Like Pope Pius XI, he was convinced that the forces that had secularized France and Italy were at work in Poland, and he set out to oppose them. But his publishing efforts were aimed at the lower middle class, and the *Mały Dziennik* was anything but imposing in either its contents or format. The bishops wanted a Catholic daily that would also attract a more educated readership. They sought it in the *Głos Narodu* (Voice of the Nation) out of Kraków. For some years *Głos Narodu* had been the official organ of the Christian Democratic party (*Chadecja*), but in 1936 it became officially non-partisan and was taken over by Catholic Action and the Archdiocese of Kraków. Edited by Father Jan Piwowarczyk and ultimately responsible to Archbishop Adam Sapieha, *Głos Narodu* was published far more professionally than the *Mały Dziennik,* but had nowhere near the circulation or influence of its competitor. In spite of more exalted ambitions, its impact remained provincial.

4. A Catholic Poland?

No matter what the level of readership or the format or frequency of issue, every publication produced under Catholic auspices was required to represent strict orthodoxy. To guarantee that end, the bishops by their office were expected to supervise all Catholic publishing, and exercising surveillance over the bishops was the papal nuncio. To carry the label

Catholic, periodicals and journals had to represent the thinking of the Holy See. The very purpose of the Catholic press was to articulate and defend papal teaching on such matters as church-state relations, marriage, and Catholic education. And according to papal teaching, states as well as individuals owed homage to God and deference to the true church. It was therefore the task of Catholic Action and the Catholic press to make nations like Poland not only factually, but formally, more Catholic.

The concept of a Catholic Poland could not help but make a large Jewish presence problematic. Poland in the 1930s was caught between two totalitarian superpowers, led by two of the most ruthless criminals in the twentieth or any century. Yet it is no exaggeration to say that the Polish Catholic clergy and press were just as exercised over liberalism as over nazism and communism. This was no peculiarity of Polish Catholicism, since it was papal teaching that liberalism had paved the way for communism. A priest, writing in this same vein for other priests, was not untypical when he blamed class conflict and the chaos in the world on capitalistic liberalism. He was sure that Roman Dmowski spoke for the whole of Catholic society when he identified Polishness with Catholicism. To separate the nation from the Church would damage the very fabric of the nation.[90]

In the last months before the invasion of Poland by Nazi Germany, the editor of the Jesuit *Przegląd Powszechny* confidently described Poland as a bastion of freedom and Christianity in Europe.[91] He had no doubt but that Poland's politics corresponded to those of the Vatican. The highest moral authority in the world, the successor of Saint Peter, was with them. Poland would fight Germany's neo-pagan racism. But joining with the democracies of the west did not mean identifying with them. The priest assured his readers that Poland would continue to distance itself from their "secularity and masonry."

It goes without saying that such an attitude bore ramifications for Poland's Jews.

---

[90]*Przegląd Homiletyczny*, 15 (1937): 216–18.

[91]*Przegląd Powszechny*, 222 (1939): 403–9.

Chapter 2

Liberalism: The Masonic-Jewish "Alliance"

"I must warn you, as Christ once warned the apostles," Pope Pius XI told a group of Polish pilgrims to the Vatican (October 4, 1929). "Be watchful and pray. Be watchful, for dangers and insidious traps are threatening you. The enemy of all good is working in your midst. Here above all I have in mind the Masonic sect, which is spreading its perverse and destructive principles even in Poland." The warning was not forgotten by the Polish Catholic press and repeated several years later by the Pope's legate to the Polish Synod of bishops, Cardinal Marmaggi.[1]

The Polish Catholic attitude toward Jews between the wars cannot be understood apart from the Roman Catholic attitude toward Freemasonry, liberalism, and the emergence of the modern secular state. The literature on each of these subjects is immense, involving the French Revolution, the Risorgimento to unify Italy, and the so-called laic laws of the Third Republic in France. The "Jewish-Masonic conspiracy," widely forgotten today, was a staple in the antisemitic arsenal of the 1930s, particularly in Catholic regions of Europe. In Poland it was a major, for some even consuming, concern. Though its origins appear to be German, its classical expression and most numerous exponents were French.

---

[1] *Mały Dziennik*, July 25, 1938.

Freemasonry and Liberalism

The origins of modern Freemasonry date back to early eighteenth century England. Church building had declined in the seventeenth century, and lodges of working Masons in England had begun admitting non-working members into their numbers, sharing secret symbols and passwords with them. When these "honorary" Masons outnumbered the operatives, the lodges became schools of morality which used the older symbols to inculcate ethical lessons.[2] Four such lodges banded together in London (June 24, 1717) to form the Grand Lodge of England. In an era torn by religious dissention, it was decided not to make religious affiliation a test for membership. Not only members of the established church of England but dissenters and even Roman Catholics could join their ranks. According to the 1723 constitution, written by Presbyterian minister James Anderson, a Mason "will never be a stupid Atheist, nor an irreligious libertine." Masons were obliged to obey the moral law and adhere to those aspects of religion "in which all men agree, leaving their particular opinions to themselves."[3]

The religious "landmarks" or principles of Freemasonry were Deist in origin. They included belief in God and in the immortality of the soul and the acceptance of a sacred law, such as the Bible. Points of dissention were bracketed off for the sake of "conciliating true friendship." In the original Masonic conception, religion, like politics, were not to be discussed within lodge meetings. Other landmarks were the equality of all Masons within the lodge, no matter what their religious affiliation or social class and the right of Masons to visit other lodges. As a consequence, Freemasonry became an attractive opportunity to enter into socially elite circles, especially for outsiders like Roman Catholics and Jews.

Within less than a decade, Freemasonry spread to Ireland and the continent. By 1738 lodges had been established not only in France, Germany, and the English colonies, but in Spain, Portugal, and Italy. Upon the establishment of lodges in Tuscany, Pope Clement XII issued

---

[2] By its own definition, Freemasonry is a "peculiar system of morality, veiled in allegory and illustrated by symbols." Alec Mellor, *Nos frères séparés, les francs-maçons* (Paris: Mame, 1961), 246.

[3] Mellor, *Nos frères séparés*, 78–79.

in 1738 the first of a series of papal condemnations (*In eminenti*), excommunicating any Catholics who joined the Freemasons. The principal reason offered for the condemnation was the Masonic oath of secrecy, which constituted, in the Pope's words, a "strong suspicion" that Freemasons were "acting ill." Along with the secrecy were "other just and reasonable causes known to ourselves," but left unexplained by the Pope.[4] The condemnation was repeated (1751) by Pope Benedict XIV (*Providas Romanorum Pontificum*). Once again the reasons given were not heresy or philosophical errors but secrecy and the Masonic oath.

Despite the papal prohibitions, Catholics continued to enter the ranks of Freemasons. In Ireland some lodges were composed entirely of priests and Catholic laymen like the patriot, Daniel O'Connell. A Masonic apron was sent as a gift to George Washington by the nuns from a convent in Nantes. Daniel Carroll, the brother of Bishop John Carroll, the first Roman Catholic bishop of the United States, was both a Catholic and an active Mason. When asked his opinion on the matter, Bishop Carroll wrote in 1794 of the papal ban: "I do not pretend that these decrees are received generally by the Church, or have full authority in this diocese."[5] According to ancient church practice, a doctrine or law had to be "received" by the church in order to have "full authority." In the view of at least one bishop, more than fifty years after its appearance, the papal ban against Freemasonry was being "generally" ignored by the Church.

An event which certainly helped to change all that was the publication in 1797 of a four volume work by Abbé Augustin Barruel, *Memoires pour servir d'histoire au Jacobinisme.* It was a best-seller and made its author the "father of modern anti-Masonry."[6] An emigré living in London, Barruel had already written sixteen volumes on the French Revolution and the disestablishment of the Catholic church in France, none of them with the slightest anti-Masonic allusion. His *Memoires,* however, took up and popularized a thesis raised earlier (1791) by a Eudist priest named Lefranc. Barruel ascribed the French Revolution, especially its excesses, to a Masonic plot to overthrow Christian

---

[4] William J. Whalen, *Christianity and American Freemasonry* (Milwaukee: Bruce, 1958), 101–2.

[5] Whalen, *Christianity and American Freemasonry,* 103.

[6] Mellor, *Nos frères séparés,* 273.

civilization. Barruel's book earned its author a fortune with translations into English, Italian, Spanish, and Russian.[7] It also supplied new reasons for the papal condemnations against Freemasonry.

Modern scholarship recognizes that eighteenth century Freemasonry in France was aristocratic more than republican, rather to be found among the emigrés and victims of the Revolution than among its adherents. Freemasonry neither provoked nor facilitated the events of 1789.[8] But by the latter part of the nineteenth century, the myth of Masonic responsibility for the Revolution had become a commonplace, accepted by France's Freemasons themselves. By that time they were anti-clerical Republicans, happy to take credit for the Revolution even as their monarchist Catholic adversaries reviled them for it.[9]

When the Napoleonic empire replaced the First Republic, the liberal ideas of 1789 spread to Italy. There they gave rise to the Carbonari, a secret society dedicated to the Risorgimento, the movement for a politically united Italy, to be governed either as a constitutional monarchy or a republic. At first even Catholic clergy joined its ranks. Though neither generated by nor affiliated with Freemasonry, the Carbonari were influenced by Masonic symbolism. The two organizations, theoretically distinct, so interpenetrated each other that they became indistinguishable. In 1821 Pope Pius VII condemned the Carbonari as an imitation of the Masons. In 1831, when the military failures of the Carbonari convinced Giuseppe Mazzini to form his own organization, Young Italy, once again those who joined him were Masons.[10]

The pontifical condemnations did not distinguish between English and North American Masons who avoided political involvement and those of the Grand Orient lodges on the continent who did not. Neither were distinctions made between Masonic and other secret societies, nor between anti-clericals and those Christian liberals who claimed a Christian basis for democratic principles. All were identified with

---

[7] Mellor, *Nos frères séparés,* 273–78.

[8] For a detailed refutation of the legend, see Alec Mellor, *Histoire de l'anticlericalisme français* (Paris: Mame, 1978), 224–34.

[9] Robert F. Byrnes, *Antisemitism in Modern France* (New Brunswick, NJ: Rutgers University, 1950), 1:126, n. 61.

[10] Mellor, *Nos frères séparés,* 296–98.

wanting to overturn the existing social order and, in the case of Italy, posing a very real threat to the Pope's temporal sovereignty over the Papal States. In 1832, Pope Gregory XVI (1831–1846) issued an encyclical (*Mirari vos*) against the "errors" and "evils" of those "shameless lovers of liberty" and those Catholic reformers who suggested that the church needed to change. "Absurd and erroneous" (*insanis*) was the Pope's description of what he called "indifferentism," the "shameful" idea that "liberty of conscience must be maintained for everyone." Likewise assailed were "immoderate freedom of opinion, license of free speech" and the "never sufficiently denounced freedom to publish any writings whatever."[11]

Gregory's successor, Pope Pius IX (1846–1878), was mistaken at first as sympathetic to liberal ideas because of political reforms he inaugurated at the beginning of his pontificate. He insisted, however, that temporal sovereignty over the papal territories was essential for the autonomy and freedom of the Holy See and for that reason inalienable. But the encroachments of the Risorgimento continued, and by 1860 the unification of Italy was a reality. Piedmont brought under its aegis the remaining principalities of Italy, except for Rome, and the Roman Question came to absorb the popes for the next several decades together with political liberalism.

In Italy liberal measures began in Piedmont under the pressure of a middle class increasingly adverse to ecclesiastical privilege. In 1850 the jurisdiction of church courts in civil and criminal cases involving clergy was abolished, and in 1855 there began a process of secularizing the schools. Attempts at compromise by moderate liberals failed because of more radical anti-clericals in the government and adamant churchmen resistant to any change in their former status.[12] These events constituted the background to Pope Pius IX's 1864 encyclical, *Quanta cura,* and its both celebrated and berated Syllabus of Errors.

The Syllabus consisted of a catalogue of eighty propositions already censured individually by the pope but brought together as the "chief errors" of the day. Some of the propositions were purely religious and

---

[11] Claudia Carlen, I.H.M., *The Papal Encyclicals, 1740–1981*. 5 vols. (1981; reprint, Ann Arbor, MI: Pierien Press, 1990), 1:235–41.

[12] Roger Aubert, *The Church in a Secularized Society,* The Christian Centuries Series, vol. 5 (New York: Paulist Press, 1978), 81–83.

philosophical. Other reprobated errors were much more political: that the papacy would benefit by its abrogation of temporal power; that church and state should be separated; that public schools should be under the state and removed from the control of the church; that civil authority should sanction divorce. The word "liberalism" has acquired a variety of meanings over its long career, depending on its context. For our purposes here and throughout this study, I shall assume the definition given to it by the Vatican Documents that condemned it. "Liberalism" according to the Syllabus of Errors was the "absurd principle" that the state should treat all religions alike without distinction.[13]

With the onset of the Franco-Prussian war, French troops were removed from Rome and the pope lost his sovereignty over the city (1870). A moderate Law of Guarantees (1871) tried to provide for the independence of the pontiff in his new situation, but Pius IX would have none of it. He refused to accept the new state of affairs as permanent and became a self-imposed prisoner of the Vatican.

By forbidding Italian Catholics to serve in the government or even vote in general elections (*Ne eletti ne elettori*), Pope Pius IX left an open field to anti-clericals who, from the 1880s on were spearheaded by Italian Masons.[14] Chairs of theology at state universities were abolished (1872). The compulsory payment of tithes to the church was declared illegal (1887). Religious instruction in public schools, previously mandated by law was rendered first optional and then banned altogether (1888). In the 1890s the considerable holdings of religious orders were expropriated and charitable enterprises under church auspices were taken over by the state.[15] In comparison to measures taken in France and Spain, even Catholic historians recognize the moderation of these laws and their uneven implementation.[16] But for the clergy trained in this era and who set the tone in the Catholic church for the next several decades, liberalism

---

[13] Carlen, *Papal Encyclicals*, 1:381–85. *The Dublin Review*, NS 4 (April 1865): 513–529.

[14] Aubert, *Church in a Secularized Society*, 84, n. 18.

[15] J. Salwyn Schapiro, *Anticlericalism: Conflict between Church and State in France, Italy, and Spain* (Princeton, NJ: Van Nostrand, 1967), 79–81.

[16] Aubert, *Church in a Secularized Society*, 83; Jose M. Sanchez, *Anticlericalism: A Brief History* (Notre Dame, IN: Notre Dame University, 1972), 151.

was the political program of Freemasons who oppressed Christianity and opposed its values.

The accession of Pope Leo XIII (1878–1903) brought some change to papal policy. He encouraged French Catholics to abandon their chimerical ideas of restoring a Christian monarchy and to exploit their constitutional liberties in behalf of the church's cause. But Leo was no liberal, and he reaffirmed his predecessors' pronouncements on Christian society, liberalism, and Freemasonry. In 1885 (*Immortale Dei*) he declared that government could take any form, but derived its authority from God, not from the people. Societies, like individuals, were obliged to express public worship.[17] Pope Leo's encyclical *Libertas* (1888) was considered a moderate document, representing the concessions he thought the Catholic church could make toward liberalism.[18] States too had duties to God and were bound to profess the true religion, he wrote; separation of church and state was a "fatal theory." The Catholic Church was not to be treated by the state "like any voluntary association of citizens." It was "quite unlawful to demand, defend, or grant unconditional freedom of thought, of speech, of writing, or of worship, as if these were so many rights given by nature." With an obvious eye on pluralistic societies, however, the Pope added that "freedom in these things may be tolerated" when there is "just cause" and "moderation."[19]

Pope Leo apparently saw neither just cause nor moderation in the secularizing legislation enacted by Freemasons in the Italian government. In 1884 he published the longest and most detailed papal denunciation of the international fraternity then or since (*Humanum genus*).[20] The reasons were no longer simply secrecy and the Masonic oath. The kingdom of Satan led by Freemasons was at war with God in their struggle against the church and Christendom. The ultimate purpose of the Masons was "the utter overthrow of that whole religious and political order of the world which Christian teaching has produced," replacing it with a new order based on "naturalism." By this, the pope explained, he

---

[17] Carlen, *Papal Encyclicals*, 2:107–19.

[18] Guido de Ruggiero, *The History of European Liberalism*, trans. by R. G. Collingwood (London: Oxford University Press, 1927), 400.

[19] Carlen, *Papal Encyclicals*, 2:169–81.

[20] Carlen, *Papal Encyclicals*, 2:91–101.

meant using only human reason to resolve matters of state, taking no account of Catholic church teaching to determine public policy. Concretely this meant separation of church and state and the "great error of this age," namely, treating the Catholic church as equal to other religions.

Pope Leo charged Freemasonry with responsibility for depriving him of his temporal sovereignty and for introducing civil marriage, divorce, and secular education into Italy. People were equal in their origin, nature, and destiny, wrote the Pontiff, but Masons went beyond this to teach equality of rights, which leads to socialism and communism. The Pope concluded with reference to Masonic misunderstanding of the true meaning of liberty, equality, and fraternity. Barruel's linkage of Masonry with the ideals of the French Revolution had apparently made an impact upon the highest echelons of the church. Eighteen years later Pope Leo would imply the connection once again, describing Freemasonry as "the permanent personification of revolution."[21]

Several times Pope Leo XIII repeated his condemnation of Freemasons for their political liberalism. More than once he described them as operating with "satanic intent" and as "possessed by the spirit of Satan, whose instrument they are."[22] The fact that Italy was simply following other nations in Western Europe was perceived as only confirming that this "anti-Christian system" was the result of a "conspiracy" endangering Christian civilization.[23] Though often employing other hands, Masonry was inspiring and promoting "persecution" of the church, declared the Pope. He called upon Italian Catholics to wage war against it with a Catholic press, schools, congresses, and clubs. Catholics were to avoid familiarity or friendship not only with suspected Masons but also with "those who hide under the mask of universal tolerance, respect for all religions, and the craving to reconcile the maxims of the Gospel with those of the revolution."[24]

In France the establishment of the Third Republic (1875) brought to power not merely a democratic form of government but a secular faith

---

[21] *Acta Apostolicae Sedis,* 34 (1901-1902): 526.

[22] Carlen, *Papal Encyclicals,* 2:226, 302.

[23] Carlen, *Papal Encyclicals,* 2:226, 297.

[24] Carlen, *Papal Encyclicals,* 2:302, 304.

in the principles of 1789, principles which for French Catholics evoked memories of suppression, confiscation of church property, and persecution. A political struggle between royalists and liberal republicans resulted in a resounding triumph for the republicans who promptly set about secularizing the school system (1881–1882), requiring civil marriage (1881), and permitting divorce (1884). In reaction to the crisis caused by the Dreyfus Affair, more radical liberals succeeded in passing legislation that dissolved all but authorized religious orders (1901). Four years later the 1801 Concordat Napoleon made with the Vatican was formally rescinded. The ties between the Catholic church and France were severed by the separation law of 1905.[25]

Despite the fact that the church was now freed from considerable control by the French government (e.g. in the naming of bishops), Pope Pius X condemned the separation law as the work of the church's Masonic enemies.[26] There is no denying that Freemasons played a leading role in the Third Republic. Every important government minister was a Freemason (Leon Gambetta, Jules Ferry, and Emile Combes). Under Combes in particular, the Grand Lodge of Paris served virtually as a shadow government, a think-tank for anti-clerical legislation. *"Le clericalisme, viola l'ennemi"*—was more than an empty catch phrase for these secularizing republicans. For their French Catholic adversaries as well there was no doubt as to who was the enemy—*le judeo-maçonnerie.*

Freemasonry and Jews

The first known instance of a Jew being admitted to a Masonic lodge was in London in 1732. There is no indication that the authors of the English constitutions intended their toleration of Christian diversity to provide for Jewish membership. But, when Jewish candidates applied, the principle was extended to them as well. And, since membership in a Masonic lodge offered access to social elites and thereby considerable business advantages, significant numbers of Jews applied and were admitted. The same was true in Holland. In France, the 1755 constitution of the Grand Lodge made baptism a requirement for admission; only in the wake of

---

[25] See Sanchez, *Anticlericalism,* 112–19; Schapiro, *Anticlericalism,* 57–69.

[26] Carlen, *Papal Encyclicals,* 3:45–48, 67–69.

the Revolution did Freemasonry follow the Republic and become open to French Jews. The Grand Orient of France eventually eliminated belief in God and the immortality of the soul as requirements for membership (1877), whereupon the Grand Lodge in England and its affiliates severed their ties with it.

In Germany Jewish efforts to join the Masonic lodges were resisted. Although barriers against Jewish membership were let down gradually in some areas, antisemitic forces bent on preserving the old social order and its values prevailed well into the late nineteenth century.[27] So it was that Eduard Emil Eckert's book, *Der Freimauer-Orden in seiner wahren Bedeutung,* made little impact in Germany. He argued that Masonry was under the influence of Jews, and that both groups were in an alliance to undermine traditional society. In Germany Eckert's book was dismissed even by those who were in principle antagonistic to Freemasonry. When it appeared (1854) in French translation, however, Eckert's book found more fertile ground. Jews were well represented in French Masonic leadership. Adolphe Cremieux, the most prominent Jewish Freemason in France, eventually became head of the Scottish rite.

Gougenot de Mousseaux, a Catholic theologian, took up Eckert's thesis in his book, *Le Juif, Le Judaisme, et la judaisation des peuples chrétiens* (1869), but he treated it incidentally, alongside the deicide charge and blood libel.[28] For E. N. Chabauty, however, a village priest, Jews were the covert grand masters of Masonry, a thesis he made into the central theme of his book, *Franc-Maçons et Juifs, sixième Âge de l'Eglise d'après l'Apocalypse* (1880). By this time the loss of the Pope's temporal sovereignty and the secularizing program of the Third Republic convinced Chabauty that both Masons and Jews were agents of the devil. As for who was directing whom, it was clear to the priest: "The Jew with his gold and his genius had seized supreme power within Masonry and secret societies."[29] Jews gave the commands and Masons carried them out. Such allegations were hardly credible in countries like Germany where antisemitism was present within the lodges themselves or in Great

---

[27] Jacob Katz, *Jews and Freemasons in Europe, 1723–1939,* trans. by Leonard Oschry (Cambridge, MA: Harvard University Press, 1970), 15–19, 208–18.

[28] Katz, *Jews and Freemasons,* 148–57.

[29] Katz, *Jews and Freemasons,* 270, n. 55.

Britain where lodges were determinedly apolitical. But in France, where lines were drawn between royalist Catholics and secular republicans, Jews and Freemasonry were easily associated in the popular mind.

With more than some justification, French Catholics saw their church as the most important institutional victim of the French Revolution. And they blamed Masons, the self-appointed protagonists of the Revolution, and Jews, arguably its foremost beneficiaries.[30]

Chabauty's book was too prolix to be popular, but its title contributed a new slogan to the antisemitic arsenal, and between 1882 and 1886 some twenty volumes appeared in print describing the "Judeo-Masonic plot."[31] In 1884 Alfred Rastoul began publishing *La Franc-Maçonnerie démasquée,* a monthly that would see forty-two volumes in quarto before its demise. Here readers could learn of the "princes of Judah" hidden somewhere in Europe, governing Catholic nations with the help of Masons and the Catholic supporters of liberal republicanism. Here one could read how the biblical symbolism of Masonic ritual (King Solomon, Hiram of Tyre, Solomon's temple) supposedly demonstrated the Jewish origins of Freemasonry.[32]

In 1886 Eduard Drumont's two volume *La France juivé* appeared and within twenty-five years went through two hundred editions. A journalist, not an historian, Drumont attempted to give his work a scholarly air by the sheer mass of anecdotes and details. His purpose, however, was the pseudo-scientific comparison of chivalrous, unselfish Aryans (traditional, Catholic France) with greedy, scheming Semites (liberal, Masonic Jewish France). Exemplifying the latter were Adolphe Crémieux, the Rothschilds, and, despite his French mother and early Catholic education, Leon Gambetta, whom, because of his Genoese-Jewish father, Drumont titled "the Jewish emperor of France." The longest part of Drumont's book was taken up with the "persecution" of Catholic France by Masons and Protestants, both under the influence of Jews.[33]

---

[30] Katz, *Jews and Freemasons,* 157–59.

[31] Robert F. Byrnes, *Antisemitism in Modern France* (New Brunswick, NJ: Rutgers University, 1950), 127; Pierre Pierrard, *Juifs et catholiques français: De Drumont à Jules Isaac, 1886–1945* (Paris: Fayard, 1970), 29–30.

[32] Pierrard, *Juifs et catholiques français,* 29–30.

[33] Pierrard, *Juifs et catholiques français,* 38–44.

Drumont presented himself as a Catholic writing for Catholics, and his book was warmly received by the Catholic press. Encouraged, he admitted, by the clergy, he went on to help found the *Ligue nationale antisemitique de France* and its antisemitic daily newspaper, *La Libre Parôle* (1892).[34]

During the Dreyfus Affair (1894–1906), Drumont associated Dreyfus' "treachery" with a Jewish plot to rule France.[35] It can be argued that, thanks to Drumont, antisemitism became an integral part of Catholic anti-Masonry. By 1900 there were three periodicals taken up with Masons and Jews, each sponsored by an anti-Masonic organization: *La France chrétienne,* later renamed *La France antimaçonnique,* a weekly; *La Franc-Maçonnerie démasquée,* a weekly; and *À bas les tyrants,* a weekly. In 1912 Abbé Ernest Jouin founded *La Revue internationale des Sociétés Secretes,* which was to become the most important periodical dedicated to the struggle against the "Jewish-Masonic conspiracy" and published right up to the Second World War. In its pages one could perceive the emergence of a veritable network of forces, combining antisemitism and anti-Masonry with the anti-modernist integralism of Pope Pius X and the anti-liberal nationalism of Charles Maurras and his *L'Action Française.*[36]

Maurras was himself an agnostic, but he advocated a program of "integral nationalism" that identified France politically with monarchy and culturally with Catholicism. Under his direction, *L'Action Française* emerged as a league at the height of the Dreyfus Affair (1899); in 1908 it began publishing its newspaper under the same name, both dedicated to the destruction of the French Republic for favoring "religious influences directly hostile to traditional Catholicism." The Roman church for Maurras was the only force in France capable of withstanding "the Jewish army." It was its Roman heritage that he valued in Catholicism, its hierarchical authority and discipline, not the Jewish Jesus, whose gospel he disdained. Maurras' theological heterodoxy and blatant political use of the church eventually served to have his works put on the Index

---

[34] Pierrard, *Juifs et catholiques français,* 18, 33.

[35] Richard I. Cohen, "The Dreyfus Affair and the Jews," in Shmuel Almog (ed.) *Antisemitism through the Ages* (Oxford: Pergamon, 1988), 301.

[36] Pierrard, *Juifs et catholiques français,* 159–60.

of Forbidden Books, but not until his league had attracted support for its crusade against Masons and Jews from among the highest circles in the church.[37]

The "Jewish problem" figured intrinsically in the persistent clash between Catholic conservatives and liberal republicans. The point at issue between them was no less than defining what it meant to be French. Active in the debate were the Assumptionist priests who published France's most influential Catholic daily, *La Croix*. With a circulation of almost two hundred thousand and fraternal ties to the French hierarchy, *La Croix* described itself as "the most anti-Jewish newspaper in France."[38] Like *L'Action Française*, *La Croix* saw Jews and Masons as the natural enemies of Catholic France. Jews were the revolutionaries par excellence, whose long history of insurrection began "at the foot of Calvary" and whose two dominant desires were "to fight the religion of Jesus Christ and to dominate the world by the power of money."[39]

Political anti-clericalism became one of the casualties of World War I, when all parties, even the most extreme right and left, were compelled to unite in the common defense of France. Catholic valor on the battlefield demonstrated Catholic loyalty to the Republic, and after the war more moderate forces came to determine policy, both in the French government and in the church in the persons of Pope Benedict XV and Pope Pius XI. The Vatican was willing to make its peace with both the French Republic and modern pluralist society. At least, it would seem, when it could do nothing else.

Pius XI was no advocate of democratic principles. His horror of bolshevism (see chapter on Communism) inclined him to a strong preference for authoritarian governments. His inaugural encyclical, *Ubi arcano Dei* (1922), made it quite clear that he intended to uphold the teachings of his predecessors on issues like church-state relations and the social and political rights ("prerogatives") of the church and the Holy See. There was a species of legal and social modernism to be

---

[37] Charles Maurras and Leon Daudet, *L'"Action Française" et le Vatican* (Paris: Ernest Flammarion, 1927); Oscar L. Arnal, *Ambivalent Alliance, The Catholic Church and the Action Française, 1899–1939* (Pittsburgh, PA: University of Pittsburgh, 1985), 16–22, 78–79.

[38] Arnal, *Ambivalent Alliance*, 33.

[39] Arnal, *Ambivalent Alliance*, 38.

condemned, he declared, no less than theological modernism.[40] This explains the anti-Masonic warning the Pope gave in 1929 to the pilgrims from Poland. The state of war between the Catholic church and liberalism had clearly not been altered. Only the field of battle.

Liberalism and Freemasonry in Poland

Freemasonry came to Poland in 1738 with one of the earliest lodges in Europe. Though subsequently banned, it reappeared in the last years of Polish independence, when it could claim King Stanisław-August (1764–1795) as a member. Before the partitions, Polish Freemasons agitated for social reforms, including granting rights to townspeople and peasants but also confiscating the land holdings of bishops. During the partitions, the lodges in Prussian Poland were associated with German liberal movements. In the Congress Kingdom and Russian Poland as well, Masons attracted a following of liberal intelligentsia until they were suppressed because of Masonic involvement in the Polish uprising of 1830.

With the end of World War I, eight lodges were organized in Poland and a Grand National Lodge in Warsaw, *Polacy Zjednoczeni* (Reunited Poles). Several Freemasons participated actively in Piłsudski's 1925 coup d'etat and in the subsequent government, among them the prime minister, Kazimierz Bartel. Even though Piłsudski governed as a dictator, he enjoyed the sympathy of liberal circles in Europe as well as Poland. Polish Freemasons were bourgeois intellectuals at odds with the program of Endecja. Though they favored the workers' movement, they were not revolutionary. Rather, the program of interwar Polish Freemasonry called for: enhancing the republican form of government; separation of church and state; dominance by the state in the secular education of youth; recognition and respect for the rights of national minorities.[41]

---

[40] Carlen, *Papal Encyclicals,* 3:236–37.

[41] Leon Chajn, *Polskie Wolnomularstwo, 1920–1938,* 2nd ed. (Warszawa: Czytelnik, 1984), 110–11. Norman Davies, *God's Playground: A History of Poland* (New York: Columbia University, 1982), 2:58–59. Ludwik Hass, "Grandeur et declin de la franc-maçonnerie en Europe centrale et orientale, 1926–1938," *Poland at the 14th International Congress of Historical Sciences in San Francisco,* Bolesław Geremek and Antoni

Because of their humanist ethic, the Polish lodges contained atheists and liberals of various shades but also some self-proclaimed "practicing Catholics." Between the wars, even within the Catholic church, liberalism was not without its partisans, as the complaints of their adversaries made clear. "There is no lack of progressive Catholics today," wrote Dr. E. Muszyński in *Wiara i Życie*. Such Catholics wanted the church to modernize and were embarrassed by the anti-liberal stance of the papal encyclicals. Muszyński acknowledged and defended the church's intolerance. "The Catholic church is fully aware that it alone is the orthodox guardian of revealed religion, that to it belongs governance over the conscience of the world." To recognize other churches and religions alongside itself would be moral suicide for the church, a betrayal before God. "A doctrinally tolerant Catholicism would cease to be Catholicism." Although in practice the church accepted freedom of conscience for the sake of the commonweal, "theoretical and doctrinal intolerance of other faiths follows from the very principles of Catholicism."

Muszyński admitted that some adherents of the French Revolution were consistent and sincere, but insisted that in no other period of history was freedom of conscience violated to such an extent. A century later, another religious war in France saw defenseless monks driven out from their cloisters, treated as traitors for their loyalty to the pope (a foreign monarch), until their valor in battle proved otherwise. But now, claimed Muszyński, "radicals" in Poland were using the same old arguments Gambetta did, tolerating Catholicism as a private sentiment, but crying "clericalism" if the church tried to exercise political influence. Tolerance might be a "fashionable" word among Polish liberals, but it masked a fanatic hatred for religion, Muszyński claimed. Whether under the aegis of liberalism, free thought, or religious indifference, liberals were hypocrites who praised tolerance but acted otherwise.[42]

Writing in *Pro Christo,* a monthly published by the Marianist priests, Stefan Kaczorowski was also concerned about Poles who looked to western Europe and liberal principles to solve Poland's "Jewish question." Centuries before, western Europe had driven out masses of Jews who then settled in Poland. Now, wrote Kaczorowski, with liberal thinking on the decline in almost all of western Europe, Jews were

---

Brykczyński (eds.), (Wroclaw/Warsaw: Ossolineum, 1975), 287–316.

[42] *Wiara i Życie,* 12 (1932): 173–78.

imposing liberal views on Polish society. Out of their own self-interest, he said, Jews were encouraging Poles to embrace the materialistic, liberal ideas of a century ago, especially that of equality before the law. The sons of tenants and saloon keepers had prospered and become merchants and industrialists. Their grandsons were becoming doctors, lawyers, engineers, and professors. Kaczorowski was concerned that "before long half the intellectuals in Poland will be Jewish." These Jews had a command of the Polish language, history, literature, and art, but, he insisted, they were not in the least affected by the "spirit" of Poland's national culture.

The Jewish middle class, wrote Kaczorowski, had a great economic advantage over the Poles. With the financial help of their parents, Jewish students did not have to work as well as study, and thus had a much better chance of completing their higher education. Combined with political equality, this economic advantage added up to factual privilege. Justice, Kaczorowski insisted, demanded that the state protect Christians by depriving Jews of political equality. He argued on the basis of the social structure of the middle ages, which did not grant equality to all, but was nonetheless accepted by the Catholic church as a just social order. The church could not have erred. If justice did not require political equality in that era, then it did not do so now, Kaczorowski insisted. Moreover, if Jews were deprived of political equality, they would leave Poland. Then he concluded, Poland would be Poland and not "Judeo-Poland."[43]

Father St. Bednarski, S.J., agreed: if Poland would not be Catholic, it would not be Poland at all. The French Revolution represented hatred of religion and war with God. Liberals in Poland, he wrote, were masking their true intentions under words like progress, but their intention was the removal of all life from the influence of the church.[44]

Efforts by freethinkers and Masons to secularize Poland on the model of western Europe were of central concern to Catholic leaders like Cardinal Hlond.[45] Father Edward Kosibowicz, S.J., of the Jesuit *Przegląd Powszechny* followed suit by warning against specific sources

---

[43] *Pro Christo—Wiara i Czyn,* 9 (1933) 7:410–19.

[44] *Wiara i Życie,* 14 (1934): 193–96.

[45] A. Hlond, "Znaczenie Jubileuszu Odkupienia," *Ruch Katolicki* 4 (1934): 401–7.

of laic thinking: Besides periodicals like *Wolnomyśliciel* (The Freethinker) and *Kurier Poranny* (Morning Courier), there was the *Wiadomości Literackie* (Literary News), which in Jewish fashion (*po żydowsku*) was having a destructive influence on "a whole host" of people. There was the overwhelming majority of medical doctors and a great number of women working with the *Związek Pracy Obywatelskiej Kobiet* (Women's Civil Service Union). Disseminating secular ideas among the youth was the *Legion Młodych* (Legion of Youth) whose periodical *Państwo Pracy* had declared war against clericalism as the "black occupation." Singled out as the "chief apostle of laicization" was literary critic and author, Tadeusz Boy-Żeleński (1874–1941), who had translated more than one hundred volumes of classic French literature into Polish. Boy-Żeleński had earned the ire of church leaders by his efforts in behalf of artificial birth control. His being named a member of the Polish Academy of Literature was declared to have been a "slap in the face" of Polish Catholics.

These Polish freethinkers, it was avowed, were only second-rate copyists, introducing discredited ideas into Poland from radicalized France. Kosibowicz pointed to Gambetta, Ferry, Victor Hugo, and Clemenceau as Masons who hated the Catholic church. Their claim that clericalism was the enemy was only a subterfuge for secularizing schools. God, for them, was the source and mainstay of despotism. The laic laws of the Third Republic supposedly began as a war against clericalism but ended as a war against religion and a campaign against God. The church and clergy in Poland could not be indifferent to similar efforts to secularize marriage, schools, science, politics, and the arts.[46]

The Jesuit journal conceded that the leaders in the effort to secularize Poland (Boy-Żeleński, Stpiczyński, Ułaszyn, Rzymowski, et al.) had formerly been Catholics. Father Nikodem L. Cieszyński had to acknowledge that Ferdynand Machaj, "one of the most radical Catholic authors," was a priest. Gathered around the *Związek Młodzieży Wiejskiej* (Union of Village Youth) and its periodical *Wici,* were liberal writers critical of the church like Wojciech Szuza, Stanisław Młodożeniec, Leon Lutyk, Tadeusz Rek, Stanisław Kot, Tomasz Nocznicki, Stanisław Thugutt, and Ignacy Solarz. These critics were writing things like, "The pagan Gandhi is closer to Christ than the Vatican is." They had an

---

[46] *Przegląd Powszechny,* 200 (1933): 576–93; 204 (1934): 423–33.

especial disdain for Catholic Action and the Catholic press, especially for the *Rycerz Niepokalanej* and the *Mały Dziennik*. Standing out for their philosemitism among these liberals, Father Cieszyński complained, were Dr. Jaworski and Ignacy Solarz.[47]

These liberals and church critics were "apostles of immorality," claimed Father Edward Kosibowicz. While their attacks against faith were not enjoying much success, their attempts to undermine Catholic principles of morality were much more worrisome. Besides the Masonic lodges in Poland, there were any number of organizations without formal ties to Freemasonry but under its influence and serving its ends. Medical doctors and university professors, educators, writers, journalists, and social workers were at war with the "integralism of Catholic ethics." Many of them, Kosibowicz admitted, claimed to be Christian and to be working for reform of the church. But their efforts could only lead to the destruction of Christian faith.

Influenced by Masonic ideas of freedom, these Christian liberals were pressing for liberation from the church's moral discipline, he asserted. They wanted coeducation and sex education in the public schools, an end to compulsory religion classes and religious practice. They wanted secular cemeteries and the confiscation of church property for the sake of schools.

Although the numbers of militant atheists were relatively few, the apostles of immorality constituted an army, including the *Towarzystwo Reformy Obyczajów* (Society for the Reform of Morals) and the *Towarzystwo Krzewienia Świadomego Macierzyństwa* (Society for the Promotion of Birth Control). Was birth control, the priest asked, the way for Poland to become a great power? This kind of thinking was also used by Jews who were "organized in their hatred for Christianity." An "international Jewish mafia," wrote Kosibowocz, was using debauchery and pornography in its "war against Christianity."[48]

Written in the same vein was a pamphlet on freethinking and freedom, published by the Kraków Jesuits in their inexpensive (five *groszy*) and popular *Głosy Katolickie* series. Following the same logic as Pope Pius XI, the anonymous author lumped Freemasons together with socialists and communists. All were in a united front that wanted to come to power

---

[47] Nikodem Ludomir Cieszyński, *Rocznik Katolicki* (Poznań: 1938), 258–63.

[48] *Wiara i Życie*, 15 (1935): 1–8.

in Poland the way they had in Russia and Mexico. Differences among the groups were unimportant. All of them hated and persecuted the church under the guise of freedom of conscience. All of them were trying to remove crucifixes and priests from schools, hospitals, and the army. All of them, but primarily Jews (like Dr. Rubinraut and Maks Boruchowicz) and periodicals serving Jewish interests, were trying to undermine the family and nation by encouraging Poles to practice birth control. Polish Jews, declared the Jesuit publication, were promoting contraception because they feared overpopulation in Poland. They were trying to limit the growth of the Poles so as to secure in advance a place for themselves.[49]

At the opposite end of the spectrum from *Głosy Katolickie* was the *Przegląd Powszechny*, also published by the Jesuits but aimed not at the educated elite. The editor, Father Jan Rostworowski, S.J., was aware that the Masons were not a united fraternity, and that organizations like the Rotary Clubs were not "officially" Masonic. But Rotary, *La Ligue des droits de l'homme*, and the like were allied to Masonry in spirit. That spirit, wrote the Jesuit, was anti-Christian from its very beginning, because it championed natural reason against supernatural religion. Rostworowski admitted that the persecution of the church in Mexico, the anti-Catholic activities of revolutionaries in Spain or of radicals in France and the like—were not the work of one hand, or even of a secret group of oligarchs, like the "Elders of Zion." But one and the same spirit of Masonry was behind them. The spirit of Masonry lay behind the corruption of morals everywhere—from movie theaters and cabarets to beaches and gymnasia, wherever freedom was being demanded from the moral discipline of Christian culture.[50]

If the Jesuits at the *Przegląd Powszechny* did not believe that a group of Jewish "elders" were conspiring with Masons to control the world, the same could not be said of the priests like Father Marian Wiśniewski who published *Pro Christo* or the Franciscans who published *Rycerz Niepokalanej* and *Mały Dziennik*. More than once Wiśniewski described a meeting he and Father Maximilian Kolbe had in May 1926, with Andrzej Strug, a 33rd degree Mason and at that time the Grand Master

---

[49] *Głosy Katolickie*, 35 (February 1935): 27–28.

[50] *Przegląd Powszechny*, 204 (1934): 423–33.

in Poland. Strug acknowledged Masonic efforts on behalf of secular schools, civil marriage, and divorce. He admitted that Masons wanted to limit the influence of Rome, since they regarded it as being too involved in Polish affairs. But Strug denied any Masonic partnership with Jewry. Wiśniewski did not believe him. Masons practiced not only deception but secret assassination. The lowest Masonic "pawns" might belong to the lodge to advance their careers, and the higher "masters" for the sake of power and influence. But at the highest unseen levels, where no gentile could enter, the goal was the domination of Israel over the nations.[51] From the articles that appeared in *Rycerz Niepokalanej* and *Mały Dziennik*, Father Maximilian Kolbe and the Conventual Franciscans at Niepokalanów were apparently of the same mind.

Niepokalanów and the Masons

When the young Maximilian Kolbe founded the Knights of the Immaculate in Rome, he did not name his fledgling organization arbitrarily. The martial designation arose in reaction to the secularizing efforts of Italian Freemasonry. For every *Rycerz Niepokalanej* (Knight of the Immaculata) and for the inexpensive little monthly published under the same name, Masons were the archenemy persecuting the church. From their publishing center at Niepokalanów, Kolbe and his associates warned Catholics to be alert: a "synagogue of Satan" consisting of a small group of freethinkers was working for the devil. Masonry practiced tyranny even over its own members, compelling them to follow strictly directions given from on high. In Warsaw they sponsored a meeting (November 1934) with various Protestant sects to organize a movement for separation of church and state. In France the Great Lodge (Scottish Rite) was concerned solely with political, anti-clerical intrigues. In Mexico a "conspiracy of Jewish-Masonic powers" was behind the closing of churches and arrests of priests.[52] Freethinkers wanted marriages, even for Catholics, to be officiated not by a representative of Christ but by a

---

[51] *Pro Christo—Wiara i Czyn*, 10 (1934): 803–5. *Kielecki Przegląd Diecezjalny*, 25 (1938): 164–68.

[52] *Rycerz Niepokalanej*, (1935): 17–20, 24, 99.

state representative, who might be an atheist or a Jew.[53]

From its very inception, Kolbe's Franciscans at Niepokalanów dedicated the *Mały Dziennik* to the cause for which Pope Pius XI wanted a Catholic daily newspaper in Poland in the first place, the struggle against secularism. In its first week of printing, the paper criticized the Polish constitution for making inadequate references to God. When Witold Wyspiański, a professor from a junior college (gymnasium) gave a "godless" lecture to a group of freethinkers on the origins of religion, the Catholic daily declared him unfit to teach Polish youth.[54]

But, viewed as the chief agent of secularity, the most frequent object of *Mały Dziennik*'s invective was Masonry, by which it meant secret organizations of any kind. A local pastoral letter by the bishop of La Rochelle in France would have received scant notice in Poland except for the bishop's call for a continued war against Masonry. For this it received front page headlines: Masons were endangering the Christian world by agitating for secular public schools, divorce, and separation of church and state. Catholics were not allowed to vote for Masons and were bound to work to change laws passed under Masonic influence. The French bishop left no doubt but that Pope Leo's 1885 condemnation had lost none of its force.[55]

Likewise imported from France was the invariable association of Masonry with Jews. When a new lodge of Odd Fellows was established in Łódź, it was announced that most of its members were Jews.[56] Criticism of Kraków's Archbishop Sapieha by newspapers was declared to be a campaign by the "Jewish-Masonic press" to malign the clergy and draw people away from God. "Foreign elements and those imbued by foreign influence" were de-christianizing Poland.[57]

Mały Dziennik regularly reported anti-Masonic news from France. Efforts there on behalf of coeducation were Masonic propaganda to

---

[53] *Rycerz Niepokalanej,* (1935): 44–45, 141–43.

[54] *Mały Dziennik,* April 13, 1935.

[55] *Mały Dziennik,* May 8, 1935.

[56] *Mały Dziennik,* May 11, 1935.

[57] *Mały Dziennik,* June 4, 1935.

"laicize" women.[58] The French-Soviet alliance was the result of Masonic, Jewish, and socialist intrigue. Romania was financially dependent on cliques of Masonic-Jewish capitalists. Masons were hostile to Poland and trying to instigate a war between church and state.[59] The People's Front in France and the League of Nations in Geneva were critical of fascist Italy and its invasion of Abyssinia, because they wanted a return of Masonic and red parties to power. The League of Nations was being used as an instrument to "Masonize" Italy once again. Christians could thank fascism for returning crosses to Italian schools and institutions, "putting an end to the era of Masonic liberalism." In contrast, Poland was honoring the political stance of the Vatican with regard to Italian fascism.[60] A universal religious revival, Italian fascism and the "healthy national sense" of the right-wing in France convinced the editors of the *Mały Dziennik* that the "death of Masonry's omnipotence" was nigh. "Tomorrow does not belong to them."[61]

On the eve of the Spanish Civil War, the Catholic daily described the election of the leftist coalition in Spain as the "Masonic-Red People's Front." Arrests of right-wing leaders and suspension of the right-wing press was a "Masonic-red terror." But the real concern for *Mały Dziennik* was the Popular Front government in France, which was fortunately more moderate than that in Spain. The example of Spain simply proved that "some countries are not ready for democracy and it was not right to leave them prey to the most barbarous of tyrannies in order to comply with democratic doctrines" (see chapter six on Spain).[62]

In the *Mały Dziennik's* unremitting campaign against liberalism and Jews, one attack in particular stands out for being directed against a man who subsequently become both a hero and a martyr of the Holocaust, Dr. Janusz Korczak. An innovative educator and director of two orphanages, one for Jewish children and another for Christians, Korczak, though born Jewish (Goldszmit), was not observant. He regarded himself simply as a Pole. For the editors of *Mały Dziennik,* this was inconceivable: "Dr.

---

[58] *Mały Dziennik,* August 3, 1935.

[59] *Mały Dziennik,* October 1, 1935.

[60] *Mały Dziennik,* November 14, 1935.

[61] *Mały Dziennik,* January 24, 1936.

[62] *Mały Dziennik,* July 19, 1936.

Goldszmit is a freethinker," an "atheist, an enemy of Catholicism." The Catholic daily accused Korczak of favoring Jewish children, because they received outside adult help for their lessons and the Christian orphans did not. Its chief concern, however, was that a Jew was having a decisive influence on the character development of Catholic children. To put these children "under the care of our enemies" was a "disgrace." *Mały Dziennik* called for government intervention to put an end to Korczak's activity, which it called "hostile and harmful to the Polish cause."[63]

Jews and Atheism

Korczak was not an exception. Jews were regularly associated with liberalism and secularism in general but atheism as well.

With headquarters in Warsaw and branches in other cities, the *Polski Związek Wolnej Myśli* (Polish Free Thought Union) was especially odious to Poland's Catholic leadership. Its publications, the *Wolnomyśliciel Polski* (Polish Freethinker) and the more popular *Błyski Wolnomyśliciel-skie* (Freethinking Flashes) repeatedly criticized the Catholic clergy and offended Catholic sensibilities with disrespectful references to Jesus and Mary, going so far as to omit capitalizing the words God and Christ. One of its most prominent leaders and representatives was Józef Litauer, a Jew who had become a Roman Catholic, then an Orthodox Christian and finally a militant atheist. Despite his several apostasies, Litauer was regularly identified in the Catholic press as a Jew. The Union was regarded as closely related to such Masonic organizations as the *Stowarzyszenie Obrony Wolności i Sumienia w Polsce* (Society for the Defence of Freedom and Conscience in Poland), the *Liga Obrony Praw Człowieka i Obywatela* (League for the Defense of Human and Civil Rights), and *Polskie Stowarzyszenie Etyczne* (Polish Ethical Society).[64]

For Father Jan Urban, S.J., the Union's self-description as freethinking was only a euphemism for atheist. Whether freethinkers, atheists, or socialists, their program called for breaking the concordat with Rome, separating church and state, taking religion out of the public schools, civil

---

[63] *Mały Dziennik,* January 7, 1936.

[64] *Przegląd Powszechny,* 210 (1936): 11–28; *Gazeta Kościelna* (1935): 106.

marriage, and divorce. They viewed the Catholic clergy as "an occupation" in service of a foreign power. As a tactic to weaken the Catholic church, the freethinkers called for equal rights for all confessions and sects in Poland. But their real aim was to weaken all religion, "not sparing even Judaism, from which most of our atheists come."[65]

The *Mały Dziennik* did not agree with the last point. If the *Wolnomyśliciel* was so concerned about progress and humanitarianism, why did it show so little sensitivity for the "macabre conditions" in the Jewish community? Why no anger at the thousands of Jewish boys rendered "senseless with the scholastic subtleties" of the Talmud? Why no attacks on the "idolatrous cult" of the rabbis, especially the miracle-working hasidic *tzaddikim,* or on the condition of Jewish women, abandoned by their husbands, victims of a "monstrous marriage law"? Why, asked the Catholic daily, were Messrs. Litauer, Landau, Jabłoński, and Wroński so alert for Catholic "superstition" but so silent or indifferent about Judaism, about whose weak points they were "better informed"?[66]

Although the Freethinkers' Union denied any connection with Marxism, a police search of suspected communist printing centers revealed anti-government and communist literature on its premises. The Union's periodicals and activities were suspended and the organization suppressed. Freethinking, editorialized the *Mały Dziennik,* was obviously just a variant form of communism. Teofil Jaskiewicz-Wroński, a member of the government's Foreign Affairs Ministry, was the editor of *Wolnomyśliciel,* but, according to the Catholic daily, just a "farm-hand" under the control of Jews like Jabłoński and Litauer.[67] Wroński and Litauer were subsequently tried on the charge of public blasphemy. They had translated and published excerpts of a French work alleged to contain slanders and insults against Jesus. Litauer and Wronski protested that the work was scientific. Litauer was found guilty and sentenced to one year in prison. Wroński was acquitted on the grounds that Litauer was the factual editor and translator of the objectionable piece. Wroński was only

---

[65] *Przegląd Powszechny,* 207 (1935): 3–22.

[66] *Mały Dziennik,* July 30, 1936.

[67] *Mały Dziennik,* August 2, 1936.

formally the editor but did not have any influence over the contents of the periodical.[68]

Father Urban and the editors of the *Mały Dziennik* could feel that their opinions were confirmed in the writings of Father Julian Unszlicht, a Catholic priest of Jewish background. Presumed to be in a position of one who knows, Unszlicht described Jewish intellectuals as the foremost propagators of atheism among Polish workers. Under Jewish direction, he wrote, Polish atheists would learn to abuse the names of Jesus and Mary, although one could still perceive differences between Polish and Jewish atheists. Whereas unbiased Polish atheists were able to admit the historical contribution Christianity had made to Poland, Jewish atheists saw only persecution. For a Jewish atheist, wrote Unszlicht, a Christian wife or lover was a source of pride, putting him above his fellow Jews. There was even a difference in liberated women. An atheist Polish woman would still seek a stable relationship, even as someone's lover. Atheistic Jewish women, claimed the priest, were promiscuous.[69]

Jews and Masons

As with communism and freethinking, so too Polish Jews were linked with Masonry. During World War I, according to the *Mały Dziennik*, Jewish author, Szymon Aszkenazy, was the leader of all Masonry in Poland.[70] Anarchists and communists were usually faulted for the anti-Catholic atrocities in Spain, wrote Dr. T. Szynwaldzki, but both were only instruments of an "underground empire" of Jews and Masons. After engineering the fall of the Spanish monarchy and of the more moderate republican government, Jews and Masons had prepared and directed the revolution, he claimed, The only proof the priest could give was the usual: Jews constituted the source and basis for Masonry. The goals and methods of Masonry and international Jewry agree. Jews hold the leading positions in Masonry, and it was thanks to Jews that Masonry enjoyed such success.

---

[68] *Mały Dziennik*, January 1 and 3, 1937.

[69] *Homo Dei*, (1936): 311–19.

[70] *Mały Dziennik*, August 9, 1939.

Szynwaldzki knew that Masons denied their association with Jews, and he conceded the sincerity of their protestations. But they were only pawns who made the denials. Those individual Masons who had nothing in common with international Jewry had no important position in the Masonic hierarchy and were unconsciously serving as a screen for Jewish ends. There was no gainsaying for Szynwaldzki that Masons were fighting Catholicism on behalf of Jews and thus preparing the way for the future Messiah and Jewish domination of the world. His proof was a variety of quotations by Jewish Masons on the Jewish origins of some of the Masonic symbolism. More important was the common cause Jews and Masons made with communists to weaken the Catholic church, Christian ethics, and nationalist ideals.[71]

Neither was Adam Bronowski, writing in *Pro Christo,* impressed by Masonic denials of ties to Judaism. Bronowski appealed to an article by Nahum Sokolow of B'nai B'rith in Kraków. Sokolow had written that "Masonry has nothing in common with Judaism." Jews did not initiate Masonry, Sokolow stated, although they could be proud if they had. Masonry has Jewish members because it has become an "asylum for minorities." Masonry, wrote Sokolow, did not support Protestantism or attack Catholicism but stood as an "uncompromising enemy of clericalism." Such remarks by Sokolow and the Jewish acknowledgement that Masons were not antisemitic was proof enough for Bronowski that "clear and strong ties completely joined Masonry with Judaism."[72]

Bronowski also appealed to the work of several Polish authors on Freemasonry, particularly a book that had appeared the previous year, in late 1936, by Dr. Kazimierz M. Morawski. The book, according to Morawski, had created a groundswell of discussion on Masonry in Poland, and the Polish bishops not only supported what Morawski styled his "pioneering work," one bishop even opened an "anti-masonic office" in his diocese.[73]

The nature and quality of Morawski's "research" can be culled from a paper he delivered at an anti-Masonic convention that took place June 11–12, 1938 in Warsaw. There, as reported in the *Mały Dziennik,*

---

[71] *Przegląd Katolicki,* 74 (1936): 742–44.

[72] *Pro Christo,* 13/1–2 (1937): 28–36.

[73] K. M. Morawski, *Tęcza,* (February 1937): 13–17.

Morawski stated:

- Masonry is an organization derived from Judaism, closely linked to Judaism, and serving the interests of international Jewry.
- Masonry is an anti-Catholic organization dedicated to the overthrow of the Catholic church.
- In theory Masonry acknowledges all beliefs (liberalism) but in practice it employs ruthless dictatorship (Russia).
- Masonry exercised a harmful, paralyzing influence on the independence movement in Poland.
- The influence of Masonry in Poland is considerable since behind the lodge stand united four million Jews for whom it works.

The 1938 anti-Masonic convention concluded with a resolution declaring "readiness for war on behalf of Poland's cultural and political-economic independence against Masonry and the Jews behind it."[74] Shortly thereafter, Morawski, appealing to the authority of French Catholic experts (Jouin), promoted, with obvious self-interest, the institution of a university chair of Masonic studies in Poland.[75]

The linkage between Masonry and Jews was to be found in Polish pulpits as well as the Catholic press. Writing for a homiletic journal, Father Franciszek Kwiatkowski, S.J., first invoked Pope Pius XI to call secularism the "plague of our times" and then identify the secularizers as "freethinkers, Masons, atheists, and freethinking Jews." It was well known, wrote the Jesuit, that "Jews use Masonry as a means to rule the world," to prepare the way for their Messiah. He cited Cardinal Kakowski: Masonry freethinking, radicalism and sectarianism were rampant in Poland because of an "overgrowth of freedom." Cardinal Hlond had referred to freethinkers conspiring in secret groups to secularize all of life. Archbishop Marmaggi, the papal nuncio declared (January 11, 1935) that powerful hostile powers were conspiring openly and in secret, among them "the oldest, Masonry, which despises everything and knows how to corrupt everything." The bishops, concluded Father Kwiatkowski, had given preachers more than enough

---

[74] *Mały Dziennik,* June 14, 1938.

[75] *Mały Dziennik,* July 21, 1938.

material to train people from the pulpit on how to answer atheists. He then illustrated: We will destroy all places of worship," a speaker cried out at a meeting of communists. "What will you do with the synagogues," broke in a worker, closing the communist's mouth.[76]

As Jews were being linked to communism and Masonry, the Catholic church was identified with fascism. It was a charge the Franciscan *Rycerz Niepokalanej* did not reject out of hand: for two hundred years, until Mussolini moved against the Italian lodges, the Catholic church had fought against Masonry singlehandedly. Now "the Church gained an ally, namely fascism, on the Masonic front." So too in Poland "Catholic-national groups and press" have fought against Masonry for fifteen years. The Franciscans at Niepokalanów saw themselves at the forefront of that struggle. The very reason the Knights of the Immaculata were founded was "to strive for the conversion of sinners, heretics, schismatics and especially Masons."

In case its readers did not know any Masons to convert, the *Rycerz* gave these aids in recognizing them: Although they could not reveal that they belonged to the lodge, Masons tipped their hand by spreading Masonic propaganda. There were also "half-Masons" who, without belonging to the lodge, betray the influence of Masonry on them. One could be sure that anyone speaking out against the faith or church was either a Mason or "infected" by Masonic propaganda. "Similarly, when we encounter people who cover up the destructive, demoralizing, anti-state and anti-national activity of Jews, we can be sure that these people are under the influence of Masonry, since Masonry is derived from Judaism and serves its purposes and politics." Anyone who would praise the Soviets or the "reds" in Spain was "at once a communist and Masonic agitator, since communism and Masonry not only agreed with each other but worked hand in hand toward the same goal, bringing about the savage Jewish dictatorship over the whole world."[77]

Rotary Clubs

As pointed out above, Catholic leadership made little distinction between

---

[76] *Przegląd Homiletyczny*, 5 (1937): 163–81.

[77] *Rycerz Niepokalanej*, (1938): 228–30.

apolitical British Freemasonry and the politically active Grand Orients of the continent, between Freemasons, Odd Fellows, and Knights of Pythias. All were secret societies. The negative judgment of Catholic officialdom upon Rotary Clubs may appear puzzling, therefore, since that international organization was completely open. The Church's Code of Canon Law had forbidden Catholic membership in Masonic societies and those which "plot against the Church" (canon 2335). Rotary Clubs hardly corresponded to that description, and Catholics felt free to join and participate actively. In some instances, Catholic priests had even assumed roles of leadership. Here was an organization, however, that was not under the supervision of the bishops, one in which Catholics and non-Catholics intermingled freely. In 1929 the Vatican had been asked to decide whether priests were permitted to belong to Rotary or at least attend their meetings. The reply was that it was not expedient.[78] There was no explicit Vatican prohibition for lay Catholics to belong to Rotary. But the Code of Canon Law did warn against societies which were "suspect" and which sought to "evade the legitimate vigilance of the Church" (canon 684). This was enough for the bishops of Spain and Holland and for the Catholic press in Poland.

Rotary began in Poland in 1931, and by 1936 numbered some two hundred members in nine cities, among them professionals, industrialists, and educators. Edward Johnson, the President of Rotary International, visited Warsaw in early 1936 for a convention of Polish Rotary Clubs. There were enough clubs in Poland for it to become an independent district, and the Catholic press began to take greater note of them. A proposed effort by the Polish Rotarians to improve the teaching profession required vigilance, declared the *Mały Dziennik*. It could only mean that Rotarians wanted to influence young Poles on a Masonic model. Like the League for the Defence of Human Rights, Rotary was under the influence of Masonry, a "pre-school" for the lodge. As proof for its contention, the Catholic daily pointed out that the program of Rotary International was toleration of others' political and religious convictions and the resolution of misunderstandings among nations. Here was the same phraseology as that of "conspiratorial Masonry."[79] Rotary

---

[78] T. Lincoln Bouscaren, S.J. (ed.), *The Canon Law Digest* (Milwaukee, WI: Bruce, 1934), 1:617.

[79] *Mały Dziennik,* April 25, 1936.

Clubs, the paper repeated later, were but "outposts" for Masonry, a new means for Masons to exercise influence over Poland's economic and cultural life by means of a "foreign agency."[80]

Catholic members of Rotary sent protests to *Mały Dziennik*, denying any connections with Masonry or any contradiction with Catholic principles. The paper responded by citing the bishops of Spain, who in 1929 had accused Rotary of laicism and religious indifferentism. Two-thirds of the leadership of Rotary International were Masons, claimed the daily. Masonry and Rotary shared common plans and projects. For *Mały Dziennik* it was no argument that leading Catholics in France, Italy, and the United States were Rotarians. The same was true in the early years of Masonry. Because the Vatican denied priests permission to belong or attend Rotary meetings, the Catholic daily, assumed the right to decide for all Polish Catholics: "it is not allowed to belong to Rotary Clubs." Rotary was a "very dangerous organization," indeed, more dangerous than Masonry: under cover of humanitarian slogans, "it concealed moral nihilism, religious indifferentism, and ultimately atheism."[81]

Other Catholic voices agreed with the Franciscans at Niepokalanów, among them Professor Morawski. Criticizing Polish Catholics associated with Rotary, he reminded them that Rotary was neutral with respect to religion, and, according to Pope Leo XIII: "fundamentally neutral organizations are suspect and should be avoided, for they can easily be dominated and directed by Masonry."[82] According to Father Józef Dajczak, it made no difference that there were numerous Catholic Rotarians in other countries. Rotary clubs were informally Masonic, sometimes called "white Masonry." Freemasons created Rotary in order to imbue Christian society with a Masonic spirit.[83] Both Dajczak and Father Tadeusz Kozłowski were influenced by a brochure on Rotary and Masonry by Jean de Boistel. Even though the founder of Rotary, Paul Harris, denied that he was ever a Mason, still Masons constituted two-thirds of the leadership of Rotary International. By encouraging helpfulness and "service above self," Rotary, claimed Kozłowski, was

---

[80] *Mały Dziennik*, August 4, 1936.

[81] *Mały Dziennik*, September 13, 1936.

[82] *Przegląd Katolicki*, 74 (1936): 631.

[83] *Gazeta Kościelna*, (1937): 51–52.

following a utilitarian ethic, not one based on Christian faith. To be a loyal Catholic called for avoiding neutral, unchristian organizations.[84] Clearly, associating socially with non-Catholics was viewed in itself as a danger to the faith.

Suppression

The church's campaign against Freemasonry eventually had its impact on the Polish government, aided certainly by the example of authoritarian governments in the West. In Italy Mussolini dissolved the Masons along with other sources of opposition. Upon the ascendancy of Nazism in Germany, Masonic lodges dissolved themselves. In 1935 Portugal interdicted all secret organizations as did Romania in 1937.[85] Steps like these as well as Hitler's action against Rotary were seen by Józef Czarnecki as aimed against internationalism.[86] Here, wrote Mieczysław Skrudlik, was proof against the so-called progressive, "Judaized" intelligentsia who claimed that fear of Masonry was a figment created by the clergy.[87]

The Catholic anti-Masonic campaign heated up considerably in 1938, as discussions in the Sejm on measures necessary to suppress the lodge coincided with the two-hundredth anniversary of the first papal bull against Freemasonry. Bishop Przeździecki of Podlaski forbade Catholics in his diocese from having even social relations with Masons, who were the "enemy of Poland."[88] The *Przewodnik Katolicki* lay a whole host of Poland's historic ills on the doorstep of the Masons, in league of course with Jews. And there was no better place to start than the partitions. Following the example of the French Catholic royalists, the popular weekly blamed Masons for the fall of Poland's monarchy. Masons, "not without the help of Jewish money," succeeded in putting "their man," Friedrich-August of Saxony on the Polish throne to do their bidding.

---

[84] *Ateneum Kapłańskie*, 43 (1939): 78–85.

[85] Ludwik Hass, "*Grandeur et declin de la franc-maçonnerie*," 309–10.

[86] *Przegląd Katolicki*, (1938): 85–86.

[87] *Przegląd Katolicki*, 75 (1937): 618.

[88] *Mały Dziennik*, April 9, 1938.

Thirty years later, Poland's last king, Stanisław August Poniatowski, was
a passive instrument of the lodge.[89]

The *Mały Dziennik* blamed Masons at the Peace Conference of
Versailles for weakening Catholic nations and contributing to the rise of
German nationalism by the humiliation of Germany.[90] Masons were also
accused of being in league with the Comintern. It did not matter that in
1922 the Communist International had declared Masonry hostile to the
revolution and forbidden communists to be Masons. The popes had
declared that liberalism had prepared the way for communism. Since the
Catholic church was the "only moral force" capable of withstanding
communism, criticism of the church constituted a contribution to
totalitarianism.[91]

Writing in the *Mały Dziennik,* self-styled Masonry expert Professor
Morawski once again assailed Freemasonry as a conspiracy to destroy
Christian civilization and subject it to Jewry. Masons were "foreign
agents," who placed their members in more than one political party, so
that any change in government would not prejudice their own interests
or "the interests of the Jews which they protect." Masons were to be
found both in the ruling and opposition parties, doing the bidding of
"hidden directors" in the interest of Judaism.[92]

Monsignor Stanisław Trzeciak was certainly the most prolific priest to
write against the purported Masonic-Jewish conspiracy. Trzeciak
explained to his readers in the *Mały Dziennik* how, when Masons said
that their aim was to build the temple of Solomon, they meant "helping
Jews to establish a Jewish kingdom." The French Revolution, which gave
equal rights to Jews, was but the first step in this program. The
revolutions in Russia, Hungary, and Spain were further steps toward
achieving Jewish power.[93] Polish Masons, Trzeciak contended, were in
contact with Masons in Prague and Danzig, where Poland's enemies
congregate. It was not without significance for Trzeciak that *Ogniwo,*
associated with the international Odd Fellows and having "rich Jews" as

---

[89] *Przewodnik Katolicki,* 44 (1938): 256–57.

[90] *Mały Dziennik,* April 26, 1938.

[91] *Przegląd Powszechny,* 215 (1937):175–76. *Przegląd Katolicki,* 76 (1938): 663.

[92] *Mały Dziennik,* July 15, 1938.

[93] *Mały Dziennik,* July 19, 1938.

members, was located across from the Soviet embassy in Warsaw.[94]

In the Sejm representative Budziński made similar points. *Ogniwo*'s Jewish secretary, Jakub Muszkat, had been convicted of activity harmful to the state. The *Mały Dziennik* accused *Ogniwo* of engaging in revolutionary activity, having a cell in the army and taking orders from outside the country.[95] Besides treason, the Catholic daily accused Masons of pandering to human weakness and promoting pornography with its advocacy of freedom. Masonry turned the attention of young people from religion to "sports and various foolish amusements."[96]

Along with Freemasons, Odd Fellows, and Rotarians, the Catholic campaign against Masonry in Poland included the lodges of B'nai B'rith. *Mały Dziennik* cited 1928 Jewish sources in asserting that there were nine hundred members of B'nai B'rith in Poland. Established in Poland in 1928 with its Grand Lodge in Kraków, these "Jewish Freemasons" according to the Catholic daily, had as their goal the "infection of humankind." [97]

B'nai B'rith lodges in Poland were among those affected by a decree of dissolution issued November 22, 1938, by President Mościcki. All Masonic associations were declared illegal and their property confiscated. Membership was made punishable by five years' imprisonment. The following December 15, Justice Minister Sławoj-Składkowski officially dissolved thirty-two Masonic associations, including the lodges of B'nai B'rith.[98] On the dissolution of the Warsaw lodge, *Mały Dziennik* reported that its founders had included Rabbi Ozjasz Thon and Józef Bachrach. Among its officers at the time of dissolution were Sejm representative Seidenmann, its president, and David Lichtenbaum, treasurer. Among its important members were "millionaire" Rafał Szereszewski, Prof. J. P. Majer Bałaban, Rabbi Schorr, the industrialist Hurwicz, and Prof. Sommerstein.[99]

---

[94] *Mały Dziennik*, July 20, 1938.

[95] *Mały Dziennik*, July 23, 1938.

[96] *Mały Dziennik*, July 25, 1938.

[97] *Mały Dziennik*, July 27, 1938.

[98] *Wiadomości Diecezjalne Łódzkie*, (1939) 1:12–14.

[99] *Mały Dziennik*, December 1, 1938.

Catholic opinion makers did not rest on their laurels. For *Mały Dziennik* the dissolutions were only a phase and not the end of the war with Masonry, which after all was but a means toward the goal of Jewish domination of the world. The Catholic church was the greatest obstacle to that end. That was why all the attacks of Jews and their often unwitting Masonic allies were directed against it. Political equality appeared to be the next phase for the Franciscan press at Niepokalanów. "The greatest 'achievement' of the French Revolution—the political equality of Jews—was the work above all of clever Masonic propaganda." Masons had made it a sign of high culture and enlightenment not to distinguish between Gentiles and Jews. Anything to the contrary was declared as smacking of the dark ages. "This was the great service Masons did for Jews, making it possible for Jews to penetrate Christian culture and do their destructive work." At the same time it was the "unjust liberal-capitalist system" which enabled Jews to expropriate their host-nations. The most effective war against Masonry, concluded the Catholic daily, was to overcome these alien ideas, to shake off Jewish influence, and to separate Jews from Christian peoples.[100]

Father Marian Wiśniewski decried Masonic influence on Poland's teaching profession, especially the teachers belonging to the *Związek Nauczycielstwa Polskiego* (Polish Teachers' Union). Polish youth were being thrown into the embrace of Jewish-Masonry. Masons had persistently tried to take over the Ministry of Education. By promoting separation of church and state, civil marriage and divorce, and a repeal of the concordat with the Vatican, the teachers' union was doing the "venomous work of bolshevizing, Masonizing, and Judaizing the Polish spirit."[101]

In the more serious *Przegląd Powszechny*, Father Edward Kosibowicz, S.J., acknowledged that the Catholic fear of secularist Freemasons taking over the Polish government was by any measure exaggerated. With the exception of one member of the Sejm who was excommunicated (Putek), there were no representatives or senators who were resolute enemies of the church, none who publicly flaunted their laicism. In the December, 1938 election, the Socialists disclaimed any opposition to religion and

---

[100] *Mały Dziennik*, December 15, 1938.

[101] *Kielecki Przegląd Diecezjalny*, 25 (1938): 164–69.

avoided even anti-clerical, let alone anti-Catholic slogans.[102]

By the late 1930s, the Catholic press at various levels expressed the conviction that liberalism was bankrupt. The triumph of liberal ideas, wrote S. Kamieński, had resulted in financiers achieving the power to decide the fate of states and social classes. Although liberals claimed to be champions of human rights, they declared war on the Catholic church in the name of freedom. Behind the liberal system lay Protestant individualism and Judaism. Protestantism relegated religion to the private sphere of life without any connection to education, politics, or economics. Jews, claimed Kamieński, expected a Messiah to bestow political power and material wealth on them.

The liberal system conceived of life as a war in which there are conquerors and the conquered. For liberalism the purpose of life was struggle, self-interest, getting rich, and domination over others.[103]

Catholic Totalitarianism

Since neither the Catholic church nor Poland could claim a democratic tradition of any kind, it is not surprising that the Polish Catholic press regularly betrayed a negative attitude toward democracy and parliamentary government. Prior to Piłsudski's 1925 coup, the overly powerful Sejm had been largely discredited as incapable of coping with Poland's economic problems. Usually a discrete silence was maintained with regard to democratic ideals, punctuated with occasional critical asides rather than front-on assaults as with the attack against liberalism. A major exception, however, occurred in late 1937, under the influence of the fascist governments in Italy and Germany. The editor of a nationalist weekly, *Prosto z Mostu* (Straight from the Bridge), Stanisław Piasecki, wrote an article calling for a totalitarian form of government corresponding to Saint Augustine's *City of God*. Certain Catholics like A. Niesiołowski and W. Bienkowski attacked the idea as dangerous and contrary to Catholic teaching. But Father Jerzy Pawski, the editor of the extremist *Pro Christo*, defended the concept. With a group of young Catholic nationalists, he became the champion of "Catholic

---

[102] *Przegląd Powszechny*, 221 (1939): 95–100.

[103] *Wiara i Życie*, (1939): 276–81.

totalitarianism."[104]

Pro Christo had a history of disparaging democracy. In 1934 J.
Dobrowolski wrote that rather than being canonized democracy should
be condemned for leading to anarchy and communism. "Democratism"
was a tyranny of the majority, conducive to the decay of nations, which
is why it was championed by Jews. Democracy was identical with
philosemitism. The way to ensure Christian morality in public life was
a return to monarchy.[105] By 1937, however, at a conference sponsored
by Catholic Action in Warsaw on "Social Catholicism," not monarchy but
totalitarianism was the concern of the day. The Conference speakers
criticized totalitarianism as contrary to Catholic teaching, transgressing
the natural rights to freedom and private property. *Pro Christo's* Father
Pawski disagreed. The church, he wrote, did not canonize any one system
of government. A careful reading of Pope Pius XI's encyclical on
Nazism, *Mit brennender Sorge,* revealed no word of condemnation for
totalitarianism as a concept nor for the policies of Nazi Germany as a
whole, only certain aspects of it. The same liberals, Masons, and marxists
criticizing totalitarianism criticized Polish nationalism. Despite the
Catholics brought up on liberalism, Poland too would be ruled by one
party.

Pawski criticized Germany as neo-pagan but expressed admiration for
Mussolini. Totalitarianism, he wrote, was capable of enticing the masses
to heroic efforts in behalf of collective goals. It could overcome the
egoism of small individuals and groups and organize society to maximum
self-denial and achievement, all in the name of transcendent ideals. If
Poland was to survive, wedged between two totalitarian powers, if it was
to play an active role in European affairs, Poland would have to respond
to its historic "mission" decreed by Providence. It was called to create "a
great block of nationalist Catholic states" in Eastern Europe. Catholicism
was totalitarian in its demands on its adherents, requiring the highest
sacrifices of the individual for the sake of the common good. Whereas
primitive patriotism required supreme sacrifice only in times of war,
totalitarianism required it every day. Working in close connection with
the church, Poland's government had the task to bring about the first

---

[104] For an overview of the origins of the movement, see *Pro Christo,* 13:11 (1937):
63–70.

[105] *Pro Christo—Wiara i Czyn,* 13:10 (1934): 517–26.

Catholic totalitarian system, the "ultimate expression" of Polish nationalism.[106]

That a Catholic periodical could openly commend a fascist form of government created a flurry of reaction in both the secular and Catholic press. *Pro Christo* devoted virtually an entire issue to the subject. Włodzimierz Sznarbachowski distinguished between liberal, police, and totalitarian states. *Liberal* states developed in an era in which the Catholic church had no influence. Modern culture, the press, political and economic forces were hostile to the church. Although theoretically all citizens enjoyed freedom and equality, in practice leadership in the liberal system was exercised by party bosses, elected officials, and the "conspiracies" behind them. Liberal governments tolerated opposition so long as all parties recognized and accepted the system. The parties represented not differing world views but differing interests and governed by striking compromises. Here lay the inner contradiction of liberal democracy. Government of the people was really in the hands of a few cliques.

In reaction to the "absurdities of parliamentarism," liberal democracies were disappearing and being replaced by *police* states. The similarity of the police state to totalitarianism was only formal. In compelling the entire population to work for the state, a police state was simply preserving the privileges of the ruling class. It rested on a worship of the state and operated solely on the idea of obedience to the law.

The *totalitarian* state, continued Sznarbachowski, was totally organized and consisted of one party. In this system in contrast to the others, the state played a greater role in education, with one party serving as instructor, comrade, and guide. Because it rested on a concept of what constituted a person's ultimate purpose, the totalitarian state was necessarily based on religion or ideology. What liberalism regarded as a person's most private affair, namely the free choice of faith and personal convictions, totalitarianism regarded as the proper concern of all. The issue came down to one of understanding what constituted the ultimate aim of humankind, whether or not it was conformable with the revelation of Christ as taught by the church. This was the aim of Catholic totalitarianism, to be based on the revealed and therefore true religion. There was no contradiction between Catholicism and the new spirit of the

---

[106] *Pro Christo,* 13:10 (1937) 3–23.

times.[107]

The stand taken by *Pro Christo* was forcefully attacked by the socialist and Jewish press, but approached by the Catholic press, according to Marian Reutt, with "seriousness and moderation." The Comintern was using democratic slogans to oppose fascism in Poland, because a totalitarian state, serving one truth, would be able to withstand communism. Democracy was bankrupt, bereft of political unity, with each party representing different ideas and interests. It led by a natural dialectic to victory of demagoguery. Democracy would achieve in Poland what Karensky did in Russia, the "first step" toward socialism. The fight against totalitarianism in the name of democracy was "water for the mill of communism."[108]

Tadeusz Dworak removed any doubt as to what *Pro Christo* meant by a Catholic totalitarian Poland. It meant that the state should systematically regulate all aspects of individual and social life deemed important for the community and its future. The government would "eliminate harmful competition and unnecessary discord." It would systematize the entire life of the nation according to the principles of morality, organize relationships and establish order based on the timeless principles of hierarchy. In the face of a chaos of opinions, class struggle and political discord, the modern totalitarian state must rest on a strong government with effective instruments of coercion at its disposal. Liberal republics existed in utopias. Human vice and folly transformed liberty into anarchy. The cult of personal freedom found in so-called democracies regularly debilitated the state.

Many in Poland were not convinced, Dworak admitted. They feared statism and absolutism. But a broad use of coercion was not the essence of totalitarianism, he insisted, though police powers would have to be applied wherever the government encountered the opposition of "demoralizing individuals and those working to harm Poland." Without needing to be more explicit, he simply added: "We have too many of these people in the state to allow them too much liberty." A totalitarian government would have formidable tasks to face: measures to protect the national economy so as to increase the income of Poles; measures to restrict the rights of Jews, exhaust them economically, and send them on

---

[107] *Pro Christo,* 13:11 (1937): 15–32.

[108] *Pro Christo,* 13:11 (1937): 40–46.

their way.[109]

The young Catholic nationalists gathered around Father Pawski at *Pro Christo* may have been the most ardent supporters of a Catholic totalitarianism, but they were not the only ones. Acknowledging that many Catholics were put off by the term, *Gazeta Kościelna* described *Pro Christo's* position sympathetically. Once a reaction against absolute monarchy, liberal democracy was being maintained by old men holding on to antiquated ideas. Democracy equated the votes of university professors and stable boys; it constantly compromised and invariably led to socialism. Totalitarianism was a one-party system concerned with forming the collective life of the people, refusing to compromise with critics. In its defence the popular Catholic weekly cited Saint Thomas Aquinas (law is meant to serve the common good) and Saint Augustine's acceptance of state coercion. Not all totalitarian systems were alike; unlike those in Germany and Soviet Russia, the one in Italy could be reconciled with Catholicism. The idea of a Catholic state forming all areas of communal life was not as bad as people said.[110]

Pro Christo had strong Catholic opposition. Totalitarianism contradicted Christian doctrine on human dignity, wrote Witold Powel.[111] For Janusz Rawicz in *Przegląd Katolicki*, totalitarianism necessarily led to "statolatry" and could not be reconciled with Catholicism. This, however, did not mean an affirmation of "extreme democracy."[112] Similarly Father Edward Kosibowocz had no use for the French style of democracy, which in Poland had led to changing cabinets with the seasons. Poland, he contended, needed a strong executive power. Unity was required by the threat of Poland's neighbors, its economy, and the "tragic problem of national minorities, especially Jews." Kosibowicz acknowledged the "rising tide of antisemitism," but rejected any ideas of imitating the Third Reich in Poland. Totalitarianism was radically at odds with the rights of the individual. Poland as a whole, he wrote, did not defend "ultra-democracy" but was closely allied to the democracies.[113]

---

[109] *Pro Christo,* 13:11 (1937): 60–64.

[110] *Gazeta Kościelna,* 45 (1938): 49–50.

[111] *Ruch Charytatywny,* 21 (1938): 180–83.

[112] *Przegląd Katolicki,* 75 (1937): 698–99; 76 (1938): 117–18.

[113] *Przegląd Powszechny,* 220 (1938): 392–403; 223 (1939): 171–75.

Pro Christo closed its series of articles on totalitarianism with four theses published under the title, "Good night to the Democrats":

- Nothing in Catholic teaching gave concrete directions as to a nation's economic system or form of government. On the contrary, doctrinal purity required that no attempt be made to associate Catholicism with any particular concept like liberalism, monarchy, democracy, or totalitarianism.

- Catholics, however, could not be indifferent to the fact that the "people's front" and the entire democratic movement not only struck a blow at Polish society but prepared the way for a communist revolution.

- A reasonable love of one's country, in accord with the spirit of Christ's teaching, required adoption of a system which would further the church's mission and assure Poles a leading role in their homeland.

- "Totalitarianism" was not a scientific but a political term, derived from fascist Italy and referred to a system quite different from Germany's and Soviet Russia's. *Pro Christo* had something quite different from all of these in mind when it spoke of totalitarianism in Poland: "Catholicism ought to be the governing ideology in the state, in the public laws just as it is in the hearts of individuals."[114]

Just what a Catholic totalitarianism might mean in practice was exemplified by *Pro Christo* in an article by Zenon Zimorowicz, who advocated state control of creative thought as a matter of public hygiene. Among those requiring regulation of their activities, according to Zimorowicz, were novelists, dramatists, poets, art critics, journalists, scientists, teachers, stage and screen stars, singers, and dancers. Censors would have to be alert for any cultural creations that threatened good order, custom, or the power of the state, involving anti-social behavior, abusive language, or blasphemy. But Zimorowicz was even more explicit about the kind of intellectual activity that required control: The propaganda of a Professor Michałowicz speaking out against nationalism in the name of peaceful coexistence among nations. The anti-religious

---

[114] *Pro Christo,* 14:2 (1938): 12.

propaganda of a Professor Kotarbiński in the name of pure reason and free-thought. Arguing, like Professor Witwicki, that the commands of Christian morality were harmful to good health. Disseminating religious doubts and sexual debauchery in the name of art like Parandowski. Advocating birth control to counteract unemployment like Boy-Żeleński. Undermining military authority by advocating pacifism like Tuwim. Exposing the public to exhibitionism and pornography like Zegadłowicz.

Some ideas deserved not only courteous criticism but condemnation and severe punishment, wrote Zimorowicz. As centers of socially harmful creativity he singled out the *Liga Obrony Praw Człowieka i Obywatela* (League for Defence of Human and Civil Rights), the *Związek Myśli Wolnej* (Free-thought Association), and a variety of newspapers and periodicals, including the *Wiadomości Literackie* (Literary News). Bourgeois Jews, Zimorowicz claimed, were the principal agents of these ideas together with "racially, culturally and above all morally judaized bourgeois Poles." Society had the right, indeed the obligation, to defend itself by setting up institutions of control like a Congregation of the Index. Government censors were being taken up with political issues like communism; more attention had to be directed to all publications and entertainment with a view to their morals. Serious consideration should be given to expelling the offenders from Poland.[115]

The democracy which Americans in the United States call Jeffersonian, interwar Catholic Poland called Masonic. The association of the two ideas was of a decidedly French Catholic provenance. Liberalism meant a radical restructuring of social classes and a demise of political privilege for aristocrats and ecclesiastics alike. Religious and political conservatives were not slow in seeing Freemasonry as at least partly culpable for the social upheavals of the nineteenth century. Even if one should take at face value the traditional Masonic disavowal of political activity and any intention of creating a social structure competing with the church, the lodge offered a novel opportunity for members of differing religious traditions and social classes to bracket off their differences and meet on neutral territory. The leaders of the Masonic movement might protest that

---

[115] *Pro Christo,* 14:3 (1938): 22–26.

this constituted no transgression of accepted values and in no way endangered the established political or religious order. Nevertheless, social intercourse among diverse Christian believers within the lodge was a radical innovation. The inclusion of Jews in the brotherhood constituted a revolution.

When French Freemasons came to embrace the principles of the Revolution, they necessarily put themselves at odds with Catholic traditionalists and on the same side with Jews. The forces that emancipated Jews disestablished the church. With Jews and Freemasons in the same secularist camp, it was easy for Catholics, first in France and then in 1930s Poland as elsewhere, to link assimilated Jews and Masons together and see them as the principle purveyors of all that was wrong with secular modernity. The identification, as noted above, began in the mid-nineteenth-century and reached its height during years following the Dreyfus Affair, when church and state in France were finally separated. With the definition of the nation as the issue, the analogies between the France of the Dreyfus Affair and interwar Poland are certainly striking.[116]

The respite in French Catholic antisemitism occasioned by World War I was brief. Charles Maurras and Action Française continued to receive considerable Catholic support in the struggle against liberalism and democracy. But it was Monsignor Ernest Jouin and his *Revue internationale des Sociétés sécrètes* which became the principle exponent of Catholic antisemitism in interwar France. In 1925 Jouin and his chief collaborator, Abbé Paul Boulin, greeted the rising prominence of Adolf Hitler and the Nazi party in Germany as allies (*entente*) in the struggle against the "common danger of Jewish conquest." Five years earlier Monsignor Jouin had written in his book, *Le péril judéo-maçonnique,* that "the Judeo-masonic danger" was "a question of life or death for all peoples."[117]

Jouin's book was prompted by the appearance of the notorious *Protocols of the Elders of Zion,* which the French prelate disseminated in France as the Nazis did in Germany. In Poland Monsignor Jouin's

---

[116] See, for example, the excellent book by Michael Marrus, *The Politics of Assimilation, A Study of the French Jewish Community at the Time of the Dreyfus Affair* (Oxford: Clarendon, 1971).

[117] Pierrard, *Juifs et catholiques français,* 242–45.

counterpart was Monsignor Stanisław Trzeciak. The two prelates were part of a veritable network of antisemites for whom the *Protocols* served as documentary evidence of a Jewish-Masonic conspiracy. Thanks to them and their like, the *Protocols* made an impact that is difficult to exaggerate.

Chapter 3

The *Protocols:* The Myth of World Domination

The *Protocols of the Elders of Zion* was first published in Russia in 1903, the purported plans by Jewish leaders to seize control of the major institutions of the western world. But the conspiracy it professed to report was already well established in nineteenth century France. For people who detested the liberal secularity of the modern world, Jews had become the supreme incarnation of modernity and all that threatened their traditional values. Gougenot des Mousseaux, Abbé Chabauty, and Eduard Drumont had each contributed to the idea of an unholy alliance between Masons and Jews to destroy Christianity. It required only a few more details to create the existence of a secret Jewish government which controlled the world's politics and economy through agencies like the Masons and public opinion through the press. Contributing those details and serving as an antecedent to the *Protocols* was a brief work that came to be known as *The Rabbi's Speech*.

In 1868, Hermann Goedsche, a Prussian newspaperman writing under the pseudonym of Sir John Retcliffe published a novel in Berlin entitled *Biarritz*. One of the chapters of the novel, "In the Jewish Cemetery in Prague," described a series of meetings held once every hundred years at midnight. Representatives of the world's Jews gather before a demonic apparition to report on their activities during the past century. The reports range from Jewish control of money, stock exchanges, various professions and land to the undermining of the Christian church by fostering anti-clericalism and free thought. The assembled representatives receive encouragement and instructions and look forward to a hundred years hence when their posterity will be able to announce at that graveyard that they had indeed become the princes of the world.

Four years after its initial publication, the relevant chapter was separated from the rest of the novel and published as a pamphlet, first in St. Petersburg and later in Moscow. Initially it was accompanied by the comment that, although a piece of fiction, the story had a basis in fact. By 1881 when it appeared in France, the meeting was no longer presented as fictitious and the various speeches made by the Jews at Prague were consolidated into a single speech. *The Rabbi's Speech,* as it came to be known, was paraphrased in 1901 in Prague under the title, *Speech of a Rabbi about the Goyim.* Eventually the hitherto anonymous rabbi received the names Eichhorn or Reichhorn. Circulating internationally after the First World War, the variants of the speech were used to bolster one another's authenticity.[1]

It was not by chance that first in late nineteenth century Russia a lurid piece of fiction came to be taken as portraying reality. The czarist regime constituted the last absolute monarchy in Europe and a stronghold of opposition to the liberalizing, democratizing forces associated with the French Revolution. In an attempt to discredit anti-monarchial revolutionary tendencies, czarist government agencies represented them as the work of Jews. Propaganda about a Jewish world-conspiracy was an officially sponsored, regular activity of Russia's political police, the Okhrana. This secret police, the evidence came to show, was ultimately responsible for contriving the fraudulent *Protocols* and arranging for their initial publication.

The *Protocols* consist of a series of lectures or lecture notes in which a supposed secret Jewish government, the "elders of Zion," construct a plot to achieve world-domination. They expound three principal themes: a critique of liberalism; an analysis of the methods by which world-domination is to be achieved by the elders; and a description of the world-state to be established. The earliest edition of a shortened version appeared in a St. Petersburg newspaper, *Znamya* (The Banner), in 1903. The publisher, P. A. Krushevan, did not reveal who gave him the manu-script, only that it was a Russian translation of a French original. In 1905 it appeared in its complete form as a chapter in a new edition of an apocalyptic work by Sergey Nilus, *The Great in the Small: Antichrist*

---

[1] Norman Cohn, *Warrant for Genocide: The Myth of the Jewish World-Conspiracy and the Protocols of the Elders of Zion* (Chico, CA: Scholars Press, 1981), 33–39.

considered as an imminent political possibility.[2]

Only at the end of the First World War did the *Protocols* come to the attention of the West, thanks to translations into German and English (1920) and a review in the London *Times* that took it seriously. Hundreds of thousands more began to take the work seriously because of the success of the Bolshevik revolution and the prominence of several Jews in the communist movement. To the myth of a Judeo-masonic conspiracy was joined a Judeo-communist conspiracy. In Germany sales quickly reached 120,000 copies. In France three translations appeared in 1920, one of them published in the *Revue Internationale des Sociétés secrètes* by Monsignor Ernest Jouin who subsequently edited, quoted and commented on the *Protocols* as if they were Scripture. That same year they appeared in the United States as a series of articles in Henry Ford's *Dearborn Independent* and were subsequently republished as a book, *The International Jew: the World's Foremost Problem*. In this form, for the sake of an American readership, Jewish Bolsheviks replaced Jewish Freemasons, and a half-million copies of the *Protocols* were put into circulation. Ford eventually retracted the accusations made in *The International Jew* and undertook to withdraw the book from circulation, but it was too late. *The International Jew* made the *Protocols* world-famous and was eventually translated into sixteen languages.[3]

Sales of the *Protocols* did not cool, when a year later (1921), it came to light that the book was not only a forgery but a plagiarism. Confessing its earlier lapse of judgment, the London *Times* revealed that much of the *Protocols* (over 160 passages, some two-fifths of the book) was based on passages taken from *Dialogue aux Enfers entre Montesquieu et Machiavel*, a work written in 1864 by a Parisian lawyer, Maurice Joly, not about Jews dominating the world but Napoleon III dominating France. Except for Great Britain, the unmasking of the forgery seemed to make little difference. Some supporters of the *Protocols* pretended that Joly, a baptized Catholic, was Jewish, and it did not matter from what Jewish hand it emanated. Other true believers begged the question and

---

[2] Cohn, *Warrant for Genocide*, 51–67.

[3] Pierre Pierrard, *Juifs et catholiques français: De Drumont a Jules Isaac (1886–1945)*, (Paris: Fayard, 1970), 233–35, 242–43; Jacob Katz, *Jews and Freemasons in Europe, 1723–1939*, trans. by Leonard Oschry (Cambridge, MA: Harvard University, 1970), 182–83; Cohn, *Warrant for Genocide*, 136, 152–66.

argued that authenticity was a secondary issue that did not affect veracity. The *Protocols* must be genuine since the events foretold were actually taking place. Who could deny that the age was one of wars, revolutions, and economic crises?[4]

Such circular thinking allowed Hitler to dismiss the evidence for their fraudulence and use the *Protocols* as a source for his *Mein Kampf* (1924). The Nazis distributed the forgery widely throughout Europe. When Nazi agents did so in Switzerland, the Swiss Jewish community fought back and initiated proceedings against the distributors for willful and malicious slander. The result was a celebrated trial in Berne (1934–1935), in which the court had to consider the question of the authenticity of the *Protocols*. The arguments and counter-arguments were presented by representatives on both sides. The *Protocols* were found to be largely plagiarized from Joly's book, with evidence pointing to their fabrication at the instigation of the Russian secret police. The court branded the *Protocols* a literary forgery, the creation of a hostile and malicious imagination.[5]

The Nazis counteracted and sponsored conferences to neutralize the doubts placed by the Berne trial on the authenticity of the *Protocols*. One such conference in Erfurt brought representatives together from some twenty-two nations. Its object was to build up an international network of true believers in the *Protocols* and in the existence of a Jewish world conspiracy.[6] One of those true believers, representing Poland at the Erfurt conference, was Monsignor Stanisław Trzeciak.

The *Protocols* in Poland

The *Protocols* first appeared in Polish translation early in 1920, in an abbreviated version entitled "*Baczność!*" (On guard!) that sold out within a year. Subsequent fuller editions followed in 1923, in the 1930 "*Wróg przed bramą!*" (Enemy at the gate!); and in 1934. The question of their

---

[4] Cohn, *Warrant for Genocide*, 71–76, 167; P. Pierrard, *Juifs et catholiques français*, 234.

[5] Cohn, *Warrant for Genocide*, 77–107; Katz, *Jews and Freemasons*, 196.

[6] N. Cohn, *Warrant for Genocide*, 218.

authenticity had been raised in Poland too, but for a convinced believer like Father Marian Wiśniewski "to no avail." For him, facts spoke more than verbal arguments. The program to conquer the world "was being accomplished" according to the plan outlined in the *Protocols*. Wiśniewski admitted that Jews everywhere advocated democracy while the *Protocols* despised it. But such incongruity posed no argument against their authenticity and only demonstrated "double-dealing, Talmudic tactics."

Wiśniewski was by any definition an extremist in his political views. Democracy in 1930s Poland was an unattainable ideal that could only lead to chaos and render Poles the prey of Jews. Although the priest was gratified that the right wing National Democrats (Endeks) had changed their name to the National Party, he disapproved of "the spirit of Jewish-masonic democracy" that still remained in its thinking. To think one could fight Jews and at the same time support democracy was foolish. Wiśniewski advised the right wing party to accept only practicing Catholics as members. What was needed was a "single Catholic-national front against Judeo-masonry" and a concentration of power into one hand, in short, a "return to monarchy."[7]

If its own inner contradictions were unable to dissuade true believers like Wiśniewski in the authenticity of the *Protocols,* neither were the facts brought to light during the Berne trial. Even before the final verdict was in, Jan Marcińczyk, in the *Przegląd Katolicki,* disparaged the proceedings as a fiasco orchestrated by Jews and Masons. The Russian emigrés who testified about the workings of the czarist secret police were described as deviates betraying their country. Marcińczyk was indifferent as to how the verdict would turn out; even the most naive Aryan knew well that the *Protocols* constituted the plans of Jews to build a world government on the ruins of Christian civilization. Jews were furious over the revelations made by Nilus and would stop at nothing discredit him and the *Protocols* by alleging that he had connections with the Russian secret police.[8]

---

[7] *Pro Christo,* 10 (1934): 780–87.

[8] *Przegląd Katolicki,* 73 (1935): 99–100.

Monsignor Stanisław Trzeciak

If Monsignor Jouin had a counterpart in Poland, it was undoubtedly Monsignor Dr. Stanisław Trzeciak. No Polish churchman wrote more about the *Protocols* or the "Jewish question" altogether. Although his earliest writing was on Protestantism, by 1906 he was specializing in Judaism at the time of Jesus. In 1911, as a professor at the seminary in Petersburg, he wrote a two-volume work on Jewish literature and religion, drawing from modern language translations of the Talmud. In that work, at least, his presentation of Judaism was relatively free of the antisemitism that marked his later writing.[9] His 1934 book on Jewish Messianism, however, demonstrated that whatever Trzeciak may have known of Jewish scholarship from the writings of Majer Bałaban and Heinrich Graetz, and the contemporary Jewish periodical literature, he read from the standpoint of the *Protocols*.[10]

Trzeciak gave considerable attention to the eighteenth century Frankist movement in Poland. He ignored the fact that orthodox Jews regarded Jacob Frank's movement as pseudo-messianic, sectarian and heretical. In contrast to the "spiritual universalism" of Christianity, Judaism was marked by a "materialistic" messianism. Jacob Frank was proof that the Jews had chosen Poland as the territory in which they could most easily realize their plans to establish a messianic kingdom (p. 84). Jews in areas like Galicia and eastern Poland had attained a veritable "state within a state." But this too, like Bolshevism, was only a phase toward the goal of establishing a "messianic kingdom." If less-than-orthodox Jews had given up the idea of an individual messiah, it meant that the entire Jewish people saw itself as destined to crush the nations and establish the messianic kingdom.

Trzeciak viewed Zionism along with Bolshevism as products of Jewish messianism. He described the nationalism of Vladimir Jabotinsky as an "imitation of Hitler in Israel" (p. 246). But this did not mean Jews were imitating Hitler. Quite the contrary, Hitler took his principles from Judaism. According to Trzeciak, the German boycott of Jewish

---

[9] Stanisław Trzeciak, *Literatura i religia u Żydów za czasów Chrystusa Pana,* 2 vols. (Warsaw: M. Szczepkowski, 1911).

[10] Stanisław Trzeciak, *Mesjanizm a kwestja żydowska* (Warsaw: Przegląd Katolicki), 1934).

businesses, the prohibition of social relationships and mixed marriages, Nazi concern about purity of the race—all these measures simply applied to Jews the same principles that the Talmud applied to gentiles.

No ivory-tower antisemite, Trzeciak helped to make ritual slaughter an issue for the Polish government[11], and in 1939 published a book on what the Talmud has to say about gentiles.[12] Whatever the issue, he gave the impression of scholarship by sprinkling his writings with references to Jewish publications as well as to the *Protocols* and other antisemitic sources. Among those sources was "The Speech of Rabbi Reichhorn about the Goyim" and "In the Jewish Cemetery in Prague." He did so even though he was aware that the story of the Prague cemetery had come from a novel.[13]

His writings earned him frequent criticism in the Jewish press,[14] but according to the *Mały Dziennik* the "universal respect" of Poles for his defense of national values. When Trzeciak attended the antisemitic congress in Erfurt, he was branded by his critics as "Hitler's envoy." The Catholic daily came to his defense by pointing out that Trzeciak's superiors not only had not reproved him but rather promoted him to be the pastor of one of the largest churches in Warsaw.[15]

Trzeciak's opinions were criticized, however, not only by Jews but by Polish Catholics as well. Several years before Trzeciak's book appeared, Father Wł. Szczepański, condemned the *Protocols* and the campaign being waged against Jews on the basis of their "forgery and deceit."[16] Father P. Stach agreed that it was likely that they had originated in antisemitic circles as a means of anti-Jewish agitation. Stach agreed with much in Trzeciak's book but criticized it for "too much antisemitism"

---

[11] Stanisław Trzeciak, *Ubój rytualny w świetle Biblji i Talmudu* (Warsaw: Kronika rodzinna, 1935).

[12] Stanisław Trzeciak, *Talmud o goyach a kwestja żydowska w Polsce* (Warsaw: A. Prabucki, 1939).

[13] Stanisław Trzeciak, *Przegląd Katolicki,* 74 (1936): 147; and *Pro Christo,* 13/3 (1937): 3.

[14] *Przegląd Katolicki,* 77 (1939): 363.

[15] *Mały Dziennik,* July 18, 1938.

[16] *Palestyna po wojnie światowej,* 93, cited by P. Stach, "Mesjanizm a kwestja żydowska," *Gazeta Kościelna,* 41 (December 2, 1934): 562.

and for providing grist for the mills of Poland's antisemites. Stach did not want to defend Jews, whom he considered a threat to the young Polish state, but neither did he think that Trzeciak should build his case on unsubstantiated claims. For Stach as for Trzeciak, Jews were dissatisfied with the status quo and aimed at destroying the whole legacy of Christian culture.[17]

Trzeciak's writings were cited and excerpted widely in the Polish Catholic press. His reputation was enhanced by the fact that he had been invited to testify at the Berne trial as an expert on the *Protocols*. The invitation came too late for him to attend, however, and his absence allowed his Polish admirers to dismiss the verdict. The testimony that he would have given on the witness stand, he published in a short book entitled *Program światowej polityki żydowskiej* (The Program of Jewish World Politics). It was described by *Głos Narodu,* the Catholic daily of Kraków, as "priceless" and "exhaustive," and a must-read for Polish socialists.[18]

Trzeciak acknowledged that there was no external proof of the authenticity of the *Protocols*. But he was convinced by the inner proof: their correspondence with events in Russia, Hungary, and Spain. Because of their worldly messianism, even religious Jews, saw communism as a step toward realizing their messianic hopes. The priest cited the Talmud (Sanhedrin 98a) as teaching the Jewish belief that the Messiah would not come so long as there was the least domination over Jews. Too weak to accomplish this by itself, Israel required the help of "artificial Jews," like Masons on the right and socialists on the left. Soviet collectivization was a "Jewish idea" whose purpose was to transfer land into Jewish hands.[19]

Trzeciak also admitted that the majority of Jews at the Zionist congresses were not aware of what their "conspiratorial presidium" was advising. Neither did he want to attribute plans of world domination to all Jews, certainly not to those "upright Jews whose actions also serve the non-Jewish community" nor the "loyal orthodox" who were being "persecuted" by Jewish internationalists. The Jews he had in mind were the socialists and communists who were wreaking vengeance in Russia

---

[17] *Gazeta Kościelna,* 41 (December 2, 1934): 561–63.

[18] *Głos Narodu,* July 30, 1936.

[19] *Przegląd Katolicki,* 74 (1936):132–34, 147–49.

and Spain for the persecutions and exile inflicted on their forebears.[20]

Jewish plans for world-domination were especially perceptible to Trzeciak in southeastern Poland. The *Protocols* and "Speech of Rabbi Reichhorn" both referred to Jews gradually gaining control not only over the economy and legal profession but also over the land. Ever since they received equal rights in Poland, Jews have been doing just that. By destroying the peasants with drink and the nobility with debts, Jews, wrote Trzeciak, had been able to buy up land in eastern Galicia. This was something new and particularly disturbing to the priest, since "they are the masters who possess the land." So many Jews in the southeast now owned small farms that they even established their own agricultural organizations. Their sons were registering in agricultural colleges. Trzeciak saw this as part of a systematic plan to control Galicia, aided by money coming from Jews in the west, especially from America. Trzeciak was blind to Jewish poverty. Jewish philanthropic agencies in the west, like the Alliance Israélite Universelle, had long been treated by antisemites as branches of the worldwide Jewish conspiracy, and Trzeciak continued the tradition.[21]

Trzeciak was not without suggestions as to how to withstand the Jewish "program" to dominate Poland. He quoted the widespread Polish saying attributed to Jacob Frank: "The Polish nobility are good but ignorant; we have need of them." The priest accused Poles of being good-hearted, light-headed and credulous in comparison to devious Jews for whom the end justified the means. Ever since they received equal rights, he wrote, Jews have seen Galicia as a "second 'promised land.'" The only way Poland could remain Polish was first for Jews to be deprived of their civil rights and then be removed from Poland. The alternative was bondage to Jews.[22] Writing on Trzeciak's books in *Przegląd Katolicki*, Józef Białasiewicz agreed that international Jewish activity must be met with international Catholic action. For the sake of their spiritual and

---

[20] *Mały Dziennik,* May 13, 1936.

[21] Jacob Brafmann, an apostate Jew turned Russian police spy, first published *Jewish Fraternities, local and universal* in 1868. See Cohn, *Warrant for Genocide*, 53–55. On the origins and work of the Alliance Israélite Universelle, see Michael Marrus, *The Politics of Assimilation: A Study of the French Jewish Community at the Time of the Dreyfus Affair* (Oxford: Clarendon, 1971).

[22] *Pro Christo*, 13/3 (1937): 1–9; *Mały Dziennik,* April 1, 1937.

social ministry, priests who cared about the church and Poland needed to familiarize themselves with Trzeciak's writings.[23]

Schools, the Catholic education of youth, were a serious concern for Monsignor Trzeciak, particularly in light of what "In the Jewish Cemetery in Prague" had to say about them. Despite his recognition of the work as a chapter of a novel,[24] Trzeciak nonetheless regarded it as laying the seedbed for the program found in the *Protocols*. There in the earlier work one could find expression of Jewish determination to separate schools from the influence of the church. Under the banner of progress and equal rights, schools were becoming non-confessional and Christian children were being taught by Jewish teachers. The Christian character of education in Poland was being obliterated thanks to the efforts of Masons, socialists, and the Polish Teachers' Association. Judging from the names on their roster, Trzeciak counted three thousand Jews in the association including 135 among the various officers. Trzeciak quoted the *Protocols* that gentiles were playing the sheep to Jewish wolves. Just as Jews had their own exclusive organizations, so should Poles, he argued. If Polish youth were to be protected from communist subversion, they had to be separated from Jewish youth and freed from the influence of Jewish teachers.[25]

When a representative of the Polish Sejm, Budzynski, made the public statement that all Semites were deserters, Jews understandably objected, among them five Jewish members of the Polish army who had been awarded the highest military honors for bravery. Trzeciak entered into the fray by going back to the revolt of the Maccabees and the Jewish wars with Rome as reported by Josephus Flavius. It was "a strange coincidence," he wrote, that those five Jewish heroes corresponded to the five Maccabean brothers: "everywhere one could find exceptions." Trzeciak blamed the Jewish defeats of two thousand years ago on a "socially destructive spirit." He accused Jews of betraying their own country in the year 67 and Poland in 1920. Jews, wrote Trzeciak, were and are prone to desertion, to harming the state more than defending it. "Almost all deserters, almost all communists, traitors to the Polish state

---

[23] *Przegląd Katolicki,* 74 (1936): 341–42.

[24] *Przegląd Katolicki,* 74 (1936): 147.

[25] *Mały Dziennik,* December 6, 1937.

and nation were Jews." Poland, it followed, had to put an end to giving the same rights to those who would defend it with their lives and those who would join its enemies and fight against it.[26]

For Trzeciak, ancient Jewish sources were of a piece with contemporary Jewish newspapers, and all were harmonized and explained by the *Protocols.* The second century revolt of Bar Kochba against the Rome, the messianic pretensions of Jacob Frank in eighteenth-century Poland, socialism, communism—all fit together as parts of a movement for Jews to take revenge on the nations. "Vengeance," wrote the priest, "belongs to the chief characteristics of the Jewish soul." Since communism was one of the means for them to attain that end, all manner of Jews, even the rich and religious, have a tendency toward communism. Trzeciak expressed full faith in the legend that the Bolshevik revolution had been financed by Jewish money like that of American banker Jacob Schiff.[27]

But Monsignor Trzeciak's erudition extended to more than the *Protocols.* He was able to draw from the long history of Catholic anti-Jewish writings, including those of the popes. At a lecture in Lwów sponsored by a nationalist university student group, he reminded his audience that Pope Alexander III had warned Catholics against familiarity with Jews. Decreeing that Jews should serve Christians and not the other way around, Pope Innocent III forbade Jews to serve in public office. Especially pertinent for Poles was the letter sent in 1752 to the Polish bishops by Pope Benedict XIV, in which the pope lamented the great numbers of Jews settling in Poland. In the words of the pope, quoted both by Trzeciak and the *Mały Dziennik,* "not only Jews but their synagogues and kehilas grow rich while undermining the existence of Christians."[28] When Jewish leaders denounced Trzeciak not only in the press but to high ranking members of the church hierarchy, he defended himself by drawing from Christian scriptures and tradition. The New Testament called Jews a "synagogue of Satan" (Rev. 2:9), displeasing to God (1 Thess. 3:14–16), and born of the devil (Jn. 8:44). From the church Fathers Trzeciak cited pertinent passages out of the *contra*

---

[26] *Mały Dziennik,* January 10, 1937.

[27] *Mały Dziennik,* April 11, 1937.

[28] *Mały Dziennik,* January 30, 1937.

Judaios literature. Saint Jerome wrote of Jews persecuting Christians and cursing them daily (Epist. 65; Lib. II in Cap. Isaiae). Calling the synagogue a place of perversity and godlessness, Saint Ambrose spoke out against praying for Jews or conversing with them (Epist. lib II, 12; Sermo 10, de cal. Jan.).

Trzeciak also cited church councils. The *Apostolic Canons* (canons 69, 70) forbade Christians to have relationships with Jews, as did (325) the ecumenical council of Nicaea (canon 52). The ecumenical council of Constantinople (692) forbade Christians to use the services of Jewish medical doctors. The Fourth Lateran Council (1215) prohibited Jews from assuming positions of authority in government. The Council of Vienna (1267) forbade Jews from frequenting Christian restaurants, hotels, and bathhouses, and the Synod of Valencia (1388) required that they live only in ghettoes.[29]

In the same vein, Trzeciak was able to cite numerous popes in support of his program to segregate Jews. Pope Paul IV required Jews to live in a ghetto and forbade them to own land or employ Christian servants. Saint Pope Pius V required Jews to leave the Papal States altogether, with the exception of Rome and Ancona (1569). Trzeciak quoted long excerpts from the papal bull of expulsion in which Jews were accused, among other things, of usury, disrespect for the name of Jesus, and leading the careless astray with fortune-telling and magic. These "manly decrees" of the popes, wrote Trzeciak, should give courage to national leaders to free their peoples from the "Jewish plague." With their Talmudic ethics, "quite the opposite of Christian ethics," Jews, he went on, were alien and hostile and could not be treated as equal to other peoples with equal rights. Depriving Jews of their civil rights in Poland, concluded Trzeciak, was only self-defense, founded on the teaching of the Catholic church.[30]

Antisemitism, for Trzeciak, was a necessary hallmark of Polish patriotism. He linked concern for Poland's greatness with interest in Poland's "Jewish question" and the Jewish "program" for world politics. More and more natives Poles, wrote the priest, were joining under the banner of nationalism. The internationalists were Jews, communists and Masons. Being a nationalist meant being an advocate for a Catholic

---

[29] *Mały Dziennik*, February 20, 1939.

[30] *Mały Dziennik*, March 6, 1939.

Poland. Being a Mason or espousing the values of liberty, equality, and fraternity, meant being an agent for the establishment of a Jewish kingdom.[31]

Few writers in the Polish Catholic press, aside from Monsignor Trzeciak, gave the *Protocols* even passing notice. No periodical gave them much heed besides the *Mały Dziennik*. But that Catholic daily did enjoy the largest circulation of any daily newspaper in Poland and obviously made an impact. And it bears noting that one could be a true believer in a Jewish-Masonic alliance even without giving credence to the authenticity of the *Protocols*.

From the standpoint of the last decade of the twentieth century, the bizarre provenance of the *Protocols* may beggar the imagination. But the book is still being published and distributed today. From Hitler and Himmler, to the SS overseeing the death camps, the perpetrators of the Holocaust went about the business of genocide not only without remorse but with a sense of accomplishing something important and necessary. That they could do so must remain unfathomable to people of conscience unless account is taken of their utter belief in the existence of a Jewish world conspiracy. Along with racism, the myth of a Jewish conspiracy was a central part of Nazi ideology. In Poland too the myth took its toll, particularly with the identification of Jews with Bolshevism. As already observed, for Monsignor Stanisław Trzeciak and other true believers in the veracity of the *Protocols*, communism was part of the plan for Jewish domination. Communism and Judaism for them were virtually synonymous.

---

[31] *Mały Dziennik*, July 19 and 20, 1938.

Chapter 4

The Soviet Union and "Judeo-Communism"

Five days after Pope Pius XI issued an encyclical critical of Nazi Germany (*Mit brennender Sorge*), he issued another one (March 19, 1937) on atheistic communism (*Divini Redemptoris*). The face value impression made by the timing of these two documents was that the Vatican was contending equally against the extremes of both left and right, that it was condemning with equal vigor and abhorrence both atheistic communism in the Soviet Union and fascism in Germany: communism for its materialistic atheism and National Socialism for its "aggressive paganism." Since neither document made any mention of Jews, it might also appear at first that neither bore any import on the Catholic attitude toward Jews. Both these impressions are false.

The Vatican's fear of fascism in no way equalled its apprehension and horror of the communist menace. The future Pope Pius XI witnessed first hand the attempted invasion of Warsaw by Soviet forces in 1920. His secretary of state, Eugenio Pacelli, the future Pius XII, had personally experienced the threat of a communist uprising in Munich. The absence of any reference to Jews in the encyclical on Nazism is an embarrassment that Vatican apologists still try to explain. The absence of any reference to Jews in the encyclical on communism was an omission that right wing Catholics could easily correct.

The official Catholic attitude towards communism goes back even before the publication of Marx's *Communist Manifesto*. In 1846 (*Qui pluribus*) Pope Pius IX made brief reference to it as an "unspeakable doctrine" opposed to natural law and destructive of society.[1] In 1849 (*Notis et Nobiscum*) he assailed both communism and socialism as "pernicious" theories bent on plundering "first the Church's and then everyone's property."[2] The same Pope linked socialists and communists again in his 1864 *Syllabus of Errors,* as did his successor Pope Leo XIII, who, in 1878 (*Quod apostolici*), described them as bound together in a "wicked confederacy." Socialism, wrote Pope Leo, was a "plague" caused by Protestantism, the Enlightenment, and the removal of religion from public education. He disparaged socialism not only for its ideas on property but its theory of equality, insisting that in the state too as in the church there is a hierarchy of dignity and power.[3]

When the communists seized control of Russia in 1917, the condition of Roman Catholics initially improved from those under which they had labored under the czars, and the Catholic press expressed guarded hopes.[4] But these were soon dashed with reports of priests and nuns being murdered, the looting of churches, widespread free love, and atheism being taught in the schools. Tensions heightened when a Catholic archbishop and eighteen other priests were tried and imprisoned for treason. With Stalin's continuation of Lenin's anti-religious policies, the Catholic church under Pius XI assumed the role of communism's most determined adversary. In an address to an international gathering of Catholic journalists in Rome (May 12, 1936), he declared that of all the dangers threatening society and the church, "the first and greatest and most universal danger is certainly communism in all its forms and gradations." He admitted that he was "profoundly preoccupied" by this "massive danger" that menaced all the world and had already created havoc, especially in Europe.[5]

Therefore, when Pius XI issued an entire encyclical on communism, he

---

[1] Claudia Carlen, I.H.M., *The Papal Encyclicals, 1740–1981,* 5 vols. (1981; reprint, Ann Arbor, MI: Pierien Press, 1990), 1:280.

[2] Carlen, *Papal Encyclicals,* 1:299.

[3] Carlen, *Papal Encyclicals,* 2:13.

[4] Ralph Lord Roy, *Communism and the Churches* (New York: Harcourt, Brace, 1960), 125, quoting a Catholic news service report.

[5] Domenico Bertetto, ed., *Discorsi di Pio XI* (Vatican City: Liberia Editrice Vaticana, 1960–1961, 2nd ed., 1985), vol.3, 487–88.

was simply restating and elaborating upon a long-established Catholic position. Describing communist persecution as exceeding any the church had previously experienced, he lay responsibility for the anti-clerical fury in Mexico and Spain on Moscow. Communists were the church's "most persistent enemies," directing a struggle against Christian civilization. Among their errors the Pope singled out both materialism and a "false messianic idea." With its "pseudo-ideal" of absolute equality, communism rejected all hierarchy and divinely constituted authority. In the tradition of his papal predecessors, Pius explained the rapid spread of communism by the fact that its way was prepared by liberalism. To separate church and state and eliminate religious instruction from public schools was to foster the materialism that affords a fertile soil for communism.

The Pope went on to warn against the blandishments of those who would invite Catholic cooperation with communists in humanitarian efforts. "Communism," he insisted, "is intrinsically wrong, and no one who would save Christian civilization may collaborate with it in any undertaking whatsoever." He called upon the Catholic press to "supply accurate and complete information on the activity of the enemy." He called upon the laity in the ranks of Catholic Action to disseminate papal teaching on social issues and to aid priests wherever anti-clericalism or religious indifference held sway.[6]

Nothing in these papal teachings makes reference to Jews; only Pius XI's description of communism as a "false messianic idea" could be even remotely interpreted as an allusion to Judaism. Yet Catholics, especially in Central and Eastern Europe, regularly identified communism with Jews. That they were not the only ones to do so may be exemplified by an article which appeared (February 1920) in the London *Illustrated Sunday Herald*. Entitled "Zionism versus Bolshevism—A Struggle for the Soul of the Jewish People," it described communism as resulting from "the schemes of International Jews.... Now at last this band of extraordinary personalities from the underworld of the great cities of Europe and America have gripped the Russian people by the hair of their heads and have become practically the undisputed masters of that enormous empire."[7]

---

[6] Pius XI, *Divini Redemptoris*, in Carlen, *Papal Encyclicals*, 3:537-53.

[7] Quoted in Jerry Z. Muller, "Communism, Anti-Semitism, and the Jews," in *Commentary* 86, 2 (August 1988), 29.

The author of that article was Winston Churchill. The "extraordinary personalities" he referred to would have included Leon Trotsky, commissar for foreign affairs in Lenin's first cabinet; Yakov Sverdlov, president of the Supreme Soviet; Lev Kamenev, chairman of the Moscow Soviet; Grigori Zinoviev, president of the Petrograd Soviet and leader of the Communist International; and Moisei Uritsky, head of the Petrograd secret police. Outside the Soviet Union there was Polish-born Rosa Luxembourg active in Germany, Bela Kun and Georg Lukacs in Hungary. With so many communists of Jewish origin in positions of prominence, it took little effort for outsiders to consider communism a peculiarly Jewish phenomenon. If someone like Churchill could deem communism to be a creation of "international Jews," it can be no source for wonder that the identification was accepted with alacrity by those who had long conceived of Jews as the enemy of Christian civilization.

By any logic or fair standard of judgment, the identification was mistaken. Karl Marx may have been born of Jewish parents, but they had deliberately dissociated themselves from Judaism and had converted to Lutheranism. Marx's immediate followers, like those who inspired him, were not Jewish, and he himself was acerbically critical of a Jewry he identified with capitalism. Lenin and Stalin were, of course, not Jewish, and in 1917 most Russian Jews did not support Bolshevism, since its atheism contradicted Jewish religious belief and its economic theories threatened Jewish merchants. In 1918 the rabbis of Odessa anathematized the Jewish Bolsheviks, and officials in the Jewish community looked with understandable apprehension on their prominence in the revolutionary wave.[8]

Once the civil war was under way, however, Jews began swinging toward the Bolsheviks for self-preservation. In a series of pogroms in the Ukraine, some 70,000 Jews were murdered by counterrevolutionary nationalists. With their very lives now contingent on the defeat of the counterrevolutionaries, greater numbers of Jews embraced the Bolshevik cause. They became, at least to a certain extent, overrepresented in the communist party. Most Jews were still not communist, and most communists were still not Jews. In the 1920s, Jews comprised only some five percent of the membership of the communist party in the Soviet

---

[8] Muller, "Communism, Anti-Semitism," 29.

Union, about twice their proportion in the population.[9] That five percent was highly visible, however. Jewish Bolsheviks were more highly urbanized and educated than other members of the party, more likely to be activists once in it, and more likely to rise in its ranks. From 1917 to 1922, between one-sixth and one-fifth of the delegates to the party congresses were of Jewish origin. Moreover, most of the prerevolutionary Russian civil service refused to collaborate with the Bolsheviks or were suspect in the eyes of the new leaders. Educated Jews moved into important and sensitive positions in the Soviet bureaucracy. As a result, the first encounter with the new regime for many Russians was likely to be with a commissar or secret police official of Jewish origin.

In Poland the image of the Jew as communist was especially believable because of the 1920 war over the Polish-Soviet border. Of the four man Provisional Revolutionary Committee the Soviets set up at that time, two members were Jewish.[10] Even before that, however, Poland's Jewish intelligentsia had provided leaders for the socialist movement, the most prominent being, of course, Rosa Luxembourg. Whereas the Polish Socialist Party (PPS) consistently championed the cause of Polish independence, left wing Polish Marxists like Luxembourg, an uncompromising internationalist, regarded Polish nationalism as retrogressive and bourgeois. An independent Polish state was a utopian distraction from the international proletarian revolution that was expected to sweep Europe. Jewish socialists, whether Zionists or Bundists, likewise refused to make Polish independence an objective. From its beginnings, in other words, the socialist movement in Poland was atomized, and relations among the various groups were bitter. An early leader in the right wing of the PPS, Józef Piłsudski eventually broke with it altogether.

The success of the Bolshevik revolution in Russia inspired radical socialists everywhere. In the last months of 1918, communist parties mushroomed all over Europe. In Poland the left wing Marxist groups merged (December 16, 1918) to form the Communist Workers' Party. When it refused the next year to comply with an order of the Polish government that all organizations register, the communist party became illegal. It went underground and was treated by the Polish government as subversive. When, with the encouragement of Polish communists, the

---

[9] Muller, "Communism, Anti-Semitism," 30.

[10] Muller, "Communism, Anti-Semitism," 34.

Soviets invaded Poland, their announced intention was the creation of a new socialist order, civil liberties, and land reform. But memories of czarist oppression were still fresh, and the Poles saw the Russian army, whatever its banner, simply as foreign invaders. The Polish communist party eventually reversed its stand on the issue of Polish statehood, but the masses of Poles did not soon forget the Soviet invasion and the hardships it inflicted.

The Polish communist party had to operate through front organizations. It attempted to infiltrate legal labor unions. But its approaches to the PPS and Bund in the mid-1930s to establish a united front against fascism met with rejection. Competing with the PPS and Bund, Polish communists made considerable efforts to organize economic strikes and turn them into political ones. But unemployed workers were not so much concerned about achieving revolutionary objectives as about meeting elementary human needs. Daily street demonstrations, hasty strikes, and riots came to alienate even the more militant among the jobless. The communist party's cosmopolitan makeup and ties tended to attract intellectuals. But, because of its pro-Soviet orientation, the Polish communist party never enjoyed wide backing among the working class. Its influence on interwar Poland was modest and at best marginal.[11]

Jewish socialism in Poland was represented by Zionists organized into the Poale Zion party (Workers of Zion) and the General Jewish Workers Bund, or simply the Bund. Founded in Wilno in 1897, the Bund was a self-proclaimed Marxist party dedicated to a new social, political, and economic order. In the first years after the Russian revolution, Bundists in Poland seriously considered joining the communist party as their counterparts had done in Russia. But Polish Bundists were dedicated to the principles of parliamentary democracy, which communists rejected as a vestige of capitalism, and in Poland the Bund never joined the

---

[11] M. K. Dziewanowski, *The Communist Party of Poland: An Outline of History* (Cambridge, MA: Harvard University Press, 2nd ed., 1976), 94–95, 134–35. See also his *Poland in the Twentieth Century* (New York: Columbia, 1977), 93. According to communist historians cited by Dziewanowski, during the interwar years, 59% of the Polish communist party's membership were classified as intellectuals, 10% as industrial workers, and the remainder as peasants and farm laborers. For a compilation of documentation and brief biographies of the party's leading members in Yiddish, see H. Goldfinger, M. Mirski, and S. Zachariasz, eds., *Unter der fon fun K.P.P.* (Warsaw: Książka i Wiedza, 1959).

Communist International.

Jewish religious leaders repudiated the Bund because of its professed Marxism. Likewise at odds were Polish Zionists. The Bund was diaspora-oriented and insisted that the Jewish cultural heritage was Eastern European, not Middle Eastern; that the language of the Jewish people was Yiddish, not Hebrew. Bundists generally considered themselves part of Poland. They professed a dual loyalty: culturally to their Jewish heritage and politically to Poland. Believing that only a Marxist revolution would lead to a satisfactory solution to Poland's Jewish question, Bundists argued most issues in Marxist terms. It emphasized class solidarity even over Jewish solidarity and tried to build bridges to the class-oriented parties on the Polish left, the chief representative of which was the Polish Socialist Party (PPS).[12]

Founded in 1892, the PPS made Poland's independence a prerequisite for socialism. Once independence had been achieved, it became a moderate social democratic party. Like the Bund it was dedicated to parliamentary democracy and favored full equality for all of Poland's national minorities. Despite some animosity with the Bund earlier over the issue of Polish independence, by the 1930s relations between the two socialist parties was fraternal. Jews were welcomed into the ranks of the PPS. There were even Jews among its leaders, but the percentage of its Jewish members was not very great. Asserting a strongly assimilationist Jewish policy, the PPS was the only important political organization in Poland opposed to antisemitism. It warrants recognition that—unlike the rest of the continent—a Polish political organization of considerable and even growing strength set its face squarely against the antisemitic campaign that engulfed Europe in the mid-1930s. To quote Israeli historian Ezra Mendelsohn: "Gentile opposition to anti-Semitism, therefore, was not restricted, as it was in other countries, to a courageous but lonely and isolated group of intellectuals and priests who viewed with alarm the emergence of virulent racism on the Nazi model. From the Jewish point of view, and particularly from the point of view of the

---

[12] For a general history of the Bund, see Bernard K. Johnpoll, *The Politics of Futility: The General Jewish Workers Bund of Poland, 1917–1943* (Ithaca, NY: Cornell University Press, 1967). See also Ezra Mendelsohn, *The Jews of East Central Europe between the World Wars* (Bloomington, IN: Indiana University Press, 1983), 46–53, 77–80, and passim.

Jewish left, this was a fact of some importance."[13]

The PPS won representation in several coalition governments between the wars. The Bund, thanks to the leadership role it assumed in combatting antisemitism, did well in municipal elections in the late 1930s, but it never elected a deputy to the Sejm. Although the great majority of Jews voted for Jewish parties, they did not vote Marxist, let alone pro-Bolshevik. The Jewish community was more interested in protecting civil rights than in promoting social change. As for the communist party, because it was illegal and underground for most of the interwar period, it is difficult to assess its numerical strength or the percentage of Jews within it. One estimate at the time, based on a study by the Institute for the Scientific Study of Communism in Warsaw, was that there were twenty thousand communists in Poland, eleven thousand of which (55%) were Jewish.[14] A more recent estimate puts the figure at a quarter of the party or five thousand Jewish communists.[15]

Whether the number is five thousand or eleven thousand, out of interwar Poland's 3.3 million Jews, the percentage of Jews who were communist was meager. But because the Polish communist party totaled only twenty thousand members, it did not take many Jews to make the party appear Jewish to outsiders, particularly to those who already hostile to Jews. To the image of the Jew as deicide and capitalist was now added the image of Jew as a communist. The notion was central to Nazi ideology in Germany but had its echo in right wing circles throughout Europe. In Poland those nationalist circles made "Judeo-communism" a single word (*Żydokomuna*), a concept given wide circulation in the Catholic press.

On the Soviet Union

For reasons of geography as well as politics and religion, the Soviet Union was a paramount concern for the Catholic church in Poland, and

---

[13] Mendelsohn, *Jews of East Central Europe,* 72.

[14] *Mały Dziennik,* March 15, 1937. Another figure given for total membership in the Polish Communist Party at its peak is 12,000. M. K. Dziewanowski, *Poland in the Twentieth Century,* 93.

[15] Muller, "Communism, Anti-Semitism," 34.

references to the Soviet Union appeared frequently in the pages of its press. A major theme of these references, of course, was the communist persecution of Christians, described as "martyrs" of the faith: the murder and imprisonment of bishops, priests, and religious.[16] The Soviet Union was at war with Christianity, converting churches into movie theaters and dance halls.[17] In stark contrast, Poland's Catholic news agency (KAP) reported in 1930 that the Soviet government was openly contending against antisemitism and that no rabbi in the Soviet Union had been threatened or killed.[18]

Why the Soviets persecuted Christians and not Jews required little explanation for J. B. Słoński in the *Mały Dziennik:* Jews were linked to communists by common aims. According to Stalin, as quoted in *Pravda* (November 30, 1936): "Communists, as consistent internationalists, cannot be anything but uncompromising and sworn enemies of antisemitism. In the U.S.S.R., antisemitism is persecuted as profoundly inimical to the soviet system." Molotov was quoted in the same *Pravda* article as expressing "brotherly feelings" toward the Jewish nation for having produced a genius like Karl Marx and so many heroes of the Russian revolution. The "Jewish-communist partnership," concluded Słoński, reached deeper and further than many of Poland's politicians believed.[19]

The prominence of Jews in the Soviet government was regularly pointed out in the Polish Catholic press. When one Moses Ruchinowicz received an appointment in the Soviet bureaucracy, the *Mały Dziennik* ran the headline: "Jew stands at the head of the newly formed commissariat of defense industry in the USSR."[20] Only the fact he was a Jew was the explanation of how an "illiterate" like Leib Mechlis could rise to become vice-minister of defence.[21] It was even reported that Russian nationals

---

[16] *Rycerz Niepokalanej* (October 1938): 311.

[17] *Przewodnik Katolicki*, 43(1937): 752–53; *Rycerz Niepokalanej* (February 1938): 41.

[18] *Mały Dziennik*, October 18, 1935.

[19] *Mały Dziennik*, March 18, 1937.

[20] *Mały Dziennik*, December 11, 1936.

[21] *Mały Dziennik*, January 11, 1938.

were assuming Jewish names in order to advance their careers.[22]

But it was the association of Jews with the Soviet secret police that offered the greatest potential for arousing the fears of Polish Catholics. To the secret police was attributed unlimited power over all aspects of life in the Soviet Union. It could arrest and execute whomever it would. No one could be appointed to an important position in the government apparatus without its approval. When the Soviet government singled out certain members of the secret police for recognition, J. B. Słoński in the *Mały Dziennik* extrapolated from the list of the honorees to the "Jewish character" of the secret police; of the ten who received the highest award, the Order of Lenin, three were Jewish; forty-two out of 238 recipients of the Red Star were Jewish; out of 154 recipients of the badge of honor, twenty-two were Jewish. Słoński concluded that virtually no office of the secret police was without a Jew, usually in an administrative position. It was a "Jewish" secret police that was terrorizing the people of the Soviet Union, posing a threat to Poles as well. One could be sure that there were many among Poland's Jews who dreamt of a future career in the secret police.[23]

Stalinist purges of Trotskyites and attacks on religious Jews produced no reassessment of the above conclusions or editorial stance in the Catholic daily. After visiting Moscow in September of 1936, an anonymous reporter for the *Mały Dziennik* wrote of Stalin beginning a "war" against Jews because "the red army does not want to defend a Jewish state."[24] When a Soviet periodical called for the liquidation of rabbis in Byelorussia as foreign agents, the *Mały Dziennik* did not write of persecution. It reported that the secret police believed espionage to be highly developed among Byelorussian Jews. The headline of the Catholic daily simply read: "Bolsheviks have enough of Jews."[25]

---

[22] Julian Unszlicht, *Gazeta Kościelna,* (1936): 199.

[23] *Mały Dziennik,* January 16, 1938.

[24] *Mały Dziennik,* October 2, 1936.

[25] *Mały Dziennik,* July 23, 1938.

On Polish Socialism

The widespread Catholic association of Jews with communism requires appreciating the virtual Catholic identification of communism with socialism. Communists and socialists were regarded as pursuing the same objectives. The fact that socialists abjured violent revolution and were willing to work peacefully within the law to attain their objectives did not alter the fundamental morality of their principles. For nearly a century already, the popes had made little or no distinction between them, and Polish church leaders followed suit.

Socialism was contrary to Christianity, according to the Polish Catholic press, but not to Judaism. Despite the fact that it struck at Jewish economic interests and undermined Jewish religious convictions, Jews have a well-known, widespread "almost instinctive sympathy" for socialism, wrote Father Julian Unszlicht, a Catholic priest of Jewish background. Socialism had attracted considerable numbers of Jews. Antisemites inflated the numbers, philosemites deflated them, but everyone could feel a certain strange kinship between socialism and Judaism. "One can say that the unusual number of Jews entering into government service brought about the victory of communism in Russia, and that factually Soviet Russia is ruled by Jews." In Nazi Germany, Marxism was viewed as a product of Jewish manufacture. In Russia it was widely viewed as the "victory of the 'Jewish antichrist' which is supposed to forewarn the end of the world."

The socialist idea of freeing the proletariat from capitalism, wrote Unszlicht, was not specifically Jewish. Theoretically one could have socialism without Jews, and certainly there were socialists who were not Jewish. But socialism would not be the immense worldwide force it was, were it not for Jews. Socialist materialism corresponded to the Jewish tendency "to resolve the highest questions of the human heart with earthly advantages." Because of former persecutions, socialists and communists instinctively defended Jews against Christians. Side by side socialists and communists waged war against the church as a common enemy, the mainstay, in their opinion, of capitalist exploitation of the working class and of the religious oppression of Jews. Jewish leaders wanted a dechristianized working class, hostile to the church. The more socialism progressed and the Christian masses fell away from the church, the more Jewish control would be enhanced.

Thus, Unszlicht continued, Jews could not be indifferent toward socialism, even though it struck at their "racial separateness" and financial interests. He assured his readers that the Jewish proclivity for socialism did not arise out of any real concern for the working classes. Obviously, it was possible for a Jew to be genuinely concerned about the injustice suffered by the underprivileged, but that was an exception. "Generally Jews are incapable of feeling the misery of non-Jews; they see instead the possibility of exploiting it in the interests of their own race, presenting themselves as defenders of the proletariat and promising earthly happiness under their leadership." Jewish socialists were indifferent to the suffering of the Christian masses, claimed the priest. When they talked about liberating the working class, they really meant bringing about the downfall of the church.

Unszlicht accused Jewish atheists of criticizing only the church, not the synagogue. As a consequence, even believing Jews were not indifferent to socialism. According to the Talmud, wrote the priest, Israel was destined to rule over the nations. But memories of Jesus and his crucifixion always aroused antisemitic feelings in Christians, so that even believing Jews saw the destruction of Christianity by atheistic socialism as a good thing. Jewish atheists thought they could make the church pay for the supposed injury it had done to Israel and thus, as in the Soviet Union, obliterate the name of Jesus everywhere. This would allow Jews to assume the moral leadership of humanity.[26]

Catholicism and socialism were incompatible, wrote Wojciech Grot in a similar vein. If socialists spoke about Jesus, it was only as a revolutionary, the gospel only as a document of social and political revolution. Always and everywhere, socialism was the forerunner of communism.[27]

At the First Plenary Polish Synod, the Polish bishops decreed that Catholics were not allowed to belong to, support or cooperate with socialists. In this they were only following the Holy See. There were some Catholics who considered Poland exempted from the papal warnings, because Polish socialism had assumed a less destructive form and was less inimical to the church. Jan Archita disagreed: Polish socialists took their origins and program completely from the "condemned teachings of the Jew, Marx." They made the *Communist*

---

[26] Rev. Julian Unszlicht, *Gazeta Kościelna* (1936): 199–200, 213–14.

[27] Wojciech Grot, *Przewodnik Katolicki,* 43 (1937): 146.

Manifesto their confession of faith. Those who thought that Catholics could meet socialists half way and have an influence on them were deluding themselves.

Polish socialists, continued Archita, constantly talked about toleration and respect, saying "religion is a private matter." But this was only a cunning tactic to mask their ultimate aim, which was to destroy the church's influence on social life. The socialist camp wanted to secularize the family by depriving marriage of its sacramental character. It stood out against religious schools, demanded separation of church and state, and encouraged birth control. Socialists professed to be opposing "clericalism," not religion itself, but their phrases about humanitarianism and progress were only a disguise for atheism. Socialists were arousing hatred against the clergy, destroying the authority of the church, and diminishing moral feeling. Pope Pius XI was right: religious socialism or Christian socialism were mutually contradictory terms.[28]

The identification of Jews with socialism could work both ways, not only to arouse hostile feelings toward Jews but to arouse distrust of socialism. When the PPS came out against the boycott of Jewish stores, their stance was perceived as proof that they depended on Jews for material support. For them to distribute a reputed two million pieces of pro-Jewish literature was a clear indication that the PPS was only a Jewish front, wrote the *Mały Dziennik*. The Polish Socialist Party was serving Jewish interests like a paid lackey. It was an appalling alliance, contrary to nature.[29]

When a congress of the PPS passed a resolution calling upon workers to oppose antisemitism as a capitalist creation, Father Józef Hetnal responded that "Socialists are flunkies for the Jews." Should workers fight against their fellow Poles, who were only trying to defend themselves against Jewish domination? A current of liberation from the Jewish yoke was surging throughout the country. Only the socialists were holding back and continuing to remain "flunkies" (*pachołki*) for the Jews. By supporting Jews the socialists were demoralizing society and lining Jewish pocketbooks at the expense of peasants and workers.[30]

---

[28] Jan Archita, *Rycerz Niepokalanej* (1938): 292–93, 329–31, 371–73.

[29] *Mały Dziennik*, September 25, 1937.

[30] Józef Hetnal, *Przewodnik Katolicki*, 44 (1938): 403.

When a coalition of socialists and Jews constituted a majority on the city council of Kraków, the *Przewodnik Katolicki* complained of "Jews and socialists together again."[31] Similarly, when socialists in Łódź gained control of the city council and won seats in the government of several other cities as well, the popular Catholic weekly expressed alarm and attributed the socialist gains to the numbers of Jews in those cities. Here was one more reason to eliminate Jewish influence from Poland. Poles were leaving their homeland by the thousands to work abroad, while Poland's Jews in the millions remained. Maybe Poland could solve its Jewish problem by trading Jews for its emigrés. With the possible exception of the socialists, Poles would gladly contribute to such a cause. Poland would immediately become more Polish and a significant part of the "red tide" would recede.[32]

Bundists and communists were not the only Jews explicitly identified in the *Mały Dziennik* with revolution. Jews, claimed the Catholic daily, played an influential, perhaps decisive, role in all revolutionary movements from the nineteenth century to that in Russia. Eager for social experiment, resentful of their surroundings, they are committed to overturning the social order. Besides the Bund and Kombund, the *Mały Dziennik* indicted the Independent Socialists (to which non-Jews also belonged), *Poale Zion, Zeire Zion,* and indirectly, the *Hitahdut.* There would never be peace in Poland so long as these organizations existed, charged the Catholic daily. It called upon the government to disband all revolutionary Jewish organizations and to create areas where these propagators of the Bolshevik paradise could be isolated.[33]

Socialism was bankrupt, declared the *Mały Dziennik*. The working masses could see its destructive work, paving the way for communism with its many strikes. Polish workers were by nature patriotic and were leaving the ranks of those clearly connected with Jews and Jewish interests. The PPS believed that the worse that things were for the workers, the better it was for the party. Jews in the PPS burned with hatred for non-Jews and held unlimited power in the party. Socialists were no different from communists in opposing religion and the Catholic

---

[31] *Przewodnik Katolicki,* 45 (1939): 488.

[32] *Przewodnik Katolicki,* 45 (1939): 144–45.

[33] *Mały Dziennik,* March 8, 1936.

church. The PPS was no place for Polish workers.[34]

Since there was no fundamental difference between communism and socialism, Poland's Catholic press made no essential distinction between the communist party, the PPS, and the Bund.

In Catholic eyes the Bundists were but precursors, preparing the Jewish masses to embrace communism. Bolshevism began where the Bund left off. The *Przegląd Katolicki* made much of the fact that in the Soviet Union almost the entire Bund had freely joined the communist party.[35] A later article in the Catholic weekly acknowledged that Bundists in the Soviet Union were being persecuted, but claimed that Polish Bundists were defending and promoting communism and having an impact on Polish Catholics. As proof the article cited the success they had in arousing fifteen hundred Polish workers in Wilno to participate in a demonstration against antisemitism. A report that Bundists were only a minority among Jewish workers in Lwów could only mean that communists were therefore the majority.[36]

On Communism

Bishops

Even before Pope Pius XI's 1937 encyclical, geography and history compelled the Polish bishops to be attentive to communist activity. One of their first statements as a collective body was a response to the Soviet invasion of 1920. When it seemed likely that Poland would be overrun by the Red army, the Polish bishops appealed to Catholic bishops throughout the world with what they called a "cry for help and rescue". The bishops' letter clearly indicates that they believed in the substance of the *Protocols of the Elders of Zion*, which had appeared earlier that year in Polish:

---

[34] *Mały Dziennik*, April 27, 1939.

[35] *Przegląd Katolicki*, 75 (1937): 230–31.

[36] *Przegląd Katolicki*, 75 (1937): 524–25.

The real object of Bolshevism is world-conquest. The race which has the leadership of Bolshevism in its hands, has already in the past subjugated the whole world by means of gold and the banks, and now, driven by the everlasting imperialistic greed which flows in its veins, is already aiming at the final subjugation of the nations under the yoke of its rule.... The hatred of Bolshevism is directed against Christ and his Church, especially because those who are the leaders of Bolshevism bear in their blood the traditional hatred for Christianity. Bolshevism is in truth the embodiment and incarnation of the spirit of Antichrist on earth.[37]

At their first plenary synod in restored Poland (1936), they attributed the destruction of churches in Spain to orders by the Kremlin. In Poland no churches had been burned nor priests killed yet, but there was reason for alarm, not only because of Polish communists but Poles who, though they rejected communism, allied themselves with "radicalism." By radicalism they meant publications critical of religion and movements like the "people's front," allied in Poland as elsewhere with Masonry. These agitators were the avant garde of communism, sowing the seeds of mistrust and hatred first for the church and then for the nation and state. The bishops proposed to do battle by means of Catholic Action. Communism was above all a spiritual disease and had to be combatted by spiritual means, not by reforms tied to radicalism. Any compromise with radicalism could only further the communist cause.[38]

The same year as the bishops' synod, Cardinal August Hlond, issued a pastoral letter in which he identified Jews as the "vanguard of atheism, the Bolshevik movement, and revolutionary activity." He condemned physical violence against Jews but at the same time encouraged the boycott of Jewish stores and publications. Jews were waging war against the Catholic church and one should keep away from their "anti-Christian culture."[39]

---

[37] Cited in Norman Cohn, *Warrant for Genocide: The Myth of the Jewish World Conspiracy and the Protocols of the Elders of Zion* (Chico, CA: Scholars Press, 1981), 164–65.

[38] *Mały Dziennik,* September 5, 1936.

[39] August Cardinal Hlond, *Na straży sumienia narodu* (Ramsey, New Jersey: Don Bosco, 1951), 164–65.

When Bishop Lisowski of Tarnów issued a pastoral letter on communism, he too blamed the horrors of the Spanish civil war on the communists and their massive war against God. But even more menacing were the crypto-communists secretly infiltrating not only leftist organizations but nationalist and Catholic ones as well. Their activity was all the more dangerous, because they disavowed any war against religion or the church. The popular front was preparing the way for communism by trying to unite socialist parties, trade unions, youth organizations like the Legion of Youth (*Legion Młodych*), and radical left wing Jewish organizations. To protect Poland from communism one needed to be closely attached to the church and the Holy See, defend Catholic morals, and condemn divorce and birth control.[40]

When a delegation of rabbis approached Warsaw's Cardinal Kakowski (June 7, 1934) and asked for a statement against antisemitic violence, he condemned the violence but explained that antisemitism was a reaction against the Jewish atheists and freethinkers who were insulting Christianity and the clergy. Obviously the rabbis were not responsible, but the Jewish community knew how to unite in solidarity to defend its own interests when necessary. It should be able to guarantee respect for Christian faith and tradition as well. If these atheists were young communists, they were nonetheless being supported by other Jews.[41]

Liberalism and Communism

Catholic linking of liberal movements with communism went back at least to the nineteenth century and Pope Leo XIII. Pope Pius XI reaffirmed the connection and with him Poland's bishops and Catholic press. Any movement or idea critical of the church was attributed to Moscow. From Father Maximilan Kolbe's Niepokalanów, the widely distributed *Rycerz Niepokalanej* had no doubt but that Russian Bolsheviks were directing the *Wici* movement among the peasants, accusing the clergy of siding with exploitation. Communism was operating through secret cells "led predominantly by Jews," and building upon the preparatory work of left wing movements. Liberals were preparing the way for communism under the banner of a "war of the workers and

---

[40] *Mały Dziennik*, March 15, 1937.

[41] *Wiadomości Diecezjalne Warszawskie*, (1934): 247. See also chapter 13.

peasants with fascism." By fascism they meant whatever stood in the way of their destructive work, religion, the church, the indissolubility of marriage, Catholic ethics, decent literature and art. These liberals and leftists under communist command were not working to overcome misery and promote justice. "Their goal is the corruption of people's souls and the destruction of the Polish state by joining it to the Soviets."[42]

Also from Niepokalanów, the *Mały Dziennik* took issue with liberals who held that nationalism, not communism, was the greatest danger facing Europe. Compared to the tyranny in Russia, fascism looked like the "height of liberalism." The Holy See rejected nationalistic oppression but not a healthy nationalism, recognized by Catholics as the right of every nation. A national homeland was an extended family to which one owed love and obedience. Christian nationalism led to a family of free nations. While vigilant against the dangers of aggressive German nationalism, Poles did not deny Germans their right to self-determination. But solidarity with the politics of the Holy See required that Poles join other nations against invasion by the Comintern. The Polish state must belong to the Polish people. But Jews, with the exception of a few Orthodox, were trying to mobilize international Masonry against the Poles' rights to polonize Poland. "The future of Europe belongs to Christian nationalism, not communism."[43]

By associating them with communists, Christian nationalists like the writers for the *Mały Dziennik* impugned liberals for lack of patriotism. Liberals were just like communist internationalists, opposed to a strong nationalist Poland and claiming that fascism was the enemy. Those periodicals that resisted attempts to unite the nation in a war against Jews were either communist or "tending toward communism." Those who criticized the clergy did so because of the church's struggle against communism. Attempts were being made to join Jews and Poles into a united front, but they would fail because communism was utterly foreign to Poland.[44]

The 1937 encyclicals of Pius XI on Nazism and communism naturally found their echo in the Catholic press throughout the world. In Poland

---

[42] *Rycerz Niepokalanej*, 5 (1936): 142–43.

[43] *Mały Dziennik*, August 10, 1936.

[44] *Mały Dziennik*, March 15, 1937.

the pope's contention that liberalism prepared the way for communism was developed thoughtfully by Henryk Dembiński in *Verbum*. Despite the apparent paradox, liberalism was the common parent of both communism and Nazism. Liberals espoused an "exaggerated notion of human and civil rights" that eventually led to the brutality of contemporary capitalism to which Marx reacted. Liberalism's *homo oeconomicus*, concerned only for profit, fully justified Marx's materialistic concepts. Liberalism further paved the way for communism by dechristianizing society and promoting religious indifferentism. The role of any society was to assist individuals to achieve perfection. By denying or at least neglecting the supernatural meaning of the human person, liberalism allowed the nation and state to become ends in themselves.

For communists and extreme nationalists like the Nazis, not the perfection of the individual but the welfare and interests of the class or nation took priority. Hence, both systems attacked religion, especially Christianity, for whom the spirit had priority over matter. Communists professed readiness to work for goals like human welfare and peace, it was clear that an alliance between Christianity and communism could never be possible. Nationalism, on the other hand, corresponded to human nature and embraced not only material but spiritual and cultural values. Concern for the family and about the decay of morals were political postulates that national movements took straight from the church. But the nation was never an end in itself. Communism and national socialism were extremes between which the church had to take a middle course. The fact that Christians had not always done so contributed to the present tragedies and required repentance.[45]

Trials

As proof that Poland's Jews were not only sympathetic to liberalism but provided the leadership for Polish communism, the Catholic press regularly pointed to the trials of those arrested for communist agitation. When labor unrest in 1936 led to riots in Kraków and Łódź, the semi-official Catholic Press Agency blamed communists and anti-religious radicals.[46] When similar riots in Lwów that year resulted in several

---

[45] Henryk Dembiński, *Verbum*, 2 (1937): 247–65.

[46] *Mały Dziennik*, April 24, 1936

persons being killed and scores injured, the *Mały Dziennik* printed the names of those arrested as agitators, describing them as obviously Jewish and "all active communists," agents of the Comintern using unemployment for their own ends. Polish workers were not responsible for the riots but were the victims. Those who fomented the disturbances were members of trades dominated by Jews.[47]

The *Mały Dziennik* regularly identified communism with Jews. The Catholic daily reported that, for wearing a religious medal, a Catholic student was assaulted by a group of "Jewish communist scum."[48] When discovery of a communist printing operation in Łódź led to the arrest of twenty persons, the *Mały Dziennik* found it "curious that the communists arrested were almost exclusively Jews."[49] At another trial of "thirteen Jews and two Orthodox (Christians)" in Wilno, the witnesses testified about the "illegal activity of Jewish revolutionaries working for Soviet money." Those defending the communists were described as the best Jewish lawyers from Wilno and Warsaw.[50]

The *Mały Dziennik* was sure that "the Polish nation would never allow the Comintern and their flunkies to triumph on its soil, despite all the efforts of Jewish communists." Jews were "always guided by their strictly racist interests and their eastern psyche." It was no secret that Jewish participation in the communist movement in Poland was "overwhelming," since the majority of communists arrested as agents of Moscow were Jews, as were those who owned and operated communist printing presses. Christians were found only in lower positions. The Catholic daily assured its readers that Poland would not make the mistake the Russian intelligentsia did, allowing themselves to be taken in by the Jews. "We want the Jewish enemies of Christian Poland to leave our country."[51]

For the *Przegląd Katolicki,* more than civil and juridical measures were required to stamp out the "bacteria" of Judeo-communism. The trials revealed how communists were trying to infiltrate the Polish Socialist Party, trade unions, and youth organizations, distributing handbills against

---

[47] *Mały Dziennik,* April 18, 1936.

[48] *Mały Dziennik,* April 21, 1936.

[49] *Mały Dziennik,* April 21, 1936.

[50] *Mały Dziennik,* February 11, 1939.

[51] *Mały Dziennik,* April 24, 1936.

fascism and antisemitism. The trials also brought out allegations of communist collaboration against Jewish sports clubs (Stern and Wieniawia) and cultural societies (Freiheit). The strongest communist influence, however, was revealed to be in Jewish secondary schools.[52]

Schools

Polish Catholic leaders were especially concerned about protecting Catholic youth from communist or other left wing influence. The Jesuits' *Przegląd Powszechny* reported how Polish communists were criticizing the persecution of Catholic organizations in Nazi Germany as a means of winning over Catholic youth. In France there were Catholics saying that communism could be reconciled with Catholic doctrine and could even contribute to a renewal of the church's social teaching. Fortunately, according to the Jesuit journal, Polish youth were alert to such traps. Their "social and cultural separation from Jews has not been without significance and positive influence, since it was well known that communist agents find especially fertile ground among Jewish youth and are creating cadres of communist youth among them." Catholic youth were undergoing a religious revival, symbolized by their struggle to have crucifixes placed in their schools.[53]

When the *Kurier Warszawski* reported on communist cells in Jewish girls' high schools (gymnasia), the *Mały Dziennik* proclaimed that there were, "high schools in the heart of Warsaw where eleven-year-old students are members of the communist party!" It called for the end to the "anti-government activity of Jews in Poland." Jewish primary and secondary schools could not continue to be "seed-beds of revolutionary slogans and communist propaganda." At fault were those Jews whose mentality always inclined them to glorify and embody revolutionary, anti-national currents in Catholic countries. Jews were spreading "moral decay and a spirit of conspiracy against the Polish nation, church, and state among the young generation."[54] Also tarred as infiltrated by communists was the Polish Teachers' Union (*Związek Nauczycielstwa Polskiego,*

---

[52] *Przegląd Katolicki,* 75 (1937): 798–800. See also *Mały Dziennik,* May 22, 1937.

[53] *Przegląd Powszechny,* 216 (1937): 308–309.

[54] *Mały Dziennik,* May 14, 1937.

Z.N.P.) for having embraced liberal causes deemed communist. When a Warsaw paper printed a list of the Union's leaders, the *Mały Dziennik* pointed out that the list contained virtually only Jewish names. With Jews educating Catholic youth, it was no wonder that there was a strong communist influence present.[55]

Reporting on a 1938 trial in Wilno, the *Mały Dziennik* ran the headline, "Sons of rich Jews—Communists." The story related how a group of middle school Jewish students belonged to a youth group allied to the communist party in Byelorussia. The Jewish students were accused of creating a secret revolutionary organization that praised Stalin, discussed the Spanish civil war and the popular front in France. They had also organized a collection to help the Reds in Spain. The students acknowledged the socialist tendencies of their organization but pleaded ignorance of any communist ties. But, the Catholic daily editorialized, this was difficult to believe since all the students were in their senior year.[56]

Schools, according to the *Rycerz Niepokalanej*, had become the battleground for the soul of Poland. Plans were being made by Moscow and the Masons for a nation to be built on the ashes of Poland and Rumania in which Jews would have the deciding voice. To this end a revolutionary campaign was being waged in all segments of Polish life but especially in the schools. So-called "progressives" had begun a struggle against religion for the soul of Poland's children. A small but active group in the Polish Teachers' Union had set for itself the task of "declericalizing" the schools and eliminating the church from education. Its publication, *The Teacher's Voice,* constantly incited teachers against priests as if they were some sort of hereditary enemies of teachers and children. The majority of teachers were terrorized by this minority and the officers of their Union. The fact that many Jews were active in the Union and its administration explained why there was a constant war against all that was Catholic. Anywhere communism or Masonry took charge, there was war against religion.[57]

---

[55] *Mały Dziennik,* November 19, 1937.

[56] *Mały Dziennik,* August 25, 1938.

[57] "A Teacher," *Rycerz Niepokalanej,* (April 1938): 105–108.

Emigrés

From the Conventual Franciscan presses at Niepokalanów concern was also expressed about the influence of leftist thinking on Polish Catholic emigrés in France. For the *Rycerz Niepokalanej* any organization affiliated with the people's front in France was plainly communist. That meant that Jewish communists were conspiring to destroy the national Catholic spirit of these Polish workers in France. Though they claimed to be Polish patriots and defenders of Poland's independence, these Jews constituted upwards of 80% of these "supposedly Polish" communists. But, the Catholic monthly continued, "they have no ties to Poland except for their being born on Polish soil, using the Polish language, and hoping someday to rule our country."

Leading these dangerous Jewish leftists, reported the Catholic monthly, was Ester Golde Stróżecka, the head of the *Dziennik Ludowy* (People's Daily), which claimed to be a popular democratic paper but was really an organ of the communist party. Along with her were such "Polish patriots" as Ditla Diament in Belgium, Moses Nowogrodzki, Jacob Dutlinger, and Saul Amsterdam. Unfortunately, these Jewish communists had succeeded in getting several native Poles to become their flunkies and to do their bidding for them, disseminating communist poison among the rest of the emigres.[58] Also tarred as communist was a monthly called "Free Thought," since it claimed that priests were enemies of working people and that the pope was an agent of fascism and Nazism.[59]

A Public Opinion Poll

In September, 1936, the editors of *Mały Dziennik* announced intentions to conduct a public opinion poll on whether communism was a threat to Poland. The letters published in the months that followed fully represented the editorial stance of the Catholic daily. By its own admission anything else was branded pro-communist and unobjective. From the supposedly more objective responses, the editors drew the conclusion that communists indeed did pose a serious threat to Poland, particularly in areas close to the Soviet border and where there were significant numbers of Jews. Especially susceptible to the lure of

---

[58] *Rycerz Niepokalanej*, (January 1938): 14–16.

[59] *Rycerz Niepokalanej*, (February 1938): 41–42.

communism were the unemployed and those Poles who had returned from France.[60]

A priest, designated only by his initials, responded that more Jews than just party members were responsible for the communist threat to Poland. Directly and indirectly, consciously and unconsciously, Jews were preparing the way for communism. That meant that "war with communism means war with Jews." Antisemitism did not contradict the law of love but was based on love, namely, the desire to save the Polish nation from the Jews' destructive influence.[61] According to another respondent, ever since liberals had integrated Jews into the Polish scouting movement, scouting circles had shown "signs of demoralization and communist activity."[62]

By the editorial staff's own admission (J. B. Słoński), the respondents consistently pointed out the prominent role Jews played in communism. The paper went on to explain that "the vast majority of respondents were deeply religious people and did not feel any hatred toward Jews." They were committed to truth and the command to love God and neighbor. "Precisely in the name of truth and out of love for their neighbor, above all for their own family and nation, they took part in the poll so widely and emphasized so strongly the role of Jews in communism."[63]

To say that communism arose out of poverty and injustice was only partially true, Słoński insisted. The essence of communism, he wrote, was its materialistic world view, "based upon a satanic, Jewish-talmudic mentality." Communism spread because of Moscow and the Jews, a people without a country who wanted to accomplish their ambitious plans to rule the world and who found in communism the means to do it. Słoński admitted that there were "many, too many Poles and Christians in the communist ranks," who were traitors to their faith and nation. Their blame was mitigated by ignorance, however, for many had not received a nationalist, Catholic education.[64]

---

[60] *Mały Dziennik,* June 6, 1937.

[61] *Mały Dziennik,* March 18, 1937.

[62] *Mały Dziennik,* May 20, 1937.

[63] *Mały Dziennik,* May 20, 1937.

[64] *Mały Dziennik,* May 30, 1937.

Persecution

By identifying Jews with communism, Catholics could assume the role of victims and see Jews as the persecutors. Not only in Spain but elsewhere, it was "the Jewish commune against Christianity." The *Rycerz Niepokalanej* assured its readers that communists saw Christianity, particularly the Catholic church, as their chief enemy. Communists were trying to destroy faith in God. And what they could not achieve in Poland with the help of Jews, they were trying to accomplish among Polish emigrés with the help of socialist and Masonic organizations.[65] Jews regarded whatever country they lived in as only a temporary and transitional homeland. How could Jews fight against communism when it is based on the Talmud. What the world is experiencing in communism is the moment of Jewish revenge on the Christian world.[66]

———

For Pope Pius XI and the Catholic leadership of the 1930s, communism posed a far more formidable threat to the church than did fascism, whether German or Italian. The fears latent or expressed in the Pope's encyclical and other statements on communism were surpassed in Poland, rendered exponentially more acute by its proximity to the Soviet Union.

Obviously the Catholic episcopate, clergy, and press in Poland were concerned about more than twenty thousand members of the Polish Communist Party. Since the party was illegal and underground, the numbers of its membership were uncertain, both of the party altogether and of the Jews within it. It was its participation in an international movement headquartered in Moscow that instilled fear. That movement had been linked by the Vatican with socialism and therefore by the Polish Catholic church with both the PPS and Bund. That communists were inimical to the democratic parliamentary system espoused by both the PPS and Bundists was negligible to Catholics. The popes had designated liberalism for over a half century as the precursor of communism.

Jews in Poland as elsewhere were among the chief advocates of liberal efforts to secularize the state and public education. The nationalist motto, "Poland for the Poles," meant "Poland for Roman Catholics," and

———

[65] *Rycerz Niepokalanej,* February (1938), 41–42.

[66] *Rycerz Niepokalanej,* (April 1938): 108.

effectively excluded the possibility of Jews assimilating into Polish culture in the way they had in other European countries. The exclusion compelled young Jews to seek an identity and future in either Zionism or communism, more in Zionism but enough in communism to command notice and confirm the worst fears of Polish Catholic nationalists. The vicious circle left no apparent escape.

Outside of a handful of titles appearing in an even smaller number of journals, the overwhelming number of articles identifying the communist menace with Jews came from the presses of the Franciscan priests and brothers at Niepokalanów, the *Mały Dziennik* and the *Rycerz Niepokalanej*. Their output was constant, however, and made its impact on Polish Catholics who had long been enjoined to be militant. The Vatican and Polish hierarchy both appealed regularly to the powerful historical symbol of Poland as the bastion of Western Christianity, protecting Europe from barbarism on the east. The mythic qualities of the image could produce at the same time both an incentive to heroism and an excuse for hostility, not only against Jews but any potential ally of the Soviets and any critic of the church. The image created a crusading mentality bent on saving Christian civilization. If the price was surrender of Poland's tradition of tolerance, it would have to be paid.

From the vantage point of over fifty years of history, much that appeared in the right wing Catholic press of the 1930s incurs disgrace, particularly the imputation of blame to millions of innocent Jews for the crimes of Jewish apostates. But Poles had a long tradition of admiring and imitating what came out of the west. If barbarism lay on the east, civilization and culture came out of the west. In the 1930s, however, more than a few of the western voices declaiming on civilization and *kultur* spoke German.

Chapter 5

Nazi Germany and Racist Antisemitism

When Pope Pius XI issued the encyclical *Mit brennender Sorge* (March 14, 1937) on the situation of the Catholic church in Nazi Germany, he confessed that he had signed the 1933 Concordat with the Third Reich only with "grave misgivings." Germany's Catholics, he wrote, would certainly have had to face repercussions if the negotiations begun prior to the Nazi ascendancy had fallen through. Protesting that the church had been faithful to the treaty, the pope denounced Germany for violating it as a normal policy. He singled out in particular the government's campaign against Catholic schools and the anti-Christian features of the national youth organization. On the level of principles, the pope attacked as "pernicious errors" the exalting of a race or people, the state or a particular form of the state to a level of idolatry. This was "aggressive paganism," he wrote and decried a situation in which disloyalty to the church had become the measure of loyalty to the state. He defended the Hebrew scriptures as a source of divine revelation and condemned the attempt to create a national church with a myth of race and blood. Redemption, like the church, were for all races and nations.[1]

Nowhere in the encyclical did the pope make any reference to Germany's persecution of Jews nor to their disenfranchisement in the 1935 Nuremberg race laws. The only allusion to Jews was one which spoke of Christ coming from a "people that was to crucify Him." Although the encyclical precipitated a violent reaction from the Nazis, it

---

[1] Claudia Carlen, I.H.M., *The Papal Encyclicals, 1740–1981,* 5 vols. (1981; reprint, Ann Arbor, MI: Pierien Press, 1990), 3:525–35.

was not, as some claimed, a decisive repudiation of the Nazi state and its world view. A judicious reading shows the papal document to have been quite moderate. It distinguished carefully between certain Nazi doctrines, which it condemned, and the political and social totalitarianism of the Nazi system, about which it said nothing. On the contrary, in response to a protest by Nazi Germany, Cardinal Secretary of State Eugenio Pacelli declared that the Holy See "will never interfere in the question of what concrete form of government a certain people chooses to regard as best suited to its nature and requirements. With respect to Germany also, it has remained true to this principle and intends to do so."[2]

Nazi Racism and the Vatican

In contrast to his successor whose silence on the Jews is controversial, Pope Pius XI is generally hailed as an outspoken adversary of antisemitism. A variety of Jewish leaders at his death praised him as one who defended Jews from persecution. In the words of one Jewish author: "As a million Jews were banished from public life, persecuted, spoliated, humiliated and their synagogues burned, not a single diplomatic step was taken, not one official protest was lodged, by any of the European states or by the League of Nations. As the moral abyss between Hitlerism and the civilized nations widened, no government stood up for human rights or common decency but one."[3] Given such generous praise, the measures against antisemitism taken by the Vatican under Pius XI bear reviewing here.

Even before Hitler became chancellor, the anti-Jewish ferment of the Nazis in Germany and of other nationalists elsewhere in Europe was such that a statement from the Vatican would hardly have been unwarranted. In 1928 the Vatican published what appears to have been its first explicit condemnation of antisemitism as such. For reasons that were not spelled out, the "Friends of Israel," a Catholic organization founded to promote

---

[2] Pacelli to Bergen, April 30, 1937, *Documents on German Foreign Policy,* D,I, doc. 649, 964–65, cited in Guenter Lewy, *The Catholic Church and Nazi Germany* (New York: McGraw-Hill, 1964), 158.

[3] Pinchas E. Lapide, *Three Popes and the Jews,* (New York: Hawthorn, 1967), 97–98.

conversion of Jews, was abolished by the Vatican doctrinal congregation known as the Holy Office. Inserted, almost parenthetically, into the middle of the decree of abolition was a statement that, despite their blindness, indeed because of it, the church prays for Jews: "Moved by this charity, the Holy See has always protected this people against unjust ill-treatment, and just as it reprobates all bitterness and conflicts among peoples, it especially condemns (*damnat*) the hatred against the people once chosen by God, commonly called 'antisemitism.'"[4] An oblique reference to antisemitism may also be read into a wide-ranging (1932) encyclical (*Caritate Christi compulsi*) in which Pope Pius XI criticized, among other errors, "undue exaltation" of patriotism. Misdeeds condemned for individual motives were not rendered honest when performed out of love for country.[5]

In 1934, after Hitler's rise to chancellorship, the Holy Office condemned Alfred Rosenberg's *The Myth of the Twentieth Century* and placed it on the church's index of forbidden books. The reasons given for the book's condemnation were not only its rejection of Christian teaching but its attempt to arouse a religious faith in blood. At the same time Ernst Bergmann's *Die deutsche Nationalkirche* was similarly condemned. Among the errors the Vatican singled out were the claims that the Hebrew Scriptures were morally dangerous to youth and that blood or race is the unique source of cultural progress.[6] Three years later the Vatican also condemned C. Cogni's *Il Razzismo*, an attempt to encourage racism in Italy.[7] Racism was also the topic of a letter (April 13, 1938) by the Vatican's Congregation of Seminaries and Universities to all Catholic college and seminary rectors. The letter called on Catholic educators to draw from their fields of expertise to refute the "dangerous theories" of racism.[8]

Toward the end of the decade, Pius XI made references to Nazi Germany in several of his public discourses. In a Christmas address (December 24, 1937), with no mention of what Germany was doing to

---

[4] *Acta Apostolicae Sedis*, (1928): 103–104.

[5] Carlen, *Papal Encyclicals*, 3:476.

[6] *Acta Apostolicae Sedis*, (1934): 93–94.

[7] *Acta Apostolicae Sedis*, (1937): 306.

[8] *Wiadomości Archidiecezalne Warszawskie*, 28 (1938): 283–84.

Jews, he condemned the "persecution" of the church and denied the charge that the church was meddling in politics. After Mussolini began introducing racial laws into Italy, the pope deplored "exaggerated nationalism" as detestable and unchristian (July 21, 1938). A week later the pope pointed out that the very word "catholic," which means universal, was contrary to racist, nationalist thinking. Why, he asked, was Italy disgracefully imitating Germany?[9]

None of these papal speeches, it must be noted again, made explicit mention of Jews, let alone antisemitism. It can be argued that it was not necessary to be explicit since the Jewish question was obviously at the root of Nazi racism. But antisemitism is much broader than its more modern racist variety. In this regard, the most celebrated reference by Pius XI to antisemitism was in conjunction with an audience given to a group of Belgian pilgrims from the Belgian Catholic radio (July 14, 1938). "It is not possible for Christians to participate in antisemitism," the pope said. "Spiritually we are semites."[10]

Together with these public statements on racism and antisemitism in the 1930s, one must also give consideration to the Vatican's silences. No comments were forthcoming in the aftermath of the anti-Jewish boycott in Germany, the Nuremberg race laws, or Kristallnacht. Pius XI is said to have privately prevailed upon Italian, French, and Belgian cardinals to speak out in condemnation of Nazi policies, and he publicly supported an American cardinal when he did the same.[11] But theirs was obviously not the moral weight of the papacy. The official response of the Holy See to these Nazi measures was one of silence. The semi-official response, as conveyed in the pages of the Vatican newspaper, *L'Osservatore Romano*, was one of reserve.

L'Osservatore Romano was critical of Nazi racial theories and defensive of the Hebrew Scriptures. But with respect to Nazi treatment of Jews in Germany, the Vatican paper simply reported events factually, without comment. No energetic protest was raised even after Kristallnacht. The Vatican paper let its readers know that it disapproved

---

[9] Domenico Bertetto, ed., *Discorsi di Pio XI* (Vatican City: Liberia Editrice Vaticana, 1960–1961, 2nd ed., 1985), vol. 3, 677–82, 772–75, 777–84.

[10] *Documentation Catholique,* 39 (1938): 1460.

[11] Lapide, *Three Popes,* 114. Saul Friedländer, *Pius XII and the Third Reich, A Documentation,* trans. by Charles Fullman (New York: Knopf, 1966), 6.

of Nazi brutality, but did so indirectly, by reporting the facts of Nazi persecution and then re-printing the editorial comments and condemnations of other newspapers around the world. *L'Osservatore Romano* insisted that the "Jewish question" should be resolved in civil, human, and Christian manner, and it was sympathetic to western European attempts to find places of refuge for German Jews. But even when the Vatican newspaper reprinted an article from the Jesuit journal, *La Civiltà Cattolica*, critical of Nazi brutality, the criticism was not conjoined to sympathy for the persecuted Jews. Arguing that the Nazi approach was no lasting solution to the "Jewish question," the author appealed to reason rather than to moral outrage.[12]

The Concordat

The issue of the concordat is beyond the scope of this study and too complex to be treated here at any length.[13] It suffices to say that Cardinal Pacelli, who as Vatican Secretary of State negotiated the concordat for Pius XI, was convinced that it spared the church even greater hardship than it had to endure. Though he was sure that the German government would violate it, the treaty at least provided a basis on which to lodge a protest. Pius XI expressed the same opinion when in May 1933, he told a meeting of bishops: "If it is a matter of saving souls, of averting even greater damage, we have the courage to negotiate even with the devil."[14]

No matter how much the pope and Pacelli may have privately deplored the actions of Hitler's government and its persecution of Jews, the concordat was not viewed from the outside as the lesser of two evils. Not only did the Nazi press hail it as a "moral strengthening" of Hitler's government and its reputation, Cardinal Michael Faulhaber of Munich did

---

[12] Fritz Sandmann, *"L'Osservatore Romano" e il Nazionalsocialismo (1929–1939)*, (Roma: Edizione Cinque Lune, 1976), 265–74.

[13] For the story of the negotiations, the impact of the Concordat, and further literature, see Steward A. Stehlin, *Weimar and the Vatican, 1919–1933: German-Vatican Diplomatic Relations in the Interwar Years* (Princeton, NJ: Princeton University Press, 1983), and Lewy, *Catholic Church*, 57–93.

[14] Lapide, *Three Popes*, 101–103.

so too. As he put it in a sermon he delivered as late as 1937: "At a time when the heads of the major nations in the world faced the new Germany with cool reserve and considerable suspicion, the Catholic Church, the greatest moral power on earth, through the Concordat expressed its confidence in the new German government. This was a deed of immeasurable significance for the reputation of the new government abroad."[15]

The concordat seriously undercut the effectiveness of any Catholic criticism of the Nazis. Although the German bishops were far from united on the issue, some were quite forceful in opposing Nazi policies, at least before Hitler became chancellor. Cardinal Bertram of Breslau was the first (1930) and warned against the fanatical nationalism that worships race. In the diocese of Mainz, members of the Nazi party were not allowed to attend funerals or other church services in group formation. Catholics were forbidden to belong to the Nazi party and, if they acknowledged adherence to its principles, could not be admitted to the sacraments.[16]

The example of Mainz was gradually followed by the other bishops. Catholics in Germany were forbidden to be Nazis the same way as they were disallowed from being communists or Masons. When Hitler became chancellor at the end of January 1933, however, the ban created a difficult situation for German Catholics. The ban created difficulty too for the bishops, when on March 13, according to the report of Cardinal Faulhaber, Pope Pius XI "publicly praised the Chancellor Adolf Hitler for the stand which the latter had taken against Communism."[17] On March 29, the German bishops withdrew the ban.

---

[15] Lewy, *Catholic Church,* 90.

[16] Hans Mueller, *Katholische Kirche und Nationalsozialismus. Dokumente 1930–1935* (Munich: Nymphenburger, 1963), 13–15.

[17] Lewy, *Catholic Church,* 8–10, 30–31.

The Bishops of Germany and Austria

The literature on the confrontation of the German Catholic church with Nazism is as enormous as the subject is controversial.[18] Those who have written in defense of the German bishops and Catholic press underscore the persecution of the church and insist that any further opposition to Hitler's policies would have been suicidal and doomed to failure from the start.[19] Authors more critical of German Catholic leadership point to the successful resistance of the German bishops to Nazi sterilization and euthanasia policies and their failure to mount a similar resistance either on behalf of the Jews or against Hitler's wars.[20] Another school of interpretation highlights the German Catholic response to Nazism as characterized by both opposition and accommodation, resistance and error.[21]

The analysis I am essaying here does not shed light on the factual confrontation between German Catholics and the Third Reich but rather on a particular perception of it. The Polish Catholic press could be quite perceptive of the Nazi menace, reject racism, and still prove sympathetic to the prewar persecution of Jews. In Germany and Austria as well, Catholic leadership betrayed similar ambiguities in their attitudes toward the Nazi persecution.

Antisemitism was a German word, invented by Wilhelm Marr, a

---

[18] For a recent study containing a bibliography of the more notable analyses, see Donald J. Dietrich, *Catholic Citizens in the Third Reich: Psycho-Social Principles and Moral Reasoning* (New Brunswick: Transaction, 1988).

[19] See for example Walter Adolph, *Hirtenamt und Hitler-Diktatur* (Berlin: Morus, 1965); Karl Aloys Altmeyer, *Katholicsche Presse unter NS-Diktatur. Die katholischen Zeitungen und Zeitschriften Deutschlands in den Jahren 1933 bis 1945* (Berlin: Morus, 1962); Wilhelm Spael, *Das katholische Deutschland im 20. Jahrhundert. Seine Pionier- und Krisenzeiten, 1890–1945* (Wurzburg: Echter, 1964).

[20] G. Lewy, *Catholic Church,* 258–267, 305–308; Gordon Zahn, "The German Catholic Press and Hitler's Wars," *Cross Currents* 10 (1960): 337–51; Gordon C. Zahn, *German Catholics and Hitler's Wars: A Study in Social Control* (Notre Dame: Notre Dame University, 1962); Carl Amery, *Capitulation: The Lesson of German Catholicism,* Trans. by Edward Quinn. (New York: Herder and Herder, 1967).

[21] Dietrich, *Catholic Citizens,* 294–306; Gerhart Binder, *Irrtum und Widerstand. Die deutschen Katholiken in der Auseinandersetzung mit dem Nationalsozialismus* (Munich: Pfeiffer, 1968).

Protestant journalist, and first used in 1879, the period of German history marked by the anti-Catholic campaign known as the Kulturkampf.[22] Branded by Bismarck as enemies of the Second Reich (*Reichsfeinde*), Germany's Catholics were compelled to protest their loyalty to *Volk* and *Vaterland.* Included among Bismarck's allies, participating in the anti-Catholic drive of the 1870s, were prominent liberal Jews. German Catholics mounted a defense in which anti-liberalism became synonymous with antisemitism. It was in this period (1876) that Bishop Martin of Paderborn accused the Talmud of wickedness and concluded that stories of Jewish ritual murder were true. Similarly the celebrated Bishop Paul Wilhelm Keppler of Rottenburg (1852–1926) could describe Jews as poisoning Christian culture and reducing Christian peoples to servitude with their money.[23] Bishop Wilhelm Ketteler (1862) described liberal Jewish dominance as warping German character. The periodical, *Der Katholik,* reinforced the point by claiming that Jewish influence was undoubtedly causing the weakening and de-Christianizing of public morality. A major Catholic daily newspaper denounced what it called the *Judenwirtschaft* and demanded a boycott of Jewish firms.[24]

As Catholics slowly integrated into the mainstream of German life, the Catholic Center party relinquished its earlier antisemitic politics. At the popular level, however, antisemitism continued to creep into Catholic responses to issues, and German Catholics went to lengths to prove their loyalty to the state up to and during the First World War. By 1918 they had assimilated a pattern of values in which nationalism and antisemitism were regarded as a "normal" German bias. Opposing the vices of urban-industrial civilization, Catholic leaders continued to express opposition to liberalism and reservations about the Weimar Republic itself.[25]

In this milieu the German bishops did not have to mention Jews explicitly in their pastoral letters attacking communism and free-thinking. But neither did they mention the increasingly rampant antisemitic hatred

---

[22] Moshe Zimmermann, *Wilhelm Marr. The Patriarch of Antisemitism* (New York: Oxford University, 1986). See also Bernard Lewis, *Semites and Anti-Semites. An Inquiry into Conflict and Prejudice* (New York: W.W. Norton, 1986), 81.

[23] Lewy, *Catholic Church,* 270.

[24] Dietrich, *Catholic Citizens,* 13–14.

[25] Dietrich, *Catholic Citizens,* 18, 24.

and violence being fomented by the National Socialists, unless one considers the exception that proves the rule. In 1925, Cardinal Faulhaber preached a sermon in which he declared that every human life was precious, including that of a Jew.[26] A similar statement was later made in 1936 by Poland's Cardinal Hlond. In both instances, the Cardinals undoubtedly considered their sentiments to be generous.

Before 1933, as pointed out above, organized Catholicism came into repeated conflict with the growing Nazi movement. Antisemitism, however, was not a notable source of contention. Nazism might be criticized for the extremism of its racial theories but could still be credited with possessing a core of truth. The Nazis were right, wrote Erhard Schlund, a Franciscan priest, in 1923, at least with respect to fighting Jewish dominance in finance and trying to maintain the "purity" of German blood and the German race.[27] At the same time, a book by Philip Häuser declared that Jews were Germany's cross and it was time to put them in their place. His book carried the *Imprimatur* of the diocese of Regensburg, indicating that nothing in it contravened Catholic faith or morals.[28]

Just how typical and perfectly respectable this view was within German Catholic circles can be demonstrated by the article on "Antisemitismus" in the 1930 edition of the prestigious *Lexikon für Theologie und Kirche*. The author, Gustav Gundlach, criticized racist antisemitism as unchristian because it contravened Christian love of neighbor. Political antisemitism was permitted, however, so long as it used morally admissible means to counteract the "exaggerated and harmful influence" of Jews over the economy, politics, press, science, and the arts.[29] In the same respected Catholic reference work, Jews were described as being ruthless in their use of political and economic power and having a demoralizing influence on religious and national life.[30]

---

[26] Lewy, *Catholic Church*, 274.

[27] Lewy, *Catholic Church*, 271.

[28] Dietrich, *Catholic Citizens*, 72.

[29] Gustav Gundlach, "Antisemitismus," *Lexikon für Theologie und Kirche*, 2nd. rev. ed. (Freiburg: Herder, 1930–1938), 1:504–05.

[30] F. Schühlein, "Geschichte der Juden," *Lexikon für Theologie und Kirche*, 2nd rev. ed. (Freiburg: Herder, 1933–1938), 5:687.

At the level of popular Catholic culture, the Passion Play at Oberammergau continued to present an Aryan Pilate unsuccessfully trying to save Jesus from his Jewish persecutors. At Deggendorf, Bavaria, Catholics continued to remember the legend that in 1337 the Jews of that town stole and "tortured" the Blessed Sacrament, only to have "a lovely little child" appear, whereupon the citizens of Deggendorf killed the town's Jews. In the play performed during the annual week-long commemoration, Jews were called "poison-mixers," "hordes of the devil," and the "brood of Judas."[31] Within this milieu, Josef Roth, a priest and early supporter of the Nazi movement, was able to write in 1923, that Jews were a morally inferior race who would have to be eliminated from public life, the innocent along with the guilty. "If in the course of proceeding against the Jews as a race some good and harmless Jews, with whom immorality because of inheritance is latent, will have to suffer together with the guilty ones, this is not a violation of Christian love of one's neighbor as long as the Church recognizes also the moral justification of war, for example, where many more 'innocents' than 'guilty' have to suffer."[32]

If German bishops tolerated statements like these, it comes as no surprise that they could express similar sentiments themselves, even after Hitler's rise to power. Munich's Cardinal Faulhaber, in defending the Hebrew Scriptures, declared in his 1933 Advent sermons: "People of Israel, this did not grow in your own garden of your own planting. This condemnation of usurious land-grabbing, this war against the oppression of the farmer by debt, this prohibition of usury, is not the product of your spirit."[33] In a 1939 pastoral letter acknowledging that Jesus was a Jew, Bishop Hilfrich of Limburg similarly insisted that Christianity was not influenced by Jewish characteristics. "Rather it has had to make its way against this people."[34] Archbishop Gröber of Freiburg im Bresgau likewise declared that Jews hated Jesus and that "their murderous hatred has continued in later centuries." In his *Handbuch* of contemporary religious issues, Gröber defined Marxism as founded by "the Jew Karl

---

[31] Lewy, *Catholic Church*, 273.

[32] Lewy, *Catholic Church*, 272.

[33] Lewy, *Catholic Church*, 276.

[34] Lewy, *Catholic Church*, 277.

Marx" and "led mostly by Jewish agitators and revolutionaries."
According to Gröber's handbook, most unhealthy, un-German
manifestations in art were the work of Jews or those influenced by them.
The politicizing of art was also due largely to "the uprooted and
atheistically perverted Jew."[35]

Together with antisemitic statements from bishops, note should be
given to early pro-Nazi declarations from some of Germany's most
prominent Catholic theologians. Church historian Joseph Lortz (1933)
saw basic similarities between the National Socialist and Catholic world
views, opposed as they both were to Bolshevism and liberalism;
Germany's Catholics were therefore obligated to support the new Nazi
government wholeheartedly. Karl Adam, a theologian of world renown,
hailed Hitler (1933) as "the liberator of the German genius." It was a
necessary measure, he wrote, that Jewish influence in the press, literature,
science and art be repulsed, in a spirit of justice and love of course.
Dogmatic theologian Michael Schmaus (1934) informed his readers that
the German bishops would never have revoked the ban on membership
in the Nazi party if they had thought that Catholic and National Socialist
ideas were in conflict. Whereas Catholic and liberal thinking were
necessarily at odds, Catholicism and Nazism could be reconciled, wrote
Schmaus and expressed "just concern" for maintaining the "purity" of
German blood.[36]

It is true that these theologians wrote in the early years of the Third
Reich. But it was also after the boycott of Jews businesses had already
begun and, it goes without saying, after *Mein Kampf.* With statements
like these from bishops and theologians, it is little wonder that a (January
1936) article in the clerically oriented *Klerusblatt* justified the 1935
Nuremberg race laws as indispensable safeguards for the qualitative
make-up of the German people.[37]

Less than one-percent (not quite 600,000) of Germany's seventy
million citizens were Jewish. Moreover the charge that Jews had
excessive influence over German public life was both factually and
morally indefensible. In the allegedly "Judaized" liberal press, for

---

[35] Lewy, *Catholic Church,* 277.

[36] Dietrich, *Catholic Citizens,* 114–17.

[37] Lewy, *Catholic Church,* 281.

example, less than 20 out of 400 editors were Jewish.[38] In Austria, however, Jews were over five-percent; in Vienna over fifteen-percent. There the "Jewish problem" was viewed as even more acute than in Germany. The enthusiastic embrace of Nazism by Catholic Austria at the time of the Anschluss is well known. Cardinal Theodor Innitzer has the misfortune of being remembered more for a *Heil Hitler* than for his subsequent outspoken opposition to the Nazi regime.[39] But in this context, the Viennese Catholic weekly, *Schönere Zukunft*, its editor Joseph Eberle, and Austria's Bishop Alois Hudal deserve mention even more.

Founded in the mid-1920s, *Schönere Zukunft* was obsessed with the "Jewish question." It published reports on it from every part of the globe. From the (January 28, 1938) issue of the *L'Osservatore Romano*: the Jews in the Soviet Union enjoy not only equality with other peoples but privileges (March 6, 1938). In Hungary, liberalism was Jewish in origin and spirit, viewed as a "national misfortune" by the "best of the Hungarian people" (April 24, 1938). Jews, wrote editor Joseph Eberle, foster not only liberalism but materialism, lead revolutions, and fill the stage, screen, and press with worship of Mammon and Venus (July 19, 1936). From the much reprinted statement of Hungary's Bishop Prohaszka: "We must advance nationals and put a curb on Jews.... It is not liberalism but an enslaving stupidity (*Dummheit*) to empty all the ghettos of Galatia and Poland into Hungary and let the Jews attack innocent people" (August 2, 1936).

As mentioned above, the most conspicuous representative of Austrian Catholic antisemitism at this time was Bishop Alois Hudal. Serving in 1936 at an institute for German and Austrian priests in Rome, he described Jews as poisoning the German soul with foreign ideas. While he sympathized with religiously conservative Jews, he declared (1936) that there was not the slightest reason for Catholics to defend those Jews who presumed to lead the working class.[40] Writing that same year in the Vienna *Reichpost*, Bishop Hudal saw no problem with the National Socialist movement. If Catholics did not want Bolshevism, they should

---

[38] Dietrich, *Catholic Citizens,* 71.

[39] Binder, *Irrtum,* 263, 270–80.

[40] *Schönere Zukunft,* June 7, 1936.

wish and work for a successful alliance between Nazis and conservative Christians.[41] The following year (1937) Bishop Hudal defended the Nuremberg race laws as a self-defense against foreign elements. "The walls of the ghetto were first torn down everywhere in the nineteenth century by the liberal state, not by the church." Consequently, he concluded, the church could have no objection to laws containing discriminatory provisions against Jews.[42]

Bishop Hudal's reasoning was quite the same as Adolf Hitler's. On April 26, 1933, Hitler had a meeting with Bishop Berning of Osnabruck, accompanied by Vicar General Monsignor Steinmann. Their talk was later described by the bishop as "cordial and to the point." When the issue arose of Hitler's treatment of Jews, Hitler appealed to the history of the Catholic church, which, he said, for 1,500 years had regarded Jews as parasites (*Schädlinge*) and had banished them into the ghetto. Hitler claimed that he was merely doing what the church had done and perhaps was doing Christianity a great service.[43]

The history of Nazi Germany and the Catholic church has been researched and recorded in detail—Hitler's promises of peace with the church, the concordat, the Nazi violations of its terms, the Vatican protests, the harassment of Catholic organizations, the compliance of the Catholic press. All this constitutes a backdrop to the even more researched and recorded history of Nazi Germany and the Jews. Both stories received considerable attention from the interwar Polish Catholic press. Both stories were invariably assessed in quite different ways. Hitler's Germany aroused curiosity and abhorrence in Poland but some would-be imitators as well. And if the Vatican under Pope Pius XI was outspokenly critical of antisemitism, the Catholic church in Poland did not appear apprised of it.

---

[41] Binder, *Irrtum,* 268–69.

[42] Binder, *Irrtum,* 267–69; Lewy, *Catholic Church,* 281.

[43] Mueller, *Katholische Kirche,* 118, 121.

Persecution of the Church

How the Polish Catholic press reported the treatment of Jews in Germany contrasted sharply with how it reported the situation of the church. In the same year that the Nuremberg Race Laws disenfranchised Jews (1935), it characterized the condition of German Catholics in terms of martyrdom. Hitler was said to be intent upon a new *Kulturkampf* that could only lead to a life and death struggle between the cross and swastika. Even though the concordat guaranteed freedom of religion, some 150 priests and religious had already been sentenced to prison. The German bishops' 1935 pastoral letter was confiscated, as were any Catholic weeklies that criticized Alfred Rosenberg's attacks on the clergy. Cardinal Faulhaber and Bishop von Galen were true "confessors." In schools youth were filled with hatred for Catholicism and taught that Christianity was a destructive outgrowth of Judaism.[44]

The Nazis persecuted the Catholic church as their foremost adversary, wrote the *Ateneum Kapłańskie,* because of its close-knit organization and defense of human rights. Over fifty religious groups had arisen dedicated to the purity of race and a return to German paganism. Protestants even had neo-pagans among their pastors and superintendents. The Nazi *Kulturkampf* was more ruthless than that of Bismarck, but the Catholic church was becoming stronger for it.[45] By persecuting the Catholic church, wrote Adam Romer in the *Mały Dziennik,* the Nazis were showing exactly how fraudulent it was for them to claim to be enemies of communism. Enemies like these were relished by Moscow.[46]

In contrast to the Soviet Union where the church was persecuted openly, the church in Germany, wrote Father Michał Milewski, was the victim of moral onslaught. It was forbidden to make any allusion to the Hebrew Scriptures or to the fact that Jesus lived in Palestine. Some 300 Catholic periodicals had been suspended. The honor of the clergy was being impugned in the press. Despite all this, German Catholics were still manifesting their religious convictions at every opportunity. Persecution, Milewski was sure, would only strengthen the faith and moral fiber of

---

[44] *Szkoła Chrystusowa,* 11 (1935): 170–75. See also *Mały Dziennik,* July 25, 1935.

[45] *Ateneum Kapłańskie,* 36 (1935): 504–17.

[46] *Mały Dziennik,* July 25, 1935.

German Catholics.[47]

In the view of the *Mały Dziennik,* the Vatican was using tact with Germany and continuing to seek a tolerable modus vivendi that would guarantee its freedom.[48]

Considerable attention was given to the pope's encyclical, *Mit brennender Sorge,* and the protest it evoked from the Nazi regime. The *Mały Dziennik* pointed out correctly that "the Holy Father does not condemn the national-socialist system but only those aspects of the Nazi ideology which are incompatible with Catholic dogma or whatever in practice Hitler's subordinates do against the commandments of faith." The Catholic daily viewed the Vatican concordat with Germany as proof of the willingness of the church to cooperate with any system and any state. The pope's list of Nazi errors was far from imposing a particular form of government on Germany. The pope only rejected putting the laws of the state above those of God.[49]

Along with the pope's addresses protesting Nazi persecution of the church,[50] the sermons of Munich's Cardinal Faulhaber also received widespread circulation in the Polish Catholic press. Faulhaber's 1933 Advent sermons on Judaism and Christianity, while correctly taken as an act of standing up to the Nazis, were commonly mistaken to be a defence of Judaism. When they were published in Polish, it was correctly pointed out that the Judaism he defended was that of the Bible not of contemporary Germany. Faulhaber made a fundamental distinction between the Bible and the Talmud. Against those Nazis who would purge Christianity of anything Jewish, he defended the Hebrew Scriptures as inspired and now fulfilled in Christianity. Faulhaber was defending the books of the Bible, not the Jewish people.[51] In a (November 6, 1938) sermon, Faulhaber attacked Julius Streicher for calling Catholics traitors to the state. He declared that the church and state both had a common enemy in the extreme liberalism which ultimately led to chaos and

---

[47] *Gazeta Kościelna,* (1937): 349–56.

[48] *Mały Dziennik,* April 12, 1937.

[49] *Mały Dziennik,* April 20, 1937.

[50] *Mały Dziennik,* December 28, 1937. *Wiadomości Archidiecezjalne Warszawskie,* 28 (1938): 467–69.

[51] *Gazeta Kościelna,* 1937: 428.

revolution.[52]

In 1938 the German bishops issued a pastoral letter in which they demanded that the Nazi government cease its war against Christianity in general and the Catholic church in particular. The *Mały Dziennik* described the campaign against the church as becoming ever more ruthless: attacking the pope, taking down and desecrating crucifixes, slandering priests, passing unchristian marriage legislation, accusing the church of being an ally of communism when in fact it was its chief adversary.[53]

Father Edward Kosibowicz in *Przegląd Powszechny* granted that in Germany there was not the terror to be found in Mexico or Spain. Hitler claimed that there was no religious persecution because no churches had been closed, but his intention was not to close but empty them. Not only the Catholic daily, *Germania*, but totally apolitical periodicals of Catholic organizations had been closed down. The bishops had had their pastoral letters confiscated, their residences attacked. Catholic property had been confiscated, and public schools were being filled with both an anti-Christian and anti-Jewish spirit, as the government promoted a German Christianity purged of all Jewish elements. Time and again Goebbels, "the apostate," had declared that international Marxism, Judaism, and Catholicism were the greatest enemies of the Third Reich.[54]

Persecution of the Jews

The Catholic press in Poland accorded the German Catholic church the mantle of martyrdom. But it took a different view of Nazi mistreatment of Jews.

Mały Dziennik

Nazi persecution of the church and that of Jews, declared the *Mały Dziennik*, were "two different things," arising from two different sources. Eliminating Jews from Germany's economic, political and cultural life

---

[52] *Głos Kapłański*, 12 (1938): 540–41.

[53] *Mały Dziennik*, August 30, 1938.

[54] *Przegląd Powszechny*, 221 (March, 1939): 391–98.

arose from Jewish domination in those spheres. What had once happened to Jews in Rome and Spain was now happening in Germany. The persecution of the church, though, arose from Germany's religious disunity. The Germans were trying to overcome disunity by returning to paganism. Though Germany had set upon an evil path, "we Catholics do not rush against the Germans foaming with hatred at the mouth." The Catholic daily sympathized with the Germans' tragedy and believed they would come to their senses. The situation of the Jews, however, was quite different and the result of their own megalomania."[55]

The Nuremberg race laws which disenfranchised Jews and forbad marriage and sexual intercourse between Jews and non-Jews were reported by the Catholic daily without criticism.[56] The race laws constituted a "Nazi revolution," that put an end to Jewish domination of German life. Jews, during the Weimar republic, wielded immense influence on German politics, the economy, the press, theater, and the film industry. Jews decided the course of art and literature. The Nuremberg laws forced Jews to withdraw from their positions of leadership and locked them once again into a ghetto. But even though they would not be able to vote, serve in the military, or belong to general professional organizations, they still enjoyed considerable latitude. Jews could still organize themselves freely and operate their own organizations and schools. They enjoyed the rights of minorities without participating in the life of the host nation.[57]

As late as 1938, the Conventual Franciscan press at Niepokalanów did not see self-interest as a reason for bringing Jews and Polish Catholics together in any sort of coalition. The aims and aspirations of Jews and Poles were regarded as at variance on every score. Jews and Germans were "two particularly formidable and dangerous powers," and it was in Poland's interests that they not cooperate or assist each other but remain hostile. The same was true of the hostility between Germany and the Soviet Union. Jews were attempting to discredit Germany's political antisemitism and claiming that Germany was on the brink of disaster. But this was only propaganda. Jews were indifferent to Poland's interests and

---

were concerned only about persuading the world that antisemitism led nations to destruction.[58]

By mid-1939, when Hitler was saber-rattling in Poland's direction, both Polish and Jewish voices were raised calling for an end to the boycott and meeting Jews half-way, so that Poland's energies could be directed exclusively toward the German menace. The *Mały Dziennik* disagreed. The "war with the Jews" should not dissipate energies needed for a possible war with Germany, but ending the boycott would not produce more aircraft. Allowing more Jewish students at universities would not produce more military officers. Allowing Jews to dominate Polish culture would not raise the Polish soldiers' morale. On the contrary, nationalizing Poland's economic and cultural life would strengthen its military capability. Poland would have to fight for its very existence and its "holiest ideals" to defend itself from both the German and Jewish dangers.[59]

There was an almost pathetic quality to the political naivete demonstrated by the Catholic daily in the last weeks before the German invasion. The German radio and press was raising the pitch of its propaganda campaign against Poland, calling it the worse aggressor in Europe. Missing the real import and purpose of the campaign, the *Mały Dziennik* saw it only as cynical and ignorant. Lambs did not feed on wolves.[60] In one of its last issues, the Catholic daily reported on the concentration camp at Buchenwald and the sophisticated tortures used on prisoners in "cultured" Germany. Unknowingly it described the horrific lot that lay ahead for Poland: labor in stone quarries, death by beatings, torture or fatigue.[61] A month after this report, Germany invaded.

Prąd

On the opposite side of the spectrum from *Mały Dziennik* was *Prąd*, which had become the central organ for Odrodzenie (Renaissance), a Catholic youth movement. Long before Hitler became chancellor, it warned its readers of the contradiction Nazism posed to Christianity. It

---

[58] *Mały Dziennik*, March 21, 1938.

[59] *Mały Dziennik*, July 17, 1939.

[60] *Mały Dziennik*, July 18, 1939.

[61] *Mały Dziennik*, July 29, 1939.

reported on the ban prohibiting Catholics from participating in the Nazi party or voting for its candidates. Hatred of other races was unchristian and uncatholic. Nazis spoke of war against Jews and Rome because they wanted a national religion purified of Roman centralism and the Judaism of the Hebrew Scriptures.[62] A similar article appeared four months after Hitler's rise to power.[63] But *Prąd* was a minority voice in the Polish Catholic press. While they condemned Nazism, other periodicals distinguished between racist antisemitism and what they regarded as a legitimate Catholic concern for maintaining Christian civilization.

Przegląd Katolicki

Writing in this popular Catholic weekly, S. Radost saw Hitler as simply putting *Mein Kampf* into action, purging German politics, economics, and culture of Jewish influence. Radost listed the German Jews prominent in science, literature, and the arts, the Jewish doctors who, he freely acknowledged, had made German medicine respected throughout Europe. But boycotting Jewish artists would open fields up to talents that otherwise would have been kept down.[64]

In a not untypical stance, Janusz Rawicz wanted no truck with Jews or Germans. "For us Poles," he wrote, "the entire ideology of Nazism is deeply repugnant." He contrasted Christian Poland with the "wild perverse instincts" let loose by German nationalism. Suffused with Catholic culture, the Slavic soul had no room for a cult of violence. The Teutonic spirit was constant, however, and, feeling confined within their own territory, the *Herrenvolk* were already looking to other people's lands. As early as 1933 Rawicz foresaw another war coming,

Some people were puzzled as to why the Nazis were attacking Jews so ruthlessly when Jews constituted barely one-percent of Germany's population and consistently fostered German interests. Because of their "lack of moderation," Rawicz answered. Jews went beyond the measure in exploiting their success and imitating German ambition. Jews, claimed Rawicz, had gained control of almost the entire German press, the banks and the professions, all of which was intolerable to Germans. Rawicz

---

[62] *Prąd,* 19 (1930): 268–70.

[63] *Prąd,* 24 (1933): 272–74.

[64] *Przegląd Katolicki,* 71 (1933): 246–48.

decried the violence being perpetrated against Jews and their property. He sympathized with the poverty of the Jewish masses in Poland's cities. But the justifiable abhorrence Poles had of Nazi policies and ideology should not blind them to the need to wage war with Jews over the future character of Polish culture. Poland was a Catholic nation; it did not want the foreign culture being disseminated by Jewish writers and their Polish imitators. "A Poland spiritually semitized would cease to be Poland." [65]

The policy of Germany and Italy, wrote Józef Czarnecki,was not the deportation of Jews but elimination of their domination of political, economic, and cultural life. Jews had lost influential positions and now had only limited freedom of movement, but they were too deeply involved in the economy to be totally affected by the boycott. The segregation of Jews from the economy had contributed to the consolidation of Jewish companies. Compared to the Catholic clergy, Jews in Germany did not suffer as badly as people said.[66] The Catholic weekly also published a report on the antisemitic exhibit, "The Eternal Jew" in Berlin. It described signs in large letters on every wall of the exhibit, among them "Baptism and signs of the cross mean nothing. Through hundreds of generations we remain Jews all the same." Along with the opinions of classical writers (Plotinus, Cicero, Tacitus), one could read there the warnings of Pope Innocent III against Jews.[67]

Pro Christo

Stefan Kaczorowski, editor of *Pro Christo—Wiara i Czyn,* was a militant right wing Catholic whose views appeared regularly in a column entitled "On the Front of the War." In the autumn of 1933, he wrote on the wide spectrum of Polish opinion regarding Nazism. The National Democratic (Endecja) press was decidedly favorable. Its *Gazeta Warszawska*enthused over Hitler after the Reichstag fire. Endecja leader Roman Dmowski wrote a series of articles highlighting the positive elements and values which in his view predominated in Nazism. The Christian Democratic *Głos Narodu* insisted that Nazism was not to be imitated in Poland. Nazism's "pagan principle of uncritical national egoism" only led to

---

[65] Janusz Rawicz, *Przegląd Katolicki,* 71 (1933): 563–64.

[66] *Przegląd Katolicki,* 76 (1938): 213–14.

[67] *Przegląd Katolicki,* 77 (1939): 149–51.

turmoil. The attitude of the Polish government, he claimed, was one of a "strange and disturbing philosemitism." Kaczorowski regarded Jews as a danger but showed no enthusiasm for Hitler. Nazi antisemitism was barbaric and "essentially new." To cleanse a nation from harmful foreign elements was "healthy and normal," but it must be done in a way consistent with Christian principles. There was only one morality, and it obliged societies as well as individuals. The end did not justify the means. Hitler was Poland's enemy," Kaczorowski concluded, but that did not necessitate policies of "philosemitic romanticism."[68]

With the possible exception of the *Mały Dziennik*, *Pro Christo* was obsessed with Jews more than any other Catholic periodical. It viewed the "Jewish question" as one of the most important issues of the twentieth century. *Pro Christo* did not approve of the "drastic and barbaric" methods used by Hitler. Catholic principles did not allow race war and hatred. But once the French Revolution freed Jews from any restraints, wrote Kaczorowski, they contributed to the dominance of rationalism and liberalism and gave these movements their extreme anti-Christian character. Equality before the law was correct if exercised discriminantly. But the abstract application of this liberal principle had deprived the Catholic church of its influence over society, limiting its activity almost exclusively to personal life. The equality which the French Revolution gave to Jews factually amounted to privilege. The Catholic church was the highest arbiter of justice and morality; it did not condemn but allowed Jews to be segregated in ghettos away from Christians. With good reason. The Jewish intelligentsia constituted a danger for Christian culture and civilization.[69]

When a German jurist, a certain Dr. Dietrich of Hechingen, wrote that Jews should be disfranchised, Kaczorowski defended Jewish civil rights on the basis of Catholic principles and modern jurisprudence. He went on, however, to accuse the Nazis of thinking like Jews with their nationalism. To separate Jews from Christian societies and "compel them to lead normal lives on their own lands" was an honest way to resolve the Jewish question, quite unlike the one thought up by "crazy Prussian

---

[68] *Pro Christo—Wiara i Czyn*, 9 (1933): 301–09.

[69] *Pro Christo—Wiara i Czyn*, 9 (1933): 338–43.

chauvinists" who were "up to their ears in a semitic mentality."[70] Poles could be sympathetic to antisemitism only when it did not entail banditry and violence, wrote Kaczorowski. He had no illusions about a rearmed united Germany. "Can we expect a sincere peaceful attitude from people who now behave like wild animals to their own citizens?"[71]

Przegląd Powszechny

Unlike many commentators in the West, M. Bruckus took Hitler's *Mein Kampf* quite seriously. The Nazis were intent on reducing the smaller nations of Europe into provinces of the Reich. As members of the *Herrenvolk*, only Germans would have rights of citizenship. The Nuremberg race laws were not just an expression of antisemitism but of a universal racist principle. They did not distinguish between Aryans and non-Aryans but between Germans and non-Germans. They made no essential distinction between Jews, Africans, Asians, or Poles. None could be German citizens and would have to live within the Reich as guests. The conquest of any territory by the Germans would mean that the conquered peoples would lose all rights and become foreigners on their own land. The Germans had deprived not only Jews but all foreigners of their civil rights, although factually, for the time being, only the Jews were affected. But *Mein Kampf* made it quite clear that Slavic and Mediterranean peoples were of lower, less valuable races too.

Although in practice the rights of Poles were still being upheld in the Reich, theoretically they were legally dispossessed. Bruckus was quite certain that political considerations would likely change after a victorious war, when the Nazis' racist program could be put fully into effect. The Jews and Gypsies were only a beginning. Although the race laws explicitly forbad sexual relations between Germans and Jews, the government had also forbidden Germans to marry Gypsies and blacks as well.

The Nazi program consisted not only of enslaving defeated nations but populating their lands with Germans, Bruckus pointed out. *Mein Kampf* made reference to Russia and the lands under its power. Hitler's program to colonize other nations had already led to a 30% increase of the

---

[70] *Pro Christo—Wiara i Czyn*, 9 (1933): 468–72.

[71] *Pro Christo—Wiara i Czyn*, 9 (1933): 500–03.

German birthrate. The fate awaiting any nations that would be conquered by Germany was clearly indicated by that of the Gypsies, for whom sterilization had been decreed. As for the Jews, Bruckus was chillingly accurate in his perception. "There is no doubt but that physical annihilation threatens German Jews if they do not succeed in emigrating." But Bruckus' concerns were accurately much broader. German Jews were but a few hundred thousand; they could possibly emigrate. But where were the hundreds of millions of non-Germans to Germany's east supposed to go?

Mein Kampf was being required as reading for all young Germans, preparing them to accept the oppression and destruction of other nations. In it they were being taught that early Aryan civilization was founded on the slavery of conquered "lower" nations. These lower races, according to Hitler, were like animals which had to be harnessed for work, like the horse, which served humankind until the automobile made it expendable. The analogy, wrote Bruckus, was clear. Peoples with non-German blood could look forward to being treated like horses.[72]

Racism

Of all the Catholic periodicals published in Poland between the wars, *Pro Christo* was the most unabashedly extreme. Exemplifying its lack of moderation was a 1934 article signed with the pseudonym "Swastyka." The author rejected claims in the Jewish and "philosemitic" press that people hated each other simply because they belonged to different races; the only group hated, even by other Semites, were Jews. National groups tended to have distinctive characteristics: Latin peoples were excitable, Slavs sentimental, Germans self-controlled. Jews tended to trickery. "Jewish blood infects Aryan blood and spirit." Even after seven generations, Jewish converts to Christianity in Poland (Frankists) still had distinctive Jewish features. No matter what nation or religion Jews might belong to, they could not free themselves of certain features, speech, or smell.

So powerful was the "call" of Jewish blood, that "putting a stop to the penetration of Aryan blood by Jewish blood is useful, proper,

---

[72] *Przegląd Powszechny*, 222 (1939): 68–77.

understandable, and moral." Like laws that quarantine infectious diseases, laws forbidding intermarriage between Aryans and Jews might be unpleasant for individuals but were required for the general welfare. Christian morality, wrote the author, allowed the individual to be sacrificed for the good of society. Self-preservation called for separation.

Pro Christo was a Catholic periodical and therefore had to comply with the Vatican condemnation of racism. The anonymous author attempted to do so by asserting that, from a Christian point of view, racist theory was sinful only if it called for hatred of people simply because they belonged to another race. Thus, the attitudes of American whites toward blacks deserved condemnation because they hated blacks without any reason. But antagonism toward Jews was justified. Racial theory became sinful only if its adherents entered into the area of religion: if they denied the divine revelation of the Old Testament, saw Christianity only as the product of Judaism, or viewed purity of race as the highest good and our purpose for existence. Purity of race was good, but only as a means to avoid the harmful influence of Jews and thereby more easily attain the ultimate highest good that is God.[73]

Much more typical than this explicitly racist Catholic antisemitism was the stance of Father Eugeniusz Dąbrowski, Seminary and University Professor in Warsaw. Lecturing on why Jews rejected Christianity, he criticized the racial theories of Gobineau and Houston Stewart Chamberlain that Christianity was foreign to the semitic psyche and Jesus was an Aryan. Racial theory had no scientific foundation whatever and was contrary to the gospel. Rather it was Jewish separateness which caused antisemitism and caused Jews to reject Christianity, wrote Dąbrowski. He rejected the idea of racial inequality but upheld the right of Christians to self-defense "of course within the limits of Christian ethics." Jews could become Christian only if they rejected the ideology and principles of Judaism.[74]

In the *Ateneum Kapłańskie,* a journal for priests, Dr. M. Lech Kaczmarek described German racism as a compensatory mechanism. German pride first manifested itself with Fichte, after Germany's humiliation by Napoleon. Rosenberg's *Myth* appeared after Germany's defeat in 1918. Racism was the result of distorted science and a history

---

[73] *Pro Christo—Wiara i Czyn,* 10 (1934): 619–28.

[74] *Przegląd Katolicki,* 72 (1934): 767–69.

falsified by German pride.[75]

In a much more penetrating treatment, Father Józef Pastuszka described nationalism and race as the most influential ideas of the 1930s. Not only in Germany but in Denmark, Sweden, Norway, England, Holland, Belgium, Czechoslovakia, Switzerland, and France, political groups were forming around racist ideology. Hitler was attempting to build an entire social-political system on the principles of Gobineau and Chamberlain, ideas which were influencing the intellectual and political life of all Europe. Pastuszka criticized Nazi racism for its materialistic anthropology. The human spirit was not a creation of race and blood. Spirit, not biology, created culture. Racism expanded biological laws to all aspects of life, a social form of Darwinism that contradicted individual freedom and creativity. The Christian world view, on the other hand, upheld human spirituality and dignity by teaching that every human being was an image of God.

Even when defending the human dignity of Jews, Catholic authors like Father Pastuszka could betray deep-seated ambivalence. Jews, he contended, illustrated the falsehood of racial theory. For two thousand years they maintained a certain identity and features no matter what their habitat. This "psychic resistance" resulted not from racial but spiritual factors: their religious isolation; their messianic, national pride; the spiritual ghetto that has shaped them for 1800 years; the ethics of the Talmud; resentment and hatred for Christian culture. These factors, contended the priest, have created a specific Jewish mentality, have hardened this "unfortunate but dangerous though chosen people." Their historical experiences have refined their minds, enriched their feelings, and strengthened their wills, but have also made them resistant to the influences of the surrounding culture. Jews were a foreign body in the organism of European nations, not because of blood, but because of their hostility to a Christian culture foreign to the Jewish psyche. Only a sincere conversion to Christianity could change that psyche.

Father Pastuszka was no democrat. He blamed the revolutionary ferment of his day on "extreme political democracy" and modern parliamentary government. Democracy gives free reign to the lowest instincts, and Nazi Germany was but an extreme reaction. Hitler's ideology constituted what was, for the most part, an accurate critique of

---

[75] *Ateneum Kapłańskie,* 35 (1935): 381–85.

democratic governments, the priest concluded. But Hitler's racist world view created a whole new scale of values and would necessarily lead to a war of extermination. Racism and Christianity were irreconcilable.[76]

In 1938 the official organ of the Archdiocese of Warsaw published the Vatican's letter requesting Catholic educators to refute racist doctrines.[77] Two months later *Przewodnik Katolicki* reported on the pope's speeches criticizing Italy's race laws but noted that Germany was implied in the criticism. The report was careful to point out that the pope was not condemning all nationalism but only its exaggerated forms. The pope's real concern, declared the Catholic weekly, was not the mere fifty thousand Jews in Italy but the church's mission to draw all nations into one fold. Racism was condemned because it constituted an obstacle to the missionary activity of the church.[78]

The anti-Jewish stereotypes and attitudes represented in the Polish Catholic press were clearly not affected by papal condemnations of racism. The Vatican letter or the pope's speeches did not affect the position of Józef Białasiewicz in *Przegląd Katolicki* for example. He called for imitation not of Germany's anti-racial legislation but its anti-Jewish measures, the disfranchisement of Jews, and creation of ghettos. Two nations of differing race and culture could not live on the same land; the guest had to give way to the host. Legislation should be introduced to de-judaize Polish life and the professions. Bialasiewicz admitted that there would be an outcry. Demonstrations, protests and press declarations would be organized by "noble-minded" representatives of Polish culture who would appeal to Poland's "innate tolerance." But to resist Jewish power successfully required draconian measures.[79]

As is clear from the foregoing, papal condemnations of racism did not affect prejudicial attitudes based on culture or the so-called Jewish psyche. Not blood but history formed a people and their civilization, wrote Father Zabroniak in the *Gazeta Kościelna*. It was cultural separation over the centuries that gave Jews a distinctive mentality and

---

[76] *Ateneum Kapłańskie*, 40 (1937): 328–44, 441–53.

[77] *Wiadomości Archidiecezjalne Warszawskie*, 28 (1938): 283–84. See above.

[78] *Przewodnik Katolicki*, 44 (1938): 551.

[79] *Przegląd Katolicki*, 76 (1938): 5–6.

made them "racially" different from other nations.[80] Papal censures not only did not preclude antisemitism, but were able to add another reason for it. In the church all nations were equal, wrote Father Józef Kaczmarek, in contrast to "Jewish racism" which claimed that Jews were chosen and superior to other nations. When Saint Paul preached freedom from the law, wrote the priest, it was to free Aryans from the "imperialism" of insincere Jewish-Christians.[81]

Poland's Catholic press was patently concerned to demonstrate that Polish nationalism was different from Germany's and so not affected by the pope's criticism. All nationalism was not the same, declared the *Gazeta Kościelna*. German nationalism was a religion of race that put Germany above Christianity. Italian nationalism glorified Italy as the purest example of Roman culture and equal to Christianity. Polish nationalism regarded all nations as equal but with different God-given missions. Poland subordinated itself to Christianity and willed only to fulfill its historic mission.[82]

In *Ruch Katolicki,* a Catholic Action periodical, Father Szczepan Sobalkowski, seminary professor at Kielce, portrayed racism simply as a hyper form of German nationalism. The pope's sermons and the Vatican theses on nationalism and race provided negative guidelines, showing how far one could not go. But they did not exclude a positive attitude toward one's own race, blood, and nationality. Nor did they exclude a stand against Jews' dominating the economy and their destructive influence on morals. Poland should look to Hungary, where Prime-minister Imredy, a Catholic, had recently issued "fascist decrees" to eliminate harmful Jewish influence. Poland too would have to undertake difficult but necessary reforms in order to "renew all things in Christ."[83]

The Vatican's letter on racism was only a first step in the opinion of the editor of *Przegląd Powszechny*. He fully expected that there would follow a formal papal declaration of Nazism as a heresy.[84] In the same

---

[80] *Gazeta Kościelna,* 45 (1938): 556.

[81] *Gazeta Kościelna,* 45 (1938): 530–32.

[82] *Gazeta Kościelna,* 45 (1938): 529.

[83] *Ruch Katolicki,* 81 (1938): 498–17.

[84] *Przegląd Powszechny,* 218 (1938): 403–07.

issue of the Jesuit journal, Dr. Andrzej Niesiołowski tried to understand the amazing intensity and irrationalism of the Nazis. He could understand their antisemitism. During the Weimar Republic Germany's Jews had gone "too far" in organizing associations for homosexuals and flooding Germany with pornography. But these were secondary phenomena which could not explain the enthusiasm with which Nazism was being embraced by Austria's Catholics, including the bishops. The deeper roots of Nazi success, Niesiołowski suggested, lay in the drive for community. How else could one explain Cardinal Innitzer ending a letter with *Heil Hitler*? Or Austrian churches flying the swastika? Young people were generally more interested in matters patriotic than religious, and Austrian church leaders were giving the Nazis no excuse to complain that Catholics were opposed to national unification. The cult of German national unity had increased the political power of the Nazis but at the price of cultural decline. Germany's Catholics faced persecution, but perhaps Catholics and Protestants would draw closer together in a common battle against neo-paganism.[85]

The distinction between racist and Christian antisemitism was given classic expression by priest-professor Jan Czuj in the *Ateneum Kapłańskie*. All people had been created equally by God, saved by Christ, and called by the church, wrote Father Czuj. But then he detailed the traditional arguments from Saint Augustine that Jews had ceased to be children of Abraham and had become subject to Satan. Jews had been punished because they had killed Christ and remained obstinate in rejecting him. Their punishment was a witness to the world of the truth of Christianity. No races were higher or lower, chosen or rejected. The city of God was international. But that did not mean Jews had access to it. In the tradition going back to Saint John Chrysostom, Father Czuj insisted that "the prayers of Jews are fruitless and go for nothing." Jews were to be condemned not for their race but for the same reasons Jesus, the apostles, and Saint Augustine gave, for their disbelief and perversity.[86]

Obviously Poland's Catholic press did not see the Vatican's condemnation of racism as addressing Polish nationalism. Neither did it see Polish Catholics as affected by the Vatican's 1928 criticism of

---

[85] *Przegląd Powszechny*, 219 (1938): 10–24.

[86] *Ateneum Kapłańskie*, 44 (1939): 1–12.

antisemitism, defined there as a "hatred" of Jews. But this did not mean that Catholics necessarily rejected the label altogether. "Antisemitic" was not the offensive word in the 1930s that it is today. Kraków's Catholic *Głos Narodu*, for example, implicitly granted that there could be a legitimate and appropriate form of antisemitism, by distinguishing between "intelligent" and "unintelligent" or "ignorant" antisemitism. An example of ignorant antisemitism was the behavior of a woman in Berlin who refused to sit in a seat just occupied by a Jew. The most ignorant form of antisemitism was the one which claimed that Christianity was a Jewish swindle. It was not clear, claimed the Catholic daily, whom such antisemites hated more, Christians or Jews.[87]

Right up to 1939, Catholic leaders and opinion-makers distinguished between hatred of Jews for reasons of race and hostility for other (theological, political, economic, cultural) reasons. No longer was it simply a matter of holding Jews responsible for the death of Jesus or viewing them as rejected for refusing to accept Christianity. Jews had become not only alien but dangerous by virtue of their widespread embrace of modern secularity and its values. Assimilated Jews had become proponents of all that was wrong with modernity—rationalism, liberalism, socialism, communism. Even more so were Jews a threat to Catholics, if one accepted the existence of a Masonic-Jewish alliance to destroy Christianity and dominate the world. In the 1930s this kind of thinking made Jews fearsome even where there were no Jews—as in a Spain torn apart by civil war. There in Spain the list of Jewish crimes was increased to include priest-killing and church-burning.

---

[87] *Głos Narodu*, January 24, 1939.

Chapter 6

Jews and the Spanish Civil War

Aside from neighboring Germany and the Soviet Union, no foreign nation received more attention from Poland's interwar Catholic press than Spain. The reason, of course, was the civil war that ravaged Spain from 1936 to April 1939. The atrocities in that conflict generally inspired onlookers with both horror and concern. But none were more horrified than Catholics, and no Catholics more concerned than those in Poland.

The Civil War

In wake of the elections of February 1936, control of the Spanish government had passed into the hands of a coalition of liberals, socialists, and communists called the Popular Front. They were elected on the campaign promise to fully implement Spain's anticlerical constitution of 1931 and to grant general amnesty to political prisoners. That amnesty necessarily included thousands of anarchists, imprisoned for acts of industrial and anticlerical violence.[1] Immediately upon their release these

---

[1] Anarchism was founded by Russian-born Michael Bakunin and advocated the violent overthrow of existing states and institutions as a necessary step toward freedom, and an egalitarian distribution of private property among individuals. It was introduced into Spain in 1868 and spread quickly among the industrial workers of Barcelona and agrarian laborers of Andalusia. For the origins of the anarchist movement in Spain, see Gerald Brenan, *The Spanish Labyrinth, An Account of the Social and Political Background of the Civil War,* (Cambridge: University Press; New York: Macmillan, 1944), 131–69.

anarchists turned not only upon their counterparts on the Right, the fascist Falange party, but also upon the church. From February to June sporadic incidents of arson occurred in which churches were put to the torch and either totally or partially destroyed by the anarchists, abetted by common criminals who had also been released in the wholesale opening of the prisons.[2]

The government did little or nothing to quell the destruction. Instead, it began implementing the anticlerical legislation that had been passed earlier, closing religious schools all over Spain. Whatever had existed of moderate political opinion disintegrated. Mass desertion from centrist parties left the nation polarized into extremist groups on both the Left and Right. On July 18, the army under General Francisco Franco revolted against the republic. Joined by the fascist Falange, this uprising of nationalists began not only nearly three years of civil war but, in reaction, six months of anticlerical bloodletting, appropriately called "the fury."[3]

The government responded to the military-rightist uprising by arming the labor unions and left wing political organizations that supported it. On the night of July 19, after battling the rebellious military, mobs of Spaniards loyal to the republic turned upon the churches and the clergy. Between July and December 1936, thousands of churches were set on fire. Thirteen bishops were killed, as well as nearly seven thousand priests, monks, nuns, and seminarians. Wherever the anarchists were numerous and beyond the control of the Popular Front government, priests and religious were hunted down and murdered, identified with the nationalist rebellion as enemies of the republic. Not merely executed, in some instances they were tortured. Besides the nearly seven thousand clergy (an estimated one-quarter of all the male clergy behind republican lines), thousands more lay people were killed simply for being related to clerics, harboring them, or being well-known churchgoers. Neither was the fury limited to murder and arson. Religious objects were profaned

---

[2] Brenan, *Spanish Labyrinth,* 301, 311; Hugh Thomas, *The Spanish Civil War,* (New York: Harper & Row, 1977), 160–62; José M. Sanchez, *Reform and Reaction: The Politico-Religious Background of the Spanish Civil War,* (Chapel Hill: University of North Carolina Press, 1962), 207.

[3] Sanchez, *Reform and Reaction,* 205–13.

and sacred ceremonies burlesqued. The tombs of nuns were opened and their petrified mummies displayed for ridicule.[4]

More than fifty years later, discussion of the Spanish civil war is still clouded by rival mythologies. One is that the republic was a fledgling democracy fighting an unholy triumvirate of wealthy landowners, military officers, and priests. The other myth is that General Franco was a national savior putting an end to persecution of the church and bringing order to a land governed by Bolshevik anarchists. The complex issues and events surrounding Spain's civil war and the vast literature it engendered lie obviously beyond the scope of this study. What is germane, though, are the uses to which the war was put by church leaders and the international secular and religious press, including that in Poland. Few reports made honest attempts at objectivity. One was either for the republic or against it. The church was either all right or all wrong, a hapless victim of persecution or the guilty oppressor of the Spanish people. There was little or no middle ground.

The Spanish Bishops

The Catholic press in Poland, like that around the world, took its lead from the Spanish bishops, especially from the collective letter they issued in the summer of 1937.[5] The letter justified the Franco rebellion as a "civic-military movement" in defense of order, civilization, and the rights of God. The Popular Front, the bishops contended, had attained power by means of election fraud. They, the Popular Front, were the revolutionaries, inspired, directed, and financed by the Soviet Comintern. The letter, addressed to Catholic bishops outside Spain, was intended as a defense against the charges that the Spanish church was a wealthy landowner and had provoked the anticlerical violence by being too closely identified with monarchy and the upper classes.

The bishops pointed out correctly that the church's landholdings were comparatively sparse and that the vast majority of Spanish priests were

---

[4] José M. Sanchez, *The Spanish Civil War as a Religious Tragedy* (Notre Dame, IN: University of Notre Dame Press, 1987), 9–11.

[5] The authorized English translation appeared in the *New York Times,* September 3, 1937, 4–5.

recruited from the lower class poor. The letter acknowledged the causes of the war to be complex. It cited not only malice in the government but careless blunders. Not taking aggressive action against the anarchists in the militia was cowardice. But the bishops did not doubt that the primary responsibility for the anticlerical violence and destruction of churches lay not in Spain but in Russia. It was "exported by Orientals of perverse spirit."

Spain, declared the bishops, was but a national battlefield for an international struggle on which there hung the fate of Europe. It was a struggle between "irreconcilable ideologies." On one side was materialistic communism, bent on the abolition of the Catholic religion in Spain, slaughtering priests, profaning sacred relics, plundering and destroying churches and works of art. On the other side were the nationalists, defending Christian civilization and representing Spain's true spirit. As for charges that the nationalists had also committed atrocities against captured republicans, the bishops answered that there was no comparison between the "excesses" of the nationalists and the "outrages against justice" committed by the Marxist republicans.

The bishops' letter was not simplistic. It admitted that not all republicans were fighting for communism and not all government leaders were malicious. But the bishops could not concede that the church in any way shared in the responsibility for the fury that had been unleashed against it. Culpability had to lie outside the church and preferably outside Spain, for whom the church had served for centuries as the primary moral educator. The bishops found a ready explanation for the violence against the church in the claim of a communist conspiracy contrived in Moscow. It was not a new thought. As early as 1931, a commonplace accusation against Spain's political Left was that of being a "Moscow agent."[6]

What the Spanish bishops failed to mention, however, was that in the election of 1936 a negligible sixteen out of 473 seats had gone to the communists. No mention was made of the fact that Soviet aid was not forthcoming until several months into the war, after most of the frenzy of church burnings had spent itself. Nor did the bishops consider that anticlerical violence had been a Spanish tradition long before Marxism

---

[6] David T. Cattell, *Communism and the Spanish Civil War* (Berkeley: University of California Press, 1955), 208.

or the Bolshevik revolution. In at least four periods of upheaval before the advent of Spain's Second Republic, (in 1822, 1834, 1868, and 1909), priests were killed and churches set ablaze.[7] It was a peculiarity of Spain that, in revolutionary situations, the arson of churches had come to be expected.

True, the church in Spain had been deprived of most of its lands in the mid-nineteenth century. But this had just made it all the more dependent on the rich for its support. The clergy had become alienated from the urban working class, which saw the church as allied with its wealthy oppressors. Alienated too were the intellectual, liberal elites, even though the church, in virtual control of all Spain's secondary schools, had helped educate them. Many of them now gathered in Masonic lodges, opposed to violence but intent on disestablishing the church and creating a secular Spain. But from the perspective of the Spanish bishops, any and all forces favoring separation of church and state were communist-inspired and subversive.

The most authoritative studies on the issue reject the notion that communists were the motivating power behind the anticlerical fury. Quite the contrary, Spain's communists wanted an end to the terror so as to be able to attract democratic support for the republic. The roots of the fury lay in Spain's history and in domestic issues.[8] But that was too much to admit. It would be too stinging an indictment for church leaders even to conceive that, after centuries of Catholicism, thousands of Spaniards could turn against the church of their own accord. It was easier to represent Spain's anticlerical Catholics as unwitting instruments of outside forces and declare the military uprising a religious crusade in defense of Christian civilization.[9]

The Vatican followed the suit of the Spanish bishops. In an address to a group of Spanish refugees, Pope Pius XI implicitly but unmistakably laid blame for the conflict in Spain on communism. He spoke of forces subverting order "from Russia to China, from Mexico to South America,"

---

[7] Sanchez, *Spanish Civil War,* 47–48.

[8] Burnett Bolloten, *The Spanish Revolution: The Left and the Struggle for Power during the Civil War* (Chapel Hill: University of North Carolina Press, 1979), 57–59, 104–105; Cattell, *Communism and the Spanish Civil War,* 208.

[9] Victor Manuel Arbeloa, "Anticlericalismo y Guerra Civil," *Lumen,* 24 (1975) 162–81, 254–71.

intent on subjecting the whole world to "absurd and disastrous ideologies." Calling the Catholic church the "one real obstacle" to these subversive forces and warning against any Catholic collaboration with them, the pope once again drew a direct connection between communism and attempts by liberals to separate church and state. Limiting the church's political influence was laying the groundwork for communism: "Whenever war is being made on religion and the Catholic Church and her beneficent influence on the individual, on the family, on the mass of the people, that war is in alliance with the forces of subversion, by these same forces and for the same disastrous purpose." [10]

The pope is said to have vacillated privately in his view of the war and of the role the Soviet Union was playing in it. But this address remained the Vatican's principal statement on the Spanish civil war. [11] Privately the pope may have regarded Franco's nationalists to be as bad as the republicans in committing atrocities. But in May 1938, the Vatican gave formal recognition to the nationalist regime, while still refusing to normalize relations with the republican government. It was a diplomatic coup for Franco. Aside from its allies in the civil war (Nazi Germany, Fascist Italy, and Portugal), this was the first recognition of the Franco regime by a major power. [12]

No reference was made to Jews in either the pope's address or the letter of the Spanish bishops. But by blaming the anticlerical fury directly on communists and indirectly on liberals, the Vatican and bishops' letter left the way open for that further connection to be made by more outspoken Catholic partisans on the Right, including highranking members of the Spanish hierarchy.

Even without Jews, antisemitism was woven into much of Spain's Catholic culture. Not without reason traditionalist Catholic Spaniards identified Jews with liberalism. The Second Republic's 1931 constitution which separated church and state had also granted political equality to Jews. The conservative Spanish press had attacked it as the result of a world Jewish conspiracy. In the general elections of 1933, Jews, Masons,

---

[10] *Acta Apostolicae Sedis,* 28 (1936) 373–81. An English translation of the Italian original was published in *The Catholic Mind,* 34 (1936) 385–94.

[11] Sanchez, *Spanish Civil War,* 123–24.

[12] Sanchez, *Spanish Civil War,* 130.

and communists together were pilloried as responsible for all revolutionary disorder. Similarly, in the very first months of the civil war, generals assisting Franco described their conflict as one against "Freemasons, Jews, and similar parasites." Jews and Freemasons—labeled as "camouflaged Jews"—were "enemies of Christ." The Spanish struggle was "not a Spanish civil war but a war for Western civilization against world Jewry."[13]

Similar rhetoric came from the leadership of the Spanish church. Cardinal Isidro Goma, archbishop of Toledo and primate of the church in Spain, designated the war as a punishment for secularism: "the Jews and Masons had poisoned the national soul with absurd doctrines."[14] Manuel de Castro Alonso, the archbishop of Burgos, wrote in a pastoral letter (February 14, 1937): "The Popular Front was nothing more than a conglomeration of atheists, Masons, Jews, and enemies of God and Spain." Feliciano Rocha Pizarro, bishop of Plasencia, denounced "communism, Judaism, and Masonry in an infernal amalgamation to destroy in a few hours the civilization we cherish." Albino G. Menendez Reigada, bishop of Tenerife, (June 1937) attacked "international Marxists and the great Jewish press lords" for publishing calumnies against Spain.[15] Antonio Garcia Garcia, bishop of Tuy, in a pastoral letter (September 19, 1936) wrote: "It is evident that the present conflict is one of the most terrible wars ever waged by Antichrist, that is by Judaism, against the Catholic Church and against Christ."[16]

Taking a lead from their bishops, priests behind nationalist lines preached sermons with sentiments like the following by a priest in Burgos: "You who call yourselves Christians! You are to blame for much that has happened. For you have tolerated in your midst, yea, and even employed in your service workmen banded together in organizations hostile to our God and our country. You have heeded not our warnings and have consorted with Jews and Freemasons, atheists and renegades,

---

[13] Caesar C. Aronsfeld, *The Ghosts of 1492, Jewish Aspects of the Struggle for Religious Freedom in Spain, 1848–1976*, (New York: Columbia University, 1979), 42–44. See also Thomas, *Spanish Civil War*, 760–61.

[14] Thomas, *Spanish Civil War*, 512.

[15] Arbeloa, "Anticlericalismo," 171, 260, 264.

[16] *Social Justice*, August 21, 1939.

so helping to strengthen the power of the very lodges whose aim it was to hurl us all into chaos."[17] Coming from church leaders on the scene, the idea that Freemasons, communists, and Jews were responsible for the atrocities of the civil war in Spain was given wide circulation in the conservative Catholic press throughout the world. Particularly in Poland the conspiracy theory found ready credence, where it fed both the fears and crusading mentality of the Polish church.

Poland's Catholic Press

Polish periodicals aimed at priests gave particular attention to the Spanish bishops' letter on the civil war.[18] The bishops left little to the imagination in describing the anticlerical violence. Their letter made references to limbs cut off and tongues cut out, eyes gouged and victims burned alive or chopped to death with axes. The blessed sacrament had been taken from churches and profaned. Cemeteries had been desecrated, corpses robbed for their rings and gold teeth, the exhumed skull of a bishop used as a football. All this, of course, the work of communists. Such descriptions in periodicals for priests filtered down into sermons and the popular Catholic press. There to graphic verbal descriptions of the atrocities were added photographs: Spanish militia men firing rifles at a statue of Jesus and "communists in Barcelona" hanging an exhumed corpse on the walls of a cloister.[19]

From the perspective of the *Mały Dziennik*, the events which led up to the Spanish uprising constituted a "Masonic-Red Terror." The paper wrote of the "tyranny of the Left," closing right wing newspapers and using draconian measures to repress Catholic solidarity. The former monarchy and patriarchal dictatorship of Primo de Rivera were like paradise compared to the bloody oppression of the republic. With a clear reference to Poland's own situation, the paper contended that, "some countries are not ready for parliamentary democracy, and it is not right,

---

[17] Quoted in Thomas, *Spanish Civil War*, 511.

[18] It appeared in Polish translation in the *Wiadomości Archidiecezjalne Warszawskie*, 1937, 494–505, and was reported in detail in the *Ateneum Kapłańskie* 40 (1937) 405–10.

[19] *Głos Narodu*, August 20, 1936; *Wiara i Życie*, 17 (1937), 327.

for the sake of satisfying democratic doctrines, to hand them over as prey to the most barbarous of tyrannies." The events in Spain were a warning. The Soviet Union might not be ready for open warfare just yet, but in a variety of countries "Jews and swindlers" in leftist movements were serving as the tools of Moscow.[20]

When news of the Spanish civil war broke in Poland, the Catholic daily was sure that victory by the Popular Front would mean a communist revolution. The nationalist uprising was inevitable in the face of the barbarism perpetrated by "foreign agents residing in faraway Moscow or concealed in Masonic lodges." The churches and their priceless works of religious art were being destroyed by the "savage lackeys of Moscow." In Poland the "socialist and Jewish press" were disturbed by the uprising, claiming that the Spanish people were happy with their left wing government. This the *Maly Dziennik* vigorously denied and ascribed the electoral victory of the Left solely to the disarray on the Right where the true majority of Spaniards were represented. A fear of fascism in Spain was ridiculous, declared the Catholic daily. "Can one even compare the abuses of fascism to the anarchy in Spain and the crimes of the communists?"[21]

In the opinion of *Nasz Przegląd,* Warsaw's Polish-language Jewish daily newspaper, the atrocities taking place in Spain were the work of the Spaniards themselves. Jews could not be implicated in them for the obvious reason that there were virtually no Jews in Spain. The *Maly Dziennik* disagreed. It conceded that Jews constituted barely .018% of the population, but statistics alone did not tell the whole story. Could Catholic Spaniards be responsible for burning their own priceless works of art? The supposedly absent Jews had certainly been involved, the Catholic daily insisted. Granted, these Jewish "ambassadors of the antichrist" did not set fire to the churches and monasteries themselves, but they were still responsible indirectly. "They who rule the Comintern and Masonry are responsible for the barbarism in Spain."[22]

---

[20] *Maly Dziennik*, July 19, 1936.

[21] *Maly Dziennik*, July 25, 1936.

[22] *Maly Dziennik*, July 28, 1936.

In a letter to the Spanish bishops, the bishops of Poland described the Spanish church's "martyrdom" as the result of a plot.[23] In his address to the Spanish refugees, mentioned above, Pope Pius XI did the same implicitly. But Warsaw's archdiocesan press left no doubt: it translated the pope's "absurd and disastrous ideologies" into "absurd communist ideologies."[24] Even more forthright, the *Mały Dziennik* ran headlines about the "barbarisms of Red Spain."[25] It asked if western Christian culture would sink into "Asiatic barbarism?"[26]

The Jesuit *Przegląd Powszechny* might have been expected to be more nuanced and moderated, since its far smaller readership consisted primarily of clerics and intellectuals. But such was not the case with regard to events in Spain, where Jesuits were particularly hated by the Left. *Przegląd Powszechny* viewed all the left wing parties as "persecuting" the church.[27] Its editor, Father Jan Rostworowski, S.J., was disturbed not only by the war but by the reporting of it in the Poland's liberal press. The crimes of the republic, directed and financed by Moscow, had reproduced Dante's Inferno. Streets were strewn with corpses as the rabble marched, drunk with crime, and celebrated their triumph with wild cries of "liberty and progress" over "slavery and darkness."

Rostworowski was incensed that the Polish press was defending the Spanish government and accusing the Franco uprising of being a revolt against lawful authority. Is it a revolt, he asked, to offer armed resistance against a band of thieves and murderers? Is it not rather a revolt to thrust the horror of communism on a people whose vast majority is Catholic? Trustworthy sources assured the Jesuit editor that "cruelty, crime, and all sorts of atrocities were to be found exclusively in the Red camp," whereas in the camp of the uprising there were no more than "acts of perhaps severe but necessary repression." He was also assured that the vast majority of Spanish people greeted the liberating armies of the nationalists with enthusiasm.

---

[23] *Wiadomości Archidiecezjalne Warszawskie,* 26 (1936), 425.

[24] *Wiadomości Archidiecezjalne Warszawskie,* 26 (1936), 465–70.

[25] *Mały Dziennik,* August 12 1936.

[26] *Mały Dziennik,* August 14, 1936.

[27] *Przegląd Powszechny,* 209 (1936) 422–27.

The crimes of Spain's communists, Rostworowski continued, awakened realization of the need for a united front against the "Red plague." It did not matter whether this united front was fascist or not, because communism was "the greatest enemy humanity has ever had" along with its "misguided and perverse partisans and defenders." Rostworowski criticized the Polish government for tolerating the left wing press. Communist agitation was everywhere, and the not too distant future would see a massive struggle between the church and the communist antichrist. Nonetheless, the Jesuit had no illusions about Nazi Germany. In a war between the swastika and Soviet star, the church could not expect anything but persecution. One should not expect Satan to drive out Satan.[28]

Obviously the Polish clergy and press viewed the Spanish civil war with self-interest and not just sympathy. In the *Ateneum Kapłańskie* Father A. Bogdański described it as an international conflict on which hung the future of Europe if not the world. It had been precipitated by two lethal external agents: Masonry from France and communism from Soviet Russia. Masons had attained the most responsible positions in government and the army, and had allowed communists to agitate the masses.

To Father Bogdański, the Comintern's strategic plan was now clear. Their objective was Spain not for its own sake but as a base of operations to create a communist France. The war in Spain was one of Satan and anarchism against God and the Roman Catholic church. In virtually every country there stood the Trojan horse of atheistic communism. In Poland too among the educated classes, there was widespread religious indifference and a falling away from the faith. The Polish church needed to remove the sources of revolt from among the masses: poverty, illiteracy, and social inequities. But it also needed to promote Catholic Action with more vigor, to mobilize an army of Catholic laity for the war that was surely close at hand.[29]

Such opinions were confirmed by the Spanish clergy. Father James Murillo, S.J., one year after the war's outbreak, claimed that 13,400 priests had been killed (over twice the actual number), victims of "the most terrible religious persecution history has ever known." But this

---

[28] *Przegląd Powszechny*, 211 (1936), 370–77.

[29] *Ateneum Kapłańskie*, 38 (1936), 501–10.

should be no surprise since Moscow had given the order that "all the clergy must die." Not sparing his readers the lurid details, the priest told of a church being converted into a dance hall with holy communion used for snacks. Spain sent a powerful signal to other countries for whom a similar fate might be imminent.[30]

Writing from France, Father Julian Unszlicht saw little danger of anticlerical violence, since the goal of a secular state had already been attained. If one looked at the French Revolution and Spanish civil war, it was obvious that the violence against the clergy was the result of many years' planning. The perpetrators, having lost any sense of moral or religious values, treated the clergy, who represented those values, with contempt. Secular schools in places like Poland were working to accomplish the same thing. In France all the priests were talking about organized conspiracy and whether or not to prepare for persecution.[31]

The *Gazeta Kościelna* reported how almost all the foreign correspondents in Spain were non-Catholics with Masonic tendencies, and so were sympathetic to the communist cause. The Masons hated Franco for suppressing their lodges. The majority of soldiers in Franco's army were not regulars but deeply religious volunteers who saw themselves as engaged in a crusade. This was the truth about Spain, declared the Catholic weekly, which was quite contradictory to what was being reported in the Jewish press and on Polish radio. The Jewish *Nasz Przegląd* had run a story describing Franco's soldiers as "rabid dogs." Catholic listeners were indignant at the biased reports about the civil war over Polish radio. But things could not be otherwise, when one considered the "Jewish personnel" employed by the Polish radio network.[32]

Towards the end of the war a story out of Paris appeared in the *Mały Dziennik* about huge profits being made by Jews who were smuggling weapons to government loyalists in Barcelona. A list of names showed all the smugglers to be Jews. The story ended with the question: "With such clear proof could anyone doubt that the Spanish nationalist army is fighting for the very life and being of the Spanish nation which Jews

---

[30] *Wiara i Życie*, 17 (1937), 324–27.

[31] *Ateneum Kapłańskie*, 40 (1937), 379–85.

[32] *Gazeta Kościelna*, 1937, 181.

have wanted to enslave?" The same issue of the Catholic daily carried an interview with an unofficial representative of Franco who linked Spain's civil war with the 1920 Soviet invasion of Poland. Also featured was a quotation ascribed to a Jewish editor in New York to the effect that Jews could hope to make progress only within a communist system.[33]

The Pulpit

The Catholic press in Poland directly influenced thousands, perhaps hundreds of thousands of ordinary lay Catholics who read either of the two daily newspapers or any of the popular periodicals. Indirectly millions more were influenced by the priests who read these and the more clerically-oriented journals. The interpretation of the Spanish civil war contained in their pages obviously affected the thinking that came out of the pulpit. One can only conjecture on the impact of those sermons. We do not have extensive reports or preachers' notes. We do have, however, the text of a sermon that was preached by Fr. F. Kwiatkowski, S.J., in Kraków (October 4, 1936), subsequently published in a periodical for preachers and intended precisely as a model for other sermons on the topic. We can only surmise how many priests used his text as the basis for their own sermons and how many did not need to do so in order to preach a similar message. Given the periodical literature reviewed above, there is no reason to consider the sermon as untypical.

The occasion for the sermon was a religious service held for the persecuted Catholics of Spain, or as the priest put it, those "murdered by the communists," for it was known to all that "the same communist hand which directed the massacres in Hungary, Mexico, and Russia, formed the Popular Front." Fr. Kwiatkowski did not restrain his oratorical skills as he described the atrocities of the Spanish fury: priests crucified, nuns raped, the severed heads of victims carried through the streets on bayonets. Skeletons had been taken from graves and used for play, churches robbed of their sacred vessels. "Red militiamen dress themselves in sacred vestments and dance wildly by the light of burning churches."

The Jesuit preacher then proceeded to draw implications closer to home: humanitarians should have raised a collective cry of protest against

---

[33] *Mały Dziennik,* July 23, 1938.

such outrages, should have proclaimed a crusade against the incendiaries. Instead they take the part of the "Jewish torturers" in Russia. Polish socialists shed tears of sympathy over the defeats of the Red Spanish Front and collect money to help them. Poland's Jewish socialists send a telegram to the Reds in Spain declaring that "your cause is our cause."

Spain, Kwiatkowski continued, is bleeding for the whole world. "On its victory or defeat hangs in great measure the collapse or triumph of the Red minions of the Antichrist." Spain's civil war was religious more than political. In former times Spain struggled against the foreign invasion of the Muslims. "Today it suffers foreign invasion once again, by the atheist Masonic-Jewish-Bolshevik enemy." The Nationalists, like the Maccabees, were waging a holy war in defense of God and fatherland.

After reminding the congregation of the 1920 "miracle on the Vistula" and Poland's title, "bastion of Christianity," Father Kwiatkowski quoted at length the words of Vatican Secretary of State, Eugenio Pacelli, the future Pope Pius XII. As reported in the *Mały Dziennik* (September 27, 1936), Pacelli had told a group of Poles in Rome: "As once your fatherland defended the nations of the West from the Muslim horde, so now it appears that your noble nation has been singled out by a particular decree of Providence to be a safeguarding bulwark to defend Western civilization against the barbarism of the North-east and its wretched, insane doctrine, which attempts in a perverse way to destroy private property for the benefit of the commune and even dares to blaspheme insolently the majesty of God." The Jesuit preacher could only hope that these words about Poland would be a true prophecy. It was a miracle of grace and faith that Poland, neighboring Soviet Russia, was not yet communist. "We trust that it never will be."[34]

Besides sermons like the above there were also lectures on Spain like those of Monsignor Stanislaus Trzeciak. Lecturing in Kraków on the civil war, Trzeciak declared that what was happening in Spain in the 1930s was revenge by the Jews for what their ancestors suffered there four hundred years earlier during the Spanish Inquisition. He explained how prominent republicans in the government came from Jewish families and how Jews were conspiring to control commerce and the press, eliminate religion from public schools and destroy Catholic marriage. Jews were the great enemy, and Catholics must know their plans so as to defend

---

[34] *Nowa Biblioteka Kaznodziejska* (1936), 387–97.

themselves and their religion. In its report on Trzeciak's lecture, *Głos Narodu*, the Kraków Catholic daily, added that, after listening to him, a group of nationalist students left the hall and went to Kraków's market square shouting epithets against "Jewish communism" (Żydokomuna).[35]

The interpretation the Polish Catholic press gave the Spanish civil war was not idiosyncratic. It was imported from the west, given wide circulation throughout the Catholic world, (in the United States by Father Charles Coughlin), and ultimately based on statements by Spain's Catholic bishops. Scholars today generally concede that the anticlerical fury of the first months of the civil war was "at bottom a spontaneous movement" by Spanish loyalists against people perceived as enemies inside the lines.[36] The atrocities committed by right wing forces were comparable to those committed by the Left and ultimately greater in number. There were summary executions on both sides. The communists in Spain denounced the anarchists and took a protective attitude toward the church.

The Spanish bishops could have exercised a moderating influence during the civil war. They chose not to.[37] No bishop issued a word of criticism against the terror on the Right.[38] This failure was confessed and repented in 1971. That year a representative assembly of Spanish bishops and priests meeting in Madrid passed by majority vote the following resolution: "We humbly recognize and ask forgiveness for the fact that we failed to act at the opportune time as true ministers of reconciliation among our people who were divided by a war between brothers."[39]

---

[35] *Głos Narodu*, November 1937.

[36] Brenan, *Spanish Labyrinth*, 318; Bolloten, *Spanish Revolution*, 57–58.

[37] It is worth noting that when Jacques Maritain, the leading French Catholic philosopher, whose wife was Jewish, criticized the notion of the Nationalist uprising as a holy war, he was denounced by the right wing press as "the Jew Maritain." Thomas, *Spanish Civil War*, 513; Sanchez, *Spanish Civil War*, 165.

[38] Brenan, *Spanish Labyrinth*, 322–23.

[39] Sanchez, *Spanish Civil War*, 203.

When reflecting on the Spanish civil war, one is not likely to consider the impact that it had on people in far-off Poland. Note is made that in Spain church leaders and others on the Right identified the government and the anticlerical fury with communism. Little importance is attributed to the connection Spanish conservatives made between the civil war and the Jews, since the number of Jews in Spain was so insignificant. But the numbers of Jews were not insignificant in Poland. Communists, Jews, church-incendiaries, priest-killers—were equations that could be found in right wing circles throughout Europe and the Catholic world. But in Poland the effects of those equations were more devastating, for sheer numbers if no other reason.

Polish Catholics alluded regularly to the fact that Poland was home to the largest Jewish community in Europe. If Jews were a danger even in Spain, where there were no Jews, how much more reason was there for self-defense in Poland? If antisemitism was rampant throughout Europe, where else was it more justified than Poland?

Chapter 7

Everywhere Else: Why not Poland?

The Catholic press acknowledged openly and without discomfort that antisemitism was widespread in Poland. Why should Poles be embarrassed about anti-Jewish attitudes, when antisemitism was rampant everywhere? It was hardly peculiar to Poland, only all-the-more justified, since Poland served as "host" to the largest concentration of Jews in Europe. Such obviously self-interested assertions were not unfounded. The First World Jewish Congress, meeting in Geneva (1936), confirmed that, with some few exceptions, antisemitism was troubling Jews everywhere. Kraków's Catholic *Głos Narodu* took due note of the fact.[1]

The example of Nazi Germany had inspired emulation throughout Europe, and it had long been a tactic of antisemitic authors to cite one another as expert witnesses to confirm their own opinions. Reports and editorials on antisemitism and the Jewish question outside Poland appeared regularly in the Catholic press, especially in the pages of *Mały Dziennik*. There Adam Romer characterized the "wave of antisemitism" sweeping Europe as a popular return to "traditional religious, political and social concepts." People had come to recognize that Jews had been leading all those so-called "progressive" movements which were chiefly responsible for Europe's troubles.

Ever since the Russian revolution, wrote Romer, people realized that communist and socialist Jews were "radicalizing the masses." Jews had been behind Bela Kun's coup d'état in Hungary, and in the first years after the war controlled political and economic life in Germany. In

---

[1] *Głos Narodu*, October 8, 1936.

France they were the mainstay of international Masonry and its war against the church. Jews in Czechoslovakia and Romania controlled commerce and industry, and, before the Fascists came to power in Italy, Rome's Jewish mayor had the crucifixes taken down from the walls of the public schools. While there was no excuse for criminal violence, the popular anti-Jewish sentiment should come as no surprise to anyone, Romer concluded. It was a direct reaction to Jewish involvement in communism and the moral depravity of the Jewish masses.[2]

While satisfied that they were in no way singular in their attitude toward Jews, Poles were generally convinced that Poland had been treated singularly. From the Polish perspective, Jewish representatives during the 1919 Paris peace conference persuaded the Allied powers that Poland should be bound by an international agreement that would regulate the treatment of its national and religious minorities. Poland's fledgling leadership signed the Minorities' Treaty, but only under duress; they could not afford alienating the victorious powers. Blaming Jews for having engineered it, all shades of political opinion resented the Minorities' Treaty as an outside interference and infringement on Polish sovereignty.[3]

Emboldened by Nazi denunciations of the League of Nations and Treaty of Versailles, the Polish government invited all the powers in the League to sign the Minorities' Treaty. The invitation constituted an excuse for its own withdrawal, a step Catholic nationalists regarded as an act of self-liberation. "Nations must be treated on an equal footing," the *Mały Dziennik* declared. "We are the masters of our own house." If anything, the rest of Europe owed Poland a debt for having taken in Jews they had driven out. Poland, concluded the Catholic daily, had been "too hospitable" for too long.[4]

From the nationalist perspective, Jewish influence on international affairs did not cease with the Paris peace conference. Poland's Catholic press viewed the League of Nations as consistently defending Jewish interests. This, contended the *Mały Dziennik*, was attributable to the fact

---

[2] *Mały Dziennik*, November 28, 1935.

[3] Ezra Mendelsohn, *The Jews of East Central Europe between the World Wars*, (Bloomington: Indiana University, 1983), 35–36.

[4] *Mały Dziennik*, July 31, 1937.

that the League's personnel was largely Jewish, descended from Jewish families or, in the case of Sir Eric Drummond, the League's General Secretary, a known friend of Jews. As one could see from merely surveying the names of its personnel, Jews controlled the politics of the League, including issues of Polish concern. The Catholic daily bore no regrets for the League's decline. The grand edifice that housed the League was a "mausoleum" and the League itself an "anecdote" that no one took seriously any longer.[5]

Jews were not wanted anywhere, and Polish nationalists could ask for no clearer proof than the 1938 conference President Roosevelt called in Evian, France, to deal with the problem of Jewish refugees from Germany and Austria. Twenty-nine nations attended, but, with the exception of the Dominican Republic, largely limited themselves to stating what they could not do. On the insistence of Great Britain, Palestine was not to be discussed, and the United States refused to allow discussion of any of its own immigration quotas. An Inter-governmental Committee on Refugees (IGCR) was established to negotiate with the Nazis so as to allow emigrants to retain some of their property and thus facilitate finding countries to accept them.[6]

The Polish government was critical of the Evian Conference, and the *Mały Dziennik* agreed. The Conference should not have limited its concern to Jews in Germany and Austria. This was a "disastrous approach" to Europe's "Jewish problem," wrote Adam Romer, clearly meaning Poland's "Jewish problem." To offer international assistance to Jews only where there was persecution was to invite radical groups to imitate the Nazis, especially in countries where there were severe population pressures. Roosevelt had used the occasion of the Conference to refer to North America as a haven for the persecuted. Why doesn't he just invite all the Jews to the United States, Romer asked.

The Evian Conference, he continued, had produced lovely phrases but no results. Belgium, Holland, Canada, and Argentina all claimed to be unable to accepts immigrants because of the depression. Some South American nations were willing to accept Jewish immigrants, but only on the condition that they come with cash or other valuables; the Reich, however, was limiting the amount of currency and possessions Jewish

[5] *Mały Dziennik*, July 26, 1938.

[6] Yehuda Bauer, *A History of the Holocaust* (New York: Franklin Watts, 1982), 129.

emigrants could take out with them. Britain agreed at most to investigate the possibility of settlements in East Africa. But Africa, Asia, Australia, and America had plenty of wide open spaces to accommodate Jews from Poland, Hungary, and Romania, Romer insisted. "Do the philanthropic gentlemen from the democratic powers want to wait until these nations, compelled to safeguard their own people, also withdraw hospitality from the Jews in a ruthless manner?" Cursing antisemitism did no good. It would be better to find a solution before it was too late.[7]

In November 1938, the Jewish refugee problem intensified with the events of Kristallnacht. The inter-governmental committee established at Evian tried to find open doors for the frantic Jews attempting to leave the Reich. The *Mały Dziennik* cited Italian fascist, Virginio Gayda, writing in the *Giornale d'Italia,* as witness to the fact that the great democracies possessed unpopulated areas that could easily be colonized by Jews. But nobody wanted the Jews, not even the Soviet Union, declared the *Mały Dziennik,* adding that obviously Jews were "faring best in Poland."[8] Nationalists writing in the Polish Catholic press knew why nobody wanted Jews. And if there were exceptions, those could be explained too.

Belgium

For the *Mały Dziennik,* the "Jewish question" was international because everywhere Jews were the same. When anyone accused of wrongdoing was Jewish, the Catholic daily then gave close attention to the "Jewish question" outside Poland. It reported, for example, that a bank scandal in Belgium was caused by two Jewish bankers, brothers who had been given a loan by the National Bank of Belgium, "even though it was well known that Jewish bankers engage in deceptive practices." The brothers were accused of forgery and fraudulent bank practices involving one hundred million francs. Their bankruptcy inflicted serious financial losses on thousands of people.[9]

---

[7] *Mały Dziennik,* July 26, 1938.

[8] *Mały Dziennik,* November 22, 1938.

[9] *Mały Dziennik,* October 27, 1937.

Czechoslovakia

When the Tiso government dissolved Masonic lodges in Slovakia, a government paper, the *Slovak,* justified the action by explaining that Masonry is "under Jewish influences." That comment moved the *Mały Dziennik* to reflect on how disastrous the year 1938 had been for Jews in Europe. Czechoslovakia, up till then, could have been called a Jewish paradise. With the annexation of Austria and the Sudetenland to Germany, Jews in Central Europe had lost their most important strongholds outside Poland. Dissolution of the Masonic lodges weakened the philosemitic elements and strengthened Slovak Catholic influence in the Prague government. When it came to Jewish issues, Tiso in Slovakia took an opposing view to the politics of Masaryk and Benes. But the Catholic daily foresaw even the Czechs changing their attitudes, after their trust in the omnipotence of Masonry and Jewry had proven illusory.

Writing in 1938, at the height of the Polish nationalist obsession with Jews, the editors at the *Mały Dziennik* gave at least one clue as to why it was sweeping Poland precisely then, far more than earlier in the decade, when the effects of the world depression were severer. The idea of an all-powerful world Jewry capable of hurting Poland or influencing the world powers against it had been dispelled. The antisemitic policies of Hitler and Mussolini had in no way produced any harmful conse-quences for Germany and Italy. England's policies in Palestine were not friendly to Jews, and in France too one could perceive an unexpected growth of antisemitism. Lithuania was quietly but effectively eliminating Jewish influence on its economy. In Romania, Jews who entered the country after 1918 were being deprived of their citizenship, and the anti-Jewish regulations issued under the Goga and Cuza regime were contin-uing in effect. Only in the Soviet Union did Jews enjoy a favorable position, and even there fears were growing. Virtually all of Poland's neighbors were waging a more or less overt war against Jews: Germany and Hungary decidedly so, with Czechoslovakia now leaning in that direction. Poland should do the same, the *Mały Dziennik* concluded. It would be absurd if Poland alone continued to fear taking decisive and effective means to resolve its "Jewish question" once and for all.[10]

---

[10] *Mały Dziennik,* October 21, 1938.

France

The writers and editors at the *Mały Dziennik* were obviously ignorant of the wave of antisemitism that had spread over France at the turn of the century. So it was found peculiarly revealing that the *Revue de Paris* had published an article by a self-described "authentic Frenchman" and "one-hundred percent Aryan." The Polish Catholic daily deemed such a reference as unthinkable a year or two earlier; it would have been regarded as backward and uncouth. Here it was a clear indication that anti-Jewish attitudes were spreading in France, too. In their pursuit of political power, French Jews had been too sure of themselves, declared the *Mały Dziennik*. They had been carelessly greedy and fanned the flames of antisemitism "where before there were none." But now, not only in Germany but in virtually all of central Europe, the political, economic and cultural influence of Jews was being overthrown. Jewish influence was waning everywhere, and Jews were being gripped by a sense of impending catastrophe. One could not hold back the course of history. Throughout the world the situation of Jews deteriorated daily, and no one could could do anything about it.[11]

Great Britain

In the popular *Przegląd Katolicki,* Józef Radomski drew from antisemitic and fascist sources in discussing Jews and English politics. He referred to the time of Cromwell, when Jews, he wrote, took "revenge" for having been driven out of England in 1290. Cromwell's soldiers, singing the psalms of David, pillaged, burned, and murdered Catholics. Thereafter, English Protestantism clearly went in the direction of being "judaized." By means of providing war loans (the "classic trick"), Jews managed not only to return triumphantly to England but to take control of its economy. By the late nineteenth century, English and Jewish interests became identical, Radomski claimed, citing the opinion of the English Catholic, Hilaire Belloc. Indeed, the entire modern capitalistic system could be attributed to northern Europeans and Jews.

---

[11] *Mały Dziennik,* May 11, 1938.

The Anglo-Jewish alliance had been promoted, Radomski assured his readers, by Masonry. With the help of Masons, Jews had come to dominate not only England but the British empire. To be a Mason was to be an "imitation Jew," and that cost money. Although Masons constituted less than one percent of the English population, they were twenty-five percent of those with wealth. Once Jews had entered the ranks of Masonry, laws were passed facilitating Jewish immigration and naturalization in Britain. The Walpoles opened the way to Jewish influence upon the economy and then Jewish entrance into British aristocracy. "From the beginning of the 18th century," wrote Radomski, "Jews have warped the whole moral fiber and national spirit of English aristocracy with their influence and poisoned it with their blood , with Masonry, a Jewish creation, playing no small role."

Beginning with Benjamin Disraeli, whom he described as putting Jewish interests above all else, Radomski listed the names of prominent Jews in England. On the basis of a pamphlet entitled "Our Jewish Aristocracy," he claimed that there were forty aristocratic families who were completely Jewish, another forty significantly so. Among Britain's six hundred members of parliament, there were nineteen Jews, including the one communist. Jews were influential at the universities of Oxford and Cambridge; they controlled the British Broadcasting Company and several leading daily newspapers. The Balfour Declaration was, of course, a primary example of Jewish influence on England. It was evident, wrote Radomski, quoting Alfred Rosenberg, the Nazi ideologist, that England had become "the greatest Jewish power on earth." But ultimately "proud Albion" was forced to capitulate. By becoming the guardian of Jewish interests, Britain was made to suffer numerous difficulties and even humiliation.[12]

Adam Romer, in the *Mały Dziennik*, was sympathetic to Great Britain's plight regarding the question of Palestine. England was trying not to antagonize the Muslim world. The majority of Arabs did not want to give Jews even the smallest part of Palestine, and Jews wanted the whole thing. Even the "immense Jewish influence in England" could not overcome Britain's fears about the safety of its oil pipeline and the defense of Gibraltar. Jewish capital was a powerful factor in England, but

---

[12] *Przegląd Katolicki*, 76 (1938), 757–59.

it would have to find some new places other than Palestine for the surplus Jews in Poland and elsewhere in central and eastern Europe.[13]

Hungary

Hungary's Jews had been profoundly disturbed by the annexation of Austria to Germany. As reported in the *Mały Dziennik*, they and other left wing elements feared that German totalitarianism and antisemitism would prove contagious. Hungarian nationalists, not unlike the Nazis, had increased their propaganda and were creating alarm. Hungary's regent, Admiral Horthy, spoke out against the scaremongering. He had taken a stand against right wing extremism, but was also determined to resolve Hungary's "Jewish question." In Hungary, as in Poland, that meant gradually removing Jewish influence by nationalizing commerce and industry. The Catholic daily reminded its readers that Hungary's Jews were the sole supporters of the communist revolution engineered there by Bela Kuhn.[14]

Italy

The *Mały Dziennik* informed its readers about the laws passed by Italy's fascist government with respect to its minuscule Jewish population: marriages between Italians and Jews were prohibited, and Italian Jews would not be permitted to serve in the Italian military or hold leadership positions in large firms. The only editorial comment the Catholic daily made on the fascist legislation was its headline declaring the laws an "act of self-defense by Italians against Jews."[15]

If Poles wanted a "rational solution" to the Jewish question, wrote Józef Czarnecki in *Przegląd Katolicki*, they should familiarize themselves with what nations like Italy were doing. Their aim was to stop Jewish domination of cultural, political and economic life and subordinate Jewish

---

[13] *Mały Dziennik*, July 10, 1937.

[14] *Mały Dziennik*, April 14, 1938.

[15] *Mały Dziennik*, October 9, 1938.

interests to those of the state. Jews had come to occupy important positions in the government and to exert influence on finances. Although the changes taking place in Italy were partially induced by Nazi racial theory, Czarnecki argued that political motives were more important. Just as England was serving Jewish interests in Palestine, Mussolini was protecting Arab-Islamic interests in the Middle East. In contrast to Nazi Germany, the antisemitism in Italy was not integral but flexible, determined by circumstances. But in neither Italy nor Germany, Czarnecki assured his readers, was it as bad for Jews as people said.[16]

Romania

In 1937 King Carol appointed a new government, led by two of Romania's most celebrated antisemites, Octavian Goga and Alexandru Cuza. The program of the Goga-Cuza regime called for removing Jews from any important positions in the economy and at universities, revoking "improperly granted" rights, and expelling those Jews who had entered Romania after the signing of the Versailles peace treaty.[17] The *Mały Dziennik* described how shortly after taking power the new administration closed several daily papers on the grounds that they were run by foreigners and consistently took stands against the interests of the nation. An official press release stated that "our government will be guided on the motto 'Romania for the Romanians' and will be based on the ideas of Christianity and monarchy as the principles of our national existence." Characterizing these first moves of the Goga government as "open antisemitism," the *Mały Dziennik* called for Poland to follow Romania's example.[18]

The *Mały Dziennik* viewed Romania's antisemitic cabinet as enormously significant for all of Europe. The new Romanian government was making a war against Jews part of its program, despite the long-held conviction throughout Europe that Jewish capital and influence over international opinion made any open opposition to Jews madness. It was

---

[16] *Przegląd Katolicki*, 76 (1938), 213–14.

[17] Mendelsohn, *The Jews of East Central Europe*, 206.

[18] *Mały Dziennik*, January 1, 1938.

presumed that any antisemitic government would suffer severe consequences. Germany's war against the Jews had already revealed that such fears were exaggerated, but its example was not enough to allay all apprehension, since Germany was a major economic power. Even though not a great power, Romania did not fear outside Jewish pressure. On the contrary, Jews in other countries were covering the matter over for fear Romania's example would prove contagious. [19]

The Goga-Cuza government lasted but two months. The economic panic it engendered and negative foreign reaction to its anti-Jewish policy prompted King Carol to engineer its fall. In Poland, *Pro Christo* described its demise as a Jewish "triumph," blaming it on the "bad press" Romania had received abroad. All the correspondents covering Romania for the international press agencies were Jewish.[20] The following year King Carol named Cuza to the Royal Council and the *Mały Dziennik* once again took the opportunity to make unfavorable comparisons between Romania and the Polish government. In Poland fears of losing the sympathy of England and France prevented the appointment of officials disliked by Jews. But Romania was not afraid. The Catholic daily viewed Romania's policies as expressions of sober realism and the sign of a powerful nation, not like those of the fainthearted in Poland.[21]

Switzerland

In the wake of the Anschluss and Evian conference, the *Mały Dziennik* reported on the criticism leveled against Switzerland for not accepting Jewish refugees from Austria. A representative of the Swiss government responded that Switzerland already had 350,000 outsiders, more than nine percent of its entire population; it had to protect itself against a wave of foreigners. Switzerland did not want Jews, and Poland must follow in its footsteps, the Catholic daily declared. "Does only Poland always have to be a place of shelter and refuge," it asked.[22]

---

[19] *Mały Dziennik*, January 4, 1938.

[20] *Pro Christo*, 14/3 (1938), 28–29.

[21] *Mały Dziennik*, June 23, 1939.

[22] *Mały Dziennik*, September 22, 1938.

United States

For Józef Radomski in the *Przegląd Katolicki,* the United States was the center of world Jewry. Jews had gained political power first in the United States, and from there established it worldwide. The 1919 peace conference was proof of the matter. Radomski cited a 1918 publication, "The Jews among the Entente Leaders," describing sixteen internationally prominent Jews. Among them were Justice Louis Brandeis, the trusted counselor to President Wilson; labor leader Samuel Gompers; former ambassador Oscar Straus; financial advisor Bernard Baruch; former ambassador Abraham Elkus; and banker Otto Kahn. These men represented Jewish influence on every sphere of American life from commerce and finance to military and foreign affairs.

But the Jewish impact on American society would never have been as profound as it was, Radomski contended, were it not for Masonry and a network of similar organizations. The Masons in America exceeded all other nations in numbers and influence. Radomski described the Rosicrucians, Odd Fellows, and B'nai B'rith as all being Masonic agents. He pointed out that President Roosevelt was a member of the Odd Fellows, and supposedly a descendent of Jews from Holland. Listing the presidents from Washington to Wilson who had been Masons, Radomski concluded that a political career in the United States was not possible "unless one is a Mason or...a Jew." Masons made up the majority of the Senate and were numerous in the House of Representatives. "As a rule, all the most important political moves take place through the mediation of Masons, and therefore by the will of the Jews."

In Radomski's opinion, the United States entered into the First World War because of President Wilson and the Freemasons. It was a war "undertaken in the name of Masonic ideals," in which General John Pershing, the commander of the American armed forces, was also a Mason. There was no doubt in Radomski's mind that the English Masons and the Jews among them had profited greatly from the war both financially and politically. American Jews and the Masons under their domination had not yet finished cashing in on the victory.

But now, once again, wrote Radomski, American Jews and Masons were being galvanized by the call for war against the dictators. Masonry in many countries was experiencing crises of life or death, and Jews in America were mobilizing for a political war. The "big four" agencies

(American Jewish Committee, American Jewish Congress, B'nai B'rith, and Jewish Labor Committee) had established a United Jewish Front as a defense agency to fight antisemitism. Proof of Jewish influence was the reaction of the United States to the anti-Jewish measures in Germany, even to the extent of threatening to break off diplomatic relations with the Third Reich. American Jews and Masons were keeping close watch on any matter which impinged upon Jewish interests. They would intervene immediately, as Poles well knew, from a whole series of issues ranging from its borders to loans. American Jews were supporting Jewish credit unions with millions of złotys. It was imperative, Radomski concluded, that Poles be apprised of this power behind the scenes in the United States.[23]

Antisemitism was everywhere, and nowhere more justified than Poland, which had been too hospitable for too long to Europe's largest Jewish community. No one wanted Jews, so why should Poland? Some of the largest selling Catholic periodicals wanted Poland to follow the example, if not of Nazi Germany, then of its less radical neighbors in dealing with the "Jewish question." But along with these sentiments, one perceives once again the conviction of a Jewish-Masonic alliance. That perspective slanted everything for the interwar Catholic press in Poland, whether it was reporting on the Soviet Union, Germany, Spain, or anywhere else. The idea of a Jewish-Masonic alliance, if not conspiracy, colored everything. One did not have to accept the authenticity of the *Protocols* to believe that Freemasons and like-minded liberals were bent on secularizing traditionally Catholic societies. One could condemn racism and violence and still see assimilated, secularized Jews as an alien force, inimical to the creation of a reborn Catholic Poland.

But most Jews in Poland were not secular, and even fewer were socialists or communists. The majority of Polish Jews were religious traditionalists. But a tradition much older than the myth of a Jewish-Masonic alliance did not exempt them from Christian animosity either. The traditional religious reasons for antisemitism, though not as prominent in interwar Catholic literature as the Masonic-Jewish

---

[23] *Przegląd Katolicki,* 77 (1939), 85–87.

conspiracy myth, had not yet been officially rejected by the church's leadership. Assumed rather than proclaimed, theological reasons for antisemitism were never far beneath the surface of the political reasons.

Chapter 8

Accusations against the Talmud

The acrimony that marked the emergence of Christianity from Judaism is reflected in the literature of both religious communities. The gospels and Pauline writings mirror the quarrels first century Jewish-Christians had with those of their compatriots who were unwilling to accept Jesus as the fulfillment of Israel's aspirations. Paul argued that the church had become the true Israel, that Christians, even gentiles, because of their faith had become the true, spiritual descendants of Abraham (Rom. 9:8). In a reflection of the intense rivalry that ensued between church and synagogue after the destruction of the second temple (70 C.E.), Matthew's gospel anachronistically portrayed the Scribes and Pharisees as Jesus's bitterest adversaries. It represented Jewish leadership as peculiarly responsible for the death of Jesus, for which the destruction of the temple was divine retribution (Mt. 27:25). For John's gospel the "*Ioudaioi*" typified all who oppose the gospel and therefore have the devil for a father (Jn. 8:44). For the visionary author of the Apocalypse, Jews were simply the "synagogue of Satan" (Rev. 3:9).

Here were the sources for all the themes subsequently developed by the church fathers from Justin Martyr to John Chrysostom and Augustine in their writings *contra Judaeos*. Given the volume of that literature and the threat it represented to rabbinical Judaism, it should not be surprising that the oral tradition from the same period, eventually recorded in the Babylonian Talmud, correspondingly contains anti-Christian references. The Talmud did not develop in a vacuum. If anything is surprising, it is how relatively few its anti-Christian references are.

Even for outsiders, the Talmud constitutes what Hermann Strack appropriately described as "one of the most remarkable literary productions of antiquity." Undoubtedly the most influential document in Jewish history, it defined Judaism for virtually all Jews for over a thousand years. Traditional or orthodox Judaism views revelation (Torah) as coming down from God on Mount Sinai not only in written form (the Pentateuch) but orally as well. Passed down one generation to another, the oral Torah was committed to writing (ca. 200 C.E.) in the Mishna, both an interpretation and augmentation of the Pentateuch. In relating the discussions of the sages on what constituted divine will and holiness for Israel, the Mishna reported divergences of opinion as well as majority decisions. Subsequent rabbinical discussions and commentary on the Mishna (known as *Gemara*) were compiled together with the Mishna to form the Jerusalem Talmud (ca. 400 C.E.), and later, the larger and much more influential Bavli, or Babylonian Talmud (ca. 600 C.E.). Embracing both written and oral Torah, the Babylonian Talmud came to be seen and studied as the single most authoritative document of Judaism.

Comprising sometimes as many as twenty folio volumes, the Babylonian Talmud embodies the labors of at least eight centuries of Jewish teachers.[1] It has been compared to an immense hall filled with hundreds of voices, as one divine decree after another is examined, debated, and applied to changing circumstances. In it one finds conflicting interpretations placed side by side, rejected opinions alongside the accepted. Together with laws (*halacha*), there are also exegetical explanations of biblical passages, legends, parables, anecdotes and aphorisms (*hagada*). Amid this assembly of disparate voices are multiple references to such typical elements of the ancient middle-eastern world-view as demons, omens, astrology and witchcraft. To an outsider the Talmud could hardly appear as anything but chaos. And it was precisely its chaotic form that rendered it liable to Christian misunderstanding and antagonism.

---

[1] Among the more accessible introductions to the Talmud in English are: Hermann J. Strack, *Introduction to the Talmud and Midrash* (Philadelphia: Jewish Publication Society, 1945); Moses Mielziner, *Introduction to the Talmud* (New York: Bloch, 1968); and the many works of Jacob Neusner, especially his *Invitation to the Talmud* (New York: Harper & Row, 1984).

Talmud on Trial

As late as the thirteenth century, Roman Catholics even at the highest levels were generally unaware that the Talmud even existed. It was then that Nicholas Donin, a Jew, came into conflict with the Jewish religious establishment and converted to Christianity. Possibly influenced by the Karaites, an eighth century Jewish sect that had rejected Talmudic tradition in favor of the written Scripture alone, Donin carried his opposition to the Talmud to Pope Gregory IX. The pope wrote to the kings of Christendom, including King Louis IX of France. Jews were ignoring the written law given to Moses and following an oral law called the Talmud, said to be the most important reason why the Jews remain obstinate in their perfidy.[2] Acceding to the pope's request, King Louis had the matter investigated. The result was the celebrated Paris disputation of 1240, a virtual trial of the Talmud, in which Rabbi Yehiel ben Yosef was called upon to defend the Talmud against Donin's charges.

Judaism was regarded by the medieval Catholic church as a licit though erroneous religion. Jewish religious practice was tolerated so long as Jews did not blaspheme Christianity or do anything to hinder its practice (such as proselytize Christians). But with the Talmud it seemed that Jews had set up a later tradition to rival the Scriptures (ironically an accusation that would be raised against the Catholic church five hundred years later by the Protestant reformers). The Parisian inquisitors had identified the Judaism of their day with the belief and practice of the Hebrew Bible. They were informed by Rabbi Yehiel that the Talmud, rather than being new or extraneous, constituted the essence of Judaism.

The principal charge pressed against the Talmud at the Paris disputation was that, along with foolish, unedifying material (such as representing God as grieving over Jewish exile or acknowledging a mistake), the Talmud contained blasphemy against the Christian faith. Donin had a creditable knowledge of the Talmud and his list of blasphemies against Christianity pointed out virtually all the passages subsequently cited by Christians in their attacks against it: slurs against Jesus and Mary; the

---

[2] Hyam Maccoby, ed., *Judaism on Trial: Jewish-Christian Disputations in the Middle Ages* (Rutherford: Fairleigh Dickinson University; London: Associated University Presses, 1982), 21–22.

equation of Christians with pagan idolaters; cursing them during daily prayer; and the charge that Jews were permitted to kill Christians.

Specific references to "Jesus of Nazareth" are exceedingly rare in the Talmud, but there are also references to a "Jesus ben Stada" and "Jesus ben Pandera," the son of Miriam the hairdresser. Yehiel argued that Jesus was a common name in first century Israel and that these Talmudic passages did not refer to the Jesus of Christianity ("Not every Louis is King of France").[3] The search for offensive passages narrowed down to two: one a necromantic vision of Jesus being punished in hell (Gittin 56b); the other an account of Jesus' execution on Passover eve by stoning on a charge of seducing Israel to idolatry (Sanhedrin 43a). The unhistorical nature of both passages indicates that third century Judaism had no independent information about Jesus; Jewish memory of him had died out. Both references were obvious attempts to counter Christian missionary efforts among Jews. When censorship of the Talmud came into operation, the offending passages referring to Jesus were among the first to be excised.[4]

As for attacks against Christians, the Talmud undoubtedly contains references hostile to gentiles, idolaters ("worshippers of stars and constellations"), and Jewish heretics (the so-called *minim*). The Talmud forbids certain forms of business and social intercourse with idolaters and reports one Rabbi Simeon as saying, "Kill the best of the gentiles" (Soferim, chapter 15, 41b). Jewish tradition also calls for the daily recitation of Eighteen Benedictions (*Shemone Esreh*), in which there is included a curse against the *minim,* the Jewish heretics.

Yehiel countered Donin's charges by pointing out correctly that many Talmudic laws in relation to idolaters were not being applied to

---

[3] Even if one accepts Yehiel's defence of more than one Jesus in the Talmud (many scholars do not), the Ben Stada and Ben Pandera references influenced the development of Jewish folk tales contained in the post-Talmudic, medieval *Toledot Yeshu.* Best described as a pseudo-history or counter-gospel, the *Toledot Yeshu* comes down in a variety of versions by different authors. They describe Jesus as illegitimate, leading a checkered career as a sorcerer and eventually executed. The main scholarly work on the topic is Samuel Krauss, *Das Leben Jesu nach juedischen Quellen* (1902). See also David Berger, "Jewish-Christian Polemics," *The Encyclopedia of Religion,* Mircea Eliade, ed. (New York, 1986), 389–95; and Morris Goldstein, *Jesus in the Jewish Tradition* (New York, 1950).

[4] Maccoby, *Judaism on Trial,* 26–30.

Christians, the prohibition of trading with them for example. The Talmudic sayings about gentiles and idolaters referred to the nations of the ancient world and must be read in context, he contended. The same was true of the quotation out of which Donin sought to make the most capital, one used time and again by antisemitic critics of the Talmud: "Kill the best of the gentiles." "In time of war," was Yehiel's immediate response. This saying, which never had the force of law, arose at a time of Roman persecution after the Bar Kochba revolt (135 C.E.). It maintains that an enemy in wartime may be killed without consideration for his personal character, no matter how admirable.[5]

Rabbi Yehiel's sharp distinction between Christians and idolaters, while understandable, was, in the thirteenth century at least, ahead of its time. The *minim,* or Jewish heretics, mentioned in the curse of the *Shemone Esreh,* would certainly include Jews who had left the practice of Judaism to become Christian. It corresponds to the *anathema* or excommunication which the church imposed on Christian heretics. As for Christians being idolaters, the state of Jewish law on the matter was confused. Medieval Jews generally regarded Christianity as an idolatrous religion. But laws prohibiting interaction with idolaters were not applied to Christians with any uniformity. Though considerable adjustments had been made by the thirteenth century, some laws regarding relationships with idolaters still pertained to Christians (e.g., the prohibition against drinking gentile wine for fear it had been used for idolatrous worship). It was not until the fourteenth century that a leading authority, Rabbi Menachem Meiri created a new legal category that distinguished peoples with a moral code, hence both Christians and Muslims, from the ancient pagan idolaters.[6]

In consequence of Meiri's distinction, medieval Jews took Christians as they found them. With some justification they often regarded themselves as a civilized people living among barbarians. When Christians treated life, including Jewish life, as cheap, they were regarded by Jews as idolaters. When they lived by standards of humanity and justice and applied them to Jews as well, Christians could be regarded as

---

[5] Maccoby, *Judaism on Trial,* 30–32.

[6] See Jacob Katz, *Exclusiveness and Tolerance: Studies in Jewish-Gentile Relations in Medieval and Modern Times* (London: Oxford University, 1961), 114–28.

coming under the covenant of Noah and included among the righteous of the nations.[7]

Blood Libel

The 1240 trial of the Talmud at Paris was followed by similar disputations at Barcelona (1263) and Tortosa in Spain (1413–1414). But in the meantime, a far more serious accusation against the Talmud arose in England, endangering the lives of Jews wherever an unexplained homicide occurred. From antiquity, through the middle ages, and well into the nineteenth century, blood was popularly regarded as having curative powers.[8] Long before the middle ages, moreover, Jews had acquired a reputation for being fortune-tellers, healers, and physicians. An extensive Christian folklore concerning Jewish magic existed by the end of the fifteenth century. But by this time the association of Jews with magic had further degenerated into an association of Jews with the demonic. For both the simple faithful and learned professors of the late middle ages, Jewish magic certainly existed, and the ritual murder of Christians by Jews was taken as a fact.[9]

The first recorded case of Jews being accused of ritual murder (the blood libel) was in Norwich, England (1144). When the body of a dead boy, William of Norwich, was discovered at Easter time, mob hysteria led to the charge that he had been tortured and murdered by Jews in imitation of Jesus' crucifixion. Similar accusations of torture and crucifixion were leveled against Jews at Gloucester, England (1168); at Blois, France (1171), and Saragossa, Spain (1182). At least seven times

---

[7]   David Novak, *Jewish-Christian Dialogue: A Jewish Justification* (New York; Oxford: Oxford University, 1989), 40, 53; Maccoby, *Judaism on Trial,* 32–34.

[8] Hermann Strack, *The Jew and Human Sacrifice* (New York: Bloch, 1909), 50–76.

[9] R. Po-Chia Hsia, *The Myth of Ritual Murder: Jews and Magic in Reformation Germany,* (New Haven; London: Yale, 1988), 12. The classic study of Jewish culture in the middle ages is Joshua Trachtenberg, *Jewish Magic and Superstition,* (New York: Macmillan, 1970). On the ritual murder charge, see his *The Devil and the Jews: the Medieval Conception of the Jews and Its Relation to Modern Antisemitism* (Philadelphia: Jewish Publication Society, 1983), 124–55. There is a vast literature on the blood libel; for a select bibliography see Cecil Roth, *The Ritual Murder Libel and the Jew: The report by Cardinal Lorenzo Ganganelli (Pope Clement XIV)* (London: Woburn, 1935), 111–12.

in the twelfth century, twenty-four in the thirteenth, instances of unexplained homicides led to Jews being accused of murder because of their sadistic hatred for Christianity and the innocent. To these original motifs there arose the idea in Germany (Fulda, 1236), that Jews used blood for medicinal remedies. Later in eastern Europe a further motif originated that Jews used blood for the preparation of unleavened bread (*matzoth*), or wine for Passover.

The blood libel disappeared from western Europe after the fourteenth century, with the expulsion of Jews from England and France. It then became prominent in the German-speaking lands, where the incidence of charges, trials, and executions reached their climax in the fifteenth and sixteenth centuries. Vigorous interventions on the part of the emperors eventually contributed to the suppression of the trials and the dwindling of judicial investigations, but popular belief in child murder by Jews remained widespread and strong well into the nineteenth century.[10]

The popes gave little credence to this libel, even those who were otherwise unsympathetic to Jews. Innocent IV (1247) issued the earliest papal pronouncement on the matter and forbade the accusation under pain of suspension from office and excommunication. His successors published similar protests. Neither the thirteenth century trials of the Talmud nor the anti-Talmudic Karaites had ever accused Talmudic Jews of using Christian blood for their rituals. But despite the papal remonstrances, the allegations continued to spread eastward, from the German-speaking lands into the Slavic territories that included Poland.

The kings of Poland, like the popes and other rulers in Europe, condemned the ritual murder accusations: Bolesław V (1264), Casimir III (1334), Casimir IV (1453), and Stephan Batory (1576).[11] In two decrees (1564 and 1566), King Zygmunt August enjoined local authorities not to institute proceeding against Jews on charges of ritual murder or desecration of hosts unless substantiated by the testimony of four Christian and three Jewish witnesses. King Stephan Batory not only forbade the impeachment of Jews on the charge of ritual murder (1576), he intervened on behalf of the Jews of Poznań, where there resided a large German middle class unsympathetic to Jews. He reminded Poznań's hostile magistrates that Jews were not to be judged by the German,

---

[10] Hsia, *Myth of Ritual Murder,* 2–4.

[11] Roth, *The Ritual Murder Libel,* 100.

Magdeburg laws but by Polish common law in addition to their own rabbinical courts for internal disputes. With the death of Batory, however, charges of ritual murder became a regular occurrence in Poland, thanks not only to a hostile German middle-class but to a hostile Polish Catholic clergy.[12]

In 1589, Father Przesław Mojecki wrote a book (*Okrucieństwo żydowskie*) on Jewish cruelty, murder, and superstition; in it he enumerated some forty cases from all over Europe but especially Poland in which Jews were accused of ritual murder and host desecration. In 1618, Sebastian Miczyński, a master of the Kraków Academy, in a similar work (*Zwierciadło Korony Polskiej*) accused Jews of murder, swindling, sacrilege, and witchcraft. He called upon the government to expel the Jews from Poland as they had been in England, France, and Spain. Kraków's Jews appealed to the crown for help against the possibility of a riot, and King Zygmunt III had the book confiscated. Miczyński was denounced in the parliament as a demagogue and menace to public safety, but he was also upheld as a champion of truth. When pictures and caricatures came from Germany depicting ritual murders, a number of them found their way into Polish churches. In 1745, the first Polish encyclopedia simply took it for granted that Jews made use of Christian blood, a fact proven by the number of murder trials that had taken place. During the previous century (1556 to 1637), some twenty-one cases of ritual murder had been tried in Poland.[13]

In the opinion of a leading Jewish historian, Salo Baron, "the number of victims sentenced to death by Polish courts, including Jews condemned for alleged offenses against the Catholic faith, was always comparatively small, compared with the numbers in leading West-European nations."[14] In the eighteenth century, however, the incidence of ritual murder accusations led Poland's Jewish community to send a delegate to Rome (1758) to appeal for protection from Pope Benedict XIV . The result was the report of Lorenzo Ganganelli, a Franciscan friar who went on to

---

[12] S. M. Dubnow, *History of the Jews in Russia and Poland*, trans. by I. Friedlaender (Philadelphia: Jewish Publication Society, 1916–1920), 1:88–95.

[13] Meyer Balaban, "Antisemitismus," *Encyclopaedia Judaica* (Berlin: Eschkol: 1928–1934), 2:1002–4; Dubnow, *History*, 1:96–97.

[14] Salo Wittmayer Baron, *A Social and Religious History of the Jews*, 2nd. rev. ed. (New York: Columbia, 1976), 16:88. See also 16:101.

become a Cardinal and eventually Pope Clement XIV. The Jewish complaint was that, whenever a dead body was found anywhere, Jews in the locality would be charged with ritual murder, tried, convicted, and executed. After receiving detailed statements from the local Polish bishops, Ganganelli, convinced of Jewish innocence, submitted a report to the pope with his conclusions.

Ganganelli pointed out the long history of papal protests against the ritual murder charge and the fact that only two cases of "child martyrdom" at Jewish hands had ever been recognized by the church (Simon of Trent in 1475 and Andreas of Rinn in 1747). Those two isolated events were not enough to establish a Jewish practice, and Ganganelli criticized the assumption of guilt by association. When a corpse was discovered, Jews were suspected "by reason of the predominant prejudice against them." Ganganelli closed his report with the hope that the Holy See would protect the Jews of Poland as it had previously protected those of Germany and France.[15]

Ganganelli's report was accepted (1760) and instructions sent to the papal nuncio in Poland. Elsewhere, however, Ganganelli's report remained virtually unknown for over a century, until it was discovered in the archives of the Jewish community in Rome and published in 1888. In the meantime, despite the "age of Enlightenment," the blood libel continued to be taken seriously and at least twenty-two incidents occurred, including the celebrated Tisza-Eszlar case in Hungary (1882). In this century, at the notorious Beilis case in Kiev (1911–1913), Father Justin Pranaitis, a priest-professor at the Catholic Academy at Saint Petersburg, served as a self-styled expert and witness for the prosecution. He doggedly upheld that Jewish ritual murder was a fact. He denied the authenticity of the Ganganelli document until the defence produced a Vatican statement verifying it.[16]

For antisemites eager to believe it, the long history of accusations was evidence enough for the veracity of Jewish ritual murder charges. In 1892 the *Osservatore Cattolico* in Milan published forty-four articles on the

---

[15] Roth, *Ritual Murder Libel*, 73, 92, 94.

[16] Roth, *Ritual Murder Libel*, 17, 34–35. For a list of the incidents of blood libel from its origins through this century, see H. Bachtold-Stäubli, *Handwörterbuch des deutschen Aberglaubens* (Berlin; New York: Gruyter, 1987), 7:728–33.

certainty of the practice.[17] A series of essays in Monsignor Jouin's *Revue des Sociétés Secretes,* subsequently republished as a book (1914), did the same.[18] The practice of these antisemitic journals was to report allegations without any criticism regarding their credibility. Invariably these journals also appealed to the scholarship of Christian "experts" on the Talmud.

Christian Experts

Christian criticism of the Talmud did not end with the medieval trials nor was it limited to the blood libel. In the early sixteenth century the attacks of Johannes Pfefferkorn, an apostate from Judaism, were answered by the Christian humanist and Hebraist, Johannes Reuchlin. The ultimate outcome of the heated debate was that, instead of being condemned, the Talmud was published at the command of Pope Leo X (1520), along with a Latin translation. With the onset of the Reformation, certain Protestant groups (e.g., sabbatarians) appeared to Catholic eyes to be reverting to Judaism. Jews could counter that their adherence to an ongoing tradition and not Scripture alone gave them a greater affinity to Catholicism.

As part of that ongoing tradition, Joseph Caro, a Spanish Jew living in what is now Israel drew up the *Shulchan Aruch,* a code of Jewish law drawn from the Talmud. Published in 1565, the new code met with serious objections by European Jews, until Rabbi Moses Isserles of Kraków supplemented and explained it on the basis of European Jewish practice. When published in Kraków with his authoritative additions (1588), the *Shulchan Aruch* became accepted as the code of Jewish law *par excellence.* As such it was assailed along with the Talmud as hostile to Christians.

The first Christian "expert" to attack the Talmud and *Shulchan Aruch* was Johannes Andreas Eisenmenger, a Protestant professor of oriental languages at the University of Heidelberg. His book *Entdecktes Judenthum* (Judaism Uncovered) created the impression that Judaism contained something mysterious and esoteric which Jews wanted to keep

---

[17] Strack, *The Jew and Human Sacrifice,* 170–73.

[18] Albert Monniot, *Le Crime rituel chez les Juifs* (Paris: Pierre Tequi, 1914).

from Christian eyes. Published in 1700, it was the result of twenty years' labor—two volumes of over two thousand pages. Eisenmenger drew from over two hundred Hebrew, Aramaic, and Arabic sources for his work, quoting them in full and translating them literally into German.

Contrary to subsequent accusations, Eisenmenger did not falsify his sources. But he did read them with a conspicuous bias. His declared purpose was to help Jews recognize their errors and acknowledge the truth of Christianity. To this end he portrayed Judaism in terms of foolishness and immorality. Listing the allegations of ritual murder, he left their veracity undecided, but left no doubt as to his own suspicions.[19] His principal criticism, however, was that Jewish law was immoral, especially those norms determining behavior toward non-Jews. He charged that, when it came to interacting with non-Jews, the Talmud and subsequent rabbinic literature permitted Jews to practice deception, perjury, and disloyalty to the state.[20]

Although a bigot, Eisenmenger was an honest scholar. His translations were at times erroneous and his interpretations one-sided, but in addition to the references for his citations, he reproduced the original wording. On a much lower level of both scholarship and integrity two centuries later was the Austrian priest, August Rohling. A professor at Prague and a minor prelate, Rohling had discovered Eisenmenger's erstwhile forgotten *Entdecktes Judenthum*. In 1871 he published *Der Talmudjude* (The Talmud Jew), in which he accused the Talmud of permitting Jews to commit all manner of crimes against gentiles: deceit, perjury, destruction of property. Ritual murder, he wrote, consisted not in Christian blood being consumed but simply shed. He made the unprovable assertion that there existed a secret Jewish tradition of ritual murder handed down orally from generation to generation. Rohling's book sold thousands of copies. Christian scholars (Franz Delitzsch; Hermann Strack) criticized it severely, however, and it was soon made apparent that Rohling was disgracefully ignorant of the Talmud. The Austrian priest was unable to

---

[19] After his lengthy list of Christians alleged to have been murdered by Jews, Einsenmenger concluded: "Everyone can guess that not everything is bound to be untrue. But I leave it undecided whether the matter is or not." Quoted in Strack, *The Jew and Human Sacrifice*, 169.

[20] Jacob Katz, *From Prejudice to Destruction: Anti-Semitism, 1700–1933* (Cambridge: Harvard, 1980), 13–22.

read it in the original language and had plagiarized from Eisenmenger, copying even the erroneous numbers of his citations.[21]

Posing as a Talmudic scholar, Rohling served as an "expert" witness for the prosecution and defended the accusation of ritual murder in the Tisza-Eszlar trial in Hungary (1882). Father Justin Pranaitis did the same, as mentioned above, in connection with the Beilis case at Kiev (1911–1913). Pranaitis plundered both from Rohling and Eisenmenger for his book, *Christianus in Talmude Judaeorum* (1892). Here too the plagiarism was apparent from the errors in the citations. In Poland, Rohling and Pranaitis were imitated by Andrzej Niemojewski (1920), and in the 1930s by Ignacy Charszewski and Stanisław Trzeciak. When they could not cite the Talmud from the original, these Christian "experts" cited one another, a standard practice in antisemitic "scholarship." They also read the New Testament's polemical references to the Pharisees as if completely accurate and objective. It was inconceivable to them that the gospels could have a biased, unhistorical view of the Talmud's pharisaic sages. But this was also true of some of the most honored and influential Catholic scholars to write in the first half of this century.[22]

Père Marie-Joseph Lagrange, a Dominican priest and founder of the École Biblique in Jerusalem, is generally regarded as the father of modern Catholic biblical scholarship. His opinion of the Talmudic sages may be found in two major books he wrote on Judaism.[23] In his book *Le Messianisme chez les Juifs,* Lagrange criticized the rabbis of the Talmud for being "arbitrary and artificial" (p. 142), guilty of "deliberate dissimulation" and "equivocal goodwill" (p. 144). That his was hardly an objective evaluation is clear from the fact that Lagrange read the antisemitic arguments of his day back 1900 years: with no evidence whatever, he wrote that Jews "then like today undoubtedly had a monopoly on certain trades, to say nothing of the management of money" (p. 276). Lagrange went on to write that the educated Jews of our century should blush with shame at what the Talmud says about Jesus, but that

---

[21] Strack, *The Jew and Human Sacrifice,* 156–60.

[22] For an overview of the antisemitic bias of Catholic and Protestant theologians in this century, see Charlotte Klein, *Anti-Judaism in Christian Theology,* trans. by Edward Quinn (Philadelphia: Fortress, 1978). Her focus, however, is almost entirely on Germany.

[23] Marie-Joseph Lagrange, O.P., *Le Messianisme chez les Juifs,* (Paris: J. Gabalda, 1909); *Le Judaisme avant Jesus-Christ* (Paris: J. Gabalda, 1931).

they only feel hatred for him (p. 290). As for the Talmud's attitude toward Christians, it is to do as much harm as possible whenever possible, but, when constrained to be peaceful, to keep a careful distance (p. 292).

In his 1931 book, *Le Judaisme avant Jesus-Christ,* Lagrange went beyond his earlier work and quite beyond the polemics of Matthew's gospel. The Pharisees, he wrote, forced their interpretations of the Scripture on Israel out of pride and a presumption of an authority they did not have (p. 274). In comparison to Christianity which he characterized in terms of universal love, Lagrange faulted the Pharisees for nationalism. Indeed their main fault of was "to make religious zeal a reason for avoiding cordial relations with their neighbors and almost a duty to despise them as impure" (p. 275). The Pharisee, he wrote,

"is a hypocrite, for he pretends to be living among the saints.... he quotes the law, but in order to deceive.... our man carefully conceals his luxurious life: after nights of debauchery he presents himself behind the smiling mask of innocence.... He goes inside a house and, like a serpent, tries to seduce the innocent with his cunning words. When he has undermined one house, he passes to another and pursues his secret intrigues, insatiable as Hades."[24]

Where did Lagrange get all of this from? Not from the gospels, but—it has been perceptively suggested—from Eduard Drumont, the notorious antisemite of the Dreyfus era.[25]

Lagrange enjoyed an immense authority among Catholics in the first half of this century; his legacy was carried on by a whole subsequent generation of scholars. Among them was Joseph Bonsirven, S.J., who studied under Lagrange in Jerusalem and made the Talmud a particular focus of his scholarly interest. In his 1928 book on Judaism after Jesus,[26] Bonsirven could be effusive in expressing admiration for traditional Judaism, its "great and magnificent riches," its "pure and

---

[24] Lagrange, *Le Judaisme,* 160.

[25] Klein, *Anti-Judaism,* 88.

[26] Joseph Bonsirven, *Sur les Ruines du Temple où le Judaisme après Jésus-Christ* (Paris: 1928), cited here from the English translation, *On the Ruins of the Temple: Judaism after Our Lord's Time* (London: Burns Oates & Washbourne, 1931).

elevated moral doctrine," and "deeply religious piety." But Bonsirven apparently felt constrained to justify such novel praise for Judaism. He explained that it should come as no surprise since Judaism could draw inspiration from the Hebrew Scriptures (p. 273).

Bonsirven could still criticize Jewish faults with no comparable critique of Catholic history and practice, however. With no mention of the anti-Jewish animus of Christians, he averred that in the first centuries of Christianity the attitude of most Jews toward Jesus was one of "venomous hatred" (p. 71). Modern Jews, he admitted, were more sympathetic to Jesus, but there were still areas where "backward, closed Jewries...use their horror of Christianity as a means of preservation" (p. 73). Likewise, though more modern Jews had tempered their hostility toward Christians, "so persistent a hatred could not disappear without leaving some traces" (p. 76). Because Judaism had rejected Jesus, "the only one who could broaden and transfigure it," Jews, concluded Bonsirven, were "peevishly hostile to all strangers," guilty of a "narrow spirit" and "pitiful superstition" (p. 274–75). On the ruins of the Temple, the rabbis "surrounded the Law and the chosen people with manifold and thorny hedges; ...the walls of the Temple had crumbled and in revenge [!] they erected the somber ramparts of the Ghetto" (p. 274).

Bonsirven was equally equivocal in his two-volume work on Palestinian Judaism at the time of Jesus.[27] Rabbinic literature, he admitted, was filled with "magnificent" statements about justice and charity. One might even be tempted to conclude that the highest summits of Christian morality were already to be found in early pharisaic Judaism. But it just was not so, Bonsirven insisted. When the Talmudic sages spoke of love of neighbor, they meant only their fellow Israelites. Jewish scholars had frequently pointed out that nowhere in the Hebrew Scriptures or Talmudic tradition was there to be found the saying attributed to them by Matthew's gospel: "You shall love your neighbor and hate your enemy" (Mt. 5:43). This was the teaching of the sectarian Essenes, not of the Pharisees and their Talmudic successors. Bonsirven refused to accept the Jewish protestations to the contrary; he insisted that, although explainable and excusable, "hatred for enemies remains the ordinary and normal attitude" of Jews for pagans and apostates (p. 200).

---

[27] Joseph Bonsirven, S.J., *Le Judaisme Palestinien au temps de Jésus-Christ* (Paris: Gabriel Beauchesne, 1935). Citations in the text are from the second volume.

Bonsirven admitted that alongside particularist attitudes recommending hatred of enemies the Talmud contained universalist statements recommending love. He was sure, though, that the particularist principle remained the ordinary rule (202). Because gentiles were the enemies of God and inclined to the most odious sins, orthodox Jews avoided contact with them unless it was impossible or advantageous. Moreover, in addition to their "self-centered and hostile particularism," Talmudic Jews had a predilection for the material aspects of religion. By multiplying external observances, like the wearing of phylacteries, they were guilty of confusing the frontiers between religion and superstition (314, 317). Needless to say, Bonsirven made no references to the particularism inherent in the long-standing Catholic doctrine of no salvation outside the church, nor to the possibility that some Catholic practices might look like superstition to outsiders.

Such were the sentiments of the most eminent Catholic scholars writing on Judaism in the first half of this century. Whatever good was to be found in Judaism came from the pre-Christian Hebrew Scriptures. Whatever came after, like the Talmud, was little more than legalism, exclusivism, and hostility to outsiders. Even in the most sophisticated and scholarly Catholic circles, the tone might be more muted and the polemical charges seasoned with equivocal praise, but the centuries-old allegations and self-serving comparisons were still there. And, as in France, Catholic writers continued to raise the perennial accusations against the Talmud in Poland.

Traditional Accusations in Poland

For Father Seweryn Kowalski, writing in the Catholic Action bi-monthly, *Ruch Katolicki*, Jews were a chosen people who had been led astray from their "mission" by the teaching of the Talmud. Under the influence of blind leaders, Israel succumbed to the temptation of Satan and traded its chosenness for a "defiant claim to political, moral and cultural primacy." The Pharisees, wrote Kowalski, were "unworthy" men who had changed the religion of the one God into a "fanatical nationalism." Like other Catholic scholars of his generation, Kowalski read the gospels of Matthew and John as objective history. The Pharisees had become "renegades and apostates," the natural antagonists of Jesus' teaching.

But Jews were guilty of more than rejecting Jesus: "The anti-Christian attitude of Jews has always united this people to the spirit of the antichrist, wherever it appears. Masonry, godless communism, atheistic socialism, frivolous liberalism, consistently recruit Jewish members in significance measures; Jews are always their natural allies." But Israel's infidelity was at the basis of it all. Jews from the time of Jesus have been compelled to wander the nations of the earth, "committing terrible crimes and doing penance for them." Everywhere they were exiled and expelled, treated as despised intruders. And as the martyrs in Russia and the burning churches in Spain testified, woe to the nation that lets them come to power.

For traditionalist Christians like Father Kowalski, a 1500-year-old theology afforded a ready explanation for the calamities Jews were suffering in Europe. The "avenging hand of God" was weighing heavy on the Jewish people. Because their Talmudic spirit inclined Jews to reject any hand extended to them in friendship, the Jewish question would never be resolved. Only at the end of time would Jews convert to Jesus "whom they crucified." Although hatred of Jews was contrary to the spirit of Christianity, Christian nations had no choice but wage a war of self-defense, for any Jew living by the precepts of the Talmud was on principle an "enemy of Christianity and of every Christian." A clear proof for Kowalski were the blasphemies it contains with reference to Jesus and his mother.

The Talmud, it followed, could not be regarded as a religious book obliging Christians to practice tolerance. Those Catholics who defended Jews erred either out of ignorance or a soft-heartedness that was out of place in this matter. Jews were apostates from the faith of Abraham. The "Old Testament" was a preparation for the New Testament and found its explanation and justification in Jesus. Jews who embraced Christianity would not have to give up their scriptures, only the Talmud, "a work of human hatred and despair."[28]

The sentiments expressed by Kowalski were profoundly traditional. They need to be seen within the context of the Catholic attitude toward all other religions before the 1960s revolution that was the Second Vatican Council. That attitude was expressed at the same time in *Prąd* by Father J. Kruszyński. Buddhism, he wrote, was flawed by pessimism and Islam by fatalism. All religions outside of Christianity were based on psychological foundations, corresponding to the psychology of a given

---

[28] *Ruch Katolicki,* 6 (1936): 312–16.

nation or race. Kruszyński's self-serving comparisons were based not only on minimal experience with other religions but also an exclusivist theology of revelation. Biblical Judaism surpassed all other religions in the ancient world, because it was not a work of the human mind. But once the Talmud replaced the Bible as the foundation for Jewish faith and practice, it was for Christianity to continue the religion of ancient Israel. Kruszyński acknowledged that the Talmud contained no independent tradition regarding Jesus, only an echo of the gospel reports, recorded, however, with "prejudice and hate."[29]

Catholic journalists as well as academics interested themselves in the intricacies of Jewish law. Jakób Polak wrote an entire series of articles on it for the readers of the popular *Przegląd Katolicki*. In the tradition of Eisenmenger and Rohling, he applied to Christians without qualification what the Talmud says about idolaters. It was clear to him that Talmudic law allowed Jews to deceive Christians and to be indifferent to their misfortune. What Jews call the "ocean of the Talmud" was rather, he declared, a "smelly pool." That the *Shulchan Aruch* called for Jews to observe the law of the land, was explained by Polak as possibly some kind of "Jewish trick." [30]

Polak exemplified how Christians misunderstood Judaism by defining it in exclusively Christian categories. The functions of rabbis, he noted correctly, were quite different from those of Catholic priests. No rabbi was necessary in order to conduct synagogue services or perform ceremonies like circumcision or marriage. Any adult Jewish male could read from the Torah and speak at a service. This led Polak to question why the Polish government paid salaries for rabbis to serve as chaplains in the army. Rabbis, he insisted, had no religious function comparable to the clergy of other faiths.[31] Polak also criticized the way the Yiddish press referred to priests, as *galoch* (unshaven) or worse as *komer,* the word for a pagan priest. He singled out for criticism the traditional Jewish practice of saying or writing *le-havdil* (to be separated), to distinguish the pure from the impure. Not only would Jews use the

---

[29] *Prąd,* 31 (1936): 263–85.

[30] *Przegląd Katolicki,* 75 (1937): 117–19; 149–50; 181–82; 193–94; 327–29.

[31] *Przegląd Katolicki,* 77 (1939): 164–66.

phrase when referring to, say, a "Jew (*le-havdil*) and his horse," but when referring in the same phrase to "rabbis (*le-havdil*) and priests."[32]

As indicated above, the most extreme and unabashed expressions of antisemitism in the Polish Catholic press regularly came from *Pro Christo,* a monthly published for "young Catholics." Here one could find justifications for Catholic totalitarianism and hatred for Jews in the name of love. Here, as late as the 1930s, one could also find the ritual murder accusation taken seriously. At least two articles had appeared earlier in *Pro Christo* on the topic. A 1926 book on ritual murder by Russian emigré Eugen Brant had been favorably reviewed by Wojciech Zajęty. Much impressed by Brant's scrupulous documentation, Zajęty also expressed his esteem for ritual murder expert Father Justin Pranaitis, who had been "furiously attacked by the Jewish Masons and judeophile press."[33] A 1929 article in *Pro Christo* reminded its readers that Andreas of Rinn and Simon of Trent had both been declared blessed by the Vatican for having been "martyred" by Jews. Polish readers were reminded too of a series of articles in Rome's Jesuit *Civiltà Cattolica* (1881–1882) which had described their deaths as the result of Jewish "hatred of the faith."[34]

In 1935 the blood libel appeared in *Pro Christo* once again, this time in an article under the title, "Bloody Christian legend or bloody Jewish superstition." The author, Monsignor Ignacy Charszewski, had written a book, *Synowie Szatana* (Sons of Satan), which made mention of ritual murder by Jews. Charszewski was ridiculed in a review by Tadeusz Zaderecki, a non-Jew who actually was an expert on the Talmud, and who accused Charszewski of writing nonsense and making a fool of himself. Charszewski responded to the review in the pages of *Pro Christo* by attempting to substitute ridicule for argument.

A student of Father Pranaitis, Charszewski admitted that he was no Hebraist. But that did not prevent him from flatly asserting that "ritual murder has a basis in the religious books of Judaism." His proof consisted of several Jewish texts into which he read his anti-Jewish convictions. Against the papal statements criticizing the ritual murder

---

[32] *Przegląd Katolicki,* 77 (1939): 187.

[33] *Pro Christo,* 3 (1927): 224–27.

[34] *Pro Christo,* 5 (1929): 281–84.

accusation, Charszewski referred to the papal decrees permitting devotion to Simon of Trent and Andreas of Rinn. He concluded that ritual murder was not therefore a priori excluded by papal decree. Furthermore, he argued, Jesus himself prophesied about the practice in John's gospel: "The hour will come when anyone who kills you will think he is doing honor to God" (Jn. 16:2). Charszewski arbitrarily translated the Greek word for honor (*latreia*) as "ritual sacrifice." Even though the Russian court had found Mendel Beilis not guilty in the celebrated trial in Kiev, Charszewski had no doubt but that a ritual murder had been committed.

The reason Jews perform ritual murder, the priest continued, was that they secretly believed that innocent Christian blood purifies them from sin. Sometimes the ritual is performed with lacerations, sometimes the throat is cut as with the ritual slaughter of animals (*shehitah*), and sometimes out of fear it is made to look like an ordinary homicide. How did Christians know all this? Certainly they could not have possibly thought it up themselves. Such "Christian perfidy," wrote Charszewski, would be unthinkable.[35]

The views of Monsignor Charszewski and *Pro Christo* were extreme and not representative of the Polish Catholic press. They warrant citation here, however, because they were tolerated by those charged with surveillance of Catholic orthodoxy. Not quite orthodox from the 1930s Catholic perspective were the views of Charszewski's chief critic, Tadeusz Zaderecki. In response to him and other Christian "experts," Zaderecki published *Talmud w ogniu wieków* (The Talmud in the Fire of the Centuries) in 1936, a scholarly explanation and defense of the Talmud. He wrote of the religious significance of the Talmud and its many points of similarity to Christianity. But such views were too novel, too revolutionary, for clerics steeped in Catholic tradition.

In the *Ateneum Kapłańskie,* a monthly published specifically for priests, Father W. Gronkowski wrote a review highly critical of Zaderecki's book. Zaderecki had made a point of informing his readers that he was a Christian and not of Jewish background. With a time-honored gambit, Father Gronkowski suggested that he had his doubts. Zaderecki had a genuine command of the Talmud, the priest admitted, but knew too little about the Bible and Catholic Christianity to make an objective evaluation of Talmudic doctrine. For Zaderecki to ascribe historical value to the

---

[35] *Pro Christo,* 11/1 (1935): 38–48.

Talmud and find points of similarity between it and Christianity was to contradict so eminent a Catholic scholar as Père Lagrange. The tactics of the Talmud, according to Lagrange, were to harm Christians at every opportunity and otherwise avoid them as much as possible. Here was authority enough for Gronkowski. Christianity had points of similarity with the Hebrew scriptures because it completed and fulfilled biblical Judaism. The Talmud, Gronkowski assured his clerical readers, had no religious significance whatever for Christians. It was not the heir of biblical Judaism but its disfigurement. Talmudic Judaism was a religion of hatred unworthy of the name religion.[36]

Gronkowski did not limit his assault on Zaderecki's book to one review. In a series of articles appearing in the official monthly organ of the Archdiocese of Gniezno-Poznań, the priest criticized orthodox rabbis for neglecting the Bible and occupying themselves almost exclusively with the Talmud. He accused them of ascribing "infallibility" to the Talmud and believing in it "blindly." He then went on to apply norms of historical criticism to the Talmud that he would have certainly refused to apply to the Christian scriptures or tradition. The Talmud's teachings did not come from Moses, Gronkowski insisted; an unbroken chain of oral tradition was untenable and improbable. Tracing an oral Torah back to Moses was a "deception" of which gullible Jews were the victims. Once again Gronkowski cited Père Lagrange as contradicting Zaderecki's defense of the Talmud. He was sure that the rabbis of the Talmud were filled with such hatred for Jesus that "enlightened" Jews were embarrassed at their former teachers.[37]

Monsignor Stanisław Trzeciak, cited frequently in these pages, did not limit his assaults to Jewish communists and secularists. Religious Jews too came under attack in his book on the Talmud and gentiles.[38] Like most other antisemitic "experts" on the Talmud, Trzeciak read it in translation and misunderstood the nature of its composition. He regarded every opinion in it as binding. In the time-honored tradition, he focused on what the Talmudic sages had to say about idolaters and then applied

---

[36] *Ateneum Kapłańskie,* 38 (1936): 410–15.

[37] *Miesięcznik Kościelny,* 52 (1937): 68–74, 207–15, 287–96, 387–97; 53 (1938): 223–28.

[38] Stanisław Trzeciak, *Talmud o Goyach a Kwestja Żydowska w Polsce* (Warszawa: Prabucki, 1939).

it to Christian Poles. Here, he wrote, was a mirror of Jewish soul. It was imperative that Poles as a "host nation" know what their Jewish "sub-tenants" thought about them.

The Talmud, wrote Trzeciak, explained why Jews were "alien" and even "hostile" in their relationships to outsiders (p. 10). Its dietary precepts made it impossible for Jews and gentiles to share meals and therefore interact socially (p. 32). The Talmud, he alleged, viewed gentiles and their homes as impure, so that a Jew is contaminated and rendered ritually impure by the slightest contact with them (p. 29). Jewish law regarded gentiles with repugnance and equated them with cattle, prompting Jews to create ghettos freely of their own accord (p. 36). Jews tried to persuade "naive Christians" that the idolaters in the Talmud were the ancient pagans; they would act in an apparently friendly way toward those who did not see through them. But the priest had no doubt but that a line spoken by a character in a Yiddish novel represented true Jewish thinking: Jews deny that gentiles have souls (p. 43).

But Poles could take a lesson from Jews when it came to national consciousness and solidarity. Trzeciak appealed to the Talmud as justifying his own political and economic ideas. He cited at length Talmudic discussions about bread, fish, wine, and milk prepared or handled by non-Jews. The Talmud's dietary laws constituted an "uncompromising boycott" not only of human relationships but of life's most elementary needs. Poles could profit from its wisdom. If its laws were good for Jews, why not for Poles? (p. 11)

Trzeciak cited Pope Clement VIII, whose "great solicitude" for the church had led him to ban the printing and distribution of the "impious" Talmud. Reasonable Jews were ashamed of the respect they once showed this collection of nonsense. Its attitude toward non-Jews explained why so few Jews converted to Christianity and why Jews did harm to the church. Jesus fought against the principles of the Talmud, wrote the priest, and so had the church. So too must every Christian who wanted to follow Jesus, especially priests.

Not surprisingly, Monsignor Trzeciak's book on the Talmud enjoyed a more favorable reception in the Catholic press than did Zaderecki's. The prelate's book was "important" reading, wrote Father I. Olszewski, especially for philosemites. To know the Talmud was to take away the mask and see the Jewish soul for what it was. Olszewski did not feel competent to judge the accuracy of Trzeciak's presentation, but he was impressed by the string of quotations. Jewish blood might not be any worse than any other, but anyone influenced by the Talmud was surely uncongenial, wrote the priest-reviewer. The Talmud and learned rabbis alone were capable of making one antisemitic.[39] Similarly Janusz Koziński in the *Przegląd Katolicki* raised a suggestion made earlier in the Sejm, that the Polish government sponsor a translation of the Talmud into Polish. Koziński wanted the Polish masses to be aware of what he called "terrible blasphemies against all that is most sacred and dear for the Christian religion."[40]

In the *Przegląd Powszechny,* the Talmud came under attack by Father Józef Kruszyński, a professor at the University of Lublin and long-time antagonist of traditional Judaism.[41] Polish Catholics, he wrote, might be impressed by what appeared to be the "deep religiosity" of those Jewish masses who observed the Talmud, who refrained from smoking or taking long walks on the sabbath. But the religious life of orthodox Jews was shallow, Kruszyński assured his readers. Its essence was the formalistic performance of empty practices in order to receive one's due. Even on Yom Kippur a visit to a synagogue disclosed nothing like what Catholics called a "spirit of prayer." Judaism had broken with Moses and the prophets and at fault lay the Talmud, the "source of hatred" Jews had for gentiles, especially Christians, and the reason why Jews could not co-exist peacefully with other people.

Because of their Talmudic mentality, Kruszyński continued, religious Jews were hostile to Poland's Catholic culture and incapable of assimilating into it. But more disturbing were precisely those Jews who had given up Talmudic tradition without becoming Christian, the Jews who were active and involved in the media, arts, and especially education. Poland, wrote the priest, was being infiltrated and poisoned by Jewish thinking, by a conscious attempt to efface the values of Christian culture. Antisemitism had arisen and grown so powerful precisely as a self-defense. Kruszyński regretted the violence but, on both the economic and cultural fronts, war was necessary. German racism was a degenerate

---

[39] *Przegląd Katolicki,* 77 (1939): 386–87.

[40] *Przegląd Katolicki,* 77 (1939): 187.

[41] His earlier anti-Jewish publications included *Antysemityzm, Antyjudaism, Antygoizm* (Włocławek, 1924), and *Talmud co zawiera i co naucza* (Lublin, 1925). See Celia S. Heller, *On the Edge of Destruction: Jews of Poland between the Two World Wars* (New York: Schocken, 1980), 316, n.69.

glorification of zoological hatred, and Poland could not employ its methods. But Jews constituted a greater danger in Poland than anywhere else.[42]

Such were the interwar accusations of Polish Catholics against the Talmud, most of them centuries old. Polish critics had a long tradition of animosity to draw on. That the tradition went back virtually to the origins of Christianity is generally recognized. That the animosity was more often than not mutual may be conceded. If Jews equated Christians with pagan idolaters, the Catholic church correspondingly consigned Jews to the same fiery eternal fate as pagans, heretics, and schismatics (Council of Florence, 1442). There was a poignant irony, however, for Catholics to hold that outside the church there was no salvation and then accuse Jews of particularism and narrowness. To say nothing of Jew-hating Christians condemning Jews for hating Christians.

The best that mainstream Catholics could say about the Talmud was enunciated by Joseph Bonsirven, that there was much to admire within Jewish tradition but it came from the Hebrew scriptures. Anything arising within Judaism after Jesus and the destruction of the second temple was at best dismissed as being without religious significance or value. As a vital religious force, Judaism was regarded as having come to an end.

The Second Vatican Council (*Nostra Aetate,* 1965) is correctly seen as a revolution for the Catholic attitude toward Jews and Judaism, an unprecedented about-face. The Council, however, said nothing about the Talmud or ongoing Jewish tradition. Subsequent Vatican statements made up for that omission, particularly the 1985 Vatican *Notes on the Correct Way to Present Jews and Judaism.*[43] There we read of Judaism's "continuous spiritual fruitfulness in the rabbinical period, in the Middle Ages, and in modern times" (No. 33). The Vatican *Notes* highlighted the few positive references made in the gospels to the Pharisees, who are then correctly described as closer to Jesus than other groups in his

---

[42] *Przegląd Powszechny,* 220 (1938): 200–13.

[43] *Notes on the Correct Way to Present Jews and Judaism in the Preaching and Catechesis of the Roman Catholic Church* (Vatican City: 1985); published in *Origins* 15 (July 4, 1985): 102–107.

society. This revision of the Christian image of the Pharisees follows from the recognition within the Vatican *Notes* that controversies between Jesus and the early rabbinic sages as reported in the gospels often reflect conflicts which arose later between the synagogue and first century church (No. 29). Pope John Paul II advanced this line of thinking by speaking of Judaism as a "living heritage" and admitting that Christians have something to learn from Jewish tradition, "the faith and religious life of the Jewish people as they are professed and practiced still today" (Mainz, March 6, 1982).[44]

Such sentiments are striking reversals in Catholic attitudes regarding Talmudic tradition, a repudiation of the "teaching of contempt." It was a teaching that had an impact not only on religious attitudes in Poland but, as is so often the case, on economics as well.

---

[44] Eugene J. Fisher and Leon Klenicki (eds.), *Pope John Paul II on Jews and Judaism, 1979–1986* (Washington, DC: United States Catholic Conference, 1987), 34, 39.

Chapter 9

The Interwar Economy: Poverty and the Boycott

From the outset of Poland's recorded history, Jews played a crucial role in its economy. Anti-Jewish outbreaks brought an influx of Jewish immigrants from Germany and Bohemia, and by the twelfth century coins with Hebrew letters circulated Poland.[1] The Poles were overwhelmingly agrarian, numbering only a small number of native townsfolk, prompting successive rulers in the thirteenth and fourteenth centuries to invite Jews to create towns and develop trade. The Statute of Kalisz (1264) granted Jews, along with protection and religious freedom, the right to practice free trade. If persecution in Germany made Poland a Jewish haven, Poland at the same time profited from Jewish skills. Jews served Poland's rulers and landowners as craftsmen, bankers, managers, and tax-collectors. By the end of the sixteenth century, it is estimated that there were nearly two hundred thousand Jews in Poland. They constituted somewhat over six percent of the entire population but sixteen percent in the towns.[2]

Because Poland required the development of trade and crafts, not more agriculture, Jews were barred from settling the land. By the fifteenth

---

[1] Marian Fuks, Zygmunt Hoffman, Maurycy Horn, and Jerzy Tomaszewski, *Polish Jewry, History and Culture* (Warsaw: Interpress, 1982), 9. See also Norman Davies, *God's Playground: A History of Poland* (New York: Columbia University, 1982), 1:3–4.

[2] Joseph Marcus, *Social and Political History of the Jews in Poland, 1919–1939* (Berlin; New York; Amsterdam: Mouton, 1983), 3–5. See also Davies, *God's Playground,* 1:130–32.

century Poland had a flourishing middle class, but most of it was Jewish or German with each group competing with the other. The few Poles who engaged in commerce and industry abandoned the occupation as soon as they became wealthy enough to pass into the class of the land-owning nobility. For the Polish aristocracy, land ownership and agriculture were the only respectable occupations. Commercial and industrial activities were despised as demeaning to their status. A succession of laws in the sixteenth century actually forbade the gentry from engaging in them under penalty of losing their privileges. This attachment to land remained strong in Poland right up through the nineteenth century. Romantic writers, like Krasiński, Słowacki, and Reymont, contrasted the bleakness of urban living with supposedly carefree village life. Even in the 1930s a native Polish bourgeoisie did not exist on a scale comparable to that in western Europe.

It is a commonplace that at least up to the end of the sixteenth century, the situation of Jews was better in Poland than anywhere else in Europe. Disturbances against Jews, generally caused by their German competitors, were economically rather than religiously motivated. Laws discriminating against Jews, usually passed to please the Germans, frequently went unenforced. But with the 1648 Ukrainian uprisings and Chmielnicki massacres, Jewish fortunes declined with those of the rest of the nation. A series of wars, economic stagnation, and political anarchy rendered the situation in the eighteenth century even more disastrous. Before it was over, there were only six towns in Poland that had more than ten thousand inhabitants. The gentry, never more than ten percent of the population, had become supreme and acted more in their own class interest than in that of the nation. The peasantry, representing seventy-five percent of the population, were bound to the land and little better than serfs.

The partitions of Poland only aggravated an already grim economic situation. Policies of systematic oppression and neglect on the part of the partitioning powers, especially Russia and Austria, made it difficult for the Poles to throw off their feudal institutions. The enormous technical progress which characterized the nineteenth century in the west left Poland virtually untouched. Austrian-occupied Poland (Galicia) experienced little industrial progress. Russian-occupied Poland, though subjected to ruthless political oppression, enjoyed almost free access to the vast Russian market and became quite possibly the most developed part of the Russian empire. By western standards, however, it was underdeveloped and its people poor. Łódź, for example, a textile center and the second largest city in Poland, had no system of sewers until the First World War.[3]

For the rest of Europe, that war ended in 1918; in Poland the fighting continued nearly two more years. In economic terms the military conflict with the Soviet Union was arguably more disastrous to Poland than the previous four years, since it had to be financed from already depleted domestic resources. Even before the end of the Great War, large areas of the country had been devastated by battle. Two years later, with mines and factories idle for lack of raw materials and machinery, the country was in economic chaos. In the first years of the new Polish Republic's existence, the entire economic system had to be reconstructed from scratch. There was no integrated infrastructure, no common currency, no established financial institutions, no government agencies.[4] And in less than a decade Poland was struck by an international depression.

Jewish historians writing on interwar Poland have generally focused on the economic plight of the Jews. Contemporary Jewish accounts, usually journalistic, did the same.[5] Readers, for example, of the *American Hebrew and Jewish Tribune*, a national weekly, were informed regularly by its correspondents in Poland about Jewish poverty: how almost eighty percent of the Jewish population could not afford the dollar a year community tax, how "a potato a day is a luxury to thousands of them."[6]

Dr. Bernard Kahn, European Director of the American Jewish Joint Distribution Committee, in an appeal to American Jews, wrote that at least one million of Poland's Jews were completely destitute and looked to soup kitchens to fend off starvation. Kahn placed the blame for their plight on the policies of the Polish government and the establishment of governmental monopolies in industries such as lumber, tobacco, liquor, and salt. Jews who had previously been active in these industries were now out of work. To relieve the effects of the world depression on Poland's massive peasant population, the government issued a fifteen year moratorium on their debts, resulting in severe losses for Jewish

---

[3] Marcus, *Social and Political History,* 5–13.

[4] Davies, *God's Playground,* 2:415.

[5] See, for example, Simon Segal, *The New Poland and the Jews* (New York: Lee Furman, 1938).

[6] *American Hebrew and Jewish Tribune,* June 14, 1935, 103.

creditors. A system of taxing urban areas at a rate higher than the impoverished countryside meant that the government was taxing precisely those areas where Jews were concentrated most heavily.[7]

Equally disturbing to Jews in 1936 was the apparent change of governmental policy with regard to the boycott of Jewish merchants. Under Roman Dmowski the National Democrats had been encouraging a boycott of Jewish enterprises since 1912. With a slogan amounting to "patronize your own," (*swój do swego*), Endeks sought to convince Poles that Jews were the primary obstacle to their own economic advancement. But Piłsudski had kept the National Democrats on a short leash, and the boycott had little effect. It was only after the his death in 1935, that the Endeks saw an opportunity to make the boycott work. They heated up their campaign until, to all appearances, the government finally caved in to Endek pressure. In a June 6, 1936 speech to the Polish Sejm, Premier Sławój-Składkowski declared: "An honest host does not allow anybody to be harmed in his house. Economic struggle—yes (*owszem*)! But no harm." Similarly the government (February 21, 1937) condemned "arbitrary and brutal anti-Jewish acts" but went on to endorse "cultural self-defense" and the "tendency of the Polish people toward economic independence."[8]

In the wake of this apparent change in governmental policy, the American Jewish Congress addressed a memorandum (July 12, 1937) to the U.S. State Department. It accused the Polish government of being "directly responsible for the present plight of the Polish Jews." The memorandum charged the government with discrimination in its hiring practices: Jews made up only one percent of the national civil service; two percent at the municipal level. The number of Jews employed in the state monopolies was similarly negligible. Although less than four percent of the employed Polish population was engaged in commerce, two-thirds of all direct taxes were levied upon commercial enterprises, in which those chiefly engaged happened to be Jews.

As a result, the memorandum continued, Jews, though only ten percent of the population, paid approximately forty percent of all direct taxes. There were Jewish traders too poor to pay their license fees and Jewish bakers denied the government credits being granted to non-Jews. The

---

[7] *American Hebrew and Jewish Tribune,* June 21, 1935, 117.

[8] Marcus, *Social and Political History,* 365–66.

cumulative effect of the unofficial boycott and official discrimination, concluded the memorandum, was the "utter impoverishment" of Poland's Jews. "Forty percent of them are unemployed and unemployment among them is more than twice as great as in the population at large." The memorandum, signed by Stephen S. Wise, requested the U.S. government to intercede with the Polish government on behalf of Poland's Jews.[9] It should be noted that the statistics cited here by Wise took into consideration only the unemployed urban population and not the masses of Polish peasants.

At a distance of some fifty years, historian Joseph Marcus has subjected interwar Poland's economic situation to more careful scrutiny and analysis. His research has led him to criticize the majority of interwar Jewish commentators on Poland for preferring political interest to objectivity. He faults them for being "champions of the Jewish cause, at a time of great economic and political difficulties." They "wrote both aggressively and plaintively, hoping to arouse compassion for and bring help to their suffering fellow Jews." In the case of Jewish relief organizations, their reports were promotional in purpose. "Polemic and protest took precedence over fair selection of facts." Marcus points out how frequently references would be made to the inferior political status of Polish Jews (which was partly due to their leaders' internal policies) but not to their superior economic status. No attention was given to the fact that the impact of the Jewish minority was greater on the majority population than vice versa.[10]

Contrary to the conventional wisdom on the matter, Marcus' research demonstrates that "between the end of the eighteenth century and 1929, the last year before the Great Depression, per capita real income of Jews went up by 350 percent, while that of the non-Jewish urban population declined" (p. 13). The credit lay with the Jewish entrepreneurs who were largely responsible for developing industry in partitioned and interwar Poland. There was a greater disparity of wealth among Jews than within Christian urban society, and certainly by western standards the average Polish Jew was poor. The main reason, however, was not Polish antisemitism. Marcus' findings are rather: "Even if all the Jews who were unemployed in 1929 had held gainful jobs at average wages and salaries

---

[9] *American Hebrew and Jewish Tribune*, July 23, 1937, 8–39, 12–13, 16.

[10] Marcus, *Social and Political History*, viii–ix.

appropriate to the occupational groups to which they belonged, only about eleven percent would have been added to the total Jewish national income in that year...leaving the people as a whole only slightly less poor than they actually were. That Jewish poverty was mainly the result of accumulated discrimination against them is a myth and it is time to expose it as such" (p. 231).

The fundamental weakness of Poland's economy was its agriculture. Thirty-four percent of all farms were five acres or less, clearly not enough for a peasant family to support itself (p. 25). In 1935 a leading agrarian expert in the Polish government estimated that a full forty-two percent of the total farm population was superfluous. A League of Nations study concurred, estimating that for the years 1931-1935, the yield of Poland's agriculture was twenty-five percent of Germany's and fifteen percent that of England and Wales. Besides the underdeveloped state of farming methods, the problem was overpopulation. The same League of Nations study concluded that to achieve the average European per capita yield, Poland would have to remove 51.3 percent of its peasants from agriculture (p. 21).

Poland was in glaring need of radical agrarian reform. Simon Segal, writing at the time, estimated that five and a half million peasants in Czechoslovakia bought three times the quantity of industrial goods purchased by twenty-three million Polish peasants.[11] Although half the agricultural land in Poland was controlled by a handful of private land-owners, they went untouched; the government limited itself to parcelling out state-owned lands.[12] The industrial workers did not fare much better. At what was then the exchange of five złotys to a dollar, the average hourly wage was a little more than a half złoty or twelve cents. The average earnings of all the workers in Warsaw in 1935 amounted to 36.89 złotys ($7.35) a week. Fifty percent of all the public employees had debts amounting to six months of their wages.[13]

The majority of the unemployed work force in interwar Poland were ethnic Poles, many if not most of them resentful of Jewish predominance

---

[11] Segal, *The New Poland,* 147.

[12] Celia S. Heller, *On the Edge of Destruction: Jews of Poland between the Two World Wars* (New York: Schocken, 1980), 94–95.

[13] Segal, *The New Poland,* 147–48.

in trade and crafts.[14] To the Polish authorities, it seemed unexceptional in the distribution of government jobs to give priority to unemployed Poles. What to Jews could only appear as discrimination, to the authorities was a policy that today they would likely describe as "affirmative action." Their motives, in Marcus' words, "were not to depress the Jews but to lift up its own nationals" (p. 238).

As mentioned above, the National Democrats campaigned for a boycott of Jewish enterprises throughout the interwar period. Encouraged by the example of the Nazis in Germany, individuals and splinter groups from the Endeks (like the eventually outlawed National Radical Camp) tried to use terror tactics and physical abuse to enforce the boycott. Right-wing students and common thugs would attack Jewish stores and market stalls and threaten Poles who dared to patronize them. Poles seeking the services of Jewish doctors and lawyers would be photographed and their pictures published with derogatory captions in hate sheets and pamphlets. At the same time, Christian merchants would advertise themselves as such by displaying pictures of Jesus or Mary in their windows or signs with slogans like "patronize your own." As Celia Heller admits, however: "it was not easy to convince Poles to abstain from patronizing Jewish enterprises."[15]

Guided by their common sense, the ordinary peasants knew very well that their plight was not due to the Jews but to oppressive governmental policies. The National Democrats did not have much success in the countryside, and antisemitism was felt much less in villages than in towns. Even during the 1937 peasant strikes, no Jews were harmed according to Marcus (p. 369). Indeed there were towns where Polish traders in 1939 petitioned local authorities to rescind regulations which for several years had required stalls at markets and fairs to be located by religion. This discriminatory legislation had led to a concentration of Jewish stalls in one recognizable section of the marketplace. Although the original purpose of the regulations had been to facilitate the boycott, they had the opposite effect. The Polish farmers would head straight to that

---

[14] When Celia Heller writes that poverty was more acute and widespread among Jews than among "urban Poles," she consciously excludes from her calculations the unemployed and landless peasants. *On the Edge,* 101.

[15] Heller, *On the Edge,* 115–16.

section of the market where the Jewish stalls were to be found (pp. 244–45).

The general failure of the boycott was hardly due to philosemitism. There was widespread envy and resentment of Jews who were prospering in business, and there was a widely-held notion that Jewish goods were shoddy. But the Polish masses could ill afford expensive products and were anxious to obtain the goods they needed at the cheapest prices. In the end, Marcus concludes that the price factor was usually decisive. "Apart from a few fanatics, most Polish consumers ignored all other considerations" (p. 245).

Government support of the boycott is generally dated from 1936 and Premier Składkowski's speech, in which he said, "Economic struggle—yes (*owszem*)! But no harm." Składkowski later wrote in his memoirs that this was not a call to boycott but merely an attempt to ward off extremists. But once the Jewish leadership and press interpreted his word as an endorsement of the boycott, it was politically expedient not to deny it (p. 366). The approach of the government was Polish self-interest, and that above all meant improvement of Poland's desperate economic situation. Although nationalization of Poland's economy was undoubtedly a long-range goal, the authorities realized that not many Poles were qualified to replace Jews in large-scale commercial enterprises, and they were left alone (p. 243). On balance, Marcus' research indicates that, during the years 1929 to 1938, though the population of Poland's Jews fell slightly, "their share of the total national income substantially increased (from 13.33 percent to almost 15 percent).... At the end of the period, the proportion of income that accrued to the upper half of the Jewish population was larger than in 1929, and the prosperous minority of Jews also owned, in real terms, more wealth" (p. 247).

In short, even in the late 1930s, the Jewish middle and lower-middle classes were holding their own. The majority of Polish Jews were more comfortable than most ethnic Poles. Government policies detrimental to Jewish economic interests were ineffective. Rather it appears that those interests were damaged more by Jewish strikes against Jewish-owned enterprises than by any government measures (p. 126–27). Marcus concludes: "The Jews in Poland were poor because they lived in a poor, underdeveloped country. Discrimination added only marginally to their poverty" (p. 231).

Marcus is not the only Jewish historian to take this patently revisionist view of interwar Poland.[16] Polish scholars have long complained that the Jewish question in interwar Poland has been studied too much in isolation, that Jewish suffering was the result of Polish poverty and underdevelopment.[17] But this clearly does not absolve the National Democrats and radical right for their campaign of terror against the most vulnerable sector of the Jewish population: the small shopkeepers and traders who sold their goods from pushcarts and stalls in the marketplaces. These were the most defenseless competitors to the radical nationalists and the most frequent victims of physical attacks.

It was against such "scoundrels in student's attire" that novelist Wanda Wasilewska raised her voice in protest: "Here fifteen, sixteen people live in one room. Here five people sleep in one bed.... The slogan of economic struggle is raised against the paupers of the Jewish street.... Why suppress when it is so easy and so safe to vent one's anger in a fight with a bowed porter, with a Jewish boy selling watches..."[18] Protests from the church against physical violence were considerably less eloquent than Wasilewska's. Against the boycott, there were none.

The spectacle of poor people striking out in anger and frustration at other poor people was hardly new nor peculiar to Poland. Noteworthy, though, was the considerable interest that Catholic opinion-makers took in economic matters. One does not ordinarily expect economic analysis and expertise from clerical publications, but the Polish Catholic press was anything but silent on such issues and hardly indifferent.

Mały Dziennik

Nationalization of Poland's economy was a concern for the Catholic press no less than for the Endeks, particularly for the *Mały Dziennik*. No issue appeared more regularly in its columns. From the first months of its publication, it advertised itself as a friend and defender of working people, which for the Catholic daily meant being an adversary to Jewish

---

[16] See Ezra Mendelsohn, "Interwar Poland: good for the Jews or bad for the Jews?" in Chimen Abramsky, Maciej Jachimczyk, and Antony Polonsky, eds., *The Jews in Poland* (Oxford: Blackwell, 1986), 130–39.

[17] See Jerzy Tomaszewski in Fuks et al., *Polish Jewry.*

[18] Quoted in Heller, *On the Edge,* 117.

economic interests (July 28, 1935). Typical of the journalism of its day, it made no sharp distinction between news reporting and editorial opinion. Its conservative Catholic and nationalistic slant appeared in all its pages, as did its hostility to Jewish interests. A news story of a strike against a lumber mill described "incredibly low pay" and "dreadful" working conditions and pointed out that the owners were Jewish, which made it a "Jewish factory" (July 28, 1935). Similarly, badly needed foreign investment being made in the shipping city of Gdynia was interpreted to mean that Poland was becoming dependent and dominated by "foreign and Jewish capital" (July 4, 1935).

From its earliest days the *Maly Dziennik* began a practice of eliciting opinions on issues it regarded as urgent. The Catholic daily, for example, asked its readers from the countryside to relate their needs and complaints (July 28, 1935). The responses to that request were suggestive of common Polish attitudes in the villages. Life, wrote one reader, was not bad in the summer, when rooms could be rented out to tourists, especially to Jews, who paid well (August 6, 1935). Another reader complained that everyone exploited farmers, but especially Jews. Cooperatives were needed as an alternative to Jewish middlemen, who bought their grain. Unfortunately, cooperatives were difficult to organize because "our farmers do not feel confident in this way of doing things and prefer to do business with Jews" (August 11, 1935).

The *Maly Dziennik* fared better in a second opinion poll directed to Catholics in trade and commerce. This hardly disinterested segment of Polish society was asked their opinions of their Jewish competitors: Would young people leaving the villages and entering into trade change the situation in which commerce was largely in the hands of people "alien and hostile" to Poles? (January 26, 1936) The Catholic store owners responded as expected. Occasional references were made to the need for Poles to learn commercial skills, but the majority of letters complained about Jews engaging in unfair business practices. Allegations were made of Jews selling inferior or defective merchandise, advertising falsely, or selling on Saturday or Sunday.

The Catholic respondents lamented having to pay rent for their stores to Jewish landlords who owned all the commercial property. The proverb, "your streets, our buildings" (*wasze ulice, nasze kamienice*) was all too true. Writers complained about Jewish credit unions subsidized by outside Jewish capital; cheap credit allowed Jews to sell cheaper. The letters acknowledged that many Poles preferred to shop in Jewish stores. More

Catholic wholesalers were needed, the respondents urged, and greater solidarity. For the "Central Association of Christian Retailers," (which had its counterpart in the "Central [Association of] Jewish Retailers"), the crucial issues were tax relief and government support. When a respondent suggested a governmental buyout of Jewish businesses tantamount to expropriation, the Catholic daily called it an "interesting project."[19]

Poverty

The effects of the depression lasted longer in Poland than in the rest of Europe. *Mały Dziennik* described the high incidence of beggars and vagrants in Warsaw resulting from joblessness (March 20, 1936). Not untypical was the story of a Polish mother who, no longer able to take in washing, made a living for herself and her children by selling cherries from a pushcart (July 18, 1936). More unusual was an article descriptive of Jewish poverty. Instead of looking for help from the government, Poles should learn from the Jews. Not only "proverbial Jewish shrewdness" helped them to get by, but also the willingness to take even poorly paid jobs. Poles preferred to remain idle than to take a job that did not pay enough, the writer claimed. Jews, by contrast, would rather work for pennies than live off charity. Women would pluck chickens and boys would sell cooked peas on street corners (March 19, 1936). Such sentiments were certainly exceptional for the *Mały Dziennik*. More typically, when several hundred Polish retailers were fined or arrested for charging inflated prices, the *Mały Dziennik* blamed the wholesalers who were overwhelmingly Jewish (October 24, 1936).

To investigate and address the problems of poverty and overpopulation in the Polish countryside, Cardinal Hlond instituted what he called a "social council." The council's recommendations were that a certain percentage of peasants be encouraged to move from the country to the cities and that the government institute land reform, subdividing and distributing Poland's larger country estates, even if it meant compulsory expropriation. *Mały Dziennik* was critical of the idea of land reform, but it enthusiastically endorsed the idea of peasants moving to cities and displacing Jews in industry and small business (November 24, 1937). The

---

[19] *Mały Dziennik,* January 28–March 4, 1936.

word overpopulation was not frequently used in the Catholic press. As one could expect, given the papal prohibition against artificial birth control, no suggestion was ever made of a need for family planning. It was easier for the Catholic daily to fault Jews: Jewish clothiers were exploiting Polish cottage workers who did their sewing (March 13, 1937); Jewish grain dealers were paying farmers as little as possible so as to keep the price of bread down for Jewish city-dwellers (November 21, 1938).

In the *Rycerz Niepokalanej,* also published by Father Kolbe's Conventual Franciscans, R. Karkowska argued from a recent report of statistics (*Mały Rocznik Statystyczny*). Given its natural resources, Poland should be self-sufficient, but, because of its neighbors, Poland required an army that consumed more than a third of its budget. Because it was under-industrialized, Poland imported goods which it should be producing itself. But, most problematic were the numbers of landless peasants. Since the outlook for land redistribution was not promising and emigration did not offer a serious option, the only solution to their problems had to be found in trade, 84% of which, Karkowska alleged, was in Jewish which was to say "foreign" hands, especially in the eastern and southern parts of the country. Nationally, 52.5% of all commercial enterprises were Jewish, but in the south it was 64.9%, and in the east 71.9%. To solve the problem of joblessness, the government was nationalizing commerce and industry, forming cooperatives and credit unions, but Jewish interests were resisting the government's efforts.[20]

In the Catholic Action *Ruch Katolicki,* Father Jan Ciemniewski blamed Poland's poverty on "Jewish capitalism." With its principles of competition and unlimited private property, capitalism had increased productivity but did not know how to divide profits fairly. Although an "aryan economic system," capitalism was influenced by "Jewish principles." Ciemniewski cited the work of Jewish economist Werner Sombart on Jews and economic life, in which Sombart claimed that contemporary capitalism and culture would not have been possible without Jews. For Ciemniewski, that meant Poland would not be able to dislodge the capitalist system without resolving the "Jewish question."

At the exchange rate of five złotys to a U.S. dollar, Ciemniewski had reason to call Poland one of the poorest countries in Europe. Near Lwów,

---

[20] *Rycerz Niepokalanej* (1938): 51–55.

an organization was founded in which each member promised one potato a day for families who had nothing other than potatoes on which to live. The national average income was somewhat less than 300 złotys per year. The "privileged" ten percent of the population had an income four times that great (1200 złotys per year). That put the income of the remaining 30 million Poles at circa 190 złotys per year. On the other hand, Jews dominated the most lucrative fields, Ciemniewski insisted, and almost all of Poland's heavy industry depended on foreign and Jewish capital. Solving the "Jewish question" in a Catholic spirit meant repudiating excesses; the Nazis contradicted the principles of the church and the values of Polish tradition. But there would be no liberation from capitalism so long as Jews dominated Poland's economy.[21]

Monopolies

The *Mały Dziennik* regularly complained about Jewish monopolies in items like salt, sugar, and meat (December 31, 1938; January 19, 1939). The Jewish wholesalers were accused of giving better prices to Jewish retailers (May 21, 1937). Poles were discouraged from eating rice, which, besides being a Jewish monopoly, the reader was assured, really did not suit Polish tastes (April 14, 1938; August 19, 1938). Krakow's *Głos Narodu* found it newsworthy that a Catholic in Warsaw was opening a fish market and so broke the Jewish fish monopoly there.[22]

Mały Dziennik encouraged its readers to inquire about the religion not only of the retailer but of the manufacturer as well (March 30, 1936). Ninety percent of the wholesale trade was in Jewish hands, the Catholic daily lamented (July 19, 1936).

The question was raised in the secular press whether there was something in the Polish temperament not conducive to commerce. Not so, answered Adolf Małyszko in the *Przegląd Katolicki.* The Polish aristocracy had erred in seeing commerce as unworthy of them. Despite that historic blunder, there were a number of areas where Poles demonstrated their entrepreneurial skills and constituted a majority (the sugar industry, publishing, retail grocery). Where the percentage of Jews was small, they

---

[21] *Ruch Katolicki,* 8 (1938): 21–24.

[22] *Głos Narodu,* August 13, 1936.

benefitted a national economy by stimulating competition; too great a
percentage deterred the development of commercial skills in the native
population. Poland's problem, Małyszko concluded, was that Warsaw
alone had three times more Jews than all of France.[23]

In eastern Poland the preponderance of Jews in commerce was
especially conspicuous and to Catholic nationalists, especially rankling.
Poles used to say that Europe ended at Warsaw's Poniatowski bridge,
wrote Antoni Chocieszyński, but it rather seemed that Poland did. The
territories east of Warsaw appeared to him like some foreign nation.
There were cities in the east where all the stores were Jewish. This called
for an "economic war" by pioneering spirits. For a Polish Catholic to
become a store owner in the east was to become no less than a "pioneer
of Polishness and a missionary of Catholicism." It was a matter not
merely of economics but of faith.[24]

The Boycott

Nationalizing Poland's economy by boycotting Jewish businesses had
been a program of the National Democrats since 1912. But its highest
and most celebrated Catholic endorsement came in 1936, when Cardinal
Hlond issued a pastoral letter on Catholic moral principles. After warning
the faithful against Nazism, communism, atheism, and Masonry, he went
on to add: "One may love one's own nation more, but one may not hate
anyone. Not even Jews. It is good to prefer your own kind when shopping, to avoid Jewish stores and Jewish stalls in the marketplace, but it
is forbidden to demolish a Jewish store, damage their merchandise, break
windows, or throw things at their homes."[25]

Reading the Catholic periodical literature subsequent to the Cardinal's
letter, one is struck at how rarely it was cited. The impression one
receives is that the Cardinal's views were hardly news and taken for
granted. The *Mały Dziennik* from its inception had treated the boycott as
an "obligation," a moral and civic duty for Polish Catholics. Regularly

---

[23] *Przegląd Katolicki,* 71 (1933): 536–37.

[24] *Przewodnik Katolicki,* 43 (1937): 710–12, 739–41.

[25] A. Hlond, Na *Straży Sumienia Narodu* (Ramsey, NJ: Don Bosco, 1951), 164–65.

it ran a banner over its advertisements, declaring that "A Pole buys only from other Poles." Among those ads, "Gloria," a manufacturer of razor blades, not only declared itself to be a Christian firm but urged, "Let's not allow ourselves to be shaved by the enemy" (August 9, 1936). *Mały Dziennik* made its point with cartoons as well. One example depicted a Polish hostess serving her guests rolls from a Jewish bakery, only to have them all fall ill with food poisoning (June 25, 1935).

No aspect of the boycott was too trivial for *Mały Dziennik*. Readers were admonished, with the advent of the school year, to buy the children's school supplies only from Christian stores. Such purchases added up and should not be considered negligible (August 29, 1938). The Catholic daily heralded the publication of a guidebook, "Christian Warsaw," that gave the names and addresses of Christian businesses, lawyers, and medical doctors (June 19, 1935). Formerly when market days fell on Jewish holidays, they had to be transferred. In Wilno in 1938, however, the market took place despite the Jewish High Holy Days, thanks to Christian merchants. Business was slower than usual, because customers presumed there would be no market, but everything was sold and no one missed the Jews. Those communities which postponed the market because of the Holy Days were guilty of "exaggerated philosemitism" (October 20, 1938).

A particular concern of the Catholic daily was to prevent cooperation between Christian and Jewish merchants. Polish firms were criticized for maintaining relations with Jewish contractors (November 23, 1938). The *Mały Dziennik* was incensed that a Christmas fair organized by the Association of Christian Retailers had allowed Jewish merchants to participate. Christian merchants did not have a moral right to work quietly together with Jews, the daily declared. Such cooperation gave the impression that Jewish firms with neutral names were Christian. Admittedly, some products were manufactured only by Jews, but one should either do without them or else organize a Polish firm to produce them (December 4, 1935). *Mały Dziennik* also railed against the Central Manufacturers Circle (*Centralny Okrąg Przemysłowy*) and those Polish chambers of commerce that included Jews in their membership. The numbers and influence of their Jewish members should be lessened if not eliminated altogether (March 2, 1938; October 26, 1938; June 14, 1939).

Other Catholic periodicals joined the *Mały Dziennik* in its campaign on behalf of the boycott. In the *Gazeta Kościelna* Father A. Sierzega wrote of the need for the clergy to support "Catholic commerce." Priests, he wrote, should patronize Catholic stores, because "the lay people follow our every step." The priest complained about Catholic retailers who bought goods from Jewish wholesalers when Catholic wholesalers were available. Such store owners were not worthy of support or of being called Catholic. Some Catholic merchants were hostile to other Catholic merchants and preferred Jewish to Catholic competition. Such attitudes deserved to be publicly condemned. Pastors, the priest continued, should call meetings of Catholic store owners in their parishes and instill a sense of solidarity among them.[26]

To get their readers thinking along the same lines, the *Przewodnik Katolicki* ran a contest, offering prizes for the best answers to questions like: What moral principles lie behind the boycott? The Catholic weekly reported over 1,500 answers from Poles in every profession, keenly aware of the "danger" of "Jewish competition." The superiority of Jewish capital threatened the very existence of Polish manufacturers, they wrote. If Poles would observe the boycott, unemployment in Poland would disappear. Supporting people who are "strange to me in faith and blood," wrote one reader, was a "sin against church and country." It meant "correcting an error made by our ancestors and assuring our children a better future." For another respondent, the boycott was an alternative to violence. Although Jews were taking away their bread, violence was unworthy of Catholic Poles and their reputation for chivalry. If Poles want to beat Jews, "let's do it on the pocketbook, not on the head."[27]

The Catholic press and church leaders plainly experienced no moral difficulties in encouraging the boycott. On the contrary, they saw the boycott as an aspect of their obligations to church and state. It was not a contradiction to Christian charity but a consequence of it. Loving one's country was analogous to loving one's family. Without despising or hating other nations, Catholics were bound by natural law and taught by the church to love their own nation more. This should be remembered when one went shopping, needed professional services, or was giving to

---

[26] *Gazeta Kościelna,* (1937): 223–24.

[27] *Przewodnik Katolicki,* 45 (1939): 248–49.

charity. Indifference with regard to one's own people was as wrong as indifference in religion.[28]

In its support of the boycott, the *Mały Dziennik* often laced its rhetoric with military metaphors. Christian merchants were described as at war with an enemy. The Catholic daily tried to bolster its readers' morale by reporting even modest breakthroughs as victories over against impressive odds (November 30, 1935). A victory was not only a Polish store opening but a Jewish store closing (February 2, 1936). One of the recurrent motifs in the *Mały Dziennik* was a call for Poles to imitate what ultimately was a widely magnified concept of Jewish solidarity (October 9, 1937; October 25, 1937). Claiming that Jews were being forbidden by their rabbis to shop in Christian stores (April 13, 1937), the daily told of a Jewish woman being attacked by other Jews for going into a Christian store (July 26, 1937). "We understand and admire the real solidarity of Jews in the defense of their interests, but want to draw some conclusions for ourselves." (November 8, 1937). Father W. Jakowski was particularly perturbed that, in a case where there was no question of cheaper prices or better merchandise, namely the Polish lottery, Poles were purchasing tickets from Jews rather than Poles (January 30, 1939).

The *Mały Dziennik* became especially aggressive in its support of the boycott during the pre-Christmas shopping season. The Catholic daily implored Poles in 1937 to think not only of their own holiday tables but those of their fellow Poles who were merchants (December 18, 1937). The newspaper's campaign was successful enough to be reported in the Jewish and "Masonic" Press, but the *Mały Dziennik* was not satisfied. There were still Poles, especially women, who regarded Jewish stores as better bargains (January 31, 1938). One still saw elegant ladies slipping furtively into Jewish stores and hiding their purchases. As well they should, wrote the Catholic daily, since they were betraying their country's best interests. Preparing properly for Christmas meant spending "not even a penny" in Jewish stores (December 3, 1938).

To guide its readers' Christmas shopping in 1938, the *Mały Dziennik* sponsored another opinion survey. Readers were asked to respond to questions like: What are the assets of the Jews in your community? What do you think of *Shabbos goyim* ("Sabbath gentiles," i.e., non-Jews hired to perform certain tasks which are forbidden to Jews on the Sabbath) who

---

[28] *Głos Misji Wewnętrznej,* 7 (1938): 364–66.

support Jews instead of helping their fellow Poles? Among the responses to such queries was complaints about the Jewish practice of price-haggling (December 12, 1938) and about Jewish wholesalers giving better goods at better terms to their co-religionists (December 19, 1938). Another reader complained that, because Jewish merchants had more capital at their disposal, they could afford to sell on credit; the unhealthy credit system was ruining Polish merchants and putting Polish customers deeper into debt (December 15, 1938). Another complained that the boycott was not working in southwest Poland, because Jews there were regarded favorably by Polish customers (December 19, 1938). Jewish firms should be nationalized and put into the hand of Poles, another reader suggested (February 23, 1939). Jews were the "grave-diggers" of Poland, carrying out the "fourth partition" (February 23, 1939).

In 1938, a "Defence of Polish Trade Week" was declared in early December. In Warsaw Polish Merchant's Day (December 8) began with a Mass in the cathedral (Decmber 10, 1938). The *Przewodnik Katolicki* reminded Poles how during the partitions they had to combat the efforts to Germanize them. They had to defend themselves from economic servitude and feelings of inferiority. Now the danger came from Jewish industrialists and international Jewish capital. Poles should prefer not only Polish stores but products made by Polish workers. Christian firms might not be well known because they did not have the money to advertise. Patriotic Polish wives should buy their husbands Polish-made shirts, even if the cut was not quite stylish.[29]

The *Mały Dziennik* admitted that Polish merchants had weaknesses to overcome. They had to learn to please customers and win their confidence. With some few exceptions, Polish merchants were unwilling to make exchanges. Likewise, one could still hear of Jewish storekeepers being gracious, while in the Polish stores they acted as if they were doing you a favor. Certain segments of Polish society, however, shopped in Jewish stores simply out of "sheer snobbery" (February 3, 1938). The reporter for the *Mały Dziennik* in Wilno complained about the "philosemitism" of the "intellectuals." There would not be any Jewish grocers in Christian neighborhoods were it not for the "white collar workers" who patronized them for the sake of cheap credit (June 7, 1939).

---

[29] *Przewodnik Katolicki,* 44 (1938): 836.

Credit Unions

The *Mały Dziennik* complained when some Jewish employers, to offset the effects of the boycott, made partial payment of their employees' salaries with coupons or certificates, redeemable only in certain Jewish stores (December 30, 1937). In some areas grain dealers were paying the farmers with certificates to Jewish stores; the farmers had no choice but to accept them since all the dealers were Jewish (December 16, 1938). But the defensive measure that aroused the most complaints in the Catholic press was the creation of credit unions where Jewish merchants, hurt by the boycott, could obtain interest-free loans or cheap credit. These credit unions had been made possible primarily by the American Jewish Joint Distribution Committee, or "Joint," as it was called. Denouncing them as privileged institutions, harmful for Poland, the *Mały Dziennik* called for the government to set up similar credit unions for small Polish merchants.[30]

Józef Białasiewicz in *Przegląd Katolicki* saw the Jewish credit unions as a means for international Jewish interests to maintain control over Poland's economy. The Polish clergy had instituted Catholic credit unions in the fifteenth and sixteenth centuries, he wrote, but they disappeared during the partitions. After the World War the Joint instituted Jewish credit unions, first offering outright financial aid and then interest-free loans. Describing the growth of Jewish credit unions from 266 in 1928 to over a thousand in 1937, Białasiewicz cited detailed statistical reports on the amount of money they had loaned each year since 1928. With this money Jewish manufacturers were able to purchase raw material with interest-free credit or at factory price. With a network of correspondents, the central organizing agency of the Jewish credit unions (the C.K.B.) served, in Białasiewicz's view, as the "command center for Jewish economic espionage" in Poland.[31]

A book by the leader of the C.K.B., Isaac Bornstein, proved to be a boon to advocates of the boycott. Entitled *Rzemiosło żydowskie w Polsce* (Jewish Industry in Poland), Bornstein's book provided all the statistics Alfons Prabucki needed to prove Jews were controlling Polish commerce.

---

[30] *Mały Dziennik*, August 13, 1935; December 24, 1935; April 15, 1936; May 13, 1938; June 27, 1938.

[31] *Przegląd Katolicki*, 75 (1937): 51–53.

He listed various areas of manufacture and the percentage of Jewish ownership: hats—97%; boots—85%; leather and watch-making—75%; glass-making—72%; sheet metal—70%; tailoring—65%; furs—56%; photography—55%; barbers—58%; bakers—48%. Here, declared Prabucki, was a Jewish source confirming that Jews commanded "close to 50% of the sum total of manufacturing positions" in Poland. From Bornstein too he detailed the growth of Jewish credit unions supported by the Joint. When one added those not supported by the Joint, the numbers had to be over a thousand, Prabucki concluded, a vast and organized Jewish network.[32]

Without the benefit of statistical evidence, Józef Radomski exaggerated the number of Jewish credit unions in Poland to be four thousand with an operating capital of 150 million złotys. He contrasted this imposing network with the five hundred Christian credit unions that were just beginning with only "several thousand" members and operating capital of perhaps a million złotys. The Christian credit unions were hardly comparable to their "privileged" Jewish counterparts, lamented Radomski, but that was just one more example of the tradition that "a guest is always honored in Poland."[33]

"Dishonesty"

One obvious reason *Mały Dziennik* promoted the boycott so vigorously was its apparent need to do so. That "Jews sell cheaper" (*U Żyda taniej*) was virtually proverb in Poland (July 17, 1935). How they did it, the Catholic daily alleged, was by using "talmudic" business practices (November 7, 1935). Not only did Jewish merchants use dishonest scales and false advertising, but such "tricks" as lowering prices on some items, even below cost, and then importuning customers to buy higher-priced goods as well (June 14, 1936). Polish peasant farmers were described as victims of the Jewish city slickers who bought their grain (September 28, 1938). Neither were these peasants up to competing with Jews when they came to the city to work in Christian stores. According to the Catholic daily, these country folk felt out of place and had a "certain inferiority complex" when dealing with city people. They needed to be made more

---

[32] *Pro Christo*, 13/8–9 (1937): 21–26.

[33] *Przegląd Katolicki*, 76 (1938): 389–90.

self-assured in their new urban environment so as not to be cheated by Jewish swindlers (September 17, 1938).

Jewish merchants were also regularly accused of selling adulterated goods and junk. When a reader wrote in to the *Mały Dziennik* complaining about poor service in a Jewish store and buying a radio that would not work, the editors commented, "That's what always happens when you buy from Jews" (March 15, 1936). Reporting on actions taken by Warsaw's health department, the Catholic daily ran the banner, "Filth and vermin at Jewish bakeries" (May 16, 1936). Jews, declared the *Mały Dziennik*, were ruining Poland's economy. They were destroying any possibility of Poland enticing foreign markets by producing goods so shoddy that they created "disgust in civilized countries" (May 6, 1938).

Another regular complaint of the *Mały Dziennik* was that Jews traded illegally on Sundays. Early on independent Poland had passed a Sunday rest law, putting Jewish merchants who observed the Sabbath (a majority in Poland) at an economic disadvantage. Claims have been made that the law was impoverishing, but Jewish leadership was divided in its attitude toward the law, and there were Poles sympathetic to modifying it for Jews.[34] Despite the rest law, de facto Sunday shopping "at the back door" was widespread. Polish workers and peasants often found Sunday the only convenient time to make purchases. The *Mały Dziennik* found the practice "dishonest and dirty." It was intolerable that Jews were "breaking our holy days," and compelling Christian merchants who want to compete to do the same (January 12, 1936). Yet when a reader wrote in to the *Rycerz Niepokalanej* to inquire if it was allowed to buy bread from Jews on Sunday, the answer was positive. The practice was allowed because it was a widespread custom; it was not the Jewish bakers but the Polish Christian customers who were the chief cause of the Sunday rest being violated.[35]

For Jewish merchants to adopt Polish names and modern rather than traditional Jewish dress was another form of "dishonesty," according to *Mały Dziennik* (December 13, 1937). The daily regularly complained

---

[34] Marcus maintains that whatever loss was suffered as a result of the Sunday rest laws was not large, and that the Jewish artisan, allegedly condemned to idleness for an extra day of the week, suffered more from lack of demand than from lack of work. *Social and Political History*, 213–15.

[35] *Rycerz Niepokalanej* (1935): 340.

about Jews who used neutral or Polish names for their stores and about Polish papers which accepted Jewish advertising (February 16, 1936). Here was the height of deceit, declared the Catholic daily, admitting that its own staff had erred more than once in accepting advertizing from Jewish firms with apparently Polish names (November 4, 1936). A regulation requiring store owners to display their full names in their windows had been passed by the government but was not effective. Jewish stores were using other names or were printing their names too small. The paper advised its readers to ask owners if theirs was a Christian store and not to accept as an answer that it was a Polish store (August 14, 1937; July 1, 1938).

Mały Dziennik expressed the hope that the regulation would be extended to include not only store owners but other groups as well. "Work in Poland must be only for Poles," it insisted (January 18, 1939). It likewise warned its readers against Jewish firms that tried to deceive Christian customers by hiring Christians or hanging somewhere prominently a Christian religious picture or a sign saying, "Christian firm." The Catholic daily questioned the honor of Christians willing to work as fronts for Jewish merchants. It called for legislation to ferret out such firms and require that they display a sign designating them as Jewish (March 11, 1939; June 5, 1939).

Ritual Slaughter

No issue in the interwar period aroused as much agitation between Polish Catholics and Jews as did *shehitah,* the halachically-defined method by which animals are slaughtered. No other issue, according to Joseph Marcus, aroused as much Jewish protest nor took up more debate in the Sejm (about half of its parliamentary time between 1936 and 1938).[36] The issue was of the utmost importance to observant Jews, since it determined whether or not the meat derived was kosher. But non-traditional, even the socialist Jews of the Bund recognized its wider implications and joined in the fray.

Jewish tradition required that kosher slaughtering be performed with an exquisitely sharp knife being drawn across the animal's throat, severing

---

[36] Marcus, *Social and Political History,* 358.

the jugular veins and arteries so that it bled to death. According to Moses Maimonides, Judaism's foremost medieval philosopher, the purpose of the law was that the death of the animal be as easy and painless as possible. The act was preceded by a benediction and performed by a rabbinically recognized slaughterer (*shohet*). Only meat slaughtered by a *shohet* was kosher. With *shehitah* under its direction, the religious leadership of a local Jewish community thus had monopolistic control over the sale of kosher meat. Income from *shehitah* came to be employed not only to defray expenses involved in the procedure itself but also to underwrite other community endeavors, charity and education. A "*shehitah* tax" often became the mainstay of a community's income.[37]

As early as the late nineteenth century, criticism arose against *shehitah* as cruelty to animals. Jewish religious authorities did not allow the animal to be stunned before its throat was cut, nor could it be decapitated. Switzerland outlawed the practice in 1893, Norway and Bavaria in 1930, Germany as a whole in 1933. In some instances the motives behind the efforts to ban *shehitah* were genuinely humanitarian: in others, as in Nazi Germany, they were simply antisemitic. In Poland they were also uniquely economic.

Poland's was not only Europe's largest Jewish population but also its most observant. Even more anomalous, the meat-packing industry, except for the western provinces, was almost entirely in Jewish hands, the slaughtering being performed by *shohtim* (butchers) according to the halachic procedure. The added expense of the *shehitah* tax was passed on by the meat-packing industry to the consumers, in the case of most non-Jews, without their knowing. In other words, as its critics argued, Catholic Poles were paying an indirect tax to the Jewish community.

The question of *ubój rytualny* (ritual slaughter) became a *cause célèbre* in Poland when the humane society of Warsaw sponsored a lecture on the subject by Monsignor Stanisław Trzeciak (March 21, 1935). Trzeciak claimed that ritual slaughter was not required by Mosaic law and therefore did not enjoy the protection of religious freedom afforded by the Polish constitution. The biblical law of Moses forbade the consumption of blood but said nothing about the method of animal slaughter. Saying a benediction before the slaughter did not render it a religious act, since Jews offer benedictions before all manner of activities, including

---

[37] *Encyclopaedia Judaica* (New York: Macmillan, 1971), 14:1337–44.

the most natural. Ritual slaughter was a "concoction" (*wymysł*) of the rabbis, Trzeciak insisted. It should be banned as a relic of "eastern barbarism" from the dark ages.[38]

Trzeciak's lecture created a sensation throughout Poland's religious and secular press. Within days Rabbi Schorr, a professor at the University of Warsaw, published a response in the Jewish daily, *Nasz Przegląd* (March 26, 1935). Schorr argued that the Jewish method of slaughter resulted in an instant loss of blood to the brain, so that the animal immediately lost consciousness. He pointed out the distinction between the Mosaic law or written Torah in the Bible and the oral Torah later recorded in the Talmud. *Shehitah*, he insisted, was a fundamental norm of the Jewish religion. As a rebuttal Trzeciak simply claimed that Rabbi Schorr was ignorant of the Talmud.[39]

More conducive to arousing public sentiment than the humanitarian or religious aspects of *shehitah* was its economics. Trzeciak continued his assault by giving statistics: in Warsaw, Bialystok, Kielce, and Łódź, 100% of the cattle were ritually slaughtered by *shohtim;* in Lwów and Rowno, 95%; in Lublin and Wilno, 90%. Since the meat-packers paid the *kahal* as much as ten złotys per head of cattle slaughtered, it meant that Christians were unwittingly paying huge amounts of money to the Jewish community in higher meat prices. Trzeciak gave statistics, once again drawn from Isaac Bornstein, a 1929 article on "The Budgets of religious Jewish communities in Poland": nearly half of the income (44.9%) of the 503 Jewish communities Bornstein studied came from *shehitah*, a total of over six million złotys a year. In some small towns the ritual slaughter tax underwrote the entire budget.[40] Bornstein's article received wide attention in the Catholic press. The official organ of the Archdiocese of Warsaw called for action to end this barbarism properly described as the "ritual murder of animals."[41]

---

[38] *Przegląd Katolicki*, 73 (1935): 270–72, 299–300, 318–20. Later expanded and published as *Ubój Rytualny w świetle Biblji i Talmudu* (Warsawa: A. Prabucki, 1935).

[39] Trzeciak, *Ubój Rytualny*, 20.

[40] *Kwartalnik Statystyczny*, 6 (1929), 3. Cited in Trzeciak, *Ubój Rytualny*, 57–66. See also *Przegląd Katolicki*, 73 (1935): 557; 74 (1936): 179–81; 197–98.

[41] *Wiadomości Archidiecezjalne Warszawskie*, 25 (1935): 311–12.

Nationalists sympathetic to Trzeciak's views saw this as an opportunity to embarrass the government.[42] In February 1936, Janina Prystor, a deputy to the Sejm, introduced a bill requiring animals to be stunned before being slaughtered. The Catholic press portrayed *shehitah* as a sadistic anachronism and medieval torture.[43] *Nasz Przegląd*, the Jewish daily, recognized that it would serve no purpose to marshall evidence to the contrary. The bill pending in the Sejm was purely economic in motivation, intended to remove Jews from the meat-packing industry.[44]

The economic issues were certainly the ones emphasized by the *Mały Dziennik*. When the leading rabbis of Poland entreated the Jewish community of Warsaw to do all it could to prevent the bill's passage, liberal Jewish organizations, including the Bund, joined in the effort. Such solidarity, concluded the *Mały Dziennik*, was proof that ritual slaughter was not at all a religious matter but "exclusively economic" (February 11, 1936). Religion was but a smoke screen to cover the real issue, which it said was an indirect tax on Christian consumers to support Jewish institutions (February 13, 1936).

Rabbis from all over Poland met in Warsaw to convince the government that Trzeciak's claim was false. They insisted that ritual slaughter was one of the chief principles of Judaism and that the slightest change in the prescriptions, especially stunning before slaughter, would render the meat inedible for observant Jews (February 15, 1936). Some local communities began passing ordinances even before the national government considered the matter. Appeals for prayers and support were made to Jewish communities outside Poland. *Mały Dziennik* denied that the attempt to ban ritual slaughter was just an attempt to get Jews out of the meat-packing industry. This "asiatic murder of animals" should have been stopped long ago, it insisted. "Only a harsh and very cruel race could agree to such a custom" (February 15, 1936; February 26, 1936).

Unlike the Catholic press, the Polish government saw the issue of *shehitah* as "unusually complicated," involving not only humanitarian and economic but also religious and legal aspects. The Jewish people had a right to kosher meat guaranteed by law. Thanks to the government's

---

[42] Marcus, *Social and Political History*, 357–58.

[43] *Przegląd Katolicki*, 73 (1935): 490–91.

[44] *Przegląd Katolicki*, 74 (1936): 354–55.

efforts, the bill to ban ritual slaughter altogether was defeated and replaced by one that limited the practice to the "factual needs" of the Jewish community (March 21, 1936). The *Mały Dziennik* criticized the government's position as too lenient. The paper was pleased that the government was finally paying attention to the "Jewish question," but complained that too much consideration was being given to minority rights. In the view of the Catholic daily, the Polish constitution, was written "especially for the majority" (March 21, 1936; March 22, 1936).

With ritual slaughter restricted to the needs of the Jewish community (January 1, 1937), public passions over the issue subsided. The practice was now limited to only 15% of Poland's meat production, and eventually kosher meat became twice the price of ordinary meat (August 18, 1939). But the editors of *Mały Dziennik* were still not satisfied. Outlawing ritual slaughter altogether was an obvious way of encouraging observant Jews to leave Poland, and in the last months before the invasion by Germany, the Catholic daily expressed its hopes for a total elimination of the practice from Poland. In March 1939, the Sejm passed a measure that would have outlawed *shehitah* altogether by 1942. But before the Senate had a chance to consider it, Germany invaded Poland and decided the issue for them.

Religious Articles

If interwar Poland was unusual for the number of Catholics who ate kosher meat, so too was it peculiar for the Jews who made crosses and sold rosaries. There could hardly be a more telling symptom of the underdeveloped state of manufacture and trade among ethnic Poles. Nor was there an area in the Polish economy where a widespread Jewish presence was more exasperating to Catholic nationalists. The word most used to describe it was "humiliating." As the *Rycerz Niepokalanej* put it: "We ought to be ashamed that Jews are manufacturing even religious articles for us, as if Catholics could not manage to establish a proper business to supply such needs."[45]

The *Mały Dziennik* took a leading role in a campaign that, like ritual slaughter, quickly found its way to the Sejm. The number of Jewish

---

[45] *Rycerz Niepokalanej*, (1935): 2, 54.

candle firms was especially exasperating to the Catholic daily since 25% of candles were purchased by churches (March 30, 1936). It was an "outrage" that a Jewish candle manufacturer would call his firm "Honeybee" so as to appear Polish and then send its price list to Catholic churches (March 14, 1936). The paper decried the "brazenness" of Jews who manufactured not only candles but articles used in Catholic prayer and worship: crosses, medals, prayer books, pictures, rosaries. For Jews to "market" such devotional objects was a "profanation." Not satisfied with encouraging Catholics to boycott such Jewish businesses, the *Mały Dziennik* went on to question the right of Jews to engage in such trade at all (May 9, 1936). When a Jewish photographer advertised a free breakfast and gifts to all children making their first holy communion, the daily denounced his action as a Jewish "trick" and reason enough to boycott all Jewish photographers (June 4, 1936).

To counteract the Jewish trade in Catholic religious goods, Częstochowa, the national center of Polish pilgrimage, became a center for organizing a Catholic wholesale firm to supply religious articles to Catholic dealers. The Society of Polish Merchants in Częstochowa estimated that 80% of the wholesale in Catholic religious goods was owned by Jews who earned upwards of 60 million złotys a year.[46] But at the hands of Monsignor Stanisław Trzeciak, the figures swelled along with the rhetoric.

Trzeciak was distressed that Jews were manufacturing and selling 80 to 100 percent of the crucifixes in Poland, symbols of Jesus' death and of Jewish "cruelty." The descendants of those who paid Judas thirty pieces of silver were now reaping 60 to 80 million złotys a year from religious articles. With the help of Jewish investors abroad, Jewish manufacturers were flooding Poland with their devotional wares, which Catholics were buying because they were cheaper. Jews, wrote Trzeciak, were even supplying oil for sanctuary lamps and wine for Mass. In contrast to Polish "tolerance," Jewish law required that Jewish religious articles (prayer shawls, mezuzahs, tefillin) be prepared only by Jews. Even wine had to be produced only by Jews to be regarded as kosher. Fair was fair, and for Trzeciak that meant priests should refuse to bless religious articles which came from Jews. And only those Catholic dealers

---

[46] *Mały Dziennik*, June 18, 1936; June 30, 1936.

who could prove that their manufacturers and wholesalers had been Catholic should be allowed to sell religious goods near a church.[47]

Once Catholic leaders calculated just how much Jewish firms were supplying to churches as well as to the faithful, it became commonly accepted that they were making profits of 80 million złotys a year. To put an end to such a "scandalous and intolerable" situation, a cooperative association was created in Warsaw to fire up the "passive and inert" masses to national-economic-religious action.[48] Father Stefan Downar, a deputy in the Sejm, took more direct action and introduced a bill into the Sejm requiring that objects used in the devotion of a particular religion be manufactured and distributed only by members of that religion.[49] The bill passed into law (March 25, 1938), giving businesses acting otherwise two years to liquidate their inventories.[50] Two years was too long to wait, complained the *Mały Dziennik* and suggested that Jewish merchants should have their Catholic religious objects confiscated (December 16, 1938).

There is no question but that Poland's interwar economy was in drastic need of radical reform: land redistribution, industrial development, creation of equal opportunities for all segments of society. Clearly there were inequities which needed to be rectified. But it is something else altogether to suggest that the "Jewish problem" in interwar Poland was essentially economic. Certainly anti-Jewish feelings among average Poles were heightened by poverty, joblessness, and major population shifts from agriculture to the urban industrial work force. But, as I have argued here, for Polish nationalists and the Catholic clergy, there was more to the issue than economics. It was not in the depths of the depression that the antisemitic campaign of the 1930s reached its height, but rather in the period of gradual recovery. And for the *Mały Dziennik,* at least, the

---

[47] *Mały Dziennik,* August 15, 1936; reprinted in *Przegląd Katolicki,* 74 (1936): 584–86.

[48] *Mały Dziennik,* August 23, 1936.

[49] *Mały Dziennik,* August 29, 1937; *Przegląd Katolicki,* 75 (1937): 243–44.

[50] *Wiadomości Archidiecezjalne Warszawskie,* 28 (1938): 245–46.

demise of Jewish businesses was announced with equal satisfaction as the development of "Christian trade."[51]

The clergy and Catholic press, above all the *Mały Dziennik*, were not on the sidelines but very much in the forefront of the effort to "nationalize" Poland's economy, as they put it. They worked as energetically as the National Democrats to solve Poland's economic problems at the expense of Poland's Jews. Cardinal Hlond was but the highest-ranking churchman to voice what the rest of the bishops and priests took for granted: Polish Catholics had the same right as Jews "to prefer" their own kind. Polish church leaders saw the boycott as a peaceful and ethically proper means to offset the economic advantages which Jewish merchants enjoyed. Poles trying to enter the marketplace to make a living were in their view underdogs in a mismatch. Centuries of commercial experience had given Jewish merchants a more than competitive edge.

What is remarkable is that ordinary Poles by and large did not adhere to the boycott. One reads of various segments of Polish society, from farmers to white collar workers, preferring to do business with Jews, whether for the sake of cheaper prices, the traditional way of doing things, credit, or courtesy. With a rhetoric betraying almost frantic desperation, the *Mały Dziennik* regularly bemoaned the Catholic Poles' lack of solidarity. If peasant farmers and workers can be credited for putting economic self-interest ahead of prejudice, it should be remembered that they and not the clergy comprised the overwhelming majority of Poland's population.

The Polish clergy may be forgiven for not appreciating the complexity of economics. It is more difficult to excuse their innocence in thinking that Poland's economic needs could be met by farm boys learning the art of selling. It is almost pathetic to observe that a Catholic opening a fish market in Warsaw could make news in Kraków. Equally pathetic was the naivete that could see attracting customers by lowering prices on some items as a "trick." To fault people for not being ahead of their time is unfair. It was not yet the era of ecumenism. But it hardly required farsightedness to recognize that Poles required precisely the kinds of skills that Jews could offer, skills that could be learned. As a matter of fact, there were Christian Poles who served as apprentices under Jews

---

[51] *Mały Dziennik*, January 2, 1938.

who were masters in their craft. But for conservative Catholic nationalists, that was "monstrous." To be an apprentice meant being part of the master's family, and that could only result in Polish apprentices being "warped" and alienated from their own.[52]

In surveying what the Polish Catholic press had to say on economic issues, one cannot help but be struck that, by far, the overwhelming number of articles appeared in one paper, the *Mały Dziennik*. If it were not for that Catholic daily, there would be relatively little to relate. Here is but one more indication that for Poland's Catholic leaders, economics was not the only nor even the central issue. In their view, whatever economic benefits might accrue to Poles from cooperating with Jews was far outweighed by other considerations, for Jewish influence in the economy meant Jewish influence in education, the arts, and literature. Cooperating with Jews would mean allowing the secularizing influences at work in the west to destroy Poland's traditional Catholic culture. For the Catholic leadership of the 1930s, poverty in a Catholic Poland was preferable to prosperity in one that was secular.

---

[52] Stanisław Fijalski, Director of the Christian Manufacturers Association, *Mały Dziennik*, December 29, 1938.

Chapter 10

A Culture Catholic or else not Polish

The Roman Catholic rejection of the modern secular state translated into Polish as a struggle for a Poland whose laws and culture represented Catholic norms and values, in short, a "Catholic Poland." Such an ideal affected not only the principle of separation of church and state but art, education, marriage laws and divorce. In a phrase quoted often in the nationalist and Catholic press, "Poland would be Catholic or it would not be Poland." Conservative Polish Catholics described religiously neutral states as "Masonic democracies." But when any aspects of modernity clashed with what was viewed as traditional Polish Catholic culture, the cry that went out was "Judaization."

The word "judaization" rings clumsy and foreign in the English language. As early as 1869, however, it was used in France to describe the changes taking place in European society.[1] That same year composer Richard Wagner wrote of the judaization (*Verjüdung*) of modern art.[2] The neologism passed into Polish as *zażydzenie,* a word which came to describe not only Poland's urban population and economy but also the "threat" Jews posed to its historic Roman Catholic culture. The "threat"

---

[1] In that year Henri Gougenot des Mousseaux published his *Le Juif, le Judaisme et la Judaisation des Peoples Chrétiens.* See Jacob Katz, *From Prejudice to Destruction, Anti-Semitism, 1700–1933* (Cambridge: Harvard, 1980), 142.

[2] Von K. Freigedank (pseudonym of Richard Wagner), *"Das Judenthum in der Musik"* (Judaism in Music), *Neue Zeitschrift fuer Musik,* 1850, 101–107, 109–112. Cf. Katz, *From Prejudice to Destruction,* 186.

came not only from Jews who regarded themselves as Poles and entered enthusiastically into Poland's cultural and intellectual life. It came also from any Poles, like the Masons, who attempted to advance liberal ideas and attitudes. For traditionalists bent on preserving the identification of Polish culture with Catholicism, judaization became another word for secularity.

The Polish Catholic press was fond of providing statistics to demonstrate the peculiarity of Poland's social situation and the extent of its judaization. For example, it was not enough to say that there were some three and a half million Jews in Poland or 11% of its population. This was over 42% of all the Jews in Europe. The two and a half million Jews in Soviet Russia were only 2% of its population. Romania's one million Jews and Hungary's half-million were only 5% of their respective populations. Only the United States had a larger Jewish population than Poland (somewhat over four million), but among 120 million inhabitants altogether, they constituted less than 4% of the total.[3]

Moreover, Poland's Jews were concentrated in cities and in the southern, central, and eastern areas of the country. There were few Jews in western Poland, formerly under Germany during the partitions. But Warsaw alone, according to the 1931 census, had 352,659 Jews, more than all the Jews of England (320,000) or of France (250,000), more than seven times the 50,000 Jews in all of Italy. With 30% of its population Jewish, Warsaw was second only to New York in numbers; Vienna (178,000 Jews) was 8th; Berlin (161,000 Jews) was 10th. In short, Warsaw was far more *zażydzona* than either Vienna or Berlin were *verjüdet*.

Population statistics, the Catholic press insisted, did not tell the entire the story. As pointed out above, the economy was shown to comprise greater disparities. The masses of poverty-stricken Jews were generally ignored; emphasis was placed on such figures like the claim that Jews, from within and outside the country, owned over 60% of all investments in Poland.[4] The 1931 government census offered further fuel to Catholic concern about Poland's judaization. In Warsaw and environs, Jews made up 32% of the lawyers and over 66% of the medical doctors. They also

---

[3] *Przewodnik Katolicki* (1932): 733; *Mały Dziennik*, November 13, 1938; February 23, 1939.

[4] *Mały Dziennik*, November 24, 1938.

owned over half of the businesses large enough to pay wages to hired help.[5] In some areas (where Jews constituted the majority of the urban population), the discrepancies were even greater. In southern Poland (Małopolska), barely one lawyer in ten was not Jewish.[6]

One does not have to be a Marxist to acknowledge the impact that economics has on culture. People living at a subsistence level of income do not patronize theaters or the arts. Poland's upper and middle class Jews not only had the means to patronize cultural productions but the capital and skills to create them: books, newspapers, motion pictures, theater. Jews were already having a marked influence on Polish culture. Even more troubling to Catholic nationalists was the fact that many had the means to facilitate their children's higher education. That could only mean an increase of Jewish influence in the future. Dedicated to the wedding of Polish culture with Catholicism, Poland's Catholic leadership had reason for alarm.

Christian Culture

For more than economic reasons, wrote St. Radost in the *Przegląd Katolicki,* Jewish capital and culture were beginning to overwhelm Polish social life. The Catholic world view, he argued, valued eternal realities above the merely temporal, whereas Jews gave greater consideration to life here and now. Like other Christian critics of Judaism, Radost interpreted this as materialism. While Christianity upheld excellence as an ideal, Judaism, he claimed, upheld affluence. Jewish dreams of a kingdom of God on earth had led to opportunism and the Bolshevik intention to rule the world.

On the other hand, wrote Radost, a falsely understood esteem for self-denial, patience and suffering had led to a certain Christian passivity in the face of supposedly divine decrees. Poland's Catholic masses tended

---

[5] *PrzeglądPowszechny*(1938): 126–33. According to Rafael Mahler, there were 4,488 Jewish medical doctors in private practice in Poland in 1931, 56% of the total; there were 6,454 lawyers and notary publics, 33.5% of the total. See Ezra Mendelsohn, *The Jews of East Central Europe between the World Wars* (Bloomington: Indiana University, 1983), 27.

[6] *Przegląd Katolicki,* 73 (1935): 118.

mistakenly to ascribe everything to God's providence rather than recognize that much of their "martyrdom" was due to their own failures. "In an era of streetcars, radio, newspaper, and poison gas," wrote Radost, Christians could not afford to look at life as only a pilgrimage. Christians had to acquire Jewish know-how and learn to use modern technology. They had to imitate Jewish solidarity and organize themselves. They had to learn patience and perseverance not only in suffering but in work. Polish Catholics had to make their presence felt in all the "shamefully neglected" areas of life, where they were an "insignificant minority."[7]

Criticizing Christians for being passive, or for their lack of modern sophistication was hardly typical for the Polish Catholic press. More standard practice was to blame the Jews, and Janusz Rawicz found the source of Jewish misfortune in Germany to lie not only in the brutal "teutonic spirit" but in Jewish "lack of restraint." Jews, he claimed, had come to dominate almost all of Germany's newspapers and set the tone for its literature and theater. Jews should have known that the Germans would not tolerate Jewish governance of their cultural life. But Germans were not the only ones with a right to be proud of their culture.

Poles, Rawicz argued, had drunk deep from the wells of western culture for a thousand years. They wanted the kind of Poland their ancestors had handed down to them, "national and Catholic." In the nineteenth century there were Jews who had become "Poles of the Mosaic religion" and embraced Polish culture. But now Jews wanted to create "some sort of new Jewish-Polish culture," claiming that it was the product of the Polish spirit. Worse yet, young talented Poles were falling under Jewish influence. Those who spoke out against the judaization of Polish culture were labeled as imitating the Nazis, as unprogressive or inconsistent with the tradition of Polish tolerance. Rawicz confessed his pity for the poverty of the Jewish masses in Poland's small towns, and he denounced anti-Jewish violence. But he could not accede to a Jewish "falsification" of Polish culture. His sentiments were paradigmatic: "We do not want a foreign culture, a foreign semitic-mercantile ethic, and the sexual corruption being thrust on us by Jewish authors and the profiteering Polish careerists who imitate them. We must stand up against the avalanche of increasing Jewish supremacy in Poland's intellectual

---

[7] *Przegląd Katolicki*, 73 (1935): 118–20.

life—not out of hatred for Jews but out of love for our own people and attachment to our reclaimed nation."

A war, Rawicz concluded, was being waged over the future of Polish culture, to determine whether it would remain Catholic and western or fall under Eastern, semitic influences. Repugnance for Nazism should not blind Poles to their obligation to fight against this "foreign invasion." The Jewish question concerned the soul of the nation. "A spiritually semitized Poland would cease to be Poland."[8]

Father Jan Rostworowski, the Jesuit editor of *Przegląd Powszechny,* concurred. Nazi measures were repugnant, but Christian concern for justice and love should not blind one to the fact that Poland's Jewish problem was "a hundred times more severe than anywhere else." While not dismissing its political and economic components, Rostworowski regarded Poland's "Jewish problem" as being "above all and firstly a matter related to Christian culture, a Christian world view and the realization and development of a Christian world order and structure, with the ultimate triumph of the kingdom of God on earth."

Jews, Rostworowski argued, had opposed the church from its beginnings and were responsible for virtually all the anti-church policies of governments throughout the world. If Poland was to be Catholic in more than name only, measures had to be taken to segregate Jews socially and to confine the influence of their literature and press. As much as Nazi antisemitism deserved to be condemned, no greater service could be done for Poland than that it become "asemitic."[9]

For traditionalist Catholics like Rostworowski, modernity and secularity had become identified with Jews. Secular culture was regarded as the product of eastern, "semiticized" thinking. For a thousand years the Poles had chosen to identify themselves with Western Europe, and that had meant with Roman Catholicism. For centuries they regarded themselves as the eastern outpost not only of Roman Catholicism but of Western civilization. Moreover, they shared western Europe's widespread disdain for anything eastern. For Poles that meant more than Ukrainians and Russians. Lumped together with the Turks whom they fought at Vienna were the Jews. Even after centuries on Polish soil, Jews were regarded

---

[8] *Przegląd Katolicki,* 71 (1933): 563–64.

[9] *Przegląd Powszechny,* (1936): 382–87.

as foreigners who could not hope to understand, let alone contribute to, Poland's Christian culture.

Tadeusz Trzebiński claimed no less an authority for this view than Adam Mickiewicz: "A culture and civilization truly worthy of humankind—must be Christian." Jews could hardly have a positive influence on Polish culture, Trzebiński wrote, since they had developed so little themselves. He explained how religious prohibitions against idols had prevented Jews from contributing to the fields of sculpture and painting. Neither, in his opinion, had Jews created anything significant in the field of architecture, music, drama, or technology. Only the poetry of the Bible and of Heine were worth mentioning.[10]

There was an obvious contradiction in treating Jewish cultural contributions so dismissively and yet seeing Jews as posing a threat to Poland's or Europe's Christian culture. Such partisans of the "purity" of Catholic or Christian culture were not without particulars, however. Once again it is clear that, in conjunction with culture at least, Jewish meant secular.

Literature

When the "Friends of Polish Art" had organized a festival of Polish art, the exhibit included the works by Finkelstein, Glicksman, Daniel, Greifenberg, M. Górewicz, Hochlinger, M. Litauer-Schneider, and Lili Pinkas. These Jews and their "adherents," complained Tadeusz Trzebiński, were neglecting to portray modern Polish life or else presenting it devoid of any spiritual character. This was a "conscious act against Polish art." But like other Polish champions of Catholic culture, Trzebinski was more concerned about literature. He was disturbed by the great number of Jewish authors and literary critics. By writing in Polish they were attempting to be the successors of Mickiewicz, Słowacki, Sienkiewicz, and Prus. They were "poaching on Polishness."[11]

Like their nostalgic counterparts elsewhere, the Polish critics of modernity glorified the past at Jewish expense. At a time still untroubled by the dangers of stereotypes, it was easy to draw comparisons between

---

[10] *Maly Dziennik,* February 5, 1939.

[11] *Maly Dziennik,* February 5, 1939.

all that was wrong with modern literature and supposed "elements of the Jewish psyche." For Feliks Jordan writing in *Tęcza,* such characteristics of modern literature as depicting the dark side of life, questioning idealism, or suspecting the heroic were all rooted in Jewish cynicism. "No one is great in the eyes of his butler," and for centuries Jews had been forced to serve others. Similarly Jordan attributed the theme of loneliness in modern literature to the alienation of Jews in diaspora.

More ominous and widespread was Jordan's identification of Jews with the modern relaxation of sexual mores. In contrast to Christian ethics and its insistence on personal responsibility, Jordan viewed Freud and Jewish authors after him as mitigating the idea of personal guilt by emphasizing the unconscious. Jews were not alone in their practical relativism, Jordan admitted, but among non-Jews, it was a matter of thoughtlessness. Among Jewish writers it was an act of "conscious and deliberate deceit." Jordan accused Jewish authors of "manic sexualism," expressing erotic feelings with descriptions at once refined and filthy.[12]

Catholic anti-modernists accused Jews of disdaining all that was noble and heroic in Poland's past, but admitted that the Jews were not alone. Aiding them were a "legion" of Poles who had become semitic at heart and now stood arm-in-arm with the Jews. In the words of one such "true" Pole: "Native Polish writers are starving today, while almost all the leading positions in cultural and artistic institutions are occupied either by Jews or their philosemitic protectors." Coming in for particular criticism was Poland's leading literary weekly, the *Wiadomości Literackie* (Literary News). Masonic-Jewish influence was held responsible for its liberal stance. Its "perfidious" activity was viewed as all the more dangerous because of its sway over young Polish talent and its ability to make or break literary reputations.[13]

Nationalist Catholics were particularly galled that Julian Tuwim, Poland's leading Jewish poet, was read in Polish schools as a Polish poet, being translated and cited abroad as a native Pole. According to the *Przegląd Katolicki,* Tuwim's "pacifist" writings were an affront to the Polish army and should be confiscated along with those of other Jewish pacifists: Wittlin, Antoni Słonimski, Anatol Stern, and Aleksander Wat. As for that other Jewish "genius," Antoni Słonimski, his depictions of

---

[12] *Tęcza,* (1937) February, 35–38; May, 33–35.

[13] *Mały Dziennik,* February 26, 1939.

Poles drinking, carrying guns, and involved in criminal activity was a mockery. The Polish masses needed to read the Polish classics and not the "communizing-pacifist-pornographic nonsense" of Jews and their "aryan followers and hirelings."[14] Another critic in the *Mały Dziennik* had a more radical solution: "Jews should not be writing books in the Polish language."[15]

The Press

Much of the influence Jews enjoyed over contemporary Polish literature and art was ascribed to their supposed influence over the press. Already in 1933, Wacław Sas-Podolski in the *Przegląd Katolicki* recognized the Nazis to be enemies of Poland, but he resented the attention being given in Poland's daily papers to Germany's persecution of Jews. The ill-treatment of Poles in the Third Reich was being given at best second place, he complained, as was the persecution of Christians in Russia and Catholics in Mexico. He blamed the "Jews, crypto-Jews, and half Jews" who had come to dominate Poland's intellectual life. Besides their own Yiddish or Polish language papers, Jews had "infiltrated" editorial positions in newspapers published by Poles. With the exception of newspapers belonging to the nationalist (Endek) camp, Poland's dailies were being judaized, as a result of "unwarranted Polish tolerance." Jews did not hire Poles on their papers, so why should Poles hire Jews?

Because of "massive" Jewish influence, claimed Sas-Podolski, Warsaw's dailies were bereft of Christian culture and pandered to the lower instincts of the masses. Crimes, scandals, sports, and theatrical reviews were receiving more coverage than intellectual matters. Every day Jewish editors and writers were "poisoning" hundreds of thousands of readers with their spiritually foreign mentality. Some Jewish writers might be sincerely attached to Polish culture, Sas-Podolski conceded, but their materialistic, internationalist world view was simply foreign to Christianity.[16]

---

[14] *Przegląd Katolicki,* 77 (1939): 282.

[15] *Mały Dziennik,* February 26, 1939.

[16] *Przegląd Katolicki,* (1933): 387–88.

Concerns about Jewish influence in the press were raised in 1936 in the Sejm. Nationalist deputy Budzyński complained that all the correspondents for the Polish press in Great Britain were Jewish. Similarly in France, Jews held leading positions for Polish newspapers. Jews likewise headed the foreign affairs department of the Polish radio network. Deputy Budzyński, admitted his antisemitism; but as a former cavalry officer who once fought foreign domination, he was now fighting "internal occupation." He demanded that the government replace its personnel or face an antisemitic reaction. "A Jew may not hold any rank in Polish culture," he insisted. In response to Budzyński, Prime Minister Składkowski insisted that Poland, despite its minorities, was one nation and that the best qualified people would be hired for their positions. The Prime Minister agreed with those who regarded Poland's press as "exceptionally honest" and working for Poland's best interests.[17]

As in the field of literature, so too in the press the problem was not only Jews but "liberals, democrats, and other free-thinkers favorable to them." These "Judaized Aryans," complained B. Malczewski in the *Mały Dziennik*, were helping Jews to "semiticize" Polish opinions and attitudes. Reuter, Haavas, the Associated Press, all the great international press agencies were influenced by Jews. Poland was no better. Malczewski bemoaned the influence of Jewish advertisers and the "democratic" papers that were "multiplying like mushrooms" and waging war against Polishness, nationalism, and Christianity. Malczewski too agreed that "Jews should not be writing in Polish."[18]

Theater, Radio, Motion Pictures

Writing in the *Przegląd Katolicki*, Wacław Sas-Podolski decried "neo-paganism" on the Polish stage. Theatrical art had been debased by rubbish from Paris, by nudity, filth, and communist propaganda like the "Three Penny Opera." Poles were allowing the semitic spirit to triumph on the stage. Jewish theatrical directors simply could not understand the Christian character of Polish culture. The Jewish public had its own tastes and materialistic world view, which were at odds with Christian idealism.

---

[17] *Mały Dziennik*, December 24, 1936.

[18] *Mały Dziennik*, March 9, 1939.

Tuwim, Hemmar, and Włast were writing lyrics for cabaret songs that were either nonsensical, cynical, or pornographic. Although Catholic Poles were avoiding cabarets, theaters, and music halls, that was not enough, Sas-Podolski insisted. Catholics had to take the offensive against the "pagan-Jewish theater." They must not allow the Polish theater to be dominated by non-Poles or Poles who had lost any feeling for their own national culture.[19]

"Dirty" songs were not being limited to theatrical audiences. Phonograph records and Polish radio also came in for Catholic disapproval. Sejm Deputy Budzyński, who had protested the judaization of the press, had the same complaint about Polish radio. A Jewish cartel, he insisted, was favoring Jewish music. The *Mały Dziennik* concurred. Despite the fact there were plenty of good Polish music directors, the Polish radio orchestra was under Jewish directors Jerzy Fitelberg and Grünberg-Górzyński.[20]

Similar complaints were raised against the Polish film industry. Pope Pius XI had already expressed concern about the potentially harmful ability of motion pictures to sway impressionable minds. To Tadeusz Trzebiński in the *Mały Dziennik,* it was distressing that Jews not only owned many of the movie theaters, but that Jewish film producers were filling the screen with pornography and "all kinds of Jewish humor." Especially troubling to Trzebiński was the attempt by Jewish film-makers to produce movies based on Poland's literary classics. Even the finest acting by Poles could result only in "weird parodies," if the directors were Jewish. Jews simply could not feel the Polish spirit which was so foreign to them. To avoid profaning them, Jewish film producers should not be allowed to touch national literary treasures.[21]

One of the more ominous recurring complaints about the judaization of Polish culture was that of pornography. Jews had often been blamed for demoralizing Poles with alcohol.[22] Modern technology now allowed conservative Catholic nationalists to link Jews with pornographic movies,

---

[19] *Przegląd Katolicki,* 71 (1933): 437–39.

[20] *Mały Dziennik,* January 18, 1938; May 7, 1938.

[21] *Mały Dziennik,* February 5, 1939; February 23, 1939; May 16, 1939.

[22] *Mały Dziennik,* September 14, 1937; September 16, 1937; September 8, 1938; *Pro Christo,* 13/3 (1937): 2.

picture postcards, books, and periodicals. Film studios, wrote Tadeusz Hoszowski, were deliberately producing lewd movies in order to deprave society. Most of the studios were owned by Jews. "Jewish-Masonic hands can do anything and find helpers everywhere."[23]

Cultural Warfare

For some years Polish nationalists had been waging an economic war against Jews, wrote the *Mały Dziennik* in 1939, but now it was time for a "cultural war," which was just as important and perhaps even more important. Polish culture, art, literature, the press, theater and film were all under the powerful influence of Jews. It was a threat against which Poles must "wage war without delay." All traces of Jewish influence were to be shaken off and a return made to a Catholic Christian way of life, both public and private. Unfortunately, such a war meant contending with more than Jews, since many Poles had been "infected" by the Talmudic ethic.[24]

Repeatedly those who wrote about de-judaizing or "nationalizing" Polish culture conceded that their opposition was more than anti-Jewish. Poles who defended Jews and Jewish contributions to Polish culture were disparaged by the *Mały Dziennik* as "knights of the yarmulke." Surely such Poles were either Masons, of Jewish descent, or else had been bought by Jewish money.[25] The Catholic daily wrote of "various organizations and Polish parties" helping Jews not only quietly but quite openly. Younger nationalists found fault with the entire "older generation."[26]

The policy of the *Mały Dziennik* was not to publish opinions at odds with its own editorial position. At least once, though, the editors did admit that they had received mail praising Jewish contributions to Polish culture and critical of their campaign. The editors dismissed the criticism and insisted that what was "advertised" as Jewish culture was parasitic,

---

[23] *Wiara i Życie*, 13 (1933): 178–83.

[24] *Mały Dziennik*, March 13, 1939.

[25] *Mały Dziennik*, February 16, 1939.

[26] *Mały Dziennik*, March 23, 1939.

simply living off the culture of different peoples. On what basis could Jews develop a culture? Their diaspora had embittered them and hardened their consciences. What did Jews know of patriotic struggle, chivalry, or idealism? Their purpose in life was money, their culture materialism in the worst sense. Only Christian culture was worthy of a person.[27]

The campaign to de-judaize Polish culture had to be primarily economic, wrote Józef Mitkowski. He pointed to the "minimal" interests of the Catholic peasant and working class masses in science, literature, music, and the arts. Those interests had to be developed; creativity among Catholic scholars and artists had to be encouraged. But how could one appeal to Catholic writers to dedicate their talents to Catholic causes, if they could not make a living from it. The issue came down to economics. "Cultural warfare" meant that Poles had to boycott books, periodicals, and newspapers written or published by Jews.[28]

Another *Mały Dziennik* reader, J. Holewiński, was more radical. Since it only affected Jews in the lower and middle classes, an economic boycott was not sufficient to nationalize Polish life and culture. The only way to de-judaize Poland, he wrote, was through legislation leading to "massive emigration."[29]

With such invective as its standard fare, the *Mały Dziennik* had to answer the charge that it was contradicting Jesus' commandment to love your neighbor. The editors felt constrained to assert that their campaign to de-judaize Polish life was not racist. Italy, with 180 times fewer Jews than Poland, was waging a ruthless war against Jews based on racist principles, but the call to nationalize Polish life was a matter of "self-defence." Love of neighbor did not require people to act contrary to their instinct for self-preservation. Poles had not fought against three partitions for 150 years only to fall under the yoke of a "fourth cultural-economic partition." The editors of the Catholic daily expressed their resentment at being told of their Christian responsibilities by Jews and their defenders, certain "democrats, progressives, and other internationalists."[30]

---

[27] *Mały Dziennik*, February 16, 1939.

[28] *Mały Dziennik*, March 12, 1939.

[29] *Mały Dziennik*, November 20, 1938.

[30] *Mały Dziennik*, February 16, 1939.

The charge that the *Mały Dziennik* was being unchristian was serious enough to warrant further rebuttal and an appeal to authority. The daily pointed to the popes who had condemned the "enticing machinations" of Jews and synods of bishops which had passed laws intended to protect Poles from what was being touted as Jewish "culture." But critics of the *Mały Dziennik* went to the government and certain highly placed church authorities. They denounced the paper's campaign to "nationalize" Polish culture as uncatholic and conducive to paganism. Monsignor Stanisław Trzeciak came to the daily's defense. He cited the New Testament's references to the "synagogue of Satan" (Rev. 2:9), to Jews doing the works of their father, the devil (Jn. 8:44). He cited the Fathers of the church. Jews, Saint Jerome had written, "are still persecuting Our Lord Jesus Christ to this day" (Epist. 65). Christians should not pray for Jews, wrote Saint Ambrose, because such prayers will not be heard (Epist. 2,12; Jer. 7:14–16). Saint Ambrose, wrote Trzeciak, was speaking to Christian defenders of Jews. He was warning them against associating with Jews.[31]

Marriage and the Family

If secularity was a "threat" to Polish arts and letters, the danger it posed to marriage and family life was even more critical. Attempts were made in the early 1930s to reform Poland's marriage laws and model them along the lines of western secular models. Catholic church leaders, including the prolific Monsignor Trzeciak, attacked the proposed reforms. For so seasoned a campaigner for Catholic tradition as Trzeciak, no attack on the proposed marriage reform seemed more appropriate or effective than to label it Jewish.

Poland's civil marriage laws simply ratified the marriage legislation of the various religious confessions within it. Catholics were bound by the church's canon law, Jews by Talmudic law, and Eastern Orthodox and Protestant Christians by their own respective church traditions. Though putatively benign, it was a situation onerous to Poles who no longer wished to practice any religion. Purely civil marriage did not exist in interwar Poland, and, even more vexing, neither did civil divorce. This

---

[31] *Mały Dziennik*, February 19, 1939.

meant that former Christians and non-observant Jews had to be married by their respective clergy. It meant that divorce was legal for Protestants, Eastern Orthodox Christians, and Jews, but not for Roman Catholics. Roman Catholic law did not sanction divorce, only annulments. Catholics who had no grounds for an annulment or who did not wish to stigmatize their children with implications of such a declaration, had only one way out of an unhappy marriage—changing their religious affiliation. In order to obtain a divorce recognized by the Polish state and thereby enter into a second marriage, Poles of Catholic background were compelled, at least temporarily, to join another church.

The "Polish Marriage Law Project," as it was called, sought to eliminate the necessity of such stratagems. It sought to bring Polish marriage legislation into line with that in the rest of Europe, including Italy, which had just concluded a concordat with the Vatican (1929). By allowing for both civil marriage and divorce, it would have put an end to a situation in which non-religious Poles were compelled to participate in religious ceremonies in order to contract a marriage. Modernist Poles viewed the change in social legislation as long overdue. In opposition, Monsignor Trzeciak sought to stigmatize the proposed reform by painting it as a Jewish effort to impose Talmudic and even bolshevik mores on Catholic family life in Poland.

Trzeciak argued that the Talmud was the basis and inspiration for marriage laws in the Soviet Union and the proposed reform in Poland.[32] The Talmud allowed for divorce, and that for Trzeciak meant it espoused an egoistic, purely materialistic view of marriage and family life. Jews saw marriage merely as a contract, not a sacrament, and ignored Jesus' prohibition of divorce. Trzeciak cited passages from the Talmud regarding the marriage of gentile slaves and contended that they constituted the source of the marriage law project. Here was a clear proof of the contempt Jews have for gentiles, and the real purpose behind the proposed marriage reform—to lead the Polish nation into "slavery" (p. 51).

As Trzeciak saw it, the authors of the marriage project were either Jewish or inspired by a Jewish spirit (p. 49). Poles had to choose between Jesus and the rabbis of the Talmud, Jesus or Barabbas. Under the

---

[32] Ks. Dr. Stanisław Trzeciak, Polska Agencja Prasowa, Warszawa: 5–14 December, 1931. *Talmud, Bolszewizm i "Projekt prawa małżeńskiego w Polsce."* (Warszawa, 1932).

pretense of equal rights and tolerance, Jews were "imparting a spirit of decay to Christian nations and societies, intentionally striving to destroy their culture, tradition, and faith" (p. 35). And because the decay of family life inevitably leads to decay of the state, the proposed changes should be seen as part of the plans revealed in the *Protocols of the Elders of Zion*. The "conspiratorial enemy" was preparing an attack on the foundations of the Polish state by first trying to poison and shackle its spirit (p. 57). By weakening family life, the marriage project would cause a moral crisis and thereby facilitate an attack by Soviet Russia. Poles, wrote the priest, had shed their blood against the Soviet attack for the sake of the Catholic religion and the sacredness of the family. They would not stand by calmly and watch as "Jewish commissars" replaced the gospel with the Talmud (p. 53).

Trzeciak's was simply a diatribe, not a reasoned argument, but his rhetoric was too inflammatory to be ignored. Dr. Armand Akerberg responded to Trzeciak's allegations with a lengthy rebuttal.[33] Most of his response was devoted to demonstrating Trzeciak's misunderstanding or falsification of Talmudic law. The marriage law project, Akerberg argued, was not based on the Talmud but on the practical experience of jurists. There might be some similarities between the prescriptions of the Talmud and the marriage reform, but a similarity was not the same thing as a cause. Allowing for civil marriage was simply an attempt to respect people's consciences and bring Poland into line with the rest of Europe. As for divorce, Trzeciak did not argue the indissolubility of marriage on humanitarian but simply religious grounds. Akerberg proceeded to put Jesus' prohibition of divorce into its historical context, as a protection for the dignity of wives and mothers. Today, he argued, we live in completely different circumstances, when women do not need the protection Jesus afforded them (p. 116). Requiring Catholic Poles to join another religion in order to divorce and remarry was tantamount to coercing them to practice deceit (p. 119).

Trzeciak's attempt to subvert reform by labeling it Jewish was nothing new. Father Ignacy Charszewski had employed the same tactic earlier in

---

[33] Armand Akerberg, *Talmud, Bolszewizm, i Projekt Polskiego Prawa Małżeńskiego. Odpowiedź Ks. Dr. Stanisławowi Trzeciakowi.* (Warszawa: 1932).

writing against feminism.[34] Giving women equal rights with men, including the right to vote, was part of a "world conspiracy" led by leftists, Jews, and Masons. Ideological feminism, wrote Charszewski, contained all the radical tendencies of liberalism. Ever since the French Revolution (which, the priest assured his readers, was really Jewish), liberals have identified progress with equality, above all the equality of Jews with Christians. Liberalism was a radical Jewish movement which had already infected the Polish constitution by placing the Talmud on the same level as the gospel. Its aim was the destruction of Catholicism in preparation for an eventual takeover by communism.

Charszewski's book was rife with sexist stereotypes. Women were unable to think for themselves. Men had the right to rule because of their intellectual superiority; women's superiority lay in their charm, which allowed them to influence men. Feminism, declared the priest, ran contrary to the laws of nature, a revolution against God, the church, and the church's doctrine of original sin. Calling it progress, more and more Poles were practicing birth control, changing their religion, divorcing and remarrying. And behind it all were Jews and Masons, bent on destroying the family and thereby the fabric of society. Because of economic conditions created by "Jewish capitalism," women were being forced to work outside the home. Women were likewise being "demoralized" by modern fashions, by short skirts and tight-fitting clothes—all the result of a "Masonic-Jewish conspiracy aimed directly against Christian women and indirectly against Christian society" (61). The ultimate objective of "Jewish-Masonic liberalism" and "Western democracy" was the dictatorship of the proletariat, which was just a mask for the dictatorship of Jews.

It bears noting here that, even within the context of Poland's Catholic traditionalism, neither Trzeciak nor Charszewski were typical. Both priests by any definition were extremists. Yet, despite the inflammatory, often outrageous language with which they propounded their antisemitism, neither priest, to my knowledge, was publicly rebuked let alone disciplined for his writings by their ecclesiastical superiors. On the contrary, both were elevated by their bishops and the Holy See to the rank of prelate, dignified with the honorific title of monsignor.

---

[34] Ignacy Charszewski, *Niebezpieczeństwo żydowskie w niebezpieczeństwie kobiecem.* (Warszawa: 1929).

Education

Along with their efforts on behalf of civil marriage and divorce, European liberals like the Freemasons had long worked to undermine the church's influence over public education by championing the principle of religiously neutral public schools. The Vatican consistently resisted such efforts wherever they arose in traditionally Catholic countries. In Poland the government's concordat with the Vatican provided that religion be taught in public schools at both the elementary and intermediate levels. It also gave local bishops the right to determine who would teach religion to the Catholic children. But for the advocates of Christian culture, these guarantees were not enough to ensure a Catholic Poland.

In his 1929 encyclical on Christian education, Pope Pius XI insisted that among the "rights" of the family and church vis-à-vis the state was the right to a state-sponsored religious education.[35] The Pope condemned schools from which religious instruction was excluded, contending that such "neutral" or "lay" schools were bound to become irreligious. Likewise "forbidden" or at most "tolerated" under certain circumstances were the so-called "mixed" schools in which Catholic children would receive separate religious instruction but might receive other lessons in common with non-Catholic pupils from non-Catholic teachers. The mere fact a state-sponsored school provided some religious instruction did not bring it into accord with the full rights of the church, declared the Pope. For this it was necessary that "all the teaching and the whole organization of the school, and its teachers, syllabus and text-books in every branch, be regulated by the Christian spirit, under the direction and maternal supervision of the Church."[36]

Many of the Pope's demands were already enshrined in the Church's 1917 Code of Canon Law: Catholic children were not to attend neutral or mixed schools with non-Catholic children (canon 1374). It was a grave obligation incumbent on "all the faithful" to provide Catholic children with a Christian education by way of the establishment and maintenance

---

[35] Claudia Carlen, I.H.M., *The Papal Encyclicals, 1740–1981,* 5 vols. (1981; reprint, Ann Arbor, MI: Pierien Press, 1990), 3:353–69.

[36] Carlen, *Papal Encyclicals,* 3:365.

of Catholic schools (canons 1372, 1379).[37] What was new in the Pope's encyclical was his demand that Catholic education for Catholic youth, supervised by the bishops, be subsidized by the state. Promoting attainment of this goal, wrote the pope, was an important goal for Catholic Action.

Attempts had been made unsuccessfully to write the creation of separate state-sponsored religious schools into Poland's 1921 constitution. Poland's public schools were open to all students of all nationalities and religions. The Vatican and bishops had to accept the principle of mixed schools in Poland. The principle proved "tolerable" so long as segregated neighborhoods and government policy resulted de facto in separate schools. In urban areas like Warsaw, however, mixed schools became not only a principle but a reality, especially after the government began a program of deliberate integration. With regular appeals to the Pope's teaching, Poland's Catholic leadership campaigned throughout the 1930s for state-subsidized Catholic schools. In Poland, needless to say, the papal prohibition of mixed schools meant that Catholic children were not to share schoolrooms with Jewish children or be taught by Jewish teachers.

According to the government's 1928 statistical yearbook, 7.5% of the pupils in Poland's public elementary schools were Jewish (somewhat less than the overall population which was 10.8% Jewish). In the countryside somewhat less than 3% of the pupils were Jewish; in the city it was 21.7%. Besides 235,358 Jewish children in public schools, there were nearly 51,000 in private schools funded by Jewish agencies, and 100,000 in traditional orthodox schools.

At the intermediate (gymnasium) level, however, the percentages changed drastically. While the number of Catholics declined, that of Jews doubled, so that 23% of the graduates were Jewish. (Ten years later, according to the *Mały Dziennik,* Jews for the 1937/38 academic year were 19% of the gymnasium graduates.) At the college and university levels, over 19% of the students were Jewish, in some cities more: Warsaw (23.7%); Kraków (28.7%); Wilno (30.3%); Lwów (33.5%). Examining these official statistics in 1930, Father Stanisław Podoleński, S.J., regretted the lack of hard data on the number of Jewish teachers in the state school system, but it appeared to him to be negligible. Most

---

[37] *Codex Iuris Canonici,* (Westminster, MD: Newman, 1957).

Jewish teachers were apparently to be found in the private Jewish schools.[38]

Despite the fact that Poland suffered from widespread shortages of both schools and funding, Polish church leaders worked to put the principles of the Pope's education encyclical into practice. The *Przegląd Homiletyczny* (Homiletic Review) encouraged priests to preach against mixed schools. The limitation of the clergy's influence to religion classes was unacceptable, since their influence could be undone by other teachers.[39] Equally unacceptable to the *Przewodnik Katolicki* were regulations by school officials prohibiting displays of religious pictures or requiring a simple "good morning" as a greeting instead of the traditional Polish "praised be Jesus Christ." During the partitions Prussian school teachers had tried to obliterate the identification of Polish and Catholic. The Poles resisted then and would have to do so now.[40]

The quasi-official Catholic press agency (KAP) complained that, without the bishops' approval and in disregard of the concordat, school authorities had on their own authority reduced the number of hours of classroom religious instruction; in some instances from twelve hours to eight, in others from eight hours to four. Religious instruction was the most important subject in the curriculum, the Catholic press agency argued. School officials were failing in their duty to accord it its proper place.[41] For the *Mały Dziennik*, it was imperative that Polish Catholics "fight energetically against those who teach Polish youth according to the 'method of the bolsheviks.'"[42]

Certainly the most vexing problem with mixed schools from the clerical perspective was that Catholic children could be instructed by liberal, secular, or Jewish teachers. Prior to 1934, Jews and Catholics each for the most part had their own public schools. Archbishop Adam Sapieha of Kraków could write with apparent satisfaction in an official (1928) report to the Vatican: "Six elementary public schools exist in our residential city, which are de facto attended exclusively by Jews; this has

---

[38] *Przegląd Powszechny*, 187 (1930): 318–33. See also *Mały Dziennik*, June 13, 1939.

[39] *Przegląd Homiletyczny*, 8 (1930): 221–23.

[40] *Przewodnik Katolicki*, (1932): 70, 118.

[41] *Prąd*, 27 (1934): 140.

[42] *Mały Dziennik*, June 28, 1935.

been accomplished gradually, so that the evil influence of Jews over Catholic children might be eliminated."[43]

At the beginning of the 1934/35 school year, however, Jewish and Catholic children in several districts were deliberately integrated into the same schools. Jewish teachers and administrators were assigned to what had previously been exclusively Catholic schools. The Minister of Education explained that properly qualified teachers had a right to positions in any public school, no matter what the students' religious background. The former policies led to separatism, and denied Jewish teachers the right to practice their profession.

Prąd, arguably the most moderate of the Catholic-oriented periodicals, acknowledged that Jewish teachers were behaving in a most proper manner, in every respect more properly than some nominal Christians. But *Prąd* questioned the wisdom of the new regulations. Jewish teachers had a right to jobs, but integration was simply escalating antagonism between Catholics and Jews. Schoolyard quarrels and fistfights were resulting from "mutual hatred and contempt." *Prąd* explicitly rejected the "demagoguery" that depicted Jews as willfully demoralizing Christian children. But a non-Catholic teacher or administrator could not help but disturb the peace and harmony required for learning by representing something in school that conflicted with what children were learning at home and in church. The problem was trying to integrate people from "two entirely different cultures" in the classroom.[44]

With a headline that read, "A Jew may not be the teacher of a Catholic child," the *Przewodnik Katolicki* was much less sympathetic. It argued along the lines of Pope Pius XI. Parents had a primary responsibility for their children's education. Schools were meant to help parents in their duties. It followed that Catholic parents had a right to Catholic teachers for their children instead of freethinking non-believers. Jews could not be trusted to teach Catholic children in a Catholic manner since, "by background, religion, and history, a Jew was an enemy of Christianity." The minorities treaty had granted Jews a right to their own schools and to government subsidies for those schools. This, the popular Catholic

---

[43] *Relatio super statu achidioecesis Cracoviensis ab Archiepiscopo Adamo Staphano Sapieha facta, Annus 1928.* Archivo Segregato Vaticano, S. Congr. Concisst. Relat. 268, Cracovien.

[44] *Prąd,* 28 (1935): 3–6.

weekly argued, did not constitute equality with the Catholic majority but privilege.[45] It might be noted here that no protests were raised in the Catholic press about the hundreds of Christian teachers who were teaching in public schools frequented by Jews. The *Mały Dziennik* complained only that they had to teach on Sundays.[46]

While the pope had to be more general in declaring non-Catholic teachers unacceptable for Catholics, the Polish bishops and their press agency could be more specific. In the name of Catholic parents, they demanded the recall of Jewish teachers from schools attended by Catholic children. Experiments were not to be tolerated. Catholic parents were not going to allow school officials to hand their children's spiritual direction over to teachers with a "different psychology and an attitude sometimes hostile to the Christian religion."[47]

Poland's educational system faced massive problems, not the least of which were economic. The government was simply unable to find enough schools to deal with the illiteracy that was still widespread in the countryside.[48] Urban areas in Poland offered the same temptations and suffered the same problems they did elsewhere. An article in the *Gazeta Kościelna* deplored youthful promiscuity. In one school district alone there had been seven hundred cases of venereal disease, four hundred abortions, and scores of incidents of homosexuality.[49] But the intractable demands faced by Poland's teachers did not win them any more sympathy in the Catholic press than their meager salaries did, some 120 to 180 złotys (24 to 36 dollars) a month.[50] Instead Professor Ludwik Skoczylas criticized teachers for "experiments" like coeducation, sex education in schools, and such unconventional activities as a field trip that took Roman Catholic school children to an orthodox church. His major criticism of Poland's teachers, however, was their religious and

---

[45] *Przewodnik Katolicki,* 40 (1934): 642.

[46] *Mały Dziennik,* May 26, 1936.

[47] *Prąd,* 27 (1934): 141–43.

[48] *Przegląd Powszechny,* 187 (1930): 318.

[49] *Gazeta Kościelna,* (1936): 514.

[50] Figures quoted from a representative of the Christian-National Teachers' Association, *Mały Dziennik,* October 12, 1937.

moral liberalism.[51] The main proponent of this liberalism and frequent object of Catholic criticism was the Federation of Polish Teachers (*Związek Nauczycielstwa Polskiego*) or ZNP.

The ZNP consisted of some 45,000 members, over half of Poland's public school teachers, outnumbering by far in membership and influence the Association of Christian-National Teachers, which was more sympathetic to the interests of the church. Although the ZNP claimed to include "many good Catholics," they obviously were not defending the church's interests against the "anti-clericals" among their colleagues, including "radicals" who dared to criticize openly the pope's encyclical on education.

The Jesuits at the *Przegląd Powszechny* were sure that the ZNP was determined not only to reduce the amount of religious instruction in schools but eliminate it altogether. These "apostles of secular schools" denied they were opposed to religion or the church, only to clerical interference. But under the guise of courtesy and toleration, the Jesuit journal contended, lay "Bolshevik hatred for all religion."[52] Ever since its liberal beginnings in prewar Austrian Poland, the ZNP had moved further to the left, spearheading almost all the opposition to the educational efforts of the church and Catholic Action. The ZNP had immense influence on the Ministry of Education, even to the extent of getting Janusz Jędrzejewicz named to office. As such, the federation was responsible for the unhealthy atmosphere in education and causing the only area of discord between the church and the Polish state.[53]

The ZNP, wrote Father Józef Hejnał, was guilty of demoralizing youth with its materialism, secularism, and "aggressive neo-paganism." He accused it of promoting textbooks sympathetic to communism and free-thinking. Field trips were breaking down academic discipline; coeducational gym classes were contributing to sexual scandals and venereal disease. Teachers were infected by ethical liberalism. Jews and declared atheists were being assigned to teach Catholic children. Behind all this lay the "Bolshevik-Masonic influences" bent on relaxing the morals of

---

[51] *Wiara i Życie*, 16 (1936): 172–77.

[52] *Przegląd Powszechny*, 187 (1930): 318–21.

[53] *Przegląd Powszechny*, 208 (1935): 430–33.

Polish youth so as to deprave society.[54] It must be granted that the ZNP did regard the clergy as a "bastion of backwardness and reaction." At a 1930 congress, it had passed the resolution that "Poland ought to be freed of clerical influences [which were] so very harmful." [55]

Without mentioning the ZNP or Ministry of Education by name, the Polish bishops took aim against their liberal programs at their First Plenary Synod at Częstochowa (1936). With an appeal to the Pope's education encyclical, the bishops passed the resolution (No. 122): "the faithful by right and obligation must demand that teaching in the present school system correspond completely to the principles of Catholic doctrine and that youth not be subjected to religious and moral harm by an improper co-education, by mixing Catholic and Jewish youth, or by entrusting the education of Catholic youth to teachers who believe differently." Like the other resolutions of the Bishops' Synod, this one too was confirmed and approved by Pope Pius XI.[56]

For Catholic officialdom, not only were liberal Jewish teachers a problem but Jewish students as well. As mentioned above, Archbishop Sapieha of Krakow, in his 1929 secret report to the Vatican, alluded to the "evil influence" (*malus influxus*) of Jewish children over Catholics. Cardinal August Hlond expressed the same view publicly in his oft-quoted 1936 statement on Jews: "It is true that, from a religious and ethical point of view, Jewish youth are having a negative influence on Catholic youth in our schools."[57]

Such sentiments found elaboration in the Catholic press. Professor Ludwik Skoczylas praised Jewish youth for working hard at their studies and not allowing themselves to be distracted by physical education or extracurricular activities. But they regularly skipped their Jewish religion classes and tended to belong to Zionist or socialist organizations hostile or at least indifferent to Polish nationalism. Even when their numbers

---

[54] *Gazeta Kościelna*, (1936): 499–500.

[55] *Gazeta Kościelna* (1937): 259. See also *Przegląd Powszechny*, 217 (1938): 399.

[56] *Przegląd Powszechny*, 2117 (1938): 403–04. See also *Mały Dziennik*, August 29, 1938.

[57] August Cardinal Hlond, *Na straży sumienia narodu* (Ramsey, NJ: Don Bosco, 1951), 164–65.

were few, they had considerable "destructive" influence on the rest of the school, he claimed, particularly in matters pertaining to sexuality.[58]

In a lengthier analysis in the *Przegląd Powszechny*, Skoczylas expressed pleasure that the dangers being posed by mixed schools were meeting resistance. Catholic youth clubs were organizing religious exercises at which young people took vows dedicating Poland to the Virgin Mother of Częstochowa. They were demonstrating their nationalism with an "intensely (*jaskrawo*) expressed antisemitism." As I have done here, Skoczylas too placed the issue of confessional Catholic schools within the larger context of culture. The times, he argued, were marked by a "most pointed conflict between Western culture and that of the Eastern ghetto, between Christianity and atheism in all its forms: liberalism, secularism, paganism, and communism."

A spiritual war was being waged in defense of faith and nation, declared Skoczylas. Through a united faith Poles were endeavoring to create a united nation that was for them an "almost religious object of devotion (*świętość*)." The ideal of Catholic education was "faith and nation." Teachers without faith in God could not truly educate children. Yet socialist and sometimes even atheist teachers were being assigned to teach in public schools, while active Catholics were being systematically removed from administrative positions. Religion was being taught as merely one subject among others, when it should be setting the tone for all the others. All sincere Catholics and nationalists wanted confessional schools, Skoczylas claimed. Those opposed were "only Jews, a small number of Polish dissenters, and those groups in Polish society devoted to Jews."[59]

If the Catholic press was to be believed, Poland's public schools were hotbeds of subversion. When Jewish students at the upper level of intermediate school (gymnasium) were charged with distributing anti-government leaflets, the *Mały Dziennik* immediately found them guilty of forming communist cells, since communism was "an entirely natural phenomenon among Jewish youth." Catholic youth had to be protected from their subversive ideas.[60] Priest-professor Fr. Kwiatkowski attacked

---

[58] *Wiara i Życie*, 16 (1936): 175–76.

[59] *Przegląd Powszechny*, 214 (1937): 164–74.

[60] *Mały Dziennik*, December 4, 1937.

"unhealthy, uncatholic" elements in Polish education, like the leaders of the ZNP. The sources of contemporary atheism were masonry and communism, "directed by liberal Jewry."[61]

For Monsignor Stanisław Trzeciak, efforts to diminish the church's influence over schools were all part of the plot outlined in the *Protocols of the Elders of Zion*. Socialists and Masons mouthed slogans about progress and equal rights for all religions but were in actuality endeavoring to secularize Poland's schools. Examining the membership of the ZNP revealed that 3,000 of its members were Jewish, including 135 of its leaders. [It should be noted that that would make Jewish membership only some 6% of the organization.] Polish members of the ZNP, wrote Trzeciak, were working for Jewish goals, allowing themselves to be guided by Jewish principles.[62]

According to a report in *Pro Christo,* police had to be called in to break up a disturbance, when angry villagers learned that the local rabbi, before teaching his religion class, removed the crucifix from the wall.[63] For the *Mały Dziennik,* however, Poles were guilty of "shameful sluggishness" by not complying with the resolution of the Polish bishops regarding education. They should be demanding separate schools from the government. After all, here was not a casual opinion but a solemn decree, confirmed by the Pope.[64]

The *Mały Dziennik* campaigned not only against mixed schools but also against camps that integrated Catholic and Jewish youth. According to the Catholic daily, camps under Jewish direction and without prayers in their program were attempting to "deprave" Polish children (July 16, 1935; July 28, 1935). The daily described young Jewish children in such camps as already filled with a "Talmudic spirit alien to Polishness and Christianity." But contrary to the intentions of the government, incidents were arising giving evidence of "some wholly wilful and determined antisemitism" (August 4, 1935). Segregated camps were necessary lest "the negative influences of the Jewish character affect the healthy

---

[61] *Rycerz Niepokalanej,* (1937): 191.

[62] *Mały Dziennik,* December 6, 1937.

[63] *Pro Christo,* 14/3 (1938): 29–30.

[64] *Mały Dziennik,* August 29, 1938.

temperaments of Polish youth" (August 11, 1938). Catholic youth should not be sharing campfires or school benches with Jews.

In their struggle against integrated schools and secular culture, Polish church leaders harbored no doubt that they were fully in accord with the mind of the Pope. The Holy See had fought secular liberalism since the time of the French Revolution. In its campaign to maintain a Catholic culture in Poland, the Polish church was simply continuing the fight. The struggle may have been lost in France and Italy, but not in Poland. To Catholic traditionalists like Monsignors Trzeciak and Charszewski, a secular culture which treated religion as a private, personal affair was intolerable. A Poland with a secular culture would not be Poland but some new "judaized" entity. The only way to prevent such an occurrence, to stave off secularity, was to limit or eliminate altogether the influence of secular Jews. The only solution was to use any means possible and morally permissible to "de-judaize" Poland.

Chapter 11

Catholic Solutions to the "Jewish Question"

The belief that Jews were a "question" was commonplace in the Europe of the 1930s, even for Jews, most notably the Zionists. Whether worded as a "question," a "problem," or an "issue," Poland's Catholics shared the generally accepted assumption that it existed. And whatever its meaning, however vague and ill-defined, if it existed elsewhere, it was manifestly more acute in Poland, where there were more Jews having more of an impact on the economy than anywhere else in Europe. Poland's severe economic problems and population statistics were proof enough that something had to be done. Nazi Germany's anti-Jewish measures were abhorred as barbarian, but employed as a proof that Jews were a "question" even in one of Europe's supposedly most advanced and "enlightened" cultures. If a problem in Germany, where they were barely one percent of the population, Jews were obviously more so in Warsaw where they were thirty-percent.

In the United States Jews were generally not seen as constituting a "question," even though antisemitism was demonstrably widespread. Jews were only four percent of the total population, and geographic expanse and ethnic diversity militated against the prejudice being blown up into a national issue. The United States' racial problems were drawn primarily along color lines. Jews were not a threat to American culture, essentially if not avowedly secular. Jews were a minority, but so was virtually everyone else.

Not so in Poland. Not in size, population, economic development, resources, ethnic diversity, history or culture was there any comparison between Poland and the United States. So there was no ostensible reason to believe that Poland could learn from the United States in dealing with its Jewish question. For conservative Catholics, the assimilation of Jews into Polish culture was inconceivable unless it included conversion, and even then it was questionable. Poland's was a Catholic culture, and to make it secular was precisely to judaize it. Jews had begun to polonize their names, but Catholic nationalists saw that as a tactic to escape the impact of the economic boycott, or worse, to begin infiltrating Polish culture.

In the face of Jewish expressions of loyalty to the Polish state, the editor of *Pro Christo* reminded its Catholic readers of Jewish involvement in passing the hated "Minorities Treaty" at Versailles. Jews were too enamored of German culture, he continued, too prone to internationalist communism. Jewish patriotism to Poland was a "relatively new" phenomenon, explainable by self-interest, especially in the wake of events in Nazi Germany. If there were exceptions, they involved only a few individual Jews who factually assimilated only after several generations.[1] So far as the Catholic press was concerned, assimilation was not the answer to Poland's Jewish question. Neither, it seems, was conversion.

Conversion

The church from its beginning directed its missionary zeal in a special way toward Jews. Their conversion, according to Saint Paul, would mean life for the world (Rom. 11:15). Toward this end Christians endeavored to bring Jews into the church by a variety of means ranging from debates and compulsory sermons to the promise of social preferment and, as at the time of the crusades, even the choice between baptism or death. By the twentieth century those efforts, with some few exceptions, were limited to prayers. Besides the Good Friday prayer for the "perfidious Jews," Pope Pius XI had inserted a special intention for Jews in his October 17, 1925 consecration of the human race to the Sacred Heart of Jesus: "Turn thine eyes of mercy toward the children of that race, once Thy chosen people. Of old they called down upon themselves the blood

---

[1] *Pro Christo* 9 (1933): 545–48.

of the Savior; may it now descend upon them a laver of redemption and life."

Prayer for the conversion of Jews was one of the purposes of a noteworthy though short-lived association for priests known as *Amici Israel,* the Friends of Israel.[2] Anthony van Asseldonk, procurator general of the Canons of the Holy Cross, had been persuaded to found the association in Rome, 1926, by a Dutch convert from Judaism, Francesca van Leer. It did not take long before the Friends of Israel grew to include 19 cardinals, 278 bishops, and 3000 priests from throughout the world. The association was remarkable for a number of reasons. Besides prayers for the conversion of Jews, members pledged themselves not to speak of Jews as a deicide people. Antisemitic speech and mockery were to be avoided, above all stories about ritual murder. Instead, members were to teach about the peculiar love God had for the Jewish people.

Within two years of its founding, the Friends of Israel was condemned (March 25, 1928) by the Holy Office, the Vatican's bureau for orthodoxy.[3] Approved by Pope Pius XI, the Vatican decree praised the purpose of the association, namely work and prayer for the conversion of Jews. And for the first time in an official Vatican statement, antisemitism was condemned by name: "Because [the Holy See] reproves all hate and animosity among peoples, it condemns most especially the hate against the once-chosen people of God, that hate that today is called by the name of antisemitism." But then the decree continued, the Holy Office had decided that the Friends of Israel must be suppressed because of "a manner of acting and thinking contrary to the opinion and spirit of the church, to the thinking of the Holy Fathers, and to the very liturgy." No more explicit official explanation was given for the condemnation. One could be inferred, however, from a documentary article in the influential and quasi-official periodical, *La Civiltà Cattolica,* published in Rome and closely supervised by the Vatican.[4] The article explained that the Vatican condemnation was directed at both antisemitism and pro-

---

[2] See C. Hall, "Friends of Israel—Stillborn Prologue," SIDIC, 1, 3 (1968): 6-11. See also Charlotte Klein, "The Vatican and Zionism, 1897–1967," *Christian Attitudes on Jews and Judaism,* Institute of Jewish Affairs, World Jewish Congress, (June/August, 1974): 12–13.

[3] *Acta Apostolicae Sedis,* vol. 20 (1928), 103–104.

[4] *La Civiltà Cattolica,* 2 (1928): 335–44.

semitism. The pro-semitic Friends of Israel "always defended and excused Jews," while ignoring their "undeniable alliance with Freemasons" and other subversive societies, all of which constituted the "Jewish peril."

Writing for a Polish readership, Father Marian Wiśniewski shared the opinions of the Roman journal. Prayers for the salvation of Jews was one thing, teaching Catholics to respect Jews was altogether something else. The Friends of Israel were to avoid references to Jews as a deicidal people. But, Wiśniewski pointed out, Pope Pius XI himself had reminded the faithful that Jews had called down Jesus' blood upon themselves, in his prayer consecrating the human race to the Sacred Heart. Today Jews were behind the persecution of Christians in Mexico and the Soviet Union. Wiśniewski quoted the Vatican's 1928 decree without commenting on its condemnation of antisemitism. The Friends of Israel was suppressed not for trying to convert Jews but for "glorifying" them with propaganda.[5] Several years later, Wiśniewski assured his readers that his efforts were aimed at converting Jews. "We are fighting them with the boycott and exclusionary laws not from national motives but for their salvation and ours." Their conversion would result in the "ultimate resolution of the Jewish question."[6]

By 1933 the Friends of Israel and the Vatican's 1928 condemnation were only a memory. Instead the Catholic leadership in Poland had to confront racist influences coming in from Nazi Germany. Some right-wing nationalists were questioning the not only the sincerity but the legal implications of Jewish conversions: Only Poles should enjoy full rights of citizenship, they held; baptism should make no difference, since, baptized or not, Jews were incapable of being polonized. An unsigned article in *Prąd* took issue with the racism of such attitudes. All people, including Jews, were called to Christian faith. Baptized Jews could be valuable contributors to Polish civilization.[7]

The traditional Christian attitude toward Jews was inherently ambivalent. Christians were to pray for Jews and to work for their conversion while at the same time disdaining and avoiding them. The

---

[5] *Pro Christo*, 6, 2 (1930): 69–77.

[6] *Pro Christo*, 9 (1933): 518–19.

[7] *Prąd*, 24 (1933): 34–37.

contradictions were strikingly apparent when in 1934, the 1900th anniversary of Jesus' death, Pius XI appealed for special prayers for the conversion of Jews. The popular Jesuit monthly, *Posłaniec Serca Jezusowego,* used the occasion to evoke the timeworn tradition of Jews as a "living memorial of divine punishment for the blood they once called down upon themselves." Converting Jews, the Jesuit monthly continued, was difficult, because they either held fast to the Talmud or else threw off all religion and became atheists. Both groups were characteristically hostile to Christianity, especially to the Catholic church. Even though Jews were frequently associated with communist activity, prostitution, and pornography, Catholics were not to hate or persecute them. Catholics were required to pray for Jews while at the same time defending themselves from their destructive influence.[8]

Conversion, according to longstanding Catholic tradition, was the only way to resolve the problems caused by the diaspora. Father T. Radkowski represented that tradition in an article for priests. Because they rejected Jesus as the messiah, Jews had become the "eternal exile," and thereby a nation of small merchants, living parasitically off the societies where they were dispersed. But it would not always be so. On the word of Saint Paul, the "old people of God," who had been the first stones to build up the church, would in the last days become the final stones to complete the edifice.[9] The problem was how to confront the problems caused by the diaspora before the "last days." Perhaps, suggested more than one priest, the mutually opposed interests of Christians and Jews could be brought closer together by Jewish converts. Up to now they had attempted to conceal their backgrounds as quickly as possible so as to avoid suspicion from Catholics and hostility from Jews. Perhaps they could become a bridge between the two communities. In other areas the church's missionary endeavors included the fostering of local cultures and the development of an indigenous clergy. Perhaps Jewish Christians could become their own rite within the church, with their own Christian culture, customs, and clergy. Such a Jewish-Christian rite might prove attractive to religiously indifferent Jews.[10] The clerical authors of such opinions

---

[8] *Posłaniec Serca Jezusowego,* 62 (1934): 13–14.

[9] *Głos Kapłański,* 9 (1935): 485–94, 535–42.

[10] *Gazeta Kościelna,* (1935): 354–55. See also *Ateneum Kapłańskie,* July 1935.

were obviously not overly familiar with either Jews or Christians of Jewish background.

One such Catholic of Jewish heritage was Father Julian Unszlicht, a frequent critic of his former co-religionists. He had no doubt but that the labor movement in Poland would have been quite different had Jews become Christian. He too identified the demoralizing influences of modernity with the Jewish community in Poland and saw it as a "sad but unavoidable necessity for us Catholic priests to fight Jewish influence and protect Catholic souls from eternal damnation." But Unszlicht was concerned about the widespread opinion among Catholics that there was something in the Jewish psyche that made missionary outreach to Jews too daunting to undertake. Although there were Jews converting to Christianity merely for self-interest, there were also "'Christ-like' souls in Israel" who needed the ministrations of Catholic priests. Jesus himself had said he came only for the lost sheep of the house of Israel (Mt. 15:14). Along with combatting the "de-christianizing actions of the Jewish community," it was an activity dear to God to try to convert the "better" Jews.[11]

His Jewish background did not preclude Unszlicht from espousing the stock Christian opinion that Jews had been scattered among the nations as a "living memorial of God's punishment." Christians could only pray for the day when they would be freed from their blindness. In the meantime, priests needed to work for individual Jewish conversions. They could do so by convincing Jews that conversion did not mean rejection of their people; the early Christians were all Jews, and those who follow Jesus were the "true Israelites." Unszlicht was satisfied that the vast majority of priests welcomed Jewish converts and were willing to minister to their personal and pastoral needs. Such priests also had a "wide field" for working to overcome prejudice against Jewish converts. True Catholics, wrote Unszlicht, embraced sincere Jewish converts with Christian love. But there were also "occasional exceptions," and newly converted Jewish Christians had to be prepared to face "suffering and humiliation" as a sharing in Jesus' cross.[12]

As Unszlicht suggested, some priests were less than sanguine about the possibility of Jewish conversion altogether, let alone as a solution to the

---

[11] *Pro Christo*, 4 (1928): 696–98.

[12] *Homo Dei*, (1935): 112–16.

Jewish question. The issue of sincerity versus self-interest received considerable treatment in the Polish Catholic press, especially in specialized periodicals for the clergy. Any outright rejection of Jews as potential converts was out of the question, since it would have constituted the racist antisemitism condemned by the Vatican. Not Jewish blood, therefore, but something in the Jewish psyche had to be found which would explain why Jews were disinclined to become sincere Christians. Centuries of being alien, wrote Father Eugeniusz Dąbrowski, made it difficult for Jews to assimilate, so that one could even speak of the incapacity of Jews to understand the gospel. This was not a matter of race, he insisted, but a "psychic type" of religiosity which Jesus had rejected. It began in the Babylonian exile and continued to this day.[13]

Father Roman Mieliński agreed. There were Catholics, he wrote, who were expressing scandal that the clergy were not condemning anti-Jewish activity, asking why more efforts were not being made to bring Jews into the church. Mieliński's response was to blame the Jews. Jewish resentment against the Romans for the destruction of the Second Temple later developed into a hatred for Christians. In Poland as elsewhere, the church had made repeated efforts to convert Jews. Their recalcitrance was not the church's fault. Priests like the editor of *Verbum,* Monsignor Korniłłowicz at Laski, were actively engaged in the apostolate to Jews. But most priests could not afford the time for such a mission. They were too taken up with the need to resist the "hostile work" of Jews against the church.[14]

In the midst of the antisemitic wave emanating from Germany and sweeping Europe, the Vatican published as the papal prayer intention for the month of December, 1938, an increase of Catholic missionaries capable of converting Jews. The Jesuit monthly, *Posłaniec Serca Jezusowego,* used the occasion to remind its readers of their "duty" to pray for Jewish conversions, a duty that continued to bind despite the widespread disbelief in the sincerity of those conversions, despite the common conviction that it was impossible for even for converted Jews to adjust to Christian society. Jews, continued the unsigned article, might control the world's financial markets and press, might seethe with loathing for Christianity, especially for the Catholic church. But that was

---

[13] *Głos Kapłański,* 10 (1936): 473–77.

[14] *Pro Christo,* 12, 7 (1936): 1–5.

all the more reason to pray for Jews to convert, so that their resources and talents could be used for good instead of evil. Although most Jews in Poland were either fanatically religious or completely irreligious, in either case hostile to the church, there was a small number who were indifferent, from whom converts could be drawn. In the previous 150 years, barely a hundred thousand Jews had converted to Christianity, the article continued. That small number was due to "Jewish pride," a belief in the superiority of Judaism. Another reason was the closed nature of Jewish society. Proselytizing efforts from Christians, including those of Jewish background, was generally viewed as being insolent and aggressive. But the cause of Jewish conversions could be expected to go forward, so long as godly missionaries might be found who would not be discouraged at the Jews' stiff necks.[15]

By 1939 the issue of Jewish conversions became topical enough to require guidance from the bishops as to how to determine sincerity. The Archdiocese of Warsaw simply reminded priests that, according to the church's canon law, no adult was to be baptized unless properly instructed. That meant that sincere intent had to be determined carefully; offhanded instructions and superficial examinations were not enough.[16] Writing for priests, Father S. Biskupski found other dioceses in Poland more exacting in their requirements. Instructions were required to last anywhere from six months to two years, and parish priests were to consult with diocesan officials before proceeding with baptism. Such policies were required, wrote Biskupski, because, as experience indicated, cases of sincere Jewish conversions were "extremely rare."[17]

The most documented and detailed consideration of Jewish conversions was written by Father Witold Gronkowski. There were, he wrote, very few Poles adamantly against accepting Jews into the church. But there were many who were troubled about insincere conversions, motivated by a Jewish desire to penetrate non-Jewish society. One could not exclude Jews from baptism *a priori*; nationality and race were no obstacles to baptism. But Gronkowski found merit in the regulations of Pope Paul III (1542), which enjoined bishops and priests to keep a watchful eye on

---

[15] *Posłaniec Serca Jezusowego*, 66 (1938): 442–46.

[16] *Wiadomości Archidiecezjalne Warszawskie*, 29 (1939): 81–82.

[17] *Ateneum Kapłańskie*, 44 (1939): 58–60.

Jewish converts to prevent them from associating with their former co-religionists.

Although most Jewish conversions were opportunistic, an increase of sincere converts could be expected, wrote Gronkowski, thanks to the efforts of a small number of priests and religious of Jewish background. But such converts still remained Jews. Gronkowski cited Theodor Herzl and Louis Brandeis as acknowledging that Jews were a distinct people, no matter what their religious convictions. The priest did not appreciate the commonly made Jewish distinction between Jews who repudiated their religion through disbelief or non-observance and those who positively joined another community by accepting another religion. Therefore, even if there should be an increase in the numbers of Jewish converts to Christianity, no relaxation or change of tactics was called for in the war against Judaism. Religious convictions were not the issue here for Poles, anymore than it would be if all Germans were to become Catholic. The question was one of patriotism and loyalty.

Gronkowski reminded his readers of the Vatican's suppression of the Friends of Israel. Here, he wrote, was a condemnation at one stroke of both "German racism" and "Jewish racism." The priest did not see the Vatican's condemnation of antisemitism as affecting Polish attitudes. He was quite satisfied that Poles had not transgressed the bounds of social justice in their self-defense against Jews. Admittedly, there had been some isolated excesses in the effort to de-judaize Polish life, but casualties in a war were to be expected. To be effective, a war had to be waged without compromise. Poles did not violate Christian ethics, they did not hate Jews qua Jews. And it should come as no surprise that newly-converted Jews encountered Christian prejudice when one considered the hundreds of Jewish converts who later became Masons, socialists, and communists. The prejudice, contended Gronkowski, was not altogether unfounded. Experience dictated the need for greater caution when it came to Jewish converts in comparison to others. Truly sincere converts, he was sure, would not be deterred by the greater rigors demanded of them.[18]

If the foregoing priest-authors did not see conversion as the answer to Poland's Jewish question, even less could lay people be expected to do so. One of the most prominent of those Catholic laity was Zofia Kossak,

---

[18] *Ateneum Kapłańskie*, 43 (1939): 435–58.

a prominent author who during German occupation would become a leader in the Polish underground. The Jewish question, she wrote in a widely publicized article, was not religious at all but exclusively racial, national, and economic. From a Christian point of view, Jews were human beings and neighbors; there was no doubt but that they could become good Catholics. But what if, by some miracle, all of Poland's Jews became Catholic and all the synagogues became churches. Who but for the clergy and a few individuals would be happy about the miracle? The Jewish problem would be solved for the church but not for Poland. Polishness and Catholicism were not identical.

If there were only a few Jews in Poland, Kossak continued, Poles would look at their synagogues with curiosity. The issue for her was one of race, not faith. "Jews are so terribly foreign to us, foreign and unpleasant because they are of another race." It was their eastern excitability, their quarrelsomeness, their way of thinking that irritated Poles, not their religion. There was no doubt but that Jewish converts to the church would impose their traits upon the Polish psyche and thereby create a new nationality. That new nationality might well possess great value, but it would cease to be Polish.

Kossak saw Polish youth as confronting a terrible dilemma. No matter what the profession or line of work they chose to enter, a Jew was already there, "more clever, more enterprising, more relentless." Although she supported the boycott, Kossak realized that it could not solve Poland's Jewish question. With no place open to Jewish immigration, did Poles imagine that Jews would commit collective suicide? Certainly they would struggle with all their strength to survive, as was their human right. So, from all appearances, Poland's Jewish question was a situation with no way out. But such a situation, Kossak insisted, did not exist. An "honest solution" had to be found. It was a European question. No single country could solve it. No issue was more urgent. A solution had to be found which would allow Poles to maintain their national integrity without harming their neighbors.[19]

---

[19] Zofia Kossak, "Nie istnieją sytuacje bez wyjścia," *Kultura,* September 27, 1936.

Emigration

For Jews too it was a situation with no way out, but few Polish Catholics writing on the subject appeared to share Zofia Kossak's appreciation of how little opportunity for Jewish immigration existed. For decades emigration had been the normal means by which Poles dealt with the otherwise intractable problems of poverty and overpopulation. Millions of its inhabitants left partitioned Poland in the nineteenth century in the wake of recurrent, ill-fated revolutions for political independence. Likewise after 1918, the mounting difficulties which accompanied reconstruction prompted hundreds of thousands of Poles to leave in another exodus. Settling mainly in the United States, western Europe, Brazil, Argentina, and Australia, a conservatively estimated one-fourth of Poland's population left to make new lives elsewhere.[20]

The political pressure on Jews to leave Poland did not develop until the calamity of world depression. While a sizable departure of Jews from Poland had always been a long-term goal of the National Democrats, they did not present this demand categorically before 1931, when they made the "Jewish problem" a decisive element in their struggle for power. Their demands increased rapidly after the Nazi rise to power in Germany. The depression saw unemployment in Poland grow to 50% in the villages, 35% in the towns. From 1932 to 1937 social unrest was such that Poland was constantly on the brink of collapse.[21] However simplistic it may seem to us today, the massive unemployment was attributed to overpopulation, an explanation considered irrefutable at the time. In 1936 the government made large-scale emigration a major plank of its program. The problem was to find outlets not just for Jewish emigrants but for the millions of peasants and other destitute Poles even more eager than Jews to leave Poland in search of a livelihood. But the government could not publicly admit that Poles needed to emigrate or that they were in need of foreign aid. That would have offended the Polish sense of national pride. The need to emigrate was depicted as

---

[20] For an overview and bibliography, see Eva Morawska, "The Poles in Europe and America," in *Ethnicity,* Andrew M. Greeley and Gregory Baum, eds. (New York: Seabury, 1977), 30–35.

[21] Joseph Marcus, *A Social and Political History of the Jews in Poland, 1919–1939* (New York; Amsterdam: Mouton, 1983), 391–93.

confined to Jews. Emigration was viewed as a solution not to Poland's economic problems but its "Jewish problem."

All Jews could not have left Poland, but neither did they all want to. It was not altogether unwelcome to the Jewish leadership in Poland that the United States and other nations had shut off the flow of immigration in the early 1920s. For groups favoring assimilation or for communists awaiting world revolution, remaining in Poland was the correct course of action. Orthodox Jews were disinclined to break up their centers of strict religious adherence in order to immigrate to countries like the United States, notorious for non-observance. Zionist leaders were the exception in that they saw a Jewish exodus from eastern Europe as a "historical necessity." As a consequence, after 1924, the number of Jewish immigrants to the United States fell short of the number that was allowed in under the quota for Poland. Moreover, in spite of western immigration restrictions, it is estimated that 429,000 Jews left Germany, Austria, and Czechoslovakia between 1933 and 1939. That was three times the number that left Poland in those years, even though those three countries combined had only one-quarter the number of Jews Poland did.[22]

Emigration was the solution most frequently offered to Poland's "Jewish problem" in the Catholic press. If Jews would emigrate, it was argued, the masses of destitute peasants could take their places in trade and commerce. Rarely did the Catholic press acknowledge that Poland's dense population constituted a problem, and never was birth control suggested as a solution. Jan Skomorowski was an exception when he admitted in the *Mały Dziennik* that Poland's villages were overpopulated. But he added quickly that this in no way justified birth control since there were still great stretches of unpopulated land in the world, untouched by a plow. In Poland, on the other hand, there were some sixty persons per square kilometer, a striking contrast to Germany, Denmark, and Czechoslovakia where there were barely forty. Skomorowski was exceptional, too, in insisting that, along with Jews, destitute peasants should also be encouraged to leave.[23]

For most Polish Catholics writing on the issue, the problem was not the peasants. Hubert Sukiennicki admitted that Poland had one of the highest rates of population increase in Europe, but it would be solved, he was

---

[22] Marcus, *Social and Political History,* 390.

[23] *Mały Dziennik,* November 19, 1935.

sure, if Jewish emigration returned to the "normal prewar process." He had no doubt that Jews were feeling the pain of the situation and were willing to leave. Neither did he doubt that world Jewry would be able to finance this massive population move. The problem was re-opening Palestine and finding new territories for Jewish settlement.[24] Even the *Mały Dziennik* acknowledged at least once that the masses of impoverished Jews were caught in a "trap." The editors of the Catholic daily were concerned, however, that as a result they might became apt candidates for communist propaganda. With Palestine closed to further Jewish immigration, only the League of Nations could provide a way out. It was a recurrent theme in the Catholic press that an international solution was the only one possible.[25]

The discernable desperation of their situation sometimes led Poland's government leaders to seek desperate solutions. Under this category one may classify the suggestion that Poland be given colonies for its Jews. In the summer of 1937, the government's Ministry of Foreign Affairs prepared a document known as the "Colonial Theses of Poland." It stressed the critical importance of emigration for Poland's chronic unemployment and stated that Poland must possess colonial territories in common with the other great powers of Europe. In September of that year, at the 18th annual session of the League of Nations, Poland formally requested economic concessions in colonial areas for itself and other overpopulated countries. Earlier that year the government had sent a commission to Madagascar, then a French colony, to investigate the possibility of a Jewish settlement there. Neither the demand for colonies nor the so-called Madagascar Plan were taken seriously by Poland's Foreign Minister, Colonel Beck. Both were simply political maneuvers which served to divert Poles from their real problems. Inspiring jokes and satirical songs, both also proved to be deeply humiliating to Jews.[26]

No threats of forced expulsion were made by Polish government officials, and no feasible plan existed for mass emigration. But this did not prevent a veritable campaign of speeches from politicians, echoed by articles in the nationalist and Catholic press. The *Mały Dziennik* even

---

[24] *Przegląd Katolicki,* 75 (1937): 195–98.

[25] *Mały Dziennik,* June 7, 1936.

[26] Marcus, *Social and Political History,* 392–95.

anticipated the idea of colonies for Jews, characterizing them not only a necessity but a "moral right." Once the Jews left, the surplus peasant population would be able to "polonize" Poland's cities. The League of Nations was responsible for finding the colonies, since many of its members controlled underpopulated lands. The League would also be responsible for financing the move.[27]

The *Mały Dziennik* pointed to the *New York Times* and American Jewish leadership as concurring with its opinion. An editorial in the *Times* had suggested that finding underpopulated colonies for Jews would be a means of obviating future conflicts and so not merely a humanitarian gesture but a matter of enlightened self-interest. The *Mały Dziennik* viewed the editorial as representative of American Jewish opinion, quite assured that the *Times* spoke for Jewish leaders and financiers.[28] Closer to home, the view of Polish Zionists like Jabotinsky and Grynbaum were quoted as ratifying emigration as the only "rational or best solution to Poland's Jewish question."[29] The problem was that Zionists had not yet recognized the need to find other territories besides Palestine, which was already a closed case and too small anyway. Along with Madagascar, Ecuador and Abyssinia were considered possibilities.[30]

Nasz Przegląd, the Jewish Polish-language daily, acknowledging that Jewish emigration from Poland was insignificant, blamed antisemitism. Anti-Jewish propaganda had so identified Jewish with communism and anarchy that countries once open to Jewish immigration were now closed.[31] The *Mały Dziennik* was unsympathetic to the reasoning and pointed with exasperation to the numbers of Jewish emigrés returning to Poland. For every Jew that leaves, two return. Re-emigration had to be stopped. Jews, the Catholic daily complained, had left with millions of złotys and were returning penniless. Equally disturbing were the Jews

---

[27] *Mały Dziennik,* August 25, 1936. See also *Przegląd Powszechny,* 212 (1936): 255.

[28] *Mały Dziennik,* November 19, 1938.

[29] *Przegląd Katolicki,* 74 (1936): 615–16.

[30] *Mały Dziennik,* October 1, 1935; January 13, 1937; October 10, 1938.

[31] *Mały Dziennik,* April 4, 1937.

claiming to be Polish citizens but in reality refugees from Romania, entering Poland illegally.[32]

The right of Jews to remain in Poland or reenter after leaving was based on the argument that it had been their home for centuries. Jerzy Jastrzębiec took issue with the argument and the "legend" that Jews had lived in Poland for nine hundred years. He disputed too the assertion of philosemitic Polish liberals that Jews were an "integral part of the Polish people." Jewish arrival in Poland, he contended, should not be confused with the fact that Jewish merchants passed through the land in the 10th century. In the early seventeenth century there were barely 200,000 Jews in Poland, he claimed. A century later, because of the Hussite Wars in Czechoslovakia and the Thirty Years' War in Germany, there were 1,800,000 Jews in Poland. If there were over three million Jews now, it could not have been the result of natural reproduction. Jastrzębiec lay the blame for Poland's large Jewish population on twentieth-century Jewish immigration from Russia, officially estimated by the Polish government as having been 600,000 but closer, he was sure, to a million. The first great influx of Jews into Poland, he concluded, was an eighteenth-century phenomenon, favored by Poland's monarchs and defended now by its "dissidents."[33]

The other argument for their rights to remain was the fact that Poland's Jews were full and equal citizens. If virtually all writers for the Catholic press wanted Jews to emigrate, they did not all encourage disenfranchisement and expulsion. There were exceptions, however, like Father Marian Wiśniewski, an ardent exponent of expulsion who would eventually become editor of *Pro Christo*. He compared Jews to a gangrenous limb and unjust aggressors. If self-defense was permitted against a physical aggressor, all the more so against the Jewish spiritual aggressors demoralizing Poland. Depriving Jews of equal rights and removing them from Christian society was a first step to religious and national self-defense. This had to be done in a Christian manner, but that translated into dislodging Jews from their positions by means of exclusionary legislation [Aryan paragraphs] and the boycott.[34]

---

[32] *Mały Dziennik*, October 14, 1937; February 2, 1938.

[33] *Pro Christo*, 13/3 (1937): 15–23.

[34] *Pro Christo*, 9 (1933): 513–19

An anonymous writer in the more moderate *Prąd* pointed to France, which was sending back thousands of Polish workers. Germany, Austria, Czechoslovakia, and Hungary were sending back all the Jews who had been settled there for years. Poland, it was suggested, should do the same with the nearly "two-million" Jews who fled from Russia since 1905. Poverty and increasing beggary should make Jews themselves realize their need to seek new places to settle.[35]

The Christian Democratic paper, *Dziennik Bydgoski,* put no stock in the belief that Jews would leave voluntarily. The Jewish question would not be resolved so long as Jews enjoyed equal rights. The *Mały Dziennik* agreed.[36] A brochure published by the Jesuits appealed to the authority of Saint Thomas Aquinas: "Jews should be expelled from Christian societies." Jews had to leave "so that the Polish nation could live and develop normally."[37] To finance the costs of compulsory emigration, writers for the *Mały Dziennik* suggested taxing wealthy Jews or confiscating the goods of Jews who had obtained them illegally or through dishonest competition. This was regarded as solving the Jewish question in a "civilized" manner, "without prejudice," and "far from the methods of the Nazis." Compelling Jews to emigrate was the only solution, because Jews do not wish to leave voluntarily. They had it too good in Poland. It was necessary to force them out, not with physical violence but in a planned, organized economic action. Jews had to be deprived of their civil rights because they had it better in Poland than anywhere else.[38]

When the western powers initiated efforts to find places for German Jews to settle, Józef Białasiewicz expressed irritation at their short-sightedness and refusal to look at the entire Jewish question. Why did the west have compassion only for Jews in distress and not others, he asked. It seemed that nations which used "radical methods" to solve their Jewish problems were being rewarded with attention, while others were being neglected. Poland should receive prior consideration, he argued, since it had more Jews than Germany and was worse off in every way. Jews too,

---

[35] *Prąd,* 30 (1936): 170–73.

[36] *Mały Dziennik,* October 18, 1936; December 23, 1938.

[37] *Mały Dziennik,* September 19, 1938.

[38] *Mały Dziennik,* November 21, 1938; January 29, 1939; March 27, 1939.

both in Poland and abroad, needed to take measures to prevent the kind of solution in Poland that the Nazis were exercising in Germany. If a bitter fate befell the Jews in Poland, it would be their own fault.[39]

The western powers' focus on German Jews frustrated both the Polish government and the *Mały Dziennik*. Europe might be overcrowded but England, France, and Belgium had large tracts of land at their disposal. "In Western Europe the Jewish question is in every way minor, but in Poland it is a matter of the nation's very life and existence." If life was difficult for Jews in Poland, it was more so for Poles.[40] But the Catholic daily was not optimistic regarding Jewish cooperation: "With very few exceptions, Jews basically do not want to emigrate from Poland." Recent events in Germany, Austria, Romania, and Hungary had brought 200,000 more Jews to Poland. Poland had become the "classic land of Jewish immigration." As Zionist leader Nahum Sokolow had put it, "Poland is the spiritual center for all Jewry." In response to such attitude, the *Mały Dziennik* concluded: "Jews must be compelled to emigrate, not by Nazi methods but by withdrawing their citizenship and reorganizing our national economy according to the needs of the Polish people. There is no other way."[41]

As Poland's Catholics saw it, emigration was the only "rational" solution to the Jewish question. It followed that, for their own reasons, ardent nationalists like those at the *Mały Dziennik* were sympathetic to Zionist aspirations. "Jews can and should have their own homeland." Whether that homeland ought to be in Palestine, however, was another question.[42]

Zionism

Zionists had no more sympathetic supporters than the Polish government. Marshal Piłsudski and the Sanacja party had always been supportive of a Jewish homeland in Palestine, and the National Unity Camp in the late

---

[39] *Przegląd Katolicki,* 76 (1938): 738–39.

[40] *Mały Dziennik,* January 22, 1939; January 24, 1939.

[41] *Mały Dziennik,* January 27, 1939.

[42] *Mały Dziennik,* January 24, 1939.

1930s was no less so. For obvious reasons of self-interest, the Polish government did its best to promote Zionist efforts at the League of Nations and other international forums. It was critical of Great Britain's exercise of its mandate over Palestine, specifically of its restrictions on Jewish immigration. It condemned Britain's 1937 plan to partition Palestine between Arabs and Jews as providing too small a territory for a Jewish state. The Polish government virtually identified itself with the proposals of Vladimir Jabotinsky and his New Zionist Organization.

Jabotinsky had spoken out publicly on Jewish emigration as a state necessity for Poland. He said that Poland should have priority before other countries in any program of emigration.

Determining the question of a Jewish state should not be left to Great Britain alone but to a "concert" of nations in which Poland played a leading part. When in 1938 Jabotinsky's New Zionist Organization conceded that other outlets besides Palestine were required for Jewish emigration from Europe, the Polish government as a quid pro quo revised its previous stand that Palestine could be only a minor outlet: "Being well disposed to the idea of building a Jewish state in Palestine, we declare simultaneously that this country should be recognized as the *main* [italics added] direction of Jewish emigration."[43]

From the very beginning of Zionist efforts, the Vatican's stand was quite the opposite of the Polish government's. Theodor Herzl's meeting with Pope Pius X (January 25, 1904) produced only the pope's celebrated *non possumus*. Herzl wanted to assure the Pontiff that the Zionist policy vis-à-vis Christian holy places was to assign them extraterritorial status. He thereby hoped to win Vatican sympathy, or at least to remove Vatican objections to the Zionist cause. The pope responded by declaring: "We are unable to favor this movement. We cannot prevent the Jews from going to Jerusalem, but we could never sanction it. The ground of Jerusalem, if it were not always sacred, has been sanctified by the life of Jesus Christ. As the head of the Church, I cannot answer you otherwise. The Jews have not recognized our Lord: therefore we cannot recognize the Jewish people."[44]

---

[43] Marcus, *Social and Political History*, 395–98.

[44] *Encyclopedia Judaica*, (Jerusalem: Macmillan, 1971), 16:74. For a detailed presentation of the Vatican's early position on Zionism, see Sergio I. Minerbi, *The Vatican and Zionism: Conflict in the Holy Land, 1895–1925*. Trans. by Arnold Schwarz.

Pius' successor, Pope Benedict XV, appeared to have assumed a more positive attitude toward the idea of a Jewish homeland in Palestine. In a personal audience with Zionist leader Nahum Sokolow (May 10, 1917), Pope Benedict is reported to have acknowledged the Zionist program as a "great idea" and the "will of Divine Providence." The pope had no doubt but that a "satisfactory understanding" could be reached regarding the Christian shrines. "Yes," he said at the end of the Sokolow audience, "I do hope that we shall be good neighbors."[45] Pope Benedict appears to have had a dramatic change of heart. Hilaire Belloc, arguably the most influential English Catholic between the world wars, reported a very different attitude from the audience he had with Pope Benedict the year before (June 3, 1916). When the discussion turned to the Jews entering Palestine, Belloc wrote of the pope, "he kept on saying to me, '*C'est une honte! C'est une honte!* '" (It's a shame.)[46]

Rather than to any private conversations we need to look at Pope Benedict's addresses to the College of Cardinals for the official Vatican attitude toward Zionism in the years between the wars. In 1919 he told the cardinals of his fears for the Christian holy places. It would be "bitter," he said, and "painful," if they would be "handed over to those who are not Christian" and if "non-believers" were to acquire a "more advantageous and powerful position" in Palestine.[47] Obviously the pope was not speaking about Muslims who had controlled the Christian shrines for centuries. Two years later (1921), the pope reiterated his negative attitude toward the Zionist enterprise. His fears, he told the cardinals, had been realized. Giving Jews "preponderance and privilege" had led to a deterioration of the Christian position in Palestine. Centers of Christian pilgrimage were being profaned: "We must deplore the persistent efforts made by many to change the sacred character of the Holy Places, turning them into frivolous places of entertainment." The pope acknowledged the existence of Jewish rights, but did not want to see them supplant those of Christians.[48]

(New York; Oxford: Oxford University, 1990).

[45] *Encyclopedia Judaica,* 16:75–76.

[46] A. N. Wilson, *Hilaire Belloc,* (New York: Atheneum, 1984), 229.

[47] *La Civiltà Cattolica,* 70 (1919) 2:8.

[48] *La Civiltà Cattolica,* 72 (1921) 3:4–6.

These were the last official public statements of Vatican's perspective on Zionism. For those not conversant with the Latin of Vatican diplomacy, the quasi-official Jesuit publication in Rome, *La Civiltà Cattolica,* translated, interpreted and expanded upon both of these allocutions. Thanks to British Secretary Balfour and "his Jewish banker Rothschild," the holy places, it lamented, were in danger of falling into the hands of the "enemies" of Christian civilization. The "Zionist plot" was intent on destroying or at least impeding Christianity in the land of its origins.[49]

Three years later the Rome-based journal described Zionism as an "episode" to be viewed in conjunction with the domination of Jews in Russia and the revolution in Hungary, in which all the leaders were Jewish. Under the evil influence of Masonry, high finance and the press in Europe and America were abetting the "tyrannical rule of Israel." Zionists intended to make Palestine a center for their efforts at world domination. "Surely we must refrain from all violence and hatred, even against Jews. We must refrain from any hint of injustice, reprisal, or revenge, despite their ingratitude and usurpation. We are far from a non-Christian antisemitism. But we must be careful to defend ourselves and all of Christian civilization, which is threatened by Jewish domination of the world. This is a national defense and struggle, because Jews do not sincerely belong to the countries which host them; but this is also an international, *catholic* struggle, because it affects the ... future of all human society."[50] Right up to 1938, even amid the antisemitic movements spreading over Europe, *La Civiltà Cattolica* insisted that Jews must leave Palestine and give up any idea of establishing a homeland there.[51]

Confronted by the conflict of interests represented by the Vatican and Polish government, opinion in the Polish Catholic press was divided. As Poles it was in their interest to support Zionist aspirations in Palestine as offering the only truly hopeful possibility for Jewish emigration from Poland. As Catholics they owed allegiance to the announced policies of

---

[49] *La Civiltà Cattolica,* 70 (1919) 2:12–16.

[50] *La Civiltà Cattolica,* 72 (1921) 3:11–13.

[51] *La Civiltà Cattolica,* 70 (1919) 2:10–16; 72 (1921) 3:3–14. See also Charlotte Klein, "Vatican and Zionism, 1897–1967," *Christian Attitudes on Jews and Judaism,* (Institute of Jewish Affairs, World Jewish Congress), 36/37 (June/August, 1974): 11–16.

the Holy See. It is telling that in an instance when Polish and Vatican interests were not identical, the Polish Catholic press was rather more Catholic than Polish.

The views of Rome's *La Civiltà Cattolica* were echoed in a popular periodical for priests, *Głos Kapłański*. An article by A. Ostoja interpreted Zionism as an essential part of the Jewish plan to dominate the world. In stark contrast to Jesus, whose kingdom was not of this world, Judaism was a "political religion." The role of the Messiah in Jewish tradition had been to lead the Jews of diaspora back to Israel, rebuild the temple, and rule the world. Citing Nahum Sokolow, Asher Ginzberg (Ahad Ha'am), and Heinrich Kohn, Ostoja wrote that Zionists now regarded the Jewish people themselves to be the Messiah. That meant Zionists intended the Jewish people to rule the world. With a brief bow to Moses Montefiori, Theodor Herzl, and the first nineteenth-century Zionist settlers in Palestine, Ostoja credited philosopher-theologian Asher Ginzberg as being the real founder of Zionism. Ginzberg had described Palestine as not replacing the diaspora but becoming its "spiritual center." That meant a "spiritual Zionism" that transcended the narrow boundaries of a small Jewish state and embraced the whole world.

As for the divergences that existed among the various Zionist organizations and their even sharper differences with anti-Zionist orthodox Jews, Ostoja assured his clerical readers that the disputes were only apparent. Jewish leaders were united in trying to save the Jewish masses from economic catastrophe. Zionism was subordinate to the political interests of Judaism, whose ultimate goal was global power. It remained to be seen if Jews would desist from their "time immemorial war against the church and the Aryan world." Since these issues concerned Catholic leaders throughout the world, they must also be of concern to the clergy of Poland.[52]

Writing in *Pro Christo,* L. Czerniewski saw support for Zionism as a Christian middle course between two mistaken extremes. Hatred for Jews, racial and otherwise, was both unchristian and unproductive. On the other hand, being open to Jewish assimilation meant subjecting Christian societies to modern Jewish influences, to materialism, religious indifference, and ultimately loss of faith. A Jewish homeland offered a

---

[52] *Głos Kapłański*, 6 (1932): 217–27. Ostoja's article was later reprinted for the benefit of non-clergy in *Pro Christo* 11/4 (1935): 15–23; 11/7 (1935): 12–17.

way out, and Jews should be "forced" to avail themselves of it. Having their own territory and state was necessary for the "normal development" of any people. Life in diaspora was "abnormal" and subjected Jews to an abnormal parasitic existence. All nations, wrote Czerniewski, but especially Poles, should be sympathetic to Zionist aspirations. Jewish criticism of Zionism could only mean that Jews did not want a healthy, normal existence. For their own good, Jews should be deprived of their parasitic existence. They should be expelled from Poland's cultural, economic, and political life. Czerniewski admitted that it sounded cruel but it would really be an act of neighborly love, a blessing for both Jews and Poles. It was the only way to speed the creation of a normal Jewish state and return the Jewish people to health.

But a Jewish homeland did not, indeed could not, mean Palestine. Geopolitically, Palestine was just too important. "Palestine ceased to be the Promised Land for Jews ... when it became the Holy Land for us Christians." Czerniewski appealed to the tradition connecting the diaspora with blame for the death of Jesus. From the time of the "crime" they committed on Calvary, Jews lost Palestine "irretrievably." It was a matter of divine justice. No true Christian could agree to give the Holy Land back to the Jews. It was proper that the Holy See had protested Zionist experiments in Palestine. Indeed, Czerniewski had no doubt but that someday the Holy Land would be entrusted to the care of the Holy See; unquestionably, the pope could manage it. Such an outcome was not in the near offing, since the mandatory agreement and Zionist plans were at odds with the aspirations of the Vatican. In the meantime, divine judgment and political necessity combined to frustrate Zionist efforts. The simplest and only way for Jews to regain Palestine was to convert to the Catholic church. Those who refused to do so would have to create a "New Palestine" in Uganda or elsewhere. Christian nations would help, but Jews dare not delay. The earth's lands were being divided up and populated, while hatred for Jews was increasing constantly.[53]

As a daily newspaper, the *Mały Dziennik* frequently covered stories on Jewish settlers in Palestine. At a time when fine distinctions were not made between objective reporting and editorial comment, even the news stories demonstrated an undisguised bias. In Tel Aviv, for example, a school official had spoken out against Jews celebrating the Christian New

---

[53] *Pro Christo* 8 (1932): 97–104, 218–24.

Year. For the *Mały Dziennik,* that was "racist fanaticism" and a proof of Jewish "hatred" for Christianity. What could Christian settlers and pilgrims expect if Jews ever gained control of the entire country?[54] Jewish settlers in the kibbutzim were socialists imitating the very worst Soviet models. The majority of Christians in Palestine were Arabs in complete solidarity with Muslims. Nonetheless, Poles must support Zionists because the poverty among the Jewish masses in Poland was inclining them to communism (August 22, 1935).

At the 1935 Zionist Congress at Lucerne, Nahum Sokolow reviewed the condition of Jews throughout the world. The *Mały Dziennik* quoted him at length regarding Poland. Sokolow described the poverty Jews and Poles were both suffering as a result of the world depression. Jews were guaranteed equal rights by the Polish constitution, and the government had stated its commitment to equal protection to all citizens. But there was active antisemitism among "certain classes," especially among the political opposition to the government. Jews were being attacked without cause, simply because they were Jews. Sokolow, however, did not see the kind of antisemitism that was present in Germany taking root in Poland; their situations were too different. Marshal Piłsudski was contemptuous of nationalistic fanaticism that led to xenophobic violence. The danger for Jews in Poland lay not in ideologies but in the increasing poverty of the country (August 23, 1935).

In the mid-1930s the *Mały Dziennik* expressed satisfaction that thirty thousand Jews a year were leaving Poland for Palestine, the equivalent of the annual Jewish birthrate in Poland. Palestine could take another million immigrants, and it was imperative that Polish Jews have priority (September 17, 1935). The Catholic daily regularly reported government efforts on behalf of Zionism at the League of Nations and the numbers of Jews leaving. It expressed concern that bloody clashes between Arabs and Jews might lead to a decline in immigration (May 18, 1936; May 14, 1937). But it also expressed sympathy for Great Britain's situation amid the conflict. British interests in the Suez Canal and in mideast oil required a policy of not antagonizing the Arab and Muslim world, for whom a Jewish Palestine was a provocation. The *Mały Dziennik* made no outcry when Great Britain announced its partition plans and limited Jewish immigration. The League of Nations would just have find new

---

[54] *Mały Dziennik,* August 11, 1935.

outlets for Jews among their colonies. Poland was no longer able to offer hospitality to Jews, when it was faced with the difficulty of feeding its "own" people (July 10, 1937).

Poland's Jewish problem was not inextricably linked to Zionist success in Palestine, the *Mały Dziennik* decided. Other outlets would simply have to be found (August 14, 1937). Palestine in the best of circumstances could not absorb all the Jews of Europe. There were Polish Jews who voiced reservations about emigration. Perhaps, suggested the daily, Polish society should dispel those reservations with economic pressure. Jews would leave only when they no longer believed Poland was better than anywhere else (September 25, 1937). Zionists could not be sincere if Palestine alone was acceptable for a Jewish state. There were too many Arabs there; moreover, it was a holy land for Christians. Sincere Zionists were those who were willing to see Eretz Israel serve as a spiritual center for several Jewish colonies (December 23, 1938).

Taking another view, the *Przegląd Powszechny* saw Polish and Vatican interests as reconcilable so long as the security of Christian holy places was maintained. When the British government decided to partition Palestine between Arabs and Jews (1937), it published a long thoughtful article by Roman Piotrowicz critical of British policies. It expressed commiseration for Jews who had placed too much trust in Great Britain and in international documents. Jews were entering Palestine by right, not by mere toleration. The division of Palestine was contrary to the letter of Britain's mandate and harmful to the economic development of the land. The Palestinian issue involved more than the interests of Arabs, Jews, and Great Britain. The mandate should be revised to include nations like Poland. Such a revision should ensure the maximal possibility for Jews to build a homeland while at the same time entrusting the security and use of Christian holy places to Catholic nations.[55]

Writing in a periodical for Catholic youth, Zygmunt Szeliga was also sympathetic. What was a Promised Land for Jews and a Holy Land for Christians was for Arabs a Fatherland. If one took a purely historical approach, even going back to the biblical origins of the land, Arabs had lived on the land for 1300 years; they therefore enjoyed "historical

---

[55] *Przegląd Powszechny*, 215 (1937): 251–69.

rights." But Szeliga expressed understanding of Jewish feelings that their rights over the land could never lapse.[56]

No such understanding was forthcoming from the *Mały Dziennik.* When Great Britain virtually closed Palestine to further Jewish immigration in 1939, the daily interpreted the action as putting an end to exaggerated opinions about Jewish influence over British politics. The Catholic daily found it "comforting" that there was no danger of Christian holy places coming under the power of a "deicide race." As for Jewish emigration, Great Britain would now have to find some other territory for a Jewish homeland, not only for the sake of Jews but for the "healthy development of Europe and its civilization" (May 26, 1939).

"Nationalizing" Polish Life

Eliminating the threat of secularity meant de-judaizing not only Poland's economy but its culture, or, as it was put more euphemistically, "nationalizing" them. Optimally, such nationalization was to be achieved by massive Jewish emigration. Until such time as Jews left Poland, the only solution, partial as it was, seemed to be an extension of the economic boycott to all areas of Polish life and culture, in other words, professional and cultural segregation. The Catholic leader in this effort was the *Mały Dziennik.* In November 1938, it invited its readers to submit articles and letters in a series on "nationalizing Polish life." Announcing the series, the Catholic daily denied any hatred for Jews or any revenge for their "hostile and harmful activity against us and Poland." It denied any desires to hinder Jewish freedom in determining their own internal affairs. But Poles had a right to be Poles, and the *Mały Dziennik* would not tolerate what it described as Jews "intruding" into Polish affairs, "shaping our economic and cultural life." Priests and laity alike responded to the concept enthusiastically.[57]

---

[56] *Młodzież Katolicki,* 8 (1939): 13–16.

[57] *Mały Dziennik,* November 11, 1938; November 14, 1938; November 23, 1938; November 24, 1938.

Law

The judaization of Poland's legal profession had long been a sore point for Polish nationalists who pointed to the statistics with regularity. Though only 11% of the population, Jews constituted 55% of all the lawyers. Although there were fewer in western and northern Poland, over half (53%) of the lawyers in Warsaw were Jewish;the same in Kraków (54%). In Lwów Jews made up 73% of the legal profession. Even more alarming were the numbers of Jews applying to the bar. In Warsaw, 1937, 62% of the applicants to the bar were Jewish; for all of Poland, in early 1939, 73% of the applicants. To the despair of Polish Catholic nationalists, unless steps were taken, there was no end in sight.[58]

The "war" to nationalize Poland's legal profession began in 1931 with the founding of the National Association of Lawyers. According to its president, Jan Optat Sokołowski, its first years were thorny. The important professional organizations of lawyers were liberal, open to both Poles and Jews. Not only Jews but, Sokołowski admitted, "very many Polish lawyers" were adverse to the nationalistic cause. The "darkest period" were the years 1932 to 1936, when Czesław Machałowski was Minister of Justice and Stefan Sieczkowski the Vice-Minister. The November, 1935, meeting of the Chamber (*Izba*) of Advocates in Kraków provided the turning point. When efforts to address the issue of judaization were rejected, nationalists resigned their positions and galvanized other organizations of Polish lawyers throughout the country. In May, 1937, a national convention held in Warsaw succeeded in bringing together lawyers of all political leanings, determined to give Poland's legal profession a "truly Polish face" by limiting the number of Jews to be admitted to the bar. Sokołowski lamented that nationalists were not able to win a seat on the board that governed the bar in Warsaw. He did not see how nationalizing the legal profession would be possible under the present Polish constitution, which defined Poland as the "common good of its citizens," including Jews. The editors of the *Mały Dziennik* greeted with satisfaction Sokołowski's assurance that his association would work for a *numerus clausus,* eventually a *numerus*

---

[58] *Mały Dziennik,* December 18, 1937; January 19, 1939. See also *Przegląd Katolicki,* 75 (1937): 308–10.

nullus of all Jewish candidates for the bar, until Jews in the legal profession were only ten percent as in the population at large.[59]

Medicine

According to Catholic nationalists, over three thousand or 35% of Poland's nearly nine thousand medical doctors were Jewish. In Łódź 44% of the physicians were Jewish; 55% in Tarnopol. For the *Mały Dziennik* it was a "great step forward" when in 1937 nationalist physicians succeeded in breaking up the local branch of the Polish Medical Association. Instead of a single organization in which Polish and Jewish physicians would work together as heretofore, now there were two organizations, each dividing the assets of the former Association. For the Catholic daily, this was the "first unusually significant example of realizing the program of nationalizing professional life." Earlier efforts to break up the national association had failed. The *Mały Dziennik* resented the claim in the Jewish press that the separation in Łódź was the work of National Democrats. "All of Polish society" was united in the "anti-Jewish war," wrote the daily, "no matter what one's party preference."[60]

Numbers were not the only reason given for nationalizing the medical profession. Especially in the provinces, wrote one *Mały Dziennik* reader, doctors counselled their patients, and Jewish doctors were encouraging birth control. Dr. Jan Witkowski, evoked the 1581 decree of Pope Gregory XIII, who forbade Catholics to seek the services of Jewish physicians under pain of severe penalties, including denial of Christian burial. The prohibition had fallen into desuetude over the centuries, but Dr. Witkowski, with some obvious professional self-interest, insisted that it still obligated Catholics since no pope had abrogated it. More shamefully, Witkowski raised the old calumny that the Talmud allows murder of non-Jews; he gave examples of Polish kings who had died under suspicious circumstances while attended by Jewish physicians. Polish medicine would not have a "Jewish problem," he concluded, if

---

[59] *Mały Dziennik*, January 19, 1939. See also *Mały Dziennik*, May 11, 1937; December 18, 1937; March 19, 1938; March 26, 1938; *Przegląd Katolicki*, 75 (1937): 308–10.

[60] *Mały Dziennik*, December 28, 1937; January 8, 1939.

Polish Catholics would only follow the instructions of Pope Gregory XIII.[61]

Dentistry

Jews constituted 60% of the 1,800 dentists in Poland, contended dental student Platon Luszpiński; over 70% of the one thousand dentists in Warsaw. Perhaps the older generation of Poles could look at those figures with equanimity, he wrote, but not the youth. Jews were threatening their future ability to earn a living, and Polish university students were beginning to take "energetic action." In December 1938, sixty Polish students at the Dental Academy forced the Jewish students to sit on the left side of the lecture hall or leave. It was comforting to the young nationalist that none of the Academy's professors were Jewish, but he was sure that the only way for the dental profession to be nationalized was for the Academy to refuse admission to Jews for "at least twenty-five years."[62]

Pharmacy

Of Poland's ten thousand pharmacists, 30% were Jewish, wrote Piotr Kwieciński. Over 20% of the pharmacies were owned by Jews; 30% in southern Poland; over 50% in southeastern Poland. This, insisted Kwieciński, a pharmacist himself, required defense of the nation. Jews were known for their sympathies to communism, and, according to the Talmud and *Protocols of the Elders of Zion,* could poison Polish soldiers. Kwieciński called upon his fellow Polish pharmacists to begin nationalizing their profession. Concurring, the editors of the *Mały Dziennik* pointed out the "wise" 1844 law of the Czarist government that allowed only Christian pharmacists to practice in Congress Poland. The Catholic daily cited Father August Rohling in defense of the slander that Jews were permitted by the Talmud to poison Christians. It questioned the reasonableness of a Catholic Pole trusting a Jewish pharmacist, knowing of the "notoriously hostile" attitude of the Talmud and its adherents to anything Christian.[63]

---

[61] *Mały Dziennik,* January 8, 1939.

[62] *Mały Dziennik,* January 12, 1939.

[63] *Mały Dziennik,* January 22, 1939.

Veterinary Medicine

There were only 150 Jews [7%] among Poland's 2,200 veterinarians, according to Dr. Piotr Krzeczowski. Their professional organization numbered 1,200 members, sixty-four of them Jews. Veterinarians, he explained, were paid less handsomely than physicians or pharmacists, and most of them in Poland worked for national or local government agencies, where, he admitted, it was harder for Jews to get jobs. Poland had need for a thousand more veterinarians, and of the 459 students in the veterinary department at Piłsudski University, only 15 [3%] were Jewish. There was no danger of veterinary medicine in Poland being judaized, Krzeczowski admitted, and then related that in November 1937, the Association of Veterinary Doctors passed the motion not to accept any more Jewish members.[64]

Architecture

The judaization of the building trades, wrote one anonymous engineer, was easily understandable. Seventy percent of the new apartment houses going up belonged to Jews who, giving out jobs, turned first to their own. As a result, many Jewish architects had more work than they could handle and went to Polish engineers for help. The anonymous correspondent resented that Poles had to work for Jews. He resented too that there were Poles who would hire Jews rather than fellow Poles for building services. He explained that Jews would work for less and had "contacts" to get materials cheaper. Jews were also taking modern styles to an extreme. But "young Polish engineers" were beginning to "polonize" the building industry by introducing an exclusionary Aryan paragraph into the by-laws of their professional organization. Jews could no longer be members of the Association of Architects, and the membership committee would decide about "persons of Jewish background." Only Catholic architects should be hired to design churches, the architects agreed, but further limitations would be necessary to ensure the "purity of Polish culture."[65] In August 1939, Jewish members of the Architects'

---

[64] *Mały Dziennik,* January 26, 1939.

[65] *Mały Dziennik,* January 29, 1939.

Association in Łódź were informed that their names had been removed from the membership rolls.[66]

Education

Much of the impetus to nationalize Polish life came from students. Not untypical was the complaint of one such young Pole that "older people cannot understand why young people in college are fighting so energetically to de-judaize institutions of higher learning."[67] Tuition rates would have to be lowered and made more affordable to Polish students of working class and peasant backgrounds. Higher education was not just a "premium" for Jews.[68] Dr. Jan Wrotkowski agreed. In the 1936/37 academic year, he wrote, a little less than one half (46%) of the Polish Christian secondary school graduates went on to colleges and universities, but 70% of the Jewish graduates went on further, either in Poland or abroad.[69]

The nationalist effort to segregate Polish society provided the context for the so-called ghetto benches at the universities. The ghetto benches were but the first step toward segregating Polish society. Having Jewish students sit at the left side of a lecture hall was an attempt to draw attention to their numbers and, according to nationalist students, their "disproportionate" presence. The judaization of Polish life was already bad enough; given the numbers of Jewish university students in Poland, prospects were even bleaker. Never, wrote Professor Ludwik Skoczylas, had Poland faced so deep a moral crisis. The future of Catholic Polish culture was as stake.[70]

Athletics

"Sports," wrote the editor of *Pro Christo* in 1933, "are perhaps the most judaized area of Polish life," by which he meant integrated. He criticized the Sanacja government for the "privileges" which Jews had acquired

---

[66] *Mały Dziennik*, August 19, 1939.

[67] *Mały Dziennik*, February 9, 1939.

[68] *Mały Dziennik*, February 14, 1936.

[69] *Mały Dziennik*, February 9, 1939.

[70] *Wiara i Życie*, 16 (1936): 177.

over the years, like playing in the same leagues and on the same teams. After agreeing in principle that athletics should be international and non-political, he condemned Jews for nationalism, for anti-Polish name-calling at games and occasional skirmishes between players and spectators. According to *Pro Christo,* the participation of Jewish teams in the same leagues as Christian teams was leading to the "secularizing of sport." Games were being scheduled on Sundays and holidays at the same time as church services. The only answer was that Catholic Poles be separated from Jews in athletic competitions.[71]

Four years later the *Mały Dziennik* expressed its satisfaction at the "healthy impulse" finally taking place where Jewish and Polish teams and players were being segregated. The Catholic daily found it "entirely understandable and praiseworthy" that Catholic athletes were beginning to avoid "destructive" Jewish influence. In fact, Jewish athletes warranted careful watching, since Jewish teams bore names like the Maccabees, Bar Kochba, and Hasmonea, taken from Jewish history with decided political overtones. No one had a right to organize a team for ulterior or political motives. The Catholic daily regretted that there were Jewish teams which "here and there" still enjoyed popularity among some Poles. These were ties which should be broken off as soon as possible.[72]

For the editors of *Mały Dziennik,* the phenomenon of Jewish athletes constituted a "new kind of Jew", one at odds with the stereotypic talmudic scholar who neglected, even despised physical fitness. The Catholic daily was concerned. Zionist organizations like Betar were encouraging young Jewish males to engage in sporting activities and to learn how to handle weapons. Jewish paramilitary organizations were marching through the streets. Leaders of Jewish nationalism were instilling a "fighting temperament" among their young men. Pointing to the riot that had taken place at Przytyk, the Catholic daily blamed the violence on Jews who had "responded" to a peaceful boycott with gun shots. The polonization of trade and commerce should be carried on without violence, the *Mały Dziennik,* pronounced, but then wondered if

---

[71] *Pro Christo,* 9 (1933): 549–51.

[72] *Mały Dziennik,* April 4, 1937.

Catholics were not contributing to the development of Jewish paramilitary organizations by playing sports with Jews.[73]

Emigration of Jews to their own homeland was the only completely satisfactory solution to the Jewish question, according to the Polish Catholic press. Until that time, temporary measures would have to do by de-judaizing the economy through the boycott and mitigating Jewish influence on Polish culture through segregation. Catholic leaders insisted that such a nationalization of Polish life was to take place peacefully. Violence was unchristian and to be abhorred. Economic boycott, ghetto benches, and the exclusionary Aryan paragraphs were all seen as legitimate, nonviolent forms of self-defense. While Catholic leaders and writers were making clarion calls for division and discrimination within Polish society, numerous National Democrats and right wing students believed in being more physical and direct. Church leaders and journalists had called for a nonviolent war on behalf of a Catholic Poland. But wars rarely remain nonviolent.

----

[73] *Mały Dziennik,* September 11, 1937.

Chapter 12

Violence at the Universities and in the Streets

The Nazi-engineered pogrom known as Kristallnacht (November 9-10, 1938) evoked expressions of outrage from scores of religious leaders in Europe and the United States. Using as an excuse the assassination of Ernst vom Rath, a German diplomat, by a young Jew, Herschel Grynszpan, Nazis incited riots throughout Germany and Austria. Jewish homes were set on fire, Jewish shops looted, a reported ninety-one Jews were killed, and 267 synagogues partially or completely destroyed. Mass arrests followed and some 30,000 Jewish men were sent to concentration camps.[1]

Catholic dignitaries like the archbishops of London, Paris, Baltimore, Boston, and San Francisco joined a wide spectrum of political and church leaders to condemn the persecution. Mass meetings were held and joint statements issued. Much was made of Pope Pius XI's prior condemnation of Nazi racial theories and his remarks earlier that year to a group of pilgrims declaring that Christians could not participate in antisemitism because they were "spiritual Semites." Yet, curiously and conspicuously, no response to Kristallnacht came from the Vatican. The magnitude of the violence and bloodshed were not deemed to warrant anything stronger than had already been said. The official Catholic response in Rome was silence. The same was true for Poland.

---

[1] Yehuda Bauer, *A History of the Holocaust* (New York: Franklin Watts, 1982), 108-109. See also the standard reference works.

...: Polish Catholic press like the Polish bishops generally published little or nothing in comment, let alone criticism, on Kristallnacht. The exceptions were the two daily newspapers, the *Mały Dziennik* and the *Głos Narodu*, both established to present the news from a Catholic perspective. When they reported and editorialized on the German pogrom, it was in a manner at once coherent with their policies and indicative of their stance toward antisemitic violence.

The story of the assassination of vom Rath in Paris received detailed treatment in the *Mały Dziennik*. The headline announced that the murder was an act of revenge for the persecution of Jews in Germany.[2] Two days later the headlines announced not the pogrom but the death of vom Rath, followed by the subheading "Demented Jews not satisfied with the blood of a third rank official." The report went on to say that the death of vom Rath, a "victim of Jewish brutality," unleashed violent anti-Jewish manifestations in cities throughout Germany. With no further details or comment on the destruction, the report simply noted that "one can expect that now Chancellor Hitler will employ the so-called 'final' policy toward the Jews."

Instead of the reporting the plight of the Jews in Germany, the *Mały Dziennik* preferred to focus its attention on the Jewish press in Poland, which it described as raving frantically over the calamity. In the opinion of the Catholic daily, the Jewish press was trivializing a vindictive crime by describing the assassin as a lone eccentric. German Jews were justifiably fearful. Jewish journalists in Poland were rending their garments over Jews in Germany, without mention of what Jewish communists were doing in the Soviet Union.[3]

Głos Narodu, under the control of the archdiocese of Kraków, also spared its readers the details of the destruction but published a lengthy editorial on the fact that the Germans were holding all Jews responsible for the crime of an individual. The Catholic daily found the German anger "understandable." The murder, after all, was a cold-blooded act of revenge. One could not be surprised at the anti-Jewish indignation and demonstrations. The Third Reich was in the process of "breaking the shackles" that Jews had laid on Germany's economic and cultural life. Grynszpan's crime at such a moment "necessarily" roused the violent

---

[2] *Mały Dziennik*, November 9, 1938.

[3] *Mały Dziennik*, November 11, 1938.

reaction by the German masses. But the editors of the Catholic daily disapproved of the Germans' method of dealing with the Jews, even though their aim was "liberation of Germans from Jewish servitude."

While the German masses could be excused, not so the German authorities. The *Głos Narodu* found it ethically indefensible that the German government was punishing the entire Jewish community for the act of a single individual, confiscating Jewish property and interning masses of Jews in concentration camps. But then the Kraków daily went on: "Every nation—certainly Germany as well–has the right to defend itself from subjection to so foreign a nationality as the Jews and their injurious influence on social life.... But always within the limits of ethics, i.e., the limits drawn by the universal Christian morality that views every human being as a neighbor." Only a return to Christian ethics could prevent public life from becoming barbarous.

With all too accurate prescience, the *Głos Narodu* described Hitler's policies as a "war of extermination" against the Jews, yet still criticized Jews for staying in Germany, and world Jewry for "raising a fuss." Jews were "guests" in Germany as they were in Poland. Since hospitality was being withdrawn, Jews had no alternative but to sell their businesses, "even if at a loss," and to emigrate. By remaining in a country that did not want them, Jews were tempting their persecutors. Instead of protesting, Jews should emigrate from Europe as quickly as possible.[4]

The editorial elicited outrage from the Jewish community. The *Nowy Dziennik,* a Zionist paper, responded that up to now the world had been divided into those who admired Hitler's treatment of Jews and those who condemned him. The *Głos Narodu* now constituted a third camp: those who wanted to "understand" Hitler. The *Głos Narodu* found the remark appropriate. What the Nazis were doing in Germany was a "real revolution," and revolutions should not be simply condemned. The *Głos Narodu* took pride in its consistent anti-Nazi editorial stance. "No Catholic daily has informed [its readers] so exactly about what is happening in the Third Reich or fought so resolutely against neo-paganism and racism." The editors of the Kraków Catholic daily disapproved of Nazi Germany's "barbarous methods" but confessed: "we recognize the reason for its war as valid."

---

[4] *Głos Narodu,* November 16, 1938.

The *Głos Narodu* urged German Jews to emigrate as the only alternative to Nazi barbarity. Germany and eastern Europe had "withdrawn hospitality." The Catholic daily warned Polish Jews that the example of Germany might "unfortunately prove to be contagious." Again with a frighteningly accurate prescience, the editorial advised that "anyone who wants to save Jews from a fate such as the Third Reich is preparing for them, ought to begin thinking now about a place for Poland's Jews too. This is not a threat but a simple deduction of objective consideration." *Głos Narodu* was sure that Polish Jews had it in their power to leave Poland. They had influential friends in both Washington and London. It was so easy for them to obtain protests from these governments in favor of the Jewish cause. Certainly they could support Warsaw's efforts to find them colonies, if they only wanted.[5]

The *Mały Dziennik* and *Głos Narodu* did not pretend to speak for the entire Catholic church in Poland. But their influence was considerable, and their editorial opinions hardly idiosyncratic. They represented the thinking of a wide spectrum of the clergy and Catholic press, as can be seen by examining them in the context of other articles on antisemitic violence in Poland and the regularly recurring reports on university disturbances and street riots in the 1930s.

Violence at the Universities

Violence at universities and other institutions of higher learning were commonplace throughout eastern Europe between the wars.[6] In Poland Endek and other nationalist organizations incited students to antisemitic resentment by pointing to the disproportionate number of Jews in the professions.[7] Student riots came to be seen as inevitable as the seasons.[8]

To decrease the numbers of Jews in the professions, Czarist Russia had introduced into its Polish territories and elsewhere the policy of *numerus*

---

[5] *Głos Narodu,* November 19, 1938.

[6] Ezra Mendelsohn, *The Jews of East Central Europe between the World Wars* (Bloomington: Indiana University, 1983), 73, 186–89.

[7] Mendelsohn, *Jews of East Central Europe,* 27.

[8] *Pro Christo,* 13/5 (1937), 7.

clausus, whereby only a limited number of Jewish applicants were admitted into the universities. After the war Poland continued the policy so that, by the 1935/36 academic year, the number of Poles studying at universities and similar institutions was 77.8%. Jews constituted 13.1%, only somewhat more than the 10% which they represented in the population. Of the Jews who had passed entrances examinations but were not accepted into the universities because of the *numerus clausus,* there were some instances of a few converting to Christianity for the sake of a higher education. More frequent were incidents of Jews studying and receiving degrees abroad, especially in the field of medicine.[9]

But antisemitism at the universities was not caused merely by the supposedly disproportionate numbers of Jewish students. In 1934, one year after Hitler took power, there arose the *Obóz Narodowo-Radykalny* (National Radical Camp) or *Naras,* as they were called, a Polish imitation of Germany's Nazi party. After only a few months the Polish government disbanded them for antisemitic agitation and violence. They broke up into several smaller groups, like the *Związek Narodowy Polskiej Młodzieży Radykalnej* (National Association of Radical Polish Youth), a group of young fascists responsible for deliberately planning actions like the occupation of university buildings. Polish nationalists favored using universities for anti-Jewish agitation because of the long-standing tradition of university autonomy. Universities were expected to maintain order themselves and were off limits to police.[10]

From the perspective of the *Głos Narodu,* the university disturbances had to be seen as part of the total antisemitic front in Poland. One could not expect university students to be indifferent to the "Jewish question" when "the whole society" was thinking and talking about it.[11]

In the pages of the *Młodzież Katolicka* (Catholic Youth), Catholic university students expressed opinions comparable to those of their elders and church leaders. Jewish ritual slaughter was a barbarous ploy to maintain a Jewish control of the meat industry.[12] Jews were demoralizing youngsters in public primary schools by introducing coeducation and

---

[9] *Pro Christo,* 13/5 (1937), 8.

[10] *Głos Narodu,* November 29, 1936.

[11] *Głos Narodu,* October 29, 1936.

[12] *Młodzież Katolicka,* (1936), 15–17.

reducing the number of class hours for religion.[13] The Jewish "psyche" was cynical, its ethic materialistic; both posed a danger to the spiritual, idealistic psyche and ethic of Catholic Poland.[14] A sodality student quoted Austria's Bishop Gfoellener of Linz: "It is the duty of every good Christian to fight against the spirit of international Judaism, which has aligned itself with international Masonry." Such a conflict did not permit racist antisemitism, which was condemned by the Holy See, but it did mean isolating Jews so as to protect the rest of society from their harmful influence.[15]

In their determination to identify Poland with Catholicism, several student organizations succeeded in getting a crucifix hung in the Auditorium Maximum of the University of Warsaw.[16] The major campaign of right wing Catholic students, however, centered around not crucifixes but segregation of Jewish university students by compelling them to occupy so-called "ghetto benches." First at the Lwów Polytechnicum in 1935 and then at the University of Wilno, Jews were forced by the nationalist students to take seats in a particular section, usually on the left side, of the classroom or lecture hall.[17] Nationalist students saw the ghetto benches as their right and petitioned university and government officials to establish the separate seating by official regulation. The Jewish students resisted, supported by sympathetic faculty members and some of their fellow Christian students.

The Minister of Education at first declared the ghetto benches to be unconstitutional. But by 1937, the university officials in Warsaw and elsewhere capitulated to the demands of the right wing students. Separate seating was instituted by official ordinance, justified on the grounds that separate seating would be a means of avoiding further disruption and restoring order.[18] Jewish students saw it as an insult to their dignity.

---

[13] *Młodzież Katolicka,* (1936), 13–16.

[14] *Młodzież Katolcika,* (1935), 9–12.

[15] *Młodzież Katolicka,* (1934), 22–23.

[16] *Mały Dziennik,* January 23, 1936.

[17] Mendelsohn, *Jews of East Central Europe,* 73.

[18] *Mały Dziennik,* October 9, 1937.

They protested with hunger strikes and boycotts, preferring to stand silently during the lectures rather than take the segregated seating.

Even though threatened with disciplinary action, including expulsion, the Jewish students continued to pressure university administrators for withdrawal of the ghetto benches. When the Jewish students were joined in their efforts by sympathetic Polish students, the *Mały Dziennik* described these Polish students as socialists or radicals known for their leanings toward Masonry.[19] As late as August 1939, Jewish students met with sympathetic, democratically inclined professors who promised to intercede with the authorities on their behalf.[20] Professor Mieczysław Michałowicz of Warsaw, a Freemason, declared his determination to resign his chair if the segregation was not discontinued.[21] The German invasion in the following month precluded the necessity of any such action on his part.

In contrast to liberals like Michałowicz, Catholic leadership was either indifferent to or aggressively in favor of the ghetto benches. Michałowicz had forbidden the segregated seating at his lectures as unconstitutional and contrary to his conscience as a faithful Christian.[22] *Głos Narodu,* however, saw it as "natural and basically healthy" that Polish students were concerning themselves with the Jewish question. It was a "manifestation of patriotism" that student newspapers were calling straightforwardly for Poland's emancipation from its "fourth partition." The students had reason to fear they would not find employment in professions now filled with Jews.[23]

The Jewish community and its organizations joined the students in their struggle. The ghetto benches were recognized as only a first step in an attempt to segregate Jews and then eliminate them from the professions altogether. There was little reason to believe that the segregation would lead to peace in the classroom, especially when the leaders of nationalist student organizations in Warsaw issued a statement confirming Jewish fears: The Jewish question would only be resolved

---

[19] *Mały Dziennik,* October 9, 1937; October 30, 1937.

[20] *Mały Dziennik,* August 26, 1939.

[21] *Mały Dziennik,* August 10, 1939.

[22] *Mały Dziennik,* October 26, 1937.

[23] *Głos Narodu,* October 29, 1936; November 27, 1936.

when the last Jew left Poland. Until that time, the student representatives
called for such measures as: removing Jews from the army, requiring
them instead to pay a tax or do compulsory labor; removing Jews from
all jobs in national and local government; withdrawing Polish citizenship
from all Jews who obtained it after 1918; not allowing Jews or Masons
to serve as professors or lecturers in universities; not recognizing the
diplomas obtained by Jews abroad; not allowing Jews to change their
names to Polish.[24]

Not satisfied with ghetto benches at the universities, the *Mały Dziennik*
ran an article calling for their introduction into public high schools as
well.[25] As part of a series on the "nationalizing of Polish life," it
published letters from high school students echoing the sentiments of
their Catholic parents and teachers: Don't buy anything from Jews....
England, France, and Denmark don't want them; why should Poland be
the haven for the world's Jews? ... Let them find a place in Madagascar,
Cameroon, or Tanzania.[26]

While it generally condoned and even welcomed antisemitic attitudes
among students, the Catholic press was critical when those attitudes
erupted into violent behavior. In a remarkable display of inconsistency,
the *Głos Narodu* saw no causal relationship between the two: "Despite
our entire sympathy for the anti-Jewish reaction of society, we must say
that in the academic sector this movement is at times taking on unethical
and unchivalrous forms. There is no right to lynch anyone. No one may
be beaten for being a Jew." Preferring not to believe that students with
Catholic convictions were perpetrating the violence, the editors of the
Catholic daily excused the students as being carried away by passion
without thinking of the consequences.[27]

The editors at the *Głos Narodu* took pride in the fact that antisemitic
incidents in Kraków did not degenerate into violence, or "at least very
rarely." While critical of deliberate actions like student occupation of
university buildings, the editors of the Catholic daily withheld indignation
for acts supposedly committed in the heat of passion. Instead they blamed

---

[24] *Mały Dziennik*, June 8, 1938.

[25] *Mały Dziennik*, September 14, 1938.

[26] *Mały Dziennik*, March 23, 1939.

[27] *Głos Narodu*, October 29, 1936.

the students' outbursts of aggression on the "indifference of society." The older generation did not realize sufficiently the students' desperation and must replace a merely moral support with one that was real and active. This would discourage the students from any shocking excesses by making them unnecessary.[28]

A much more consistent position toward student violence was taken by Father Antoni Szymański in the pages of *Prąd*, a publication of the more democratically inclined Catholic student organization *Odrodzenie* (Rebirth). Szymański expressed sympathy for the difficulties Jews faced as a minority. He criticized student violence as social anarchy and against the commandments. Christ the Good Shepherd provided for sheep, not wolves. The priest especially decried the occasions when students used the Mass for nationalist demonstrations. They would leave church shouting antisemitic slogans and rampage in the Jewish quarter, where they would break windows and destroy property, eventually clash with the police and be arrested. It was a minority of students who acted this way, the priest granted, but their behavior should not be trivialized. It was a profanation of religion.[29]

Exactly what percentage of students engaged in these violent demonstrations is difficult to say. A memorandum of the American Jewish Congress cited a statement by Senator Malinowski (February 12, 1937), which gave the number of Polish students participating in riots as 1,500 out of 48,000 [some three percent].[30] More pertinent to my consideration here, however, is the relative silence of the Catholic hierarchy and clergy in the face of these student demonstrations. No calls came from bishops or priests against the ghetto benches and, as pointed out above, the condemnations of student violence were qualified. Professor Michałowicz's rejection of ghetto benches on the basis of his Catholic conscience received notice precisely because of its exceptional nature. And he did not go without rebuttal.

The prolific Monsignor Trzeciak responded to Michałowicz by quoting the New Testament: "If your hand or your foot causes you to sin, cut it off and throw it from you" (Mt. 18:8). Revolutionary, anti-governmental

---

[28] *Głos Narodu*, November 27, 1936.

[29] *Prąd* (1932), 239–45.

[30] *The American Hebrew*, July 23, 1937, 13.

activity was spreading like gangrene in the Jewish community. It had to be isolated and amputated. Why should ghetto benches be unconstitutional, when Jews practiced it themselves in the synagogue? Jews were an alien and harmful force in Polish society and should be isolated. University officials should not only impose ghetto benches but adopt a policy of *numerus nullus* that would close universities to Jews altogether.[31]

That same year Trzeciak argued the morality and legality of ghetto benches in a public response to Rabbi Thon. Thon had written that one could not be both a Christian and an antisemite, that antisemitism was a pagan movement. Trzeciak retorted with a reminder that John's gospel describes Jews as coming from the devil (Jn. 8:44). The church, moreover, had not only tolerated but mandated ghettoes. And how could Jews complain about separate seating in university lecture halls, when they practiced it themselves with separate seating for women in their synagogues? Jewish men discriminated daily, Trzeciak contended, when they thanked God that they were not created Gentiles, slaves, or women. Poles should draw the same lines, wrote the priest, not only at universities but in primary schools and the market place.[32]

Trzeciak was not the only voice in the Catholic press to call for excluding any more Jews at the universities. Writing in *Pro Christo,* Ignacy Zaleski warned against believing that the fall in numbers of Jewish university students would in time transform the structure of Poland's educated class. The Jewish community was too strong, wealthy, and organized; Polish students were too poor and encumbered by the indifference of the past. Jewish competition was a threat to Polish culture, like a festering ulcer that needed to be lanced. Half-measures were just band-aids. Only depriving Jews of their political rights would solve the problem, and depriving Jews of access to Polish universities was a first step in that direction.[33]

Sentiments like these had their impact, and by 1938, in some university departments at least, *numerus nullus* was de facto if not de jure in effect. For the 1938/39 academic year, no new Jewish students were

---

[31] *Mały Dziennik,* October 26, 1937.

[32] *Mały Dziennik,* May 11, 1937; October 26, 1937.

[33] *Pro Christo,* 13/5 (1937), 15.

admitted into the departments of medicine and pharmacy at the University in Kraków. In Lwów no Jews were accepted into the Academy of Veterinary Medicine or the department of mechanics at the Polytechnic. In Warsaw no Jews were accepted into the department of veterinary medicine or pharmacy. In Poznań, for the second year in a row, no Jews were accepted into the university at all.[34]

Any Catholic Pole critical of the ghetto benches or university admission policies was dismissed by the *Mały Dziennik* as guilty of serving Jewish interests and tainted by liberalism with either socialist or Masonic tendencies.[35] In the *Przegląd Powszechny,* a more scholarly consideration of the ghetto benches was given by a priest who would become one of Poland's most prolific and respected theologians, Father Wincenty Granat. Ghetto benches would be morally evil, he wrote, if they would lead to hatred and prevent the conversion of Jews to the church. But if these extremes could be avoided, separation from Jews was not only permitted but in some cases even required by Catholic teaching. The Plenary Synod of Polish Bishops had rejected the coeducation of Catholic and Jewish children in primary and secondary schools. Catholics were entitled to have their faith and Christian morals protected from spiritual disintegration. Jews constituted a high percentage of anarchists and atheists, and the declarations of popes and synods attested to their bad example. Segregation could be seen as a means of self-defence, to prevent Polish society from being spiritually disarmed or altogether lost.

Ghetto benches were not necessarily a symbol of racial hatred, Granat argued. A Catholic was not allowed to attack Jews just because they were Jews. But every race had its virtues and vices, and Poles were allowed to do battle against Jewish vices, so long as they did not embrace unchristian theories or unethical methods of warfare. Poland had not imposed ghettos. Polish Jews had free access to all spheres of cultural and economic life. The Jewish intelligentsia was free to disseminate its ideas about humanitarianism, free thought, sexual license, and "progress." It was free to assault those whom they called "clericalists" and "hooligans of the nationalist camp." Professors of the old liberal stripe trivialized the ghetto benches as an inconsequential youthful prank, the priest-theologian concluded. But college youth were a seismograph of ideological change

---

[34] *Mały Dziennik,* October 27, 1938.

[35] *Mały Dziennik,* July 12, 1937.

in search of a symbol. In an age marked by nationalist symbols like the
swastika, fasces, hammer and sickle, Polish youth considered the ghetto
benches as "one of the symbols of national rebirth."[36]

Violence in the Streets

Anti-Jewish violence was not limited to the universities, although very
often it was again inspired by nationalist youth who saw Jews as easy
scapegoats for their frustrations. By 1934 news from Nazi Germany
inspired not only National Radicals but other young Poles who would
harass Jewish shopkeepers or passers-by. In Warsaw in 1934, a group of
Jews were said to have affronted a Catholic religious procession. A group
of National Radicals, who were still legal at that time, and a young
workers organization used this as an excuse to take to the streets and
began shattering the windows of Jewish businesses and breaking into
Jewish homes. One person was killed. Twenty-two of the rioters were
arrested. In describing the trials and events, *Mały Dziennik* spoke of the
"profanation" of the procession by the Jews but omitted any moral
condemnation of the rioters.[37]

Whether a handful of hoodlums assaulting Jewish pedestrians or a full-
scale riot, the Polish Catholic press would invariably describe an act of
anti-Jewish violence as an "incident" (*zajście*). After the death of
Marshall Piłsudski in 1935, the number and seriousness of these
"incidents" increased dramatically. One of the first was at Grodno, a city
of some 50,000 in eastern Poland, two-thirds of them Jewish. A Pole had
been stabbed to death in a fight with two Jews. A riot broke out that
resulted in one death, at least six serious injuries, and an estimated
$12,000 in damage. The Polish newspapers were not permitted to report
on the riots and those that did were confiscated. A correspondent for *The
American Hebrew* related how the mayor of Grodno appealed to Polish
mothers to dissuade their children from such actions. He blamed the
nationalist youth for "causing a blot on their honor and the honor of the
city where all citizens had always lived peacefully."[38]

---

[36] *Przegląd Powszechny*, 217 (1938), 181–85.

[37] *Mały Dziennik*, October 4, 1935.

[38] *The American Hebrew*, June 28, 1935, 135.

Five months later, *Mały Dziennik* reported on the trial resulting from the Grodno riot and the "wave of anti-Jewish incidents" that were sweeping the "whole country." When the Jewish press ascribed the violence to "hooligans" and the National Democrats (*Endecja*), the Catholic daily disagreed. The issue, it wrote, was "not separate sporadic excesses but the reaction of almost all informed Polish society which intends to shake off its dependence on Jews." The Catholic daily perceived a "general psychosis of fear among Jews." This was with good reason since the Jewish question was "agitating the whole society."[39]

Beset by joblessness and labor unrest, the situation of Poland in the mid-thirties was volatile. The violence was not only anti-Jewish. In Kraków in 1936, a labor demonstration and factory sit-in precipitated a riot that left six people dead and twenty injured. Catholic leaders worried about growing numbers of workers becoming the prey of communist agitation, fomented according to the *Mały Dziennik* "almost exclusively," by Jews.[40]

In this atmosphere of economic hardship and unrest, the National Democrats not only promoted their economic boycott of Jewish businesses but tried to enforce it. Przytyk, a small town 80 miles from Warsaw, almost 90% Jewish, and had routinely enjoyed peaceful, even friendly relations with the Catholic peasants of the surrounding countryside. Young Endeks, however, made it their intention to change all that. Besides shouting antisemitic slogans, they began to stand outside Jewish shops and drive away non-Jewish customers. Non-Jews were attacked and beaten for insisting on buying from Jews. Friendly Christians warned the Jewish population of trouble brewing, and an appeal was made to the local governor for increased police protection, but he brushed the Jewish fears aside. On market day (March 9, 1936), a fight began when several Poles attempted to buy bread from a Jewish merchant. The fight sparked a riot that quickly overpowered the local police. When a shot in front of a Jewish house killed a Christian, the crowd threw off all restraint. A mob began invading Jewish homes, smashing windows, breaking furniture, and beating the inhabitants. The subsequent trial resulted in guilty verdicts for forty-three Poles and eleven Jews. A

---

[39] *Mały Dziennik*, November 23, 1935; February 4, 1936.

[40] *Mały Dziennik*, March 24, 1936; April 21, 1936.

headline in the *Mały Dziennik* declared that the Jews bore responsibility for the "incident."[41]

In June 1936, the murder of an army officer ignited an anti-Jewish riot in Mińsk Mazowiecki. It was but one of numerous antisemitic incidents that year for which Endeks were arrested and convicted. The Nationalists were inciting anarchy, charged Premier Składkowski. He blamed them for twenty-one "massive incidents" in the region of Białystok alone. Besides 161 cases of broken windows there were three deaths and ninety-nine instances of Jews being beaten.[42] Antisemites were arrested and imprisoned for organizing attacks on the police as well as on Jews. And at a market in Smerdin in the province of Siedlece, a rare if not altogether unique occurrence: Endek pickets trying to keep Polish peasants away from buying at Jewish stalls were beaten up and driven away by the peasants.[43]

In February 1937, however, the government formed the National Unity Camp (OZON) that explicitly excluded Jews. OZON embraced the boycott of Jewish businesses as a means of finding employment for Poles and committed itself to the mass migration of Jews as the solution for Poland's socio-economic problems. Those national policies did not go without impact on local government and police. In May 1937, in Brest-Litovsk, a Jewish butcher found to be selling meat illegally procured from ritually slaughtered cattle killed a policeman who had attempted to confiscate the meat. The news set off a riot that saw three Jews killed, more than fifty injured, and the Jewish quarter laid waste. Although Brest-Litovsk was the seat of the district governor and soldiers were garrisoned there, the rioting was allowed to rage for sixteen hours. The governor and police did nothing to protect the Jews.[44]

The following month in the pilgrimage city of Częstochowa, when the killing of a Pole by a Jew led to riots, once again the police did nothing. For nearly a week Jewish shops were pillaged, until finally calls for peace from the local bishop and mayor restored calm. When Jewish

---

[41] *Mały Dziennik*, August 12, 1936. See also *The American Hebrew*, July 3, 1936, 47–48.

[42] *Mały Dziennik*, January 16, 1937.

[43] *The American Hebrew*, February 26, 1937, 925–26.

[44] *The American Hebrew*, July 23, 1937; *Mały Dziennik*, May 30, 1937.

newspapers described the rioters as robbing Jewish stores, the *Mały Dziennik* accused the Jewish press of printing "lies". The mob did not rob, it threw the goods from the Jewish stores into the street.[45]

In the wake of the riots at Grodno (1935), Przytyk (1936), and Brest-Litovsk (1937), Catholic leaders in Poland could hardly keep silent on the antisemitic violence the nationalists were inciting. The head of the Evangelical Church in Poland, Dr. Boursche, denounced the antisemitism as "un-Christian." He declared that violence against Jews contradicted Christian ethics and that pastors under his jurisdiction would preach against antisemitism in their churches.[46] The Catholic press and clergy responded as well, but in a tone set by the bishops. Their criticism of the violence was much more nuanced and less denunciatory.

Certainly the most celebrated response was the 1936 statement of the Primate, Cardinal Hlond. In it he proclaimed that Nazi racial theories and violence against Jews were contrary to Christian ethics. It was "forbidden," he wrote, to "demolish a Jewish store, damage their merchandise, break windows, or throw things at their homes." It was "forbidden to assault, beat up, maim, or slander Jews." The context for these moral prescripts, however, was a statement by the Cardinal, identifying Jews with bolshevism, atheism, fraud, and prostitution. Jews, he charged, were corrupting morals and waging war on the church.[47]

Earlier in 1934, before the riots described above, a delegation of rabbis had visited Cardinal Aleksander Kakowski of Warsaw and petitioned him to issue a pastoral letter, appealing for an end to the violence that was defaming Poland's good name. Kakowski's published response was to "condemn all violence and excesses, from whatever side they come from, whether Catholic or Jewish." But then the Cardinal went on to point out that Jewish atheists were "fighting against the Christian religion" and Jewish publishers were "inundating" Poland with pornography. While not all Jews were responsible for them, such actions "helped to create antisemitic feelings in the Polish community and may have led to

---

[45] *Mały Dziennik,* June 25, 1937.

[46] *The American Hebrew,* February 26, 1937, 925.

[47] August Cardinal Hlond, *Na Straży Sumienia Narodu* (Ramsey, New Jersey: Don Bosco, 1951), 38–52.

regrettable excesses."[48] If subsequent reporting of this meeting is any measure, it was not the Cardinal's criticism of violence but his explanation of antisemitism that made the most lasting impression on Catholic consciousness.

When the Jewish press accused the Catholic clergy of not speaking out against antisemitic violence, the Catholic Press Agency (KAP) responded: "All excesses and brutal means of war are unworthy of the name Christian and ultimately do not attain their goal. The Catholic clergy certainly does not approve of any violence and does not neglect to remind the faithful that the highest commandment of Christian ethics is the command of love of God and love of neighbor without regard to race, nationality, or religion.... But Jews who complain about excesses ought to remember that they are not without fault in this regard." The statement then proceeded to advocate a "cultural separation of Poles from Jews" because of Jewish radicalism, bad example on Polish youth, and the "negative traits in the Jewish character which grate on Christians." The Jews themselves could help keep people calm by "overcoming the faults, which render mutual co-existence difficult."[49]

The tone set by the bishops and their press agency resonated in the rest of the clergy and Catholic press. Their ambiguity was exemplified by the *Głos Narodu*: violence against Jews was unethical and "primitive." Breaking windows did not solve Poland's Jewish question. Poles should leave the windows alone but empty the Jewish stores of Christian clients. That was the only effective method of ridding Poland of Jews.[50]

Violence Justified?

While Catholic leaders criticized antisemitic violence, they also explained it, and with the explanations came justification. "It is permissible to defend yourself against an aggressor," wrote Father Paul Kuczka in the Catholic Action journal, *Kultura*. Unlike that of Germany, Poland's nationalism followed Christian principles, he argued. Jews were

---

[48] *Wiadomości Archidiecezalne Warszawskie* (1934), 248–49.

[49] *Prąd* (1936), 81–82.

[50] *Głos Narodu,* July 5, 1936.

fomenting revolutionary unrest. They were capitalists, communists, socialists, and Masons. They had chosen certain Catholic countries for "subversive experiments." France was only their first victim. "The ethical stand in our war with the Jews is clear. Christian ethics allows you to defend yourself against an aggressor, even if the aggressor should thereby lose his life."

War was evil, Kuczka conceded, but in defense of superior values it was a "necessary evil." Although you may elect to suffer harm to yourself voluntarily, you may not stand by passively when the life of a neighbor or of the nation is threatened. Aggressors themselves are responsible for whatever consequences they suffer from a war. If you had a guest who demoralized your children, who took away their bread and ideals, would you hesitate to throw that guest out of your house just because he might thereby sprain an ankle? What would have happened to Poland, asked Kuczka, if its defenders had been afraid to use the sword against the invasion of the old Teutonic knights? Jews were a hundred times richer and more powerful than Poles. They could manage without Polish bread, but the Poles would perish without it.[51]

Self-defense was the standard appeal used by the Catholic press to justify the violence erupting against Jews. The problem was not only the Jewish leftists. The Talmud permitted Jews to practice a double standard, Stanisław Nowak claimed, and Christian violence was simply a reaction against the Talmud's sanction of cheating, theft, and false oaths.[52] Eugeniusz Januszkiewicz in *Kultura* pointed out that one had only to visit Warsaw's Jewish quarter, Nalewki, to experience the hostile, foreign atmosphere there. Nothing comparable could be found in Poland among Germans and Ukrainians. Polish antisemitism was a "healthy reaction against a foreign body" that required expulsion.[53] Also in *Kultura* Stanisław Nowak explained that the Polish peasant had "ceased to be a source of exploitation and experiments for others."[54]

Blaming the victims is a commonly observed reaction to violence, and the Polish Catholic press proved no exception. When Jewish pedestrians

---

[51] Paul Kuczka, *Kultura*, November 8, 1936.

[52] Stanisław Nowak, *Kultura*, July 12, 1936.

[53] *Kultura*, August 29, 1937.

[54] Nowak, *Kultura*, July 12, 1936.

were attacked by a gang in Wilno, the *Mały Dziennik* described the assaults as "incidents provoked by Jews." The daily justified its characterization on the grounds that earlier in the day Jews had manhandled a Polish youth for shouting out slogans in support of the boycott.[55] The *Mały Dziennik* agreed that the violence at Brest-Litovsk was the result of hatred, but not the hatred of Poles for Jews. Rather, it was "the incredible fanaticism of Jewish hatred." When the Jewish butcher killed the Polish policeman, there was a spontaneous, impulsive, uncontrollable reaction. Rather than railing against Poles with hatred, Jews should stop crying persecution and emigrate, the daily advised. "There is a lot of gunpowder lying around and every spark leads to an explosion." No appeals for peace and calm from the Polish side would do any good when Jews were making the sparks.[56]

The violence engendered by the nationalists aroused opposition as well as explanations. A group of leading Polish intellectuals attempted to counteract antisemitism in the pages of the *Wiadomości Literackie* (Literary News), and in 1936 planning began for a congress in Lwów under the banner of a "Battle with antisemitism." The *Mały Dziennik* called into question the Polishness and patriotism of these critics, painting them as left wing liberals associated with Masonry and under the influence of Jews. The Catholic daily could not approve of violence against Jews, but neither would it close its eyes to the violence which the "Polish-Jewish intelligentsia" was perpetrating. By combatting antisemitism, these Polish intellectuals were promoting the supremacy of Jews in all areas of Polish life. Such a Poland would be "communist-Jewish" and no longer Poland.[57]

Intellectuals were not the only Poles to criticize the antisemitic wave of the 1930s. When clerics advocated the expulsion of Jews from the country, ordinary Catholics questioned if it was christian to deprive people of a roof over their heads just because they were Jews. Then too there was the attitude that "all Jews are scoundrels, but the Jew I deal with is exceptionally decent." The *Przewodnik Katolicki* dealt with such scruples with a variety of arguments. There simply was not enough room

---

[55] *Mały Dziennik*, September 8, 1938.

[56] *Mały Dziennik*, May 20, 1937.

[57] *Mały Dziennik*, June 14, 1936.

in Poland for all the "exceptionally decent" Jews, since practically every Pole knew one. Antisemitism, according to the popular Catholic weekly, was a badge of honor. It meant you loved your own nation more than you did strangers. The contrary meant "you wear a Jewish coat and hundreds of Poles shiver from the cold for lack of work. You wear Jewish shoes and hundreds of your countrymen go barefoot, because Polish work places are not open. You give your wages to Jews, and thousands of your unemployed brethren go hungry." Catholic Poles did not need to abuse or persecute Jews, just to support their own kind.[58]

If antisemitic violence required explanation, so too did the attitudes that gave rise to it. Catholic authors had to make it quite clear that they were not expounding the racial antisemitism that had been condemned by Pope Pius XI. *Pro Christo* emphasized that it was not condemning Jews simply because they were Jews.[59]

Catholic antisemites also had to answer the objection that they were not repudiating the gospel. Jesus had commanded love of neighbor, even love of enemies. How could antisemitism be reconciled with such clear Christian teaching? The Catholic rationalizations of antisemitism took a variety of tortuous turns. One young writer, for example, a student, distinguished between the obligations of individuals and those of societies. What was admirable and proper for an individual might be irresponsible for a society. The "Jewish Question" in Poland was not one of individuals but of a Catholic society defending itself and its culture from the destructive influence of Jewish culture.[60]

Another student interpreted the commandment to love one's neighbor by distinguishing between spiritual and material interests. When it came to purely material matters, you could put your neighbor before yourself, as the Good Samaritan did. But in spiritual matters St. Thomas Aquinas taught that there was a hierarchy of responsibility: first to care about your own soul; then those who belong to you, your family and nation; and finally total strangers. As Cardinal Kakowski indicated to the rabbis, Jews were demoralizing the country. The whole Christian world was being depraved by Jews with their movies, cabarets, and modern ways of

---

[58] *Przewodnik Katolicki* (1935) 676–77; (1938), 28.

[59] *Pro Christo*, 14/9 (1938), 306–307.

[60] *Młodzież Katolicka* (1934), 24–25.

dancing. It was precisely the love of neighbor that commanded Poles to save themselves and those near to them from moral downfall. Living together with Jews hindered one's salvation. Like Jesus, Poles must drive away Satan and all those who aided him. Of course, Catholics would not use weapons except when necessary in self-defense. Economic measures, and depriving Jews of all positions of influence would be enough to make them leave.[61]

Of all Catholic periodicals *Pro Christo* was predictably the most radical. In it J. Dobrowolski maintained that Poles were bound to love their own more than they did strangers. When you defended your fellow-citizens by hanging a bandit or locking up a thief, you did injury to the aggressor but demonstrated true love for your neighbor. Poles had a right to defend themselves from Jews without worrying about the injury they might thereby inflict. Jews were like ungrateful guests who had taken over the home of their host. Jews and their judaized Polish allies were trying to blackmail Catholics with the commandment to love one's neighbor. But it was the church and its priests, not the rabbis, who gave the true interpretation of the commandment, Dobrowolski argued. "The church has always taught that war and the vindication of one's just rights in no way contradicts the Christian religion or love of neighbor." Aryans have no need to scruple when defending themselves against Jews."[62]

The lengths to which a cleric could go in justifying his antisemitism was given classic expression by Father Ignacy Charszewski. In an article on "Love and Hate" in *Pro Christo,* he responded to a Christmas poem that had appeared in a secular daily paper. The poem had described Polish children taking pity on a Jew and a German, both refugees from the Nazis. A heavenly figure then appears and breaks the traditional Polish Christmas wafer with the German, the Jew, and the Polish children. This was no less than sacrilege, fumed the priest, breaking the Christmas wafer with a non-believer and, if a German refugee from the Third Reich, then obviously a communist. Charszewski proceeded to disparage Polish sentimentality, the *"dulcis sanguis Polonorum."* Toleration was a national failing of the Poles, he wrote, and it was a falsified gospel that tried to justify it. They were "accursed liberals" who were trying to defend Jews in the name of progress and Christian love.

---

[61] *Młodzież Katolicka* (1934), 12–14.

[62] J. Dobrowolski, *Pro Christo,* 10 (1934), 262–68.

But there was no salvation outside the church, and neither was there progress.

According to Charszewski, having real love required having real hate. Real love required hating cruelty and tyranny. Real love demanded that Poles hate and fight against liberalism as well as communism, for the one led to the other. Liberals claimed to defend the oppressed, but their cold altruism and false humanitarianism was only an imitation of Christian love. Liberals accused Christians of being brutal for refusing to allow themselves to be devoured. Poland had been paradise for Jews but purgatory for its own people. There might be some exceptional and fine persons who were Jews but they all followed their leaders. The "synagogue of Satan" was in a struggle with the church, but Jews would not prevail so long as there was more true love and true hate.[63]

Charszewski's outright justification of hatred was exceptional. Much more typical of the tone set by the bishops was Jesuit Father P. Turbak in the mass-produced *Głosy Katolickie* (Catholic Voices). While anti-Jewish violence was barbarous, a political-economic-cultural "war" against Jews based on "law and morality" was imperative. War against Jews was justified not out of hatred but of a sense of responsibility toward one's own. There was antisemitism everywhere, but no where more justified than in Poland where the percentage of Jews to the rest of the population was greater than anywhere else. If, as some claimed, antisemitism was as old as the Jewish people, then Jews must themselves be to blame for it. Were Jews always the lambs, and all other people the wolves? Jews in Poland had no complaint, Turbak assured his readers. They enjoyed equality under the law, and police authorities were quite energetic in prosecuting crimes committed against them. If the police did not always succeed in apprehending all the culprits, they were only human. Father Turbak granted that this kind of legal and moral war sometimes turned violent. But wherever it did, experience indicated that there was "always some kind of provocation from the Jews."[64]

Finally, if antisemitism occasionally led to violence in Poland, Catholic writers could point out that things were worse elsewhere. Catholic nationalists took offense at the fact that Jews were sending reports to foreign newspapers about mistreatment in Poland. How could one speak

---

[63] Ignacy Charszewski, *Pro Christo,* 10 (1934), 331–60.

[64] *Głosy Katolickie,* 4 (April) 1937.

about persecution when everyday hundreds of Jews were seeking asylum in Poland to escape from Austria, Germany, Czechoslovakia, and Hungary? According to the *Przewodnik Katolicki,* Deputy Grynbaum, one of the Jewish representatives to the Sejm, stated after a trip abroad: "When you leave Poland and see what it is like, you then return gladly."[65]

In light of the foregoing, one can understand why there were no expressions of outrage at the Kristallnacht pogrom from the bishops and clergy of Poland. They were hardly in a position to condemn Germany and Austria, when they had not denounced antisemitic violence in Poland. Though they criticized antisemitic violence as unethical, the tone of the criticism was too muted and qualified to be called a denunciation. In their struggle against separation of church and state in Poland, the Catholic leadership waged war against those most interested in effecting and maintaining that separation. Their hatred of liberalism as much as their fear of communism fueled the clergy's crusade to limit as much as possible the secularizing influences of assimilated Jews and their liberal Polish allies.

The ghetto benches were both a symbol and a first step toward segregating Jews and circumscribing their impact on Polish society. The violence that erupted around the ghetto benches and economic boycott was regarded as an unfortunate but inevitable by-product of a necessary struggle. Victims of antisemitic violence were unlucky but not altogether innocent casualties of war. With the analogy of a just war as the dominant metaphor to define Catholic efforts to maintain a preferred status for the church, violence could be justified as self-defense. Hatred of those designated as enemies could be rationalized as love for family and neighbor. Indifference to, or worse, Catholic criticism of antisemitism could be interpreted as aiding the aggressor. Traditional Polish tolerance, formerly a virtue, could be rebuked as a vice to be uprooted, or at least a virtue that Poland could no longer afford.

Catholic leaders in Poland criticized the antisemitic brutality in Germany and Austria as barbarous and primitive. But self-interest

---

[65] *Przewodnik Katolicki* (1939), 83.

prevented them from criticizing too loudly. When that brutality came to Poland in September of 1939, it was too late to inaugurate a massive change of public opinion. Mental habits and attitudes had become too ingrained. The characters were already well-defined, when the German death machines began to operate on occupied Polish soil. Catholic orthodoxy had helped define them: the Poles were the victims and the Jews, if not enemies, were aliens. Certainly the numbers changed the nature of the crime, but the precedents had already been set. Antisemitic violence was always unethical, but it could be explained.

Chapter 13

The Vatican and the Polish Bishops

By mid-August 1920, the diplomatic corps had left Warsaw for safety elsewhere. The Soviet armies had invaded Poland and were marching with little resistance toward the capital. Streams of refugees poured into the city, as the demoralized Polish army retreated before the Soviet advance. Achille Ratti, titular Archbishop of Lepanto and Papal Nuncio to Poland, informed the Vatican of the gravity of the situation. He sent his archives out of the threatened city with the English ambassador who, with most other diplomats, judged it wise to leave.

Archbishop Ratti had requested permission to remain in the city, even in the event of its being taken by the invading Soviets. He would drive through Warsaw in an open carriage, so all the Poles could see he was still there, ready to share their fate, whatever it would be. On August 14, canon fire could be heard from the suburbs. It was the eve of a great feast of Mary, mother of Jesus and patroness of Poland. Heavy fighting continued for two days, as the Polish defenders of the capital held their own. Then, on August 16, news reached the city that the Soviet forces had been routed and were rapidly retreating. Marshal Piłsudski, staking everything on a desperate last-minute maneuver, had made a surprise attack on the flank of the Soviet army. For the Catholics of Poland, however, the victory was not the result of mere military prowess but of heavenly protection—the "Miracle on the Vistula" (*Cud nad Wisłą*).[1]

---

[1] Robin Anderson, *Between Two Wars, The Story of Pope Pius XI (Achille Ratti) 1922–1939* (Chicago: Franciscan Herald, 1977), 38–41.

The British ambassador at Berlin at the time, Lord D'Abernon, later described it as the *Eighteenth Decisive Battle of the World.* He was convinced that, had the Soviets armies broken through the Polish resistance, communism would have swept throughout central Europe, possibly penetrating the entire continent. D'Abernon quoted the commander-in-chief of the Soviet army: "There is not the slightest doubt that, if we had succeeded in breaking the Polish army of bourgeois and seigneurs, the revolution of the working class in Poland would have been an accomplished fact. And the tempest would not have stopped at the Polish frontier."[2]

There is no question but that the Battle of Warsaw made a profound impact on Achille Ratti. His first act on receiving the news of the Polish victory was to visit the battlefield. At Lepanto the Catholic forces had halted the advance of the Turks; at Warsaw the armies from the east were Bolshevik. The memory would stay with him long after the Titular Archbishop of Lepanto had become the Bishop of Rome, Pope Pius XI.

His Polish experience affected Ratti for the rest of his life. It was in Poland that he had learned from the refugees of the anti-God museums in the Soviet Union, of the bishops and priests who had been executed. Later in 1922, when Ratti was pope, the British Minister at the Vatican would write, "Everything in the Vatican is dominated by the pope's fear of Russian Communism, that the Soviets may reach Western Europe."[3]

As with Sobieski at Vienna, Poland had once again protected western Europe from an onslaught by the east. Convinced that the situation was hopeless, Poland's allies had left the Poles to defend themselves alone. The Catholic Poles ascribed the victory to Providence and to the role Providence had assigned to Poland. Archbishop Ratti did nothing to shake that conviction. As nuncio, the future pope was quoted as saying to the Poles, "I am convinced that God, who returned freedom to your nation in so miraculous a manner, desires to accomplish his plans through you and he will accomplish them despite everything."[4] Even on his deathbed, Pius XI is said to have expressed his faith in Poland's historic

---

[2] Cited in Philip Hughes, *Pope Pius the Eleventh* (New York: Sheed and Ward, 1937), 95.

[3] Anthony Rhodes, *The Vatican in the Age of Dictators, 1922–1945* (London: Hodder and Stoughton, 1973), 18.

[4] *Wiadomości Archidiecezalne Warszawskie* (1939): 99.

mission to be the "Bulwark of Christianity," (*Przedmurze Chrześcijaństwa*). "You are the knights of the faith; in this role you will be the best knights of Poland."[5]

If Poland had a profound affect on Ratti, so too did Ratti affect Poland. The Catholic church faced the same massive challenges in reborn Poland that the government did, reuniting populations that had been separated for nearly a hundred fifty years, people who under Prussian, Austrian, and Russian domination had been shaped by widely different fates and circumstances. Amid the most chaotic conditions, diocesan lines had to be re-aligned according to new frontiers. Twelve new bishops were named in Ratti's first six months, and Ratti himself was consecrated an Archbishop (October 28, 1919) by Cardinal Aleksander Kakowski of Warsaw. Ratti met regularly with the bishops of Poland and could not help but come to know them with some familiarity, going so far as to describe himself as a Polish bishop. "I am a friend of Poland," he is quoted as saying. "Because of Poland I became a bishop. I was consecrated a bishop in Poland by Polish bishops.... I am truly a Polish bishop."[6]

During his years as nuncio, Ratti came to know Poland's strengths, weaknesses, and problems personally. Among those problems were its large non-Catholic minorities, including well over three million Jews. It did not take Ratti long to learn what it meant for Poland to be home to the largest Jewish community in Europe. Among Ratti's papers, housed in the Vatican archives, is a file on "The Jews and the Jewish Question in Poland (1915–19)," containing letters to Ratti, memoranda, and publications, sixteen items in all, some of them extensively underlined.[7] In it one finds a seven-page article, *"Die Juden in Polen,"* with the words underlined, "Antisemitism is very strong in Poland" (*Der Antisemitismus ist in Polen sehr stark*). One finds a Jewish protest regarding the 1918 pogrom at Kielce and a 1919 pamphlet on the pogrom at Lwów. Correspondence also indicates that Ratti met with representatives of the

---

[5] *Wiadomości Archidiecezalne Warszawskie* (1939): 152.

[6] *Wiadomości Archidiecezalne Warszawskie* (1939): 99.

[7] Included among these are: P. Rohrbach, ed., *Die Juden in Polen und Westrussland* (1915); W. Kaplun-Kogan, *Die Juden in Polen, Ein geschichtlicher Überblick;* N. Goldmann, *Zum Polnisch-Jüdischen Problem, Eine Erwiderung* (1915); N. Birnbaum, *Was sind Ost-Juden* (1916).

Berlin-based *Komitee für den Osten* (Committee for the East), created to study and improve the political-economic situation of German-speaking Jews.

Among the more significant of these items is a six-page memorandum written in French, undated and unsigned, but providing an "Account of Polish-Jewish Relations" from the perspective of the Polish government. The memorandum explains that: "Because of the great number of Jews who live in Poland...their national character and above all the manner they earn their living, the Jewish question is extremely sensitive in Poland." Poland's Jews are then described as "unproductive," a "race of merchants," the great majority of them immersed in poverty. "Apart from a relatively small number of artisans, they are comprised of small shop keepers, middlemen, and usurers, or, to be precise, they are living off the exploitation of the Christian population."

There follows an account of a 1913 Zionist meeting at Łódź at which Vladimir Jabotinsky, the Russian Zionist, is reported as having called for Poland's Jews to march with Russia against the Poles. The memorandum goes on to claim that, when the war finally did come, the Jews sided with Austria and Germany. The pogrom at Lwów is deplored but explained by the fact that Austria had released all but the most dangerous criminals and made them defenders of the city. The memorandum blames these newly armed ex-prisoners for pillaging the Jewish quarter and complains that ill-intentioned elements were trying to place all the blame on Poland as being "ungovernable by itself."

The memorandum underscores the presence of Jews in the Communist movement. It disclaims any insinuation that all Jews are Bolshevik, but states that Jews play a "predominant role" in the movement both in Poland and Russia, where, with the exception of Lenin, all the leaders and communists of note are Jews. Cited by name are Trotski, Zinoviev, Ganetski and several leading Polish communists. "The government finds itself in a very delicate position. Any action against the local bolshevik movement ... is seen by the Jews as directed against them. The general headquarters of the communist movement is located in Nalewki, the Jewish quarter of Warsaw." The memorandum concludes with an assurance that the government has the well-being and safety of all its citizens at heart without distinction as to race or religion. It desires to avoid any incident.

Also among Ratti's papers were the proceedings of an anti-communist congress held in Warsaw (January 17–20, 1920). In it the war against communism is described as following from Poland's "great historic mission." Poland's intimate cooperation with the Papacy would aim at internationally uniting Christian forces "for the struggle against the common enemy, i.e., against Jewish Masons and the socialist International." Christian opposition must be marshalled against all the anti-Christian forces "preparing to pass over the corpse of Poland to conquer the entire world."[8]

Ratti's papers reveal not his opinions but only those he received. We do not know what he thought about liberals, communists, or the Jews in Poland when he was nuncio. But we do know what he thought once he became pope, especially about the broader socio-political issues which affected Catholic opinion about Jews, including the opinions of the bishops of Poland. One cannot understand the attitude of the Polish bishops toward Jews except within the context of the Vatican's attitude toward the revolutionary social and political movements that had been sweeping Europe for over a century.

Pope Pius XI

Upon his election as pope, Ratti is reported to have told the College of Cardinals that had elected him, "It is the wish of my heart to safeguard and defend all the rights of the Church and all the prerogatives of the Holy See."[9] His first encyclical, "On the peace of Christ in the kingdom of Christ," made quite clear what those rights and prerogatives were. He left no doubt but that the kingdom he had in mind was also very much of this world and that he would continue the church's struggle against political liberalism.

The church, wrote the pope, was the teacher and guide not only of individuals but of societies and nations. With a clear reference to the League of Nations at Geneva, he claimed that the church was more successful than any "merely human institution" in devising a set of international laws. Among those laws upholding the rights of Christ over public life were the Church's teaching on marriage and its right to teach

---

[8] Archivo Segregato Vaticano, Archivo di Mons. Ratti, Varsavia, 1918-1921, 1/205 and 1/206.

[9] Thomas B. Morgan, *A Reporter at the Papal Court, A Narrative of the Reign of Pope Pius XI* (New York: Longmans, Green, 1937), 41.

in public schools. The pope promised that a "holy battle" would be waged to vindicate the rights of the Church over education. He reaffirmed the traditional Catholic teaching on the proper relationship between church and state and expressed his intense interest in what had come to be called "Catholic Action."[10]

That first encyclical proved very much to be the program of Pius XI. To re-assert and promote the rights of the Church within civil affairs he instituted in 1929 the Feast of Christ the King. Government leaders, he wrote, were bound to give public honor to Christ and to his empire over all nations. It was the fault of an impious anti-clericalism that parliaments avoided mentioning Christ's name and that the Catholic church was "ignominiously" placed on the same level as "false religions."[11]

In his 1929 encyclical on education, as pointed out previously, Pius XI absolutely forbade that Catholic and non-Catholic children be mixed in schools where they would receive lessons from non-Catholic teachers. Justice, he insisted, required the State to provide Catholic pupils not only with religious instruction but with schools in which the teachers, syllabi, and textbooks were all regulated by a Christian spirit under the supervision of the church. Promoting and defending the church's rights over the education was one of the important tasks of Catholic Action.[12]

Catholic Action had had its origins with Pope Leo XIII's opposition to the separation of church and state and Pope Pius X's program to restore Catholic culture. But it was Pius XI who became the "Pope of Catholic Action." He consolidated it into an international movement and gave it its classical definition: "the cooperation and participation of the laity in the apostolate of the church's hierarchy." Promoting it frequently in his letters and addresses, he insisted that Catholic Action must remain "outside and above all party politics." But this was not to say that Catholic Action did not involve itself in political issues.[13]

In his 1937 encyclical on communism, the pope encouraged Catholic laity who were "doing battle" in the ranks of Catholic Action to make

---

[10] Claudia Carlen, I.H.M., *The Papal Encyclicals, 1740–1981,* 5 vols. (1981; reprint, Ann Arbor, MI: Pierien Press, 1990), 3:225–39.

[11] Carlen, *Papal Encyclicals,* 3:265–69, 271–79.

[12] Carlen, *Papal Encyclicals,* 3:353–69.

[13] Carlen, *Papal Encyclicals,* 3:445–58.

known the Christian solution to social problems. With a penchant for martial metaphors, the pope referred to the need for "militant" leaders of Catholic Action "properly prepared and armed." The pope accused economic and political liberalism of preparing the way for communism. He also indicted the international press for not adequately reporting the anti-Christian violence in Russia, Mexico, and Spain. There was a "conspiracy of silence on the part of a large section of the non-Catholic press of the world," he wrote, favored by "various occult forces which for a long time have been working for the overthrow of the Christian Social Order."[14]

The pope did not make explicit whom he meant by the "various occult forces" bent on overturning the Christian social order. He did not make any mention of Jews in connection with communism nor with the "conspiracy of silence" on the part of the non-Catholic press. If any group was to be singled out, it was Freemasons. In 1929, Pius XI warned a group of Polish pilgrims of "dangers and insidious traps" being set by "the enemy of all good": "I have in mind here above all the Masonic sect, which is spreading its perverse and destructive principles even in Poland."[15]

The Vatican viewed Masonic efforts to separate church and state, introduce civil divorce, and remove religious instruction from public schools with virtually the same horror as it viewed communism. Both were seen as subverting Catholic culture and civilization. Both were singled out as targets for Catholic Action. Poland was no exception. In 1936, Archbishop Francisco Marmaggi, for eight years the successor to Ratti as nuncio to Poland, repeated the warning the pope had earlier given the Polish pilgrims: "Be on guard. Vigilate! Poland is in great danger today. An especially insidious enemy is lying in wait and threatening you, plotting conspiracies against your traditions and Catholic life. It should be easy for you to guess who this enemy is. Be on guard! ... Join together, support one another, organize!"

Reporting on the Marmaggi's speech, the *Mały Dziennik* left no doubt as to who the enemy was. Defensive action had to be mounted against the "deluge of communism, Masonry, and unbelief." Polish Catholics must "without exception actively support the Catholic press and strongly

---

[14] Carlen, *Papal Encyclicals,* 3:537–54.

[15] *Mały Dziennik,* July 25, 1938.

campaign for the creation of Catholic primary and secondary schools so that our youth may be protected from the corrupting influence of Jewish and radical teachers."[16]

The pope singled out Masons as the "enemy of all good." Neither he nor Marmaggi made any mention of Jews. But when the editors of *Mały Dziennik*, the largest daily newspaper in all of Poland, interpreted such warnings as including Jews, they were not corrected, neither by the Polish bishops nor by the Apostolic Nuncio from Rome.

To say that the Roman Catholic church is both Catholic and Roman is not simply to utter an empty tautology. No church in the Roman Catholic communion is autonomous; each is part of an international network of churches centered in Rome. Bishops are not only named by the Vatican, they must report on their dioceses and be evaluated every five years. They are under the constant surveillance and scrutiny of an Apostolic Nuncio or Delegate, the Vatican's ambassador to a local church and on-the-scene source of information about it.

Serving as nuncios to interwar Poland were, after Ratti, Archbishops Francisco Marmaggi and Philip Cortesi. They, no less than the Polish bishops, reiterated frequently the equation that being Polish meant being Catholic. Ignoring Poland's minorities, Marmaggi reminded the Poles that it was because of their loyalty to Rome that they had received the title "*semper fidelis.*"[17] His successor, Archbishop Cortesi, re-echoed the theme: "Religion and Fatherland—the two loves and two lights which have covered Poland with glory forever in the annals of heroism, holiness, and Christian civilization." Docile to the teachings of the church, Poland was becoming "ever more capable of fulfilling its historic mission for which it earned the beautiful title, Bastion of Christianity."[18]

Poland had originally served as a bulwark for western Christendom against Muslims. In 1937 the pope had other hostile forces in mind, when he invoked the image in a letter to the Polish bishops on the occasion of an international congress in honor of Christ the King. It was appropriate, he wrote, that the congress be held in a land "which is rightly called the Bastion of Christianity and truly has been." The purpose of the congress

---

[16] *Mały Dziennik*, September 2, 1936.

[17] *Gazeta Kościelna* (1936), 47.

[18] *Gazeta Kościelna* (1937), 258; *Mały Dziennik*, May 22, 1937.

was not only that the reign of Christ be recognized by all, but that the public life of all peoples be subject to his "empire." Get to know the enemies of Christ, the pope warned, their power, plans, and mode of operation. The fate of the whole world can be said to hang in the balance.[19]

When the National Radical Camp and in the wake of its break-up smaller radical youth groups took it upon themselves to imitate Germany's Nazis in dealing with Jews, a Parisian newspaper reported the presence of neo-paganism in Poland. The papal nuncio, Philip Cortesi responded in defense of the Poles. The movement did not have the significance ascribed to it, in fact was "almost unknown" in Poland, he stated. Poland was simply fulfilling its providential role in the "fight for Christian civilization." Poland had been and was being faithful to its mission and willed to remain so forever.[20]

Even though they contained no explicit reference to the Jewish question as such, these official and public statements by the Holy See and its representatives certainly affected the Polish hierarchy's stance toward Jews. As for official but private, diplomatic statements, there is no record indicating that Poland's Jewish question ever arose as an issue between the Polish government and the Holy See. The Vatican eschewed commentary on Poland's minority policies except with regard to Ukrainian Eastern rite Catholics, the so-called Uniates. Of indirect significance to the "Jewish question" in Poland, Pius XI made no secret of his high regard for Marshal Piłsudski and of his distaste for Poland's right wing nationalists. The pope's condemnation of L'Action Française in 1927 was interpreted as a censure, by analogy, of Endecja. If not in France then neither in Poland was it acceptable to hide a chauvinist creed behind a facade of Catholicism. But it was clear too that the pope's confidence in Piłsudski did not extend to those who surrounded him, certainly not to the Freemasons and liberals.[21]

---

[19] *Acta Apostolicae Sedis* (1937), 335–38.

[20] *Przewodnik Katolicki* (1939), 441.

[21] For an excellent overview of the relationship between the Vatican and the Second Polish Republic, see Neal Pease, "Poland and the Holy See, 1918–1939," *Slavic Review* 50:3 (Fall 1991), 521–30.

La Civiltà Cattolica

But in addition to encyclicals and allocutions, there were other ways one could use to discern the mind of the Holy See, like carefully reading the pages of *La Civiltà Cattolica*. Founded by the Italian Jesuits in 1850, *La Civiltà Cattolica* was and is not just another Catholic periodical. Formally approved with a papal letter by Pope Pius IX (1866), later reconfirmed by Pope Leo XIII, the Jesuit journal has long been justifiably regarded as a "semi-official organ of the Holy See."[22] Its editors proposed "always and in all matters to reflect the thinking of the Holy See."[23] Not only was it scrupulous in its fidelity to Vatican directives, its editorial positions were openly known to have been given prior approval by the Vatican curia. As such, its opinions, written almost always by anonymous authors, were regularly regarded with close attention in both religious and political circles. Its merited reputation for enjoying the confidence of the popes gave it a unique authority for Catholics. Within its pages one could receive clarification for the often encoded or merely suggestive language of official Vatican documents. Certainly this was true concerning the Jewish question.

As early as 1890, *La Civiltà Cattolica* gave extensive coverage to the causes, effects, and remedies of the "Jewish Question in Europe." In 1928 the Rome-based journal returned to the issue, but this time designated as the "Jewish Danger."[24] The occasion for the 1928 article was the condemnation the previous year of the association *Amici Israel* in which the Holy See also condemned antisemitism by name. *La Civiltà Cattolica* interpreted the double condemnation as the Vatican's intention to take a middle stance between the extremes of antisemitism and what it called "semitism" (*semitismo*) a term certainly comparable to the German *Verjüdung* and the Polish *zażydzenie*.

---

[22] Roger Aubert, *Le Pontificat de Pie IX (1846–1878)* (Tournai: Bloud-Gay, 1963), 40.

[23] *The New Catholic Encyclopedia,* (New York: McGraw Hill, 1967), 13:305. See also *Encyclopedia Italiana.* (Roma: Trecani, 1949), 10:515. In its 1949 anniversary issue (2:3), the editors of *La Civiltà Cattolica* boasted of its "very special links" to the Holy See and the favor which it enjoyed from the popes.

[24] *La Civiltà Cattolica* (1928) 3: 335–44.

The most succinct description of what the Jesuit journal meant by semitism was the "social predominance (*prepotere*) in all areas of modern life, especially the economic" accorded to Jews by liberalism (p. 344). Liberalism had allowed Jews to become bold, powerful, and ever more economically dominant (*preponderante*) in modern society (p. 340). They now enjoyed the highest positions in industry, banking, diplomacy, and "even more in secret sects, plotting their world domination" (*più ancora delle sètte occulte, macchinanti la loro egemonia mondiale*). Jews together with the "liberal, masonic movement" were responsible for a religious persecution of Catholics and the clergy (p. 343).

The writers for *La Civiltà Cattolica* admitted that the authenticity of the *Protocols of the Elders of Zion* lacked sufficient proof, but that did not gainsay the "undeniable alliance" (*innegabile alleanza*) between Masons and Jews (p. 342). By favoring Jews, liberalism had allowed the "Jewish danger" to increase steadily, so that Jews now posed a "threat" to all the world, especially to Christian nations, with their "adverse interferences" (*ingerenze nefaste*) and "harmful infiltration" (*perniciose infiltrazioni*) into society (p. 341).

At the other extreme from semitism was antisemitism which the 1928 Vatican document on the *Amici Israel* defined as "hatred" for Jews. *La Civiltà Cattolica* made clear that the church did not hate Jews or harass them unjustly. In fact, contended the Roman journal, "the Catholic church intends to protect as it has in fact always protected even its enemies and fiercest persecutors (*perseciutori più accanti*) such as the Jews" (p. 340). Those guilty of the "excesses" of antisemitism were politicians and "so-called patriotic movements" who, rather than remove the cause of semitism, namely liberalism, rather repress the "inevitable effects" of liberalism with a hateful and violent form that "borders on injustice" (pp. 339–340).

Avoiding the "extremes" of semitism and antisemitism, according to *La Civiltà Cattolica*, required application of both charity and justice. Charity excluded the "excesses" of antisemitism, but justice required that the church not close its eyes to some sad realities. The Roman journal did not intend to ascribe all the ills of modern society to Jews, but it was clear that, as the Jews were involved in the French Revolution, so too was there a "prevalence" (*prevalenza*) of Jews in the Russian and more recent Hungarian Revolution with all its cruelty and horror (p. 342). To say that Russian Jews at the time of the Russian revolution favored the more democratically-inclined socialist Mensheviks rather than the Bolsheviks did not change anything. Menshevism was only a phase in the movement toward Bolshevism, as socialism was to communism (p. 342). In short, the semitism represented by *Amici Israel* was "an extreme no less dangerous" than antisemitism and, in fact, was "even more seductive" (*anche più seducente*), because it posed under the aspect of good (p. 339).

This unsigned article about the "Jewish Danger" appeared in 1929, well before the Nazis came to power in Germany. Once they began their ruthless campaign against Jews, *La Civiltà Cattolica* might have been expected to soften its charges against semitism. It did not. Writing in the journal in 1934, E. Rosa, S.J. condemned Nazi racist doctrine and deplored Nazi treatment of the Catholic church. He decried Nazism as a "new apostasy" from genuine Christianity, more radical and worse than Protestantism. But, he cautioned his readers, a condemnation of Nazi antisemitism should not be taken as an apologia for Jews or Judaism. "They have always been and still are, by their own admission, bitter and irreconcilable enemies of Christ and Christianity, especially of the integral and pure Christianity of the Roman Catholic church." This enmity, declared Rosa, was "precisely the essence (*l'essenza appunto*) of Judaism."[25]

In 1936 *La Civiltà Cattolica* re-examined the Jewish question by reviewing the book by Lèon de Poncins, *La Mystérieuse Internationale Juive*, which had appeared that year and accused all Jews of being a permanent danger for the world.[26] This it found too extreme: "Not all" but "certainly a part" and "not a few" Jews constituted a "grave and permanent danger for society" (p. 43). For the root of this danger, the journal referred to the 1928 book by Joseph Bonsirven, S.J., *Sur les Ruines du Temple,* in which the French Jesuit attributed the "frequent participation" of Jews in modern social revolutions to their materialistic concept of messianism. For the editors at *La Civiltà Cattolica,* this "authentic Jewish mentality" was responsible for the bloodshed in Bela Kun's Hungary, Bolshevik Russia, and the atrocities in Spain (p. 43).

---

[25] *La Civiltà Cattolica* (1934) 4:284–85.

[26] *La Civiltà Cattolica* (1936) 4:37–46.

As for solutions to the Jewish question, none that was satisfactory had been found yet. Assimilation would be the perfect solution, but experience had proven that assimilation was impossible so long as Jews insisted on staying Jewish. Zionism did not appear a viable solution because Palestine was too small and the Jews of Europe did not want to leave. A third solution would be the reestablishment of ghettos, such as existed before the French Revolution. But the only fully satisfactory solution would be for Jews to convert to Christianity. A life-or-death struggle between communism and the Catholic church had already begun, *La Civiltà Cattolica* declared. The salvation of the west and of the world was to be found uniquely in the Catholic church. The same was true for Jews (p. 46).

In 1937, in another unsigned article on the Jewish question, the Jesuit journal cited the opinions of the English Catholic writer, Hilaire Belloc: "Jews and Jews alone" were an "irreducible entity" and a "foreign body" that produced irritation and reaction in any organism it penetrated.[27] The solution was to eliminate the source of irritation through expulsion or segregation, neither of which would be contrary to Christian charity if done in a civil, amicable fashion without hostility. *La Civiltà Cattolica* found Belloc's plan for "peaceful segregation" a preferable alternative to Zionism, so long as ghettos could be set up with juridical and coercive restrictions but without persecution, "in a manner adapted to our times" (p. 423). It was not clear, on the other hand, that, if the Jews acquired a Zionist state, they would abandon their "messianic aspirations" to dominate the world. On the contrary, a Zionist state could well serve as a stimulus and support for that "innate messianic aspirations" and their double "preponderance" in capitalism and revolution. There already existed in Palestine "various Jewish communist colonies" in which property was held in common (p. 431).

Later that year *La Civiltà Cattolica* repeated the above themes in an article on the need for missionary activity among Jews.[28] Antisemitism was condemned as "more or less violent" and contrary to charity (p. 39). On the other hand, prudence required eliminating the danger Jews posed to Christians and restraining their disruptive power over finances and revolutionary movements. With their great power (*preponderanza*) and

---

[27] *La Civiltà Cattolica* (1937) 2:418–31.

[28] *La Civiltà Cattolica* (1937) 3:27–39.

materialistic, immoral, and irreligious ideas, Jews were exercising considerable influence (*più influiscono*) over modern life. Judaism was disintegrating as a religion. "Many and some of the most ardent" socialists and communists were Jews. Hence, all the most reason to avoid any antisemitic talk or behavior so as to help create a more favorable climate for Jewish conversions (p. 32).

Its focus on economic dominance and revolution did not mean that *La Civiltà Cattolica* absolved religious Jews or the Talmud of transgression. Traditional Talmudic Judaism, according to an unsigned 1938 article, was a "profoundly corrupt (*corrotta*) religion" and the "antithesis of Christianity."[29] Judaism was only a preamble or preparation for Christianity, which, with the coming of Jesus, "necessarily and automatically" lost its purpose for existence (p. 76). But the reason religious Judaism was so "profoundly corrupt" was its "corrupted messianism," which in contrast to Christianity was materialistic and temporal. This corrupt "Talmudic messianism" was at work not only among religious but also unbelieving and atheist Jews. It was their "fatal desire" (*fatale smiana*) to dominate the world financially and temporally that made Judaism a source of "disorder" and "permanent danger" for the world. Christian charity precluded persecution, but prudence required that Jews and Christians be segregated. Jews could enjoy "hospitality" among Christian peoples but at a distance suitable for our times (p. 77). Civil coexistence (*convivenza*) among Christians and Jews should be like that which is customary between strangers (*stranieri*).

Polish bishops or Jesuits reading *La Civiltà Cattolica* would have found an article on "the Jewish question in Hungary" quite affirmative of the views prevailing in Poland.[30] The Jesuit author, M. Barbera, described how Jews had come to dominate the professions, so that now they had become in every way the "masters (*padroni*) of Hungary" (p. 150). The 1919 revolution under Bela Kun was, according to Barbera, a "Jewish-bolshevik disaster" (p. 146). The author's justification for the phrase was not only the predominance of Jewish commissars with Kun at the head, but Jewish solidarity with one another and therefore with the Jewish revolutionaries (p. 151).

---

[29] *La Civiltà Cattolica* (1938) 2:76–82.

[30] *La Civiltà Cattolica* (1938) 3:146–53.

Antisemitism in Hungary, Barbera contended, was not vulgar or fanatic, not based on race or religion. Rather it was a movement to defend national traditions, true liberty and independence. "All or almost all" of the Jews of the intellectual and ruling class were non-believing "free-thinkers, revolutionaries, masons and organizers of masonry: anti-Christians in moral and intellectual life; capitalists in economic life, socialists or philo-socialists in social life" (p. 149). Jews had rejected not only Jesus but now the Torah and the Hebrew Scriptures.

Barbera detailed how Catholic Action in Hungary had listed among its goals the "solution of the Jewish question according to the interests of the Hungarian people" (p. 151). To that end the Catholic Action program aimed at doing away with the liberalism that had destroyed the nation's economic life. Moreover, neither Jews nor those Hungarians allied with them were to have direction or influence over the intellectual life of the nation, its press, literature, or art. This was to be accomplished without persecution but with "energetic and efficient means," such as the *numerus clausus* limiting Jewish attendance at universities to five percent, their percentage in the population at large. The same limitations should hold for Jewish activity in the press, professions, indeed, all of the nation's economic and cultural life. Barbera found these objectives of the Catholic Action program to be "inspired" by the noble tradition of Hungarian hospitality and chivalry (p. 152).

Even in late September, 1938, after Pope Pius' celebrated assertion that Christians were "spiritual Semites," *La Civiltà Cattolica* made no substantial change in its views on liberalism and "semitism."[31] Jesuit writer E. Rosa re-rehearsed and defended the same timeworn themes it had published in 1890. Jews and Masons were "natural" and "intimate" allies (pp. 4–5) Liberalism had led to a Jewish "invasion" of Europe by abolishing the old laws regulating Jews in Christian society. The segregation of Christians and Jews had been for the protection of both groups. Granting civil equality to Jews had proven harmful (*perniciosa*) to both Jews and Christians. Jews and Masons were joined together in a persecution of the church (p. 9).

The editorial writers for *La Civiltà Cattolica* eventually found it necessary to rebuff the "misuse" or exploitation (*sfruttati*) which some fascist authors were making of their positions on the "Jewish question"

---

[31] *La Civiltà Cattolica* (1938) 4:3–16.

(p. 6). *La Civiltà Cattolica* had to explain that it was only concerned for the "legitimate defense" of Christian peoples and did not draw the excessive and harsh conclusions which the fascists did.[32] Jews were always welcome into the church as sincere converts. The laws of Christian charity required one to distinguish between the innocent and the guilty.

Needless to say, the writers for *La Civiltà Cattolica* were themselves hardly exemplary in distinguishing between the innocent and guilty. As dedicated champions of the Vatican's longstanding struggle against liberalism and modern secular culture, they opposed Jewish liberals, not to speak of socialists, as enemies of the church and Catholic culture in league with Masonry. But instead of distinguishing among the shades of Jewish opinion and practice, they regularly subscribed to the myth of Jewish solidarity and spoke of Jews collectively.

As a touchstone for Catholic orthodoxy and an exponent of Vatican thinking, the significance of *La Civiltà Cattolica* is difficult to exaggerate. Its exact influence cannot be gauged with any accuracy, however, extending as it did far beyond the circle of the journal's readers, many of them influential in their own right. There is no denying that it was a bellwether for Catholic writers and churchmen everywhere, certainly for more journalists than Jesuits and more bishops than Italians.

The Bishops of Poland

Poland's bishops had a long tradition of loyalty to the Holy See. During the partitions that loyalty extended to putting the interests of Rome and the church above the cause of Polish independence. The bishops of interwar Poland certainly willed to be faithful to their office, and that meant loyalty to Rome. It meant sharing the Vatican's struggle against Masonic liberalism. It meant opposing civil marriage and divorce, separation of church and state, and religiously neutral or secular public schools. It meant striving to preserve Catholic culture within a Catholic Poland. Both collectively and as individuals, the statements and policies of the Polish bishops can be rightly understood and evaluated only in the context of their responsibilities to the teaching and policies of the popes.

---

[32] *La Civiltà Cattolica* (1938) 3:558–61.

Certainly they were acting in accord with the mind of Pope Pius XI, when they resisted any effort to attenuate the power and influence of the church over Poland's public life.

Precisely against such an effort the Polish bishops published a joint pastoral letter in 1934 on the Soul of Christianity in Poland. Singled out by name for criticism was the Women's Civil Service Union (*Związek Pracy Obywatelskiej Kobiet*) for its stand in favor of coeducation and family planning and the Legion of Youth (*Legion Młodych*) for its efforts on behalf of separation of church and state. Such a separation, wrote the bishops, could only mean war between church and state, and that could only mean succumbing to secularism ("laicism") or bolshevism.

By trying to introduce the spirit of the French Revolution into Poland, the Women's Union and Legion of Youth, continued the bishops, were embroiled in the "deep things of Satan". Elsewhere in Europe that spirit was being buried, but in Poland it was being touted as something new. Such efforts were alien to the true Polish spirit, the bishops contended. Marxism, liberalism, and capitalism were bankrupt. Rejected too was the claim of the church's critics that it was not Christ they were fighting but clericalism. The bishops denied that they had any hidden political agenda. They insisted that, though political systems might change, Catholic truth did not. Poland must remain Christian, and to that end they would accept no limitation of the church's teaching and pastoral mission.[33]

In 1934 the bishops announced their intention to hold the First Plenary Synod of the new Polish Republic. Pope Pius XI, in a letter to the bishops, welcomed the announcement, especially the fact that Catholic Action was at the top of their agenda, and with it the plan to publish a Catholic daily paper: "Your decision to begin publishing a Catholic daily newspaper as soon as possible has brought us particular pleasure."[34] Five months after the pope's letter, the first issue of the *Mały Dziennik* appeared. A tabloid selling at five groszy a copy, the cheapest in Poland, it soon attained the largest circulation of any daily paper in Poland. Though produced by the Conventual Franciscans, the *Mały Dziennik* was under the surveillance of the bishops and Papal nuncio. Since it enjoyed the largest circulation of any newspaper in the country, the churchmen

---

[33] *Wiadomości Archidiecezjalne Warszawskie* (1934), 49–60; also found in *Miesięcznik Kościelny* (1934), 49–61.

[34] *Acta Apostolicae Sedis* (1935), 301–302.

were certainly not unfamiliar with its editorial positions on Masons and Jews.

At the conclusion of their 1937 Plenary Synod, the first such meeting since the end of the partitions, the bishops issued a list of decrees regulating church life together with a lengthy statement. In it they proclaimed that, thanks to Catholic Action, the days of the church's impotence before evil were over. No longer would the church be passive or uninvolved in contemporary issues. Though they would steer clear of partisan politics, the hierarchy, with the clergy and Catholic laity, would contribute a Catholic content to social and political relationships. The bishops appealed to the Catholic faithful with the same martial imagery employed earlier by the pope. "March to the front of the battle for Christianity," they charged. "Do not forget that Catholic Action is essentially a movement, an activity, a conquest."[35]

The bishops were not vague as to whom they were opposing. The first named were communists, socialists and all those who identified the church with fascism and called it an enemy of the working class. But second and denounced at greater length were Freemasons, free-thinkers, and those who conspired to remove religious instruction from public schools. These were the individuals and groups who attacked the clergy for their "unlimited power" and were attempting to subordinate the church and its institutions to the state. They were the ones calling the Polish government to secularize hospitals and the church's charitable operations. They were the ones demanding that Poland withdraw from the concordat with the Vatican.

These were unmistakably the adversaries: those who called for the government to separate church and state, limit the church's influence, and drive it out of public life. They were promoting a secular ethic and attempting to discredit the church's hierarchy and its authority. "From them the call for freedom of conscience but conceived as a principle that does not allow the church to resist the depravation of consciences. From them the related call for religious tolerance according to which the Catholic church in Poland should be equated with any other sect."[36]

Separation of church and state could only mean a Poland without God and a nation without faith, the bishops contended. In opposition to these

---

[35] *Kielecki Przegląd Diecezalny* (1938), 95–97.

[36] *Kielecki Przegląd Diecezjalny* (1938), 98

efforts, the church would work to build a Catholic Poland and preserve its native culture. In the name of that Catholic culture, the bishops called upon the Polish faithful to demand that civil laws regarding marriage conform to those of the church and that civil divorce be disallowed. Catholics must oppose all efforts to remove religious instruction and practice from public schools. Those who influenced the direction of public life should ensure that it be governed by Catholic principles. The bishops charged the faithful with the responsibility of learning Catholic teaching regarding public life and becoming its advocates.[37]

With both communism and Nazism in mind, the bishops warned Catholics against the errors of class warfare, nationalism, and "pagan racism." The decrees of the Plenary Synod forbade Catholic Poles to join, support, or cooperate with sects, Masons, socialists, or any other organizations inimical to the church or fostering religious indifference. The faithful were encouraged to join Catholic associations. In accord with Vatican recommendations, Catholics were also to avoid associations that were "confessionally neutral" since they posed a danger to religious loyalty.[38]

The bishops made reference to Nazi Germany once again in the spring of 1939, when rumors of war filled the land. Linking Poland's radical and racist nationalists with German fascism, the bishops were confident that Poland had beaten back Nazi neo-paganism, "even when it came to us in the sheep's clothing of Slavic pretence and rituals." The bishops believed that Polish life was established solidly on Christian principles. "We do not advocate principles of violence and mastery. We do not lie in wait for defenseless neighbors. We profess the fraternal cooperation of peoples." The bishops manifestly had no sense of anything awry in Polish society. "We are certain that acting in this way we do not depart from our vocation; indeed, we cooperate with Providence and realize our mission."[39]

The bishops fought for a Catholic Poland not only as a body but as individuals. In 1934 Bishop Przeździecki of Podlesie decried the fact that Poles were greeting one another with a simple hello (*Dzień dobry*) in-

---

[37] *Kielecki Przegląd Diecezjalny* (1938), 101.

[38] *Kielecki Przegląd Diecezjalny* (1938), 45–53.

[39] *Przegląd Powszechny* (1939), 275–76.

stead of the traditional "praised be Jesus Christ." The old greeting should be used, he wrote, to distinguish true believers in Christ from his "enemies."[40] Bishop Tymieniecki of Łódź wrote against those who would limit the church's influence to private life and attacked as leading to anarchy the efforts on behalf of the "rampant freedom of the individual."[41]

The most prolific, articulate, and influential of them was undoubtedly the Primate, August Cardinal Hlond. No stranger to either the marketplace or political arena, he asserted in 1931 that in both domains the enemies of the church were also the source of Poland's misfortunes. In the midst of the international depression, he blamed joblessness in Poland and elsewhere on the "free-thinking elements among the world's wealthy classes." In the name of freedom and progress they chained the working class with the worst shackles of capitalism. They dictated laws to governments and laid financial traps for whole nations.[42]

The Cardinal did not specify any particular group among the wealthy who were responsible for the depression. In early 1932, denouncing what he called a war against God, he again described the enemies of the church as Bolsheviks, atheists, freethinkers, and those with no religion. But with an allusion to the New Testament book of apocalypse, he also referred to these enemies as the "synagogue of Satan" (Rev. 3:9). Their numbers were not great, he admitted, but they were having an impact in their attempts to secularize Polish life, attempts that could only lead to bolshevism. Clearly the fate of Polish culture and of Poland's mission to the world would be decided in the arena of religion.[43]

Two months later Hlond issued a pastoral letter in which, quoting frequently from Pope Leo XIII, he attacked the notion of a secular, non-confessional state. Catholic children must receive religious instruction in public schools. Holy days must be kept holy. Laws establishing civil marriage and divorce for Catholics were unjust. Efforts to separate church and state were "perverted," at least in "Catholic countries." It was incon-

---

[40] *Ateneum Kapłańskie* (1934), 486–87.

[41] *Ateneum Kapłańskie* (1934), 488–89.

[42] *Przewodnik Katolicki* (1931), 690.

[43] August Cardinal Hlond, *Na Straży Sumienia Narodu* (Ramsey, New Jersey: Don Bosco, 1951), 38–52.

ceivable "especially in Catholic countries" that a "circle of liberals and free-thinkers" would be allowed to influence public policy contrary to the convictions of a Catholic majority. "A Catholic should participate in politics ... with a sense of the absolute superiority of Catholic ideas above any others," he wrote. One could not have a Catholic conscience for private life and another for public life.[44]

In a 1933 statement commemorating the 250th anniversary of the Battle of Vienna, Hlond compared the church's struggle against secularism to King John Sobieski's victory over the Turks, not a chance triumph but one proceeding "with historical necessity from the superiority of the Polish spirit." The stakes were even higher in 1920, he wrote, when once again Poland saved European faith and culture from a Soviet onslaught. Now in its opposition to secularism, the Polish church was fighting "modern paganism."[45]

The struggle against separation of church and state was not just a skirmish. In a 1936 article entitled "A War of Spirits," Hlond described it as a manifestation of the great eternal war between Catholicism and the forces of irreligion, comparable perhaps only to the struggle of Christianity with pagan Rome. "We have entered into the initial era of that historic meeting between the 'church of the living God' and the 'synagogue of Satan.'"[46] Once again Hlond used the apocalyptic language of the New Testament to describe secularizing influences in Poland. This time, however, the allusion was less ambiguous. Hlond had been quite explicit two months earlier in asserting that the symbol had contemporary connotations.

The Jewish Question

Undoubtedly the most widely noted of Hlond's writings was a pastoral letter he issued (February 29, 1936) on Catholic moral principles. The National Democrats, with the death of Piłsudski, were making the "Jewish question" and the boycott a central issue of social concern.

---

[44] Hlond, *Na Straży,* 53–75.

[45] *Ruch Katolicki* (1933), 385–86.

[46] *Mały Dziennik,* April 10, 1936.

Radicals and ruffians were perpetrating acts of antisemitic violence. Hlond made use of the pastoral letter, not only to make the usual warnings against Nazism, communism, and Masonry, but to express his views on the "Jewish question." The Cardinal's celebrated statement, usually quoted only in part, merits being cited in its entirety:

So long as Jews remain Jews, a Jewish problem exists and will continue to exist. This question varies in intensity and degree from country to country. It is especially difficult in our country and ought to be the object of serious consideration. I shall touch briefly here on its moral aspects in connection with the situation today.

It is a fact that Jews are waging war against the Catholic church, that they are steeped in free-thinking, and constitute the vanguard of atheism, the Bolshevik movement, and revolutionary activity. It is a fact that Jews have a corruptive influence on morals and that their publishing houses are spreading pornography. It is true that Jews are perpetrating fraud, practicing usury, and dealing in prostitution. It is true that, from a religious and ethical point of view, Jewish youth are having a negative influence on the Catholic youth in our schools. But let us be fair. Not all Jews are this way. There are very many Jews who are believers, honest, just, kind, and philanthropic. There is a healthy, edifying sense of family in very many Jewish homes. We know Jews who are ethically outstanding, noble, and upright.

I warn against that moral stance, imported from abroad, that is basically and ruthlessly anti-Jewish. It is contrary to Catholic ethics. One may love one's own nation more, but one may not hate anyone. Not even Jews. It is good to prefer your own kind when shopping, to avoid Jewish stores and Jewish stalls in the marketplace, but it is forbidden to demolish a Jewish store, damage their merchandise, break windows, or throw things at their homes. One should stay away from the harmful moral influence of Jews, keep away from their anti-Christian culture, and especially boycott the Jewish press and demoralizing Jewish publications. But it is forbidden to assault, beat up, maim, or slander Jews. One should honor and love Jews as human beings and neighbors, even though we do not honor the indescribable tragedy of that nation, which was the guardian of the idea of the Messiah and from which was born the Savior. When divine mercy enlightens a Jew to sincerely accept his and our Messiah, let us greet him into our Christian ranks with joy.

> Beware of those who are inciting anti-Jewish violence. They are serving a bad cause. Do you know who is giving the orders? Do you know who is intent on these riots? No good comes from these rash actions. And it is Polish blood that is sometimes being shed at them.[47]

There is no question but that Cardinal Hlond, in writing these paragraphs, was sincerely attempting to be even-handed, to strike a balance between what *La Civiltà Cattolica* called the extremes of semitism and antisemitism. The Jewish daily *Nasz Przegląd* acknowledged the universalist sentiments of the Cardinal's pastoral letter. And it is striking how relatively little comment these paragraphs received in the Catholic press. After all, Hlond was not the first bishop to publicly support the boycott. Bishop Lukomski of Łomża had earlier instructed the priests of his diocese to dissuade people from "buying from peddlers" and to encourage support of Polish shopkeepers.[48] But Hlond was the highest-ranking Polish churchman to give the boycott his moral support.

Despite his presumably good intentions, the Cardinal's pastoral letter evoked criticism in both the secular and Jewish press. The Socialist *Tydzień Robotnika* (Worker's Weekly), pointed out that a Catholic boycott of Jewish shopkeepers would mean their financial ruin.[49] *Hajnt,* a Yiddish newspaper, charged that, instead of mitigating passions, Hlond had only intensified them: "One would have to go back tens, if not hundreds, of years to find such talk about Jews among the pronouncements of church dignitaries.... The letter brings back memories of days we thought were gone, never to return, when the clergy could physically and morally wallow in our blood and assault us as much as they pleased. Can such a document be used in the fight against antisemitism? No, that is (on the part of commentators) more than naive." The Yiddish commentary concluded that Jews must disabuse themselves of the illusion that they should distinguish between "delicate, sober, cultural antisemitism and...excesses."[50]

---

[47] Hlond, *Na Straży,* 164–65.

[48] *American Hebrew and Jewish Tribune,* May 31, 1935.

[49] *Mały Dziennik,* March 27, 1936.

[50] *Gazeta Kościelna* (1936), 170; *Mały Dziennik,* March 27, 1936.

The Archbishop of Kraków during this time was Prince Adam Sapieha, the man who would later ordain as a priest Karol Wojtyła, the future Pope John Paul II. In 1928 Sapieha was required to send the Vatican one of the five year reports required of all bishops of the world. He was obliged to answer a series of questions on the social and political as well as religious state of affairs in his diocese. Because the reports were secret, he could be candid in expressing his views. On the matter of schools he wrote that, "six elementary public schools exist in our residential city which de facto are attended exclusively by Jews alone. This was achieved gradually so that the evil influence of the Jews might be removed from the Catholic children." To a question on publications, Sapieha answered that a flood of obscene and irreligious books, periodicals, and daily papers were impairing good morals. Chiefly responsible for disseminating these writings were "various American sects and Jews."[51]

Ten years earlier, Cardinal Kakowski of Warsaw made a similar report to the Vatican, which found its way into the files of Papal Nuncio Achille Ratti. In it Kakowski described the people of his diocese as honest and religious, although the workers were being stirred up by socialists. "Recently agitators and bolsheviks have begun to exercise a most evil influence, among whom those prevalent are Jews." Kakowski lamented the fact that Socialists were being elected to the Polish legislature (Sejm) but assured the Vatican that the clergy would work for the election of representatives who would favor the freedom of the church. The Cardinal was not sure if there was a Masonic lodge in Warsaw, but, if so, it was totally secret or "affiliated with the Jewish sect."[52]

Cardinal Kakowski's attitude to Jews did not alter over the years, nor remain concealed in confidential reports. By June of 1934, radical nationalist Polish youth, infected by propaganda from Nazi Germany, had begun imitating Nazi treatment of Jews. A delegation of four rabbis (Kanal, Perelman, Langleben, and Fajner) made an official visit to Cardinal Kakowski (June 7, 1934), pleading for him to use his moral authority to protect hapless Jews against the young offenders. The rabbis' petition was eloquent in its appeal:

---

[51] *Archivo Segregato Vaticano*, S.Cong. Concist. Relat. 268, Cracovien., #90 and #96.

[52] *Archivo Segregato Vaticano*, Archivo di Mons. Ratti/206, 641–42.

Your Eminence! In the name of the rabbinate of the Polish Republic, we turn to you in the following painful matter. In Germany, the land of the Teutonic Knights, from time immemorial Poland's enemy, a horde of barbarous pagans has recently come to power, warring against all the laws of God, trampling upon all the important principles of the Christian faith, persecuting all their adversaries with a cruelty unknown in human history, especially all the descendants of the land of Israel.

The whole civilized world, with the princes of the Catholic church at their head, has condemned the monstrous actions of the Nazis in Germany. Unfortunately, in Poland, the land with the greatest number of God-fearing Catholic Christians, a certain faction, especially of youth, is troubling us. Shamefully calling themselves Polish nationalists, they model themselves after the example of the pagan Nazis. They attack defenseless people walking the streets of Poland's cities, because they look Jewish. Without pity they bully, beat, and injure them.

Sometimes these ruffians encounter resistance from their innocent victims and the resistance provokes even greater fury and disgraceful acts by the assailants, thereby bringing shame on Poland's centuries-old reputation for tolerance and the fear of God.

We are convinced, Cardinal, that no true Polish Catholic can be utterly corrupt, that these Polish youth persecuting Jews have been momentarily deluded and tricked by the slogans of foreign enemies. At an appeal of the Polish bishops, they will come to their senses and certainly cease this persecution of Jewish people, which defames Poland's good name. In the name of the rabbis and Jews of the illustrious Republic of Poland, we entreat you, Cardinal, to issue a pastoral appeal about this to all of Poland's Catholics. Then peace and order will reign again in this land, beloved by us all. May God's grace flow upon it. Amen.[53]

When news of the rabbis' petition and Cardinal's response made the newspapers, Kakowski felt obliged to issue a public statement explaining his position. It too deserves to be cited in its entirety:

---

[53] *Wiadomości Diecezjalne Warszawskie* (1934), 247.

Since the visit of the rabbis and the purpose of their visit to me has appeared in the press, I feel it necessary to state that I absolutely condemn all violence and excesses, from whatever side they come from, whether Catholic or Jewish. Even the most complex questions and problems should be resolved in accord with the dictates of Christian ethics. This is our fundamental position.

As chief shepherd of this diocese, I would like to take the opportunity of the rabbis' visit to point out that numerous complaints come to me about provocations and offenses by Jews against the religious sensibilities of Christians. Rather than speak in generalities, allow me to offer some examples.

The atheist movement in Poland has in recent times assumed the most aggressive forms of fighting against the Christian religion, ridiculing its dogmas, and insulting its clergy. Its leader is a Jew, David Jabłoński, editor of the *Wolnomyśliciel* (Free-thinker) and the widely disseminated paper, *Błyski*. Other free-thinking papers insulting the Catholic religion, both in Polish and Yiddish, are published by Jews. I was compelled to intervene personally with the authorities against blasphemous articles insulting Christ in the weekly *Opinia* and the *Literarische Bletter*. I do not hold you rabbis responsible for the acts of your co-religionists. But the Jewish community, which unites in solidarity to defend its own interests, should be able to guarantee respect for the faith and traditions of Christians.

Finally, I cannot refrain from expressing my regrets that the publishing companies that are offending good morals and inundating Poland today with pornography, have found so many carriers and distributors from the Jewish community. These complaints have helped to create antisemitic feelings in the Polish community and may have led to regrettable excesses. I consider it necessary to bring them to your attention, since you wished to see me about this matter.[54]

In response to the Cardinal, one of the rabbis pointed out that these Jewish atheists were communists. To this the Cardinal replied that they were, however, young Jews to whom older Jews were giving money,

---

[54] *Wiadomości Archidiecezjalne Warszawskie* (1934), 248–49.

whether from Poland or abroad. "Use your influence," said the Cardinal, "on those Jews here and abroad so that they would lend money to the Polish state instead of giving it to communist agitators."[55]

The story of the rabbis' visit and the Cardinal's reply was reprinted widely. One of those reports in the Catholic press told of a baptized Jewish woman going to the papal nuncio in Warsaw, asking him to instruct the Polish bishops to issue a collective letter in defense of the Jews. The Nuncio reportedly answered that the Polish bishops knew their duty and that it was not for him to dictate to them what they had to do.[56]

When Kakowski issued a pastoral letter to the priests of Warsaw in 1936, he made no mention of Jews, only the "enemies of the state and church: like communists, radicals, atheists, and free-thinkers."[57] Other bishops were more explicit. Archbishop Teodorowicz of Lwów, for example, called for a "militant church" in the name of a "militant Christ." Jesus' life, he wrote, was "one prolonged war with the Pharisees and synagogue." At the center of that war was a fundamental and eternal conflict between a supernatural messianism and one that was this-worldly. "The proud synagogue" did not want to enter itself into the kingdom of God announced by Christ and did not want anyone else to either. "And so they who want to follow the call of Christ must use violence to repel the Synagogue that is blocking their way, must expose themselves to its anger and persecution, must enter into a spiritual war." The war, he wrote, was between Christ's kingdom and those who agitated hatred against property owners for the sake of an earthly paradise. It was between the church and those who did not recognize Christ as king, between Christ and antichrist.[58]

While Archbishop Teodorowicz identified Jews with communists, Archbishop Sapieha identified them with both communists and capitalist factory owners. In the wake of violent labor riots in Kraków in 1936, Sapieha issued a statement in which he first criticized Christians for looking only at profits and forgetting about justice. But then he went on:

---

[55] Ibid.

[56] *Pro Christo—Wiara i Czyn* (1934), 730.

[57] *Wiadomości Archidiecezjalne Warszawskie* (1936), 201.

[58] *Ruch Katolicki* (1933), 387–90.

"We have in our society, furthermore, a considerable number of non-Christian employers who are so blinded by greed that they do not see even their own peril, ruthlessly exploiting on every front and enriching themselves by treating people unjustly. Since we are not fulfilling our obligations and not helping those without a living wage, some others are pushing themselves into leadership of the working classes: people often of a different nationality and faith, consumed by hate." The Archbishop closed his statement with an appeal for solidarity among those "in whose veins there flows Polish blood and in whose hearts there reigns the faith of Christ."[59]

The bishops obviously could not conceive of Poles and Jews working together to resolve Poland's social and economic difficulties. A 1936 pastoral letter of Bishop Teodor Kubina explained why: the world was divided into the rival camps of Christ and antichrist. Christians must embrace the battle cry, "Rule over us, O Christ." They must counteract the materialistic capitalists and communists who had embraced the "Jewish" battle cry, "We do not want Christ to rule over us."[60]

The bishops were not wont to make careful distinctions. The Jews were identified with communism, and communism with any program remotely left of center. For Bishop Lisowski of Tarnów, even more dangerous than communists were the "crypto-communists" who were preparing the way for communism to enter Poland and were even infiltrating Catholic organizations. These crypto-communists were the socialist People's Front (*Front Ludowy*), Legion of Youth (*Legion Młodych*) and various "left-wing Jewish radical organizations."[61]

Although the bishops identified Jews collectively with both capitalist factory owners and their left wing critics, obviously the great masses of Polish Jews belonged to neither camp. But even those Jews who were apolitical were regarded as "other." In a letter to Catholic youth, Cardinal Kakowksi wrote: Let no one think that we do not have to "strive for our own national interests or that we have to allow another nation or other nations to rule over us, either economically or culturally."[62]

---

[59] *Prąd* (1936), 168–70.

[60] *Mały Dziennik,* October 29, 1936.

[61] *Mały Dziennik,* March 15, 1937.

[62] *Mały Dziennik,* September 9, 1938.

In the same vein Bishop Przeździecki of Podlesie wrote about the creation of Christian credit unions for foster Catholic commerce: "It was an error of our ancestors in the past that they did not value commerce and even looked down on it. That error must be corrected. It is not antisemitism for us to become more involved in commerce now, to form cooperatives, credit unions, develop trade, form trade unions. Work is necessary, without it Poland will perish from poverty."[63] Bishop Przeździecki was correct, of course. But my point here is that there was evidently never a question of cooperation. Work was necessary, as the bishop stated, but apparently not working together.

Jewish "otherness" was also the object of criticism in the semi-official organ of the bishops' conference, the Catholic Press Agency (KAP). When the Jewish press criticized the Catholic clergy in 1936 for not speaking out against antisemitic actions, the bishops' press agency criticized violence as "unworthy of the name Christian" and ultimately ineffective. But Poles were not the only ones responsible, nor Polish youth the only radicals, as evidenced by the many cases in court against young Jewish communists. Besides the fact that Poles too had a right to economic, social, and cultural development, even Jewish writers pointed out negative traits in the Jewish character which grated on Christians. Jews themselves could contribute considerably to calming passions by not obstructing Polish development and "overcoming the faults which render mutual co-existence difficult."[64]

If one can describe Catholic-Jewish relations in Poland in terms of alienation, the case of Bishop Buczka is the exception that proves the rule. In September, 1936, on the occasion of Rosh Hoshana, Bishop Buczka of the Greek Catholic (Uniate) rite gave an interview in *Chwila,* a Jewish paper in Lwów. In the interview the bishop extended New Year greetings to the Jewish community by wishing them *Shalom* (peace). He condemned antisemitism as anti-Christian and contrary to the principles of Christian love. The Nazis "disgrace themselves" by their neo-paganism and burning of the Hebrew Scriptures. But the bishop was sure that the Jewish people could not be destroyed by antisemitism. He spoke of listening to the "beautiful Eastern melodies" of Hasidic Jews and described as fitting the Zionist aspiration for a Jewish homeland.

---

[63] *Mały Dziennik,* September 9, 1938.

[64] *Prąd* (1936), 81–82.

The bishop's interview provoked such a firestorm of reaction from both Roman and Greek rite Catholics, that he felt compelled to clarify his position with a subsequent statement. Buczka explained that he was just imitating St. Paul who had tried to be all things to all in order to convert all to Christ. He denied saying that Jewish people had been chosen by God to teach the world or that it was any credit to them that Christ was a Jew. Regarding his statement that the Jews would survive antisemitism, Buczka explained that he was basing himself on St. Paul's prophecy that Jews would convert to Christianity at the end of the world. While Zionist efforts to create a Jewish homeland were just, this did not mean that the Christian world ought to help in the effort. Moreover, Jews had no right to such a homeland in Palestine so long as they remained non-Christians. As for the peace he wished for the Jews, he explained that "this peace will be possible only when Jews fall at the feet of Christ and recognize him as their Messiah, promised by the prophets. This Messiah will certainly make it possible for Jews to rebuild their homeland."[65]

Spiritual Semites

The most celebrated Catholic reference to Jews in the 1930s was undoubtedly that made in 1938 by Pope Pius XI in which he not only denounced antisemitism but described Christians as "spiritual semites." The words of the pope were quoted around the world, and it is likely that they are remembered more than anything else he ever wrote or spoke. Allusions to the quotation usually omit its context or simply describe his words as addressed to a group of Belgian pilgrims. The circumstances surrounding them, however, are really much more pertinent to their weight. So, too, is the need for the complete attribution, in order to make any judgment about Catholic attitudes toward antisemitism in the 1930s.

A group of pilgrims from the Belgian Catholic radio were visiting the Vatican (July 14, 1938) and presented the pope with the gift of a Mass book. The pope began paging through the book until he came to the prayer in the Mass which refers to "the sacrifice of Abraham." According to the first person report of those present, the pope first read the Latin prayer, and then with feeling evident in his voice he said in French:

[65] *Mały Dziennik*, October 14, 1936.

Every time we read these words, we are seized by deep emotion. "The sacrifice of our Father Abraham." Notice that Abraham is called our Father, our Ancestor. Antisemitism is not compatible with the sublime thought and reality which are expressed in this text. It is a movement that inspires aversion (*antipathique*), a movement in which we Christians can have no part."

Here, it was reported, the Pope could no longer contain his emotion. With tears in his eyes he spoke of Christians being spiritual descendants of Abraham.

No, [he concluded,] it is not possible for Christians to participate in antisemitism. We acknowledge everyone's right to self-defense, to take the means to protect themselves against any threat to their legitimate interests. But antisemitism is inadmissible. Spiritually we are semites.[66]

On several counts this is a remarkable text. Again, I contend that, amid his voluminous outpouring of encyclicals and addresses, these words describing Christians as spiritual semites are probably the most quoted Pius XI ever spoke. Unquestionably they sprung from a deep feeling of compassion for the situation of Jews being persecuted in Germany. They were utterly spontaneous and unprepared. They were not written and, more important, they were not published—not in either the Vatican's official *Acta Apostolicae Sedis* nor its semi-official *L'Osservatore Romano*. It is an old principle of Roman law, *Quod non est in actis non est in mundo* (What is not in the records is not in the world). For Vatican diplomacy, what is not in the records had might as well not exist.

The reason the pope's words to the Belgian pilgrims were not published in the *Acta* or otherwise by the Vatican is that they were not addressed to a general audience, as is often surmised. They were spoken prior to a general audience in a conversation to three officers of the Belgian Catholic radio. Relating the pope's words and actions, the organization's president, Monsignor Picard, admitted that they would never have made them public except that the pope, at the beginning of the general audience that followed, asked them to do so. The three

---

[66] *Documentation Catholique*, 39 (1938): 1460.

officers then conferred and reconstructed their private conversation. Avowing that they had added nothing to the pope's words, they also disclaimed any official nature to their text. Despite the disclaimer, their reconstruction subsequently received wide currency, first in the Belgian and French press, and then internationally. Not, however, in Poland.

In my not inconsiderable research into the Catholic periodical literature of interwar Poland, I have found no reference to this incident. It is possible that the bishops and writers for the Catholic press simply had not heard about it. But if they had, there was no reason for it to be cited. It was unofficial and off-the-record, a reconstruction of a private conversation based on secondhand testimony. Moreover that reconstruction contained a sentence which did not receive the same press attention that the pope's reference to spiritual semites did. Pius XI is also quoted as saying, "We acknowledge everyone's right to self-defense, to take the means to protect themselves against any threat to their legitimate interests." That is precisely what the Polish Catholic bishops, clergy, and press saw themselves as doing. That is what the boycott and the struggle for a Catholic Poland were all about, what the battle against Masons, secular Jews, and liberals of every stripe was all about: engaging in "self-defense" and protecting the "legitimate interests" of the Polish people and the church.

If this examination of the historical data has uncovered anything, it is that the church of Poland was not out of step with the Catholic church elsewhere in Europe, certainly not out of step with the Vatican. For over a century already the Holy See had been waging a campaign against the fallout from the French Revolution, first in France, then Italy, and finally in eastern Europe. *La Civiltà Cattolica* represented clearly the church's stand against liberalism and therefore what they called semitism, the impact emancipated and assimilated Jews were having on the economy and culture of Christian peoples. In Poland the bishops and with them the Catholic press were simply fighting an old war on a new front.

Cardinal Hlond, as the leader of the Polish bishops, was unyielding in his criticism of nazism as "ruthlessly anti-Jewish" and "contrary to Catholic ethics." Poles who were inciting anti-Jewish violence were "serving a bad cause." It was forbidden to assault or slander Jews or to do damage to their property. One may not hate Jews, the Cardinal stated.

But that is not the way he put it. Instead he wrote: "One may not hate anyone. Not even Jews." It is his "not even Jews" that we find startling and even reprehensible today. But they were not startling in the 1930s, when Catholics generally and church leaders in particular saw Jews as allied with Masons in a war against the church.

Cardinal Hlond's "not even Jews" corresponded to "one may not hate anyone, not even enemies." His words are intelligible only in the context of the defensive campaign that for a over a hundred years Catholic church leaders throughout Europe had been waging against the onslaughts of liberalism and secularity. In Poland the bishops saw that campaign as being for Christian morality, economic equality, public decency, and Catholic culture. It set them against not only communism but the liberal secularism that the popes had said would lead to it.

One can appreciate that religious as well as secular Jews would prefer equality of citizenship in a confessionally neutral Poland to one that was officially Catholic. The fact that Jews were urban, educated, and in the process of assimilating and increasing their influence over Polish culture could only serve to make them the natural adversaries of those who championed the cause of a Catholic Poland. Those factors also made them the natural allies of Poles who shared their preference for a confessionally neutral Poland modelled after France. These were the so-called liberals and Freemasons, freethinkers and socialists who were intent on limiting the church's influence over public life. Not all were secularists. There were practicing Catholics both in and outside Poland's left wing and socialist parties who disagreed with the nationalist right wing and demonstrated their convictions at the ballot box. Their criticisms of antisemitism differed considerably in tone and substance from those surveyed thus far.

Chapter 14

By Way of Contrast:
The Polish Opponents of Antisemitism

If Christianity is more than Catholicism, and the Catholic church more than popes and bishops, interwar Poland was certainly more than the Catholic press and the Polish Catholic church. Church leaders generally regarded Jews, especially those who were no longer traditional, as a danger to Poland's Catholic heritage and cultural identity. In contrast to the bishops, who were generally more discreet, writers for the Catholic press often acknowledged quite openly that they were antisemitic. It was before the Holocaust, when antisemitism was sweeping all of Europe and was in the minds of many traditionalists a justifiable political option. Not the racist variety of Nazi Germany or the violent antisemitism of the radical nationalists, but the traditional antisemitism that saw Jews as a threat to legitimate Catholic interests and Christian culture.

Racist antisemitism, as pointed out above, did not go unopposed in Poland. Neither did its traditional form. The Nazi propaganda and example which infected much of Europe aroused denunciations from a variety of Christians, including Catholics; and liberals, including Poles. Their attitudes and arguments stand in stark contrast to those surveyed thus far. They give us another and broader view of the antisemitism that existed in interwar Poland. Contrasting those who opposed antisemitism to those who justified it gives us a better appreciation of its extent in Polish society and a clearer picture of where the real issues and problems lay.

Christian Clergy

As early as 1933 Protestant and Catholic leaders expressed moral outrage at antisemitic measures being taken in Germany by the Nazis. A collection of their statements was published in Poland in 1936 under the title, "When Hatred Rages, the Voices of the Christian Clergy."[1] Among the Roman Catholic voices cited in the collection were Cardinal Verdier of Paris, who protested the "inhuman persecution" of Jews. Bishop Ramond of Nice condemned the exclusionary decrees against Jews in Germany and against Catholics in Mexico and Spain. Bishop Balthazar Debreczyn of Hungary identified nazism with paganism, the "synagogue of Satan," and the antichrist. The bishop was sure that Jews would survive the Nazi onslaught but was concerned that Christianity would be corrupted by racist errors. Also included in the collection were statements condemning Nazi racism made by German bishops before Hitler came to power.

It is noteworthy that these early Christian condemnations of nazism, most authored in 1933, found their way into Polish translation in 1936. Obviously a Polish translation was viewed as useful and opportune. Even more notable, this collection contained only one voice from a churchman in Poland, Grzegorz Chomyszyn, the Greek Catholic bishop of Stanisławów. For Chomyszyn, interviewed in a Lwów daily in 1936, antisemitism was a consequence of chauvinist nationalism. "No one is of less value as a human being because of religion, nationality, or class." The bishop had put his beliefs into practice and told of going to the local government bureaucracy to intercede for a poor Jewish widow. Jews were a people burdened with a great mission, he wrote, chosen by Providence not for their own sake but for the good of all humankind. Any true Christian realized how perverse nationalism could be, driving insolent lunatics to the depths of sadism. Fanatical nationalists were worse than pagans and verged on bestiality. Competition between groups was ethical and healthy, but Christianity condemned violence and oppression. Nations perished not because others were powerful but because they themselves were powerless. There was no greater sign of powerlessness than brutality and the inability to contain it.

---

[1] *Gdy nienawiść szaleje, Głosy duchowieństwa chrześcijańskiego* (Warszawa: Hoesick, 1936.)

Bishop Chomyszyn's statements first appeared not in a Catholic but a secular newspaper and found little echo in the Catholic press. Why he was the only Catholic bishop in Poland who could be quoted in 1936 as denouncing nationalistic antisemitism, is perhaps most easily explained by the fact that, although a Catholic bishop in union with Rome, he was also a member of Poland's Ukrainian minority. His own minority status obviously made him more sensitive to the plight of others in the same situation. Earlier in 1933 he had written a lengthy pastoral letter on the problems Ukrainians were having in the new Polish state.[2] In it he acknowledged the longstanding enmity that existed between Ukrainians and Poles. The basic reason, he argued, was that Poles looked down upon Ukrainians as a "second-rate nation," a tribe incapable of cultural development. If the historic problems between them were to be resolved, Poles would have to stop disdaining Ukrainians as if they were lackeys.

Polish Liberals

Chomyszyn remained the only bishop, indeed the only leading Catholic churchman, who could be cited a year later when another collection of articles and statements was published, *Polacy o Żydach* (Poles about Jews).[3] After the death of Piłsudski in 1935, as antisemitic propaganda and violence increased proportionately, Polish liberals, intellectuals, and socialists raised voices of protest in a variety of publications and from a variety of viewpoints. Their statements not only contrasted with those found in the Catholic press but allow us a clearer view of the situation and the ability to assess better what the church's leaders did and did not do.

For K. R. Żywicki (*Robotnik*), Nazi racism arose in reaction to the workers' movement and the workers' sense of solidarity. Adam Próchnik (*Zew sumienia*) concurred that antisemitism in Poland was not to be found among workers but primarily among youth, who were particularly susceptible to nationalist propaganda. Workers who recognized the real enemy to be the capitalist system were by and large resisting it. The

---

[2] Grzegorz Chomyszyn, *Problem ukraiński* (Warszawa, 1933.)

[3] *Polacy o Żydach: Zbiór artykułów z przedruku* (Warszawa: Wydawnictwo Polskiej Unii Zgody Narodów, 1937).

peasantry were not antagonistic, since Jews did not constitute a source of competition. Only few Jews lived in the country, and relations between them and the Polish peasants were friendly. The peasants resented Jewish middlemen who bought their crops cheap, but equally resented non-Jewish buyers who did the same. Antisemitic outbursts were the work of youth and the middle class, who were entering into direct competition with Jewish traders and craftsmen.

The most aggressive antisemitism, according to Próchnik, was to be found among young people who were either unemployed or feared that they would not be able to find work once they left school. They were being victimized by the propaganda coming from the nationalist press and teachers, including the clergy. The nationalist camp was exploiting youth, using them in their planned agitations to do the kind of work they would be ashamed to do themselves. In a situation rife with poverty, calling for a war against Jews was not only the path of least resistance but a fraud. Like the sorcerer's apprentice, Polish nationalists were unleashing forces they would not be able to stop.

Poet and future vice-minister of culture in postwar Poland, Leon Kruczkowski analyzed antisemitism in Polish literature and culture (*Zew sumienia*). Polish artists and writers had historically maintained warm, friendly relations with Jews—from the "notoriously Judeophile" Adam Mickiewicz to Konopnicka, Żeromski, and the many in between. As they had everywhere else, Jews were playing a leading role in Poland's cultural life. Not only because of the economy but because of their avid cultural interests, Jews were numerically the most significant consumers of culture in Poland. Perhaps because of the "Judeophile tradition of Polish literature," there was little inclination towards antisemitism among truly talented Polish and artists. The Poles spreading cultural antisemitism and lamenting the so-called judaization of Poland's cultural life were mostly second-rate. They fancied themselves as victims of unfair Jewish competition, when in reality they were simply weak in their fields. Great works of art, concluded Kruczkowski, arose out of an atmosphere of political and social liberation, not nationalistic egoism.

In the view of Jadwiga Krawczyńska (*Echo Społeczne*), antisemitism for some Poles had become a monomania, encompassing their entire intellectual horizon. There was no issue untouched by Jewish influence, no misfortune without a Jewish hand. If anyone failed, it was because of Jews. If someone succeeded, look for Jewish features, because non-Jews in their estimation were presumed incapable of success. "For antisemites incompetence and failure are Polish characteristics, while energy and achievement belong to the Jews," wrote Krawczyńska. Much to the impairment not only of Jews but of Poles, this "psychosis" affected an "unfortunately not unsizable" portion of Polish society. Antisemitic propaganda was distracting attention from the real problems confronting Polish life. With or without Jews, illiteracy, unemployment, and crime in Poland were issues that needed to be addressed. There was no denying the difficulties posed by a large Jewish minority, but a mass departure of Jews would not solve Poland's educational problems, nor would it increase Polish managerial skills. Antisemitic Poles were suffering from feelings of inferiority, and the real danger of antisemitism was what it could do to Poles.

For Ludwika Wolska (*Echo Społeczne*), it was an embarrassment to have to write about antisemitism. But after repeated incidents, even decent people were becoming numb and remaining silent, as "degenerate" nationalism appeared to be triumphing. Jews were and would remain full-fledged citizens of Poland, Wolska argued. Emigration was not possible. (Where would they go?) In comparison to Poland's other [German and Ukrainian] minorities, Jews were certainly more loyal. No one could dispute that there were Jews who were real patriots, deeply attached to Poland and its culture. But the infectious example coming out of the west was aggravating prejudices arising from religious and cultural differences. Above all there was the need to find a scapegoat on which to blame the misery and despair caused by the depression. Wolska admitted that a "certain percentage" of those hard hit by the depression were falling for antisemitic slogans, as "defeated political parties" attempted to recoup their losses with demagoguery. College students in particular were resorting to violence, and newspapers, instead of condemning the students' actions, were more intent on explaining and justifying them. Students needed to realize that there was nowhere for Jews to emigrate, and that it was in Poland's best interests that they be integrated into Polish society.

For Jagiellonian University Professor Witold Rubczyński (*Czas*), the student "trouble-makers" were imitating German barbarity and ignoring Catholic tradition. They were injuring Poland's reputation and wasting the time they needed to acquire knowledge and skills to help Poland. Professor Tadeusz Kotarbiński (*Kurier Poranny*) also knew the problems first-hand. He expressed admiration for the Jewish students who stood up for their rights and had no doubt that reason and education would overcome prejudice. But Poles and Jews alike felt threatened and were becoming more nationalistic. The ghetto benches were no more than a student prank but were being raised to the level of a symbol. The government was defending the victims of attacks, but not energetically enough. Universities had traditionally been immune from outside interference, but, in a radical departure from that tradition, Kotarbiński advocated abolishing university autonomy and allowing police to enter and restore order.

For the editors of *Kurier Poranny,* abolishing the protections of university autonomy was not the answer. According to best estimates of impartial observers, the youthful troublemakers in Warsaw numbered only two or three hundred. They chose the universities for their activities because of guaranteed immunity from prosecution. The *Kurier Poranny* accused university officials of being too lenient; university guards would suffice if they acted forcefully enough. In a time of scarcity, the student troublemakers were wasting time, opportunity, and the people's money. They should be expelled. The ghetto benches were only a caprice being endowed with the dignity of a battle standard. Jewish students had good reason to resist them, because, if the "fascists" won this first battle, they would go on to demand further segregation. There was reason for Poles to be troubled. The ignorance and anarchy which marked the decline of the old republic was threatening Poland once again.

The National Democrats, wrote Professor Zygmunt Szymanowski (*Epoka*), had always preyed upon impressionistic young people. But along with the increased tempo of antisemitic propaganda in 1935, the Endeks had also been responsible for a series of planned brawls. At one such melee at the Polytechnical Institute in Lwów, sixty people were injured and fifteen had to be taken to a clinic. First small but organized groups in 1936 initiated the campaign to introduce ghetto benches in lecture halls and then began to harass Jewish students and any non-Jewish students who defended or sat with them. Most students were unorganized and wanted to study; they listened to the slogans but remained passive. Instead of punishing the guilty, university administrators only suspended classes and called for peace. Szymanowski also laid blame on Endek professors in solidarity with the trouble-making students. They claimed not to know the attackers and accused the Jewish students of provoking the incidents. But it was no coincidence that the brawls occurred in their classes. As Szymanowski saw it, German vandalism was making its mark on Poland's Endeks.

Professor Stefan Czarnowski (*Dziennik Popularny*) decried the university brawls for their cost to Polish society. They were victimizing the students who wanted to study, especially the children of workers and peasants. In failing to find a solution, academic authorities were jeopardizing their universities' territorial autonomy. Limiting university autonomy would be disastrous for academic freedom, Czarnowski believed, but society could not tolerate a situation that provided immunity for roughnecks. There was no provision in the Polish constitution for anything like second-class citizenship. Jews paid their taxes, and basic moral principles were being transgressed by precisely those who were aspiring to be the nation's intellectual elite.

In an interview in the *Trybun Robotniczy*, Professor J. Szymkiewicz also upheld the need of university autonomy for the sake of academic freedom, but he admitted that bringing peace to the universities would be difficult. Those who initiated the disorders would comport themselves civilly, then suddenly attack a stranger and immediately hide. Most students, while opposed to these actions, did not resist. The professors had to speak up, since calls for order by administrators had proved ineffective. Even those professors with antisemitic leanings were against the disturbances, but silence by the faculty was being taken by the students as encouragement.

Some professors did speak up, and gradually democratic students began standing up to the Endek and ONR students. But the militant nationalists were not deterred, according to Jadwiga Markowska (*Robotnik*). They simply insulted the professors who opposed their actions and continued to terrorize their colleagues. They were poisoning the university environment with their hate and contradicting the Polish tradition of struggle for freedom. Antisemitism was a symptom of fascism, distracting attention from the burning issues facing Poland.

When the government finally took action against the ONR (radical nationalist) students, Professor Józef Ujejski of the government's Ministry of Education pointed out on Polish radio (April 5, 1937) that Jews were not the only victims of their violence. A Polish student, beaten by them, was in danger of losing an eye. The radical nationalist students not only distributed libelous handouts, they beat workers and, in the case of a professor who disciplined them, threw a homemade explosive against his door. When they could not achieve their ends by using ideas, they resorted to crowbars, clubs, and test tubes filled with gas. When the ONR had been suppressed in Warsaw and Wilno, it was clear that only a "very small percent" of the students were involved. Speaking on the floor of the Polish Senate, Professor Mieczysław Michałowicz agreed. Both a Freemason and an outspoken opponent of antisemitism, Michałowicz acknowledged that the students involved in these brawls were "relatively few." But that was no great comfort, he argued, when the majority of other students were capable only of murmuring in a corner, afraid to speak out or actively resist.

University student Aleksander Banasiak (*Dziennik Popularny*), criticized the priests who used the pulpit to mouth National Democratic propaganda. While proclaiming love of neighbor, they sowed the seeds of racial hatred, encouraging war against atheists, Masons, and communists. Those with a different religion were bad and those with no religion worse. Likewise for Janina Strzelecka (*Kurier Poranny*), the nationalist students were "still children," twenty-year-olds passing themselves off as knightly defenders of Christianity. Instead of chivalry, they were demonstrating boorishness (*chamstwo*), giving bent to their basest instincts and calling it a crusade. When two nineteen-year-olds were apprehended for murdering two Jews in Łódź, Wanda Wasilewska (*Robotnik*) pointed an accusing finger at the right wing. They claimed a monopoly on Polishness but imitated Poland's historic enemies. The teenagers were only blind, ignorant instruments. It was the disseminators of antisemitism who were guilty of murder.

In an original, concluding chapter to the collection of articles, *Polacy o Żydach*, Kazimiera Muszałówna acknowledged regretfully that the opponents of antisemitism in Poland had erred. They had remained silent as the years of economic depression dragged on and antisemitic propaganda increased. Rebutting "arguments of exceptional stupidity" had seemed a waste of time. It seemed more important to change the conditions that generated the economic injustice that in turn gave rise to antisemitism. That was a mistake. Since 1935 antisemitic propaganda had swollen into a "wave of barbarity." Leaders in Polish society resisted the criminal violence and hooliganism but did not confront the antisemitism head on. Not infrequently the causes of antisemitism were examined in order to justify it. Instead of calls to arms against antisemitism, declarations were made about human rights. Antisemitism was taken lightly instead of as a "national treason." Liberals were ashamed to have to write about issues once thought long resolved, like human dignity and the Christian command to love one's neighbor. It was an embarrassment to have to write about separate seating, clubs, and crowbars.

There was no question for Muszałówna that the antisemitic campaign in Poland was politically motivated. She saw antisemitism in Poland as "above all, if not exclusively, political." Conservatives were determined to win at any cost, including the "unfathomable poverty of the Polish masses" or the physical safety of Jews. Only someone politically illiterate or disoriented by long unemployment could believe that Poland's economic depression would be resolved by Polish workers replacing Jews. Ousting Poland's Jews would not help the seven million Poles out of work but only increase unemployment by reducing consumers. Antisemitic ideologues realized the falsity of their arguments but were exploiting the people's poverty and lack of elementary knowledge about economics.

Antisemitism was only one component of a much wider issue, Muszałówna continued. Liberals had to mobilize their energies, not only for ethical reasons but out of concern for Poland's culture and future. Those who opposed antisemitism were defending Poland's humanitarian and libertarian traditions. By combining Jewish and communist into one concept (*Żydokomuna*), "Endek-clerical agitators" had successfully painted all their opponents as communists. Muszałówna found it at once painful and bitterly amusing to see Catholic clergy trying to reconcile anti-semitism with the Christian law of love: "It is really a remarkable proof of how spiritual ideals have fallen, that in all of Poland no leading member of the Roman Catholic clergy has spoken out against the antisemitic slogans."

Antisemitism, Muszałówna concluded, was feeding upon ignorance, illiteracy, and base instincts. Why search for difficult solutions to Poland's economic problems when there was a universal remedy at hand: expel the Jews. Here was intellectual lethargy instead of moral principles, barbarism instead of culture. Antisemites were infecting young people with inferiority feelings, telling them that Jews were more competent and industrious and that Poles would fail except with violence. Though they claimed to be defending Poland, the antisemites were in fact traitors to its culture and traditions.

A Catholic Socialist

Antoni Gronowicz was a disaffected Catholic socialist, polemicist, and poet. In December 1937, he was invited to speak in Lwów after an especially violent outburst by nationalist students at the university there. Gronowicz's presentation was later published as a book under the provocative title, *Antisemitism Is Destroying my Fatherland.*[4] In it he asserted that only a relatively small percentage of Jews were in competition with Poles and that the rest were in the same poverty, or even worse, as that of Poles. He blamed "Polish capitalists" and, as he put it, "the pulpit of my religion" for waging an unfair war against Jews. It was no accident that violence would erupt, as it did in Przytyk and Mińsk Mazowiecki, when peasants heard Sunday sermons about "Judeo-communism." Gronowicz also blamed nationalist newspapers, especially the *Mały Dziennik.*

Gronowicz was a personal friend of the grandson of Berek Joselowicz, the Jewish patriot who had fought beside Kosciuszko for Polish freedom. He pointed to the support Jews had given to subsequent efforts on behalf of Polish liberty. Today, Gronowicz lamented, their descendants could barely make a living and were repaid with violence like that at Przytyk. National Democrats described such incidents as the "healthy reaction" of an uninfected peasantry. Uninfected, Gronowicz noted with sarcasm, because ten million of them could not read.

Economics, for Gronowicz, was the principal source of antisemitism. Polish capitalists were disseminating racial and religious hatred to obstruct solidarity among workers and to distract them from the real sources of exploitation. Christian and Jewish capitalists alike oppressed Christian and Jewish workers. Hitler was not persecuting the Jewish capitalists, only the poor, confused Jewish middle class. The Nazis were using racist theories only so as to convince workers and the middle class that Jews and not capitalists were to blame for their problems.

The violence at the university in Lwów that left one Jew dead and others injured, just added to the list of crimes committed by National Democrats. The Endeks, averred Gronowicz, were no less than fascists, posing as good citizens but sowing devastation. It did not matter whether it was veiled in paganism as in Germany and Italy, or in Christianity as in Poland. Fascism was all the same. Any manifestation of freedom was viewed as a threat. The church for Gronowicz had become no more than a place to observe people. The Polish clergy were too tied, for his taste,

---

[4] Antoni Gronowicz, *Antysemityzm rujnuje moją ojczyznę* (Lwów: Nakładem Dobrego Polaka, 1938).

to Polish nationalism, a cause that could only lead to tribal hatred and warfare. Gronowicz expressed his admiration for Jesus but for the same reason he admired Karl Marx. Both were Jews who had contributed much to the human spirit. Jews were "pioneers of human progress." It was absurd to think that suddenly in the twentieth century they were responsible for the spiritual and material poverty of other nations.

A Student of the Talmud

Tadeusz Zaderecki, a journalist and former assistant editor of a Lwów newspaper, the *Kurier Lwowski,* had first published works in the area of literature, on Mickiewicz (1931) and Homer (1932). Only in response to Monsignor Ignacy Charszewski, whom he described as a "deceived deceiver," did he set out to write a defense of the Talmud in 1934. But Zaderecki had taken up study of the Talmud much earlier. He related how in 1920 he had read a book on the Talmud in which the author, Andrzej Niemojewski, engaged in a polemic against the German talmudist, Hermann Strack. Zaderecki related how proud he was of a Pole taking on a scholar the stature of Strack and how he dreamed of succeeding Niemojewski as a leader in the field.

In studying these other "experts" on the Talmud, however, Zaderecki perceived unresolvable contradictions on fundamental questions. He determined to overcome their inadequacies and write his own book on the Talmud. Because it seemed impossible to write about a religion without observing how it was lived, he went to Poland's Jewish communities. Zaderecki described how he studied and disputed with Jews, until he became familiar with peculiarities of Jewish thought. His attempt to learn Talmud was met sympathetically. He read the texts with scholars who ignored the fact he was a gentile and opened their spiritual "treasure" with pride. The deep discrepancy between what he had read about the Talmud and his own practical experience convinced him of the "ignorance and bad will" of so-called "experts" like Rohling and Pranaitis.

Zaderecki first wrote about the Talmud with respect to the blood-libel in 1934. He would later write on the controversy surrounding ritual slaughter. But his most widely distributed work was his 1936 book, *Talmud w ogniu wiekow* (The Talmud in the Fire of the Centuries), a scholarly explanation and defense of the Talmud. The book went through several editions in Polish and in short time was published in an expanded German translation, not only for the sake of Christians but also for modern, secular Jews for whom the Talmud had become a *terra incognita*.[5] Zaderecki desired, he wrote, to set straight the misrepresentations of the Talmud "in the name of the good repute of Polish science, of justice, and of truth"(p. 8).

Zaderecki first chronicled what he called the *Talmudmartyrium* in western Europe: the 1240 Paris disputation; the sixteenth century Pfefferkorn-Reuchlin debate, and the *Entdecktes Judenthum* of Andreas Eisenmenger, whom Zaderecki regarded as the "real father" of pseudo-scientific antisemitism, but next to whom Rohling and Pranaitis were "ignoramuses." Zaderecki criticized Jews who regarded the Talmud as a cause of backwardness among Jewish traditionalists. He criticized as well those Jews who regarded Talmud study as best left to the rabbis or at most honored it as a monument of the past. The Talmud, he insisted, was much more the source of Jewish progress, because of the requirements it made on those who studied it. In Zaredecki's opinion, the "almost proverbial acumen, elasticity, and agility of the Jewish intellect" was the result of studying Talmud (p. 106).

Zaderecki waxed eloquent in expressing his admiration for Talmudic ethics. "The entire Talmud," he wrote, "is imbued with striving to a higher morality." It possesses "singular beauty" and "universal human value." A pillar of strength for Jews in time of oppression, Zaderecki saw the Talmud as something "powerful, imposing, and eternal." It allowed Jews to maintain their belief in one God and taught them to suffer for it. It saved them from destruction. The admirable qualities in Jews, which even their bitterest enemy must acknowledge, Zaderecki attributed to the Talmud (pp. 109, 132). The attacks against it came from "men with bad will and from converts often with a criminal past" (p. 57). Zaderecki pointed out the major misunderstandings of the Talmud's critics. They erred, he wrote, by seeing the Talmud as a binding code of law, in which every sentence was a commandment regulating Jewish religious life. He compared the Talmud to a massive "newspaper of Jewish antiquity," where one could find all manner of material of various degrees of importance: news, scientific essays, chronicles, and gossip. Along with

---

[5] All references here are to the expanded German translation of the Polish original, *Der Talmud im Feuer der Jahrhunderte*, trans. by Dr. Minna Safier (Wien: 1937).

history and philosophy there were legends, fables, and superstitions. But amid the chaos, a knowledgeable reader could perceive order. "As a newspaper gives a picture of the day, so the Talmud gives a picture of full Jewish life at the time of its origins"(p. 81). Just as not every line in a newspaper has the same value, neither did every line of the Mishna. The Talmud was a child of its times and had to be understood within the horizons of its assumptions. Passages had various levels of religious importance. Next to binding statements were statements that had been contested, superseded, and even condemned (pp. 81–82, 95, 102).

Zaderecki was certainly ahead of his time when he described the Talmud as having importance for Christianity as well as Judaism. With remarkable foresight into the direction future scholarship would take, Zaderecki viewed the schism between the church and the synagogue as stemming from a struggle between Galilee and Jerusalem. But if one took into consideration without prejudice points of contact as well as differences between Judaism and Christianity, a bridge of understanding would arise (p. 57). What was needed was mutual acquaintance and honest, mutual soul-searching. "Christianity," wrote Zaderecki, "especially Catholicism stands fundamentally much closer to Talmudic Judaism than is generally assumed. There are many possibilities for reconciliation" (p. 105). Finding those points of contact would bring more profit to Christianity and culture than sniffing out what apparently separated them.

Zaderecki concluded his pioneering work with a reference to Christianity's debt to the Talmudic sages. The rabbis did not see Saint Jerome as an enemy when they taught him Hebrew and helped him translate difficult passages of the scriptures into the Vulgate. Like Jerome, many of the church fathers drew from the learning of the rabbis for their interpretations of the Bible (pp. 105, 140). Zaderecki left his readers with a line from the Talmud (Baba kamma 92b): "You should not throw stones into a well from which you have drunk."

Polish Writers

The *Wiadomości Literackie* (Literary News) was without question the premier literary journal in interwar Poland. As a major vehicle for liberal opinion, it was, as noted several times in the preceding chapters, a frequent object of attack by conservative Catholic writers. In April 1937, it began running a series of articles on "Polish Writers concerning the Jewish Question." The series appeared intermittently for almost a year and drew contributions from some of Poland's most distinguished authors, representing a variety of fields as well as political viewpoints. They were a minority, as intellectuals are wont to be, but not without influence. And they help us to formulate a better judgment of the Catholic leaders who claimed to be the moral leaders of Poland and who did influence the majority of Poles much more.

Aleksander Świętochowski

Regarded by many as the father of Polish positivism, Aleksander Świętochowski began the series (April 11, 1937) with an essay that aroused the most response, because it seemed so out of character with his usual liberal views. Jews were not liked, wrote Świętochowski, despite their contributions to science and literature, for a variety of economic, religious and political reasons. It was "natural and understandable" that open or latent antisemitism was a force throughout Europe, but especially where, as in Poland, there were large numbers of Jews. Although there had been antisemitism in Poland as long as Jews had lived there, it first erupted into violence when nazism began having an impact on nationalist students. And despite the efforts of government officials to contain it, antisemitic violence was increasing. Antisemitic nationalists were justifying their brutal methods with the claim that they were launching a revolution, and wars were necessarily brutal.

Świętochowski reproached liberals for condemning violence without offering a solution of their own. It would have to be an international solution, since Jews had the whole planet as their home and not just Poland. In what would later draw the most criticism from his colleagues, Świętochowski criticized the Jewish university students who were refusing to take seats at the left side of the lecture halls. Parliaments were divided into left and right according to political persuasion, he argued. Why would Jews want to sit among right wing Endek students in the first place? Świętochowski decided that it was "exceptional insensitivity and a lack of self-respect" on the part of the Jewish students to resist the segregation.

Karol Zawodziński

Literary critic and academic Karol Zawodziński also acknowledged the escalation of antisemitism in Poland (May 2, 1937). Earlier, when lecturing abroad in 1934, he had protested that, while it existed in Poland as it did everywhere else, the majority of Polish society opposed antisemitism. In 1937 he could no longer make that claim. But the reasons, Zawodziński was sure, were economic. Poland was coming too slowly out of the depression. People seemed unable to believe in a better tomorrow. Jews and Poles were like people trying to divide a loaf of bread; both were hungry and the loaf was too small. Drained by passion, neither had energy enough to enlarge the loaf so that there would be enough for all.

Zawodziński complained that no serious discussion was taking place concerning Poland's economic problems. The reason, he suggested, was that "most Poles" firmly believed that for prosperity to reign, all that was needed was to expel the Jews. In reality, a massive Jewish emigration would only cause unprecedented poverty. Jewish capital and initiative were necessary to industrialize Poland and increase its productivity. The violence by right wing groups was intended to encourage Jews to leave, but Palestine was only a dream for Zionists and antisemites. In reality, antisemitism was debilitating Poland's economic recovery by creating an "atmosphere of civil war." There could be no economic development in Poland without stability and trust.

The linkage of Jews with communism was, to Zawodzinski's mind, particularly unfounded. He could not imagine a single ethnic group less disposed to communism. For centuries the vast majority of Jews had supported themselves with trade and small businesses. Their history inclined them to individualism, to taking risks and depending on their own enterprise. Jews more than any other group were associated with capitalism. Because emancipation from the Talmud and ghetto into modern European society was not yet complete, Jews, like Poles for the greater part of the nineteenth century, had become a "revolutionary people *par excellence.*" Just as there were Jewish Bolsheviks, so too were there considerable numbers of Jews in the war against communism. Since it was the liberalism of the French Revolution that made their emancipation possible, Jews were understandably sympathetic to "progressive" politics, to the same revolutionary liberalism that lay behind Poland's struggle for independence. Liberalism continued, despite upheavals, to be an important factor in Polish political life. Communism and fascism had much more in common with each other than with liberalism, which was at war against them both.

Zawodziński was not ashamed of being called a philosemite. He remembered his not too distant youth, when antisemitism was considered unworthy of a "refined" person. But he distinguished between Jews who were Polish patriots and "Litvaks" who after leaving czarist Russia to settle in Poland harbored contempt for Polish culture. He also faulted those Jews responsible for limiting Poland's sovereignty with the Minorities Treaty. Zawodziński was not happy with the "control" Jews enjoyed over much of Poland's economy and the professions, but violence was no answer. The right wing of Polish society was being blinded by an "antisemitic monomania." More than any Jewish communists, the "brutal antisemitic movement" in Poland was rousing "dark instincts of anarchy."

Emil Zegadłowicz

In the view of Emil Zegadłowicz (May 9, 1937), the impact nazism was having outside of Germany was catastrophic. Like flying shrapnel and sparks after an explosion, Nazi slogans could be heard everywhere, starting fires all over Europe. Zegadłowicz listed some of the contributions to European culture by made by Jews like Spinoza, Heine, and Tuwim. Christianity itself was a Jewish contribution, "the grandest gift of the Jewish people" to humanity. From the Mass to the paintings of Botticelli and Michelangelo, the Jewish spirit had exerted a decisive influence on Europe. And yet antisemitism had become one of contemporary Europe's distinctive characteristics.

Zegadłowicz took serious issue with Świętochowski and denied that there was such a thing as a "Jewish question." If there were concentrations of Jews who were poor and hungry, the only human and most practical solution was to help them. Instead, nationalists, who learned about Abraham and Moses before they did about Kościuszko, were crying antisemitic slogans until they were hoarse. Under the image of the cross, Jews were being beaten up so that [in the words of the papal motto] "all things may be renewed in Christ." From the very beginning, the "Jewish question" was nonsense, and antisemites betrayed themselves as powerless and uncreative. The only way out of Poland's problems was cooperation toward building peace and the common good. For Zegadłowicz, there was no fatherland where there was injustice. It was a matter of obligation to stand on the side of the injured and to defend human rights.

Ksawery Pruszyński

For journalist and future Polish diplomat Ksawery Pruszyński (May 16, 1937), it was for Jews to decide whether they should emigrate from Poland or assimilate; it was not a matter for the Polish government to establish policies. The government had no business favoring Zionists over Hasidim, or Hasidim over assimilationists. In practice, that meant respect for the schools, customs, and regulations of the Hasidic ghetto, including ritual slaughter, so long as they did not burden the rest of Polish society economically. It meant allowing assimilationists to integrate fully into Polish society. Jews were not altogether resistant to emigration, since on the average Jews in Poland had a lower standard of living than even their co-religionists in Nazi Germany.

The "Jewish question," wrote Pruszyński, was not primarily socio-economic, as Marxists claimed, but moral. Poland needed jobs, new and improved means of productivity, and capital. That meant Poland needed Jews. It was incumbent on the Polish government to create a favorable climate for Jewish investment. An owner must be assured that his factory would not be expropriated in a year just because his name was Cohen. The government's policy of nationalization had not served to increase Polish industry but to destroy it.

As for the Jewish contribution to Polish culture, there was none greater in Pruszyński's estimation than the psalms of the Hebrew Scriptures. Kochanowski's rendition of Psalm 137 ("If I forget you, O holy land...") gave birth to Polish messianism. Certainly Polish universities were in need of complete reform, but that meant curtailing the policy of subsidizing all students. Government subsidies should be granted on the basis of scholarship and financial need. Distinctions of students should be made not on religious background but exclusively on the basis of merit.

Andrzej Stawar

A member of the communist party, Andrzej Stawar eventually worked in the Polish government's ministry of culture after the war.[6] In the pages of *Wiadomości Literackie* (May 23, 1937), he took strong exception to Świętochowski's indictment of Jews for the animosity against them. Education and cultural differences might lead to antagonism, like that

---

[6] Lesław M. Bartelski, *Polscy pisarze współcześni* (Warszawa: Wyd. Artystyczne i Filmowe, 1977).

between Germans and Poles, but the antisemitism of Poland's nationalists had become phobic. Poland's militant antisemites were viewing their war against Jews as part of a national economic renaissance. Without Jews, they believed, all of its economic problems would be solved, and Poland would be stronger, richer, and happier.

Stawar acknowledged that antisemitic attitudes had existed earlier in Poland, but the idea of a war against Jews arose only recently with the influence of nazism on Poland's radical Right. Antisemitism was not a major issue during the partitions, and at the time of the Polish uprisings, one could even speak of a certain philosemitism among Poles. Antisemitism, Stawar contended, generally arose in periods of political reaction. Only complete equality before the law could solve Poland's socio-economic problems.

Radical nationalists, in Stawar's view, were deliberately exaggerating the influence of Jews on Polish culture. What the nationalists were attributing to Jewish influences was simply the impact of urbanization on arts and letters. Ironically, no intellectual force in Polish life bore as much of a Jewish stamp as did Polish messianism.

Paweł Hulka-Laskowski

For essayist and social activist Paweł Hulka-Laskowski, antisemitism was an infallible index of a civilization in decline (June 14, 1937). Not Jews but antisemites were the real problem facing Poland. Often they were good, honest people, but honesty did not preclude shortsighted ignorance. They believed that somehow a connection existed between striking a Jew and achieving a moral economic order. They believed that a club could improve Christian civilization and advance the cause of Christ's kingdom of love and mercy. Like every other "novelty," the "Jewish question" had come to Poland from western Europe, and like other imports it would be imitated. But only half-heartedly. Maurras in France and the Nazis in Germany both rejected Christianity precisely because it was Jewish. In Poland, on the contrary, antisemites were waging war against Jews precisely in the name of Jesus the Jew.

In Germany Jews were blamed for the loss of the war, in Poland for the partitions. Such allegations, however, were always general, never specific. Antisemites regarded Jews as somehow titanic and not ordinary people. Some antisemites had become so obsessed that they began living off Jews like parasites, searching them out, looking into people's faces for Jewish features. Antisemitism had come to serve as an inverse measure for morality and culture. It was antisemitism and not Jews who had given rise to the "Jewish question."

Mieczysław Wardziński

For Mieczysław Wardziński too, Endecja's antisemitism had become a monomania (July 4, 1937). For the National Democrats any problem or difficulty could be solved with the same ready explanation. All evil and misfortune could be attributed to Masons and Jews. Their antisemitism blinded the Endeks to the real danger facing Poland. Her neighbors had carved it up once and they could do it again. This made the German and Ukrainian minorities in Poland much more dangerous than the Jews. In the event of an attack, Poland's Jewish community could provide four hundred thousand soldiers. The National Democrats portrayed all Jews as cowardly and unable to fight. But when you countered this charge by pointing to Jews who were Polish military heroes, the Endek rejoinder was that they were exceptions. It was a convenient escape from serious productive thought.

Poland was being threatened by a terrible war with catastrophic odds, Wardziński warned. Endecja's antisemitism had not gone unobserved by Germany. It was imperative that Poland be united. It had need of every one of its Jewish soldiers. But Polish Jews would first have to be convinced that their human dignity was respected. In the context of the geopolitical realities of the day, antisemitism in Poland was not only blindness but a detriment to the security of the state.

Henryk Dembiński

Henryk Dembiński (July 11, 1937) took exception to Świętochowski's attempt to defend separate seating at universities with the analogy of a parliament. University students did not vote. And if segregation was to be admissible in lecture halls, then why not in hospitals, theaters, and everywhere else? Public institutions were bound to serve all citizens without respect to religion or nationality. Poland, unlike Germany, did not distinguish between second-class citizens and the *Herrenvolk*. Ghetto benches at universities would lead to the creation of ghettos in all areas of public life. Although nationalists were trying to justify it on the basis of a "higher national need," the attempt to "de-Judaize" universities was clearly contrary to the principles of a democratic state.

Dembiński admitted that the percentages of Jews at universities was disproportionate to the general population, but there were good reasons why. Unlike the young people of peasant background, Jews lived in the urban centers where the universities were located. They had a tradition of valuing scholarship and constituted a larger percentage of bourgeoisie. Poland's peasant class made up 52% of the general population but only 9% of the university enrollment. If one took Endecja's reasons to its logical conclusion and accorded the peasantry a proportionate number of university seats, the Endek and radical nationalist students would have to be expelled as well.

Securing justice for young people of peasant origins required increasing educational opportunities for all, not limiting them for some. If Poland was to succeed in reconstructing its economy, it would need more Jewish engineers and agronomists, not more shopkeepers. If educational opportunities were extended to the agricultural and working classes, the professional structure between Poles and Jews would be equalized. The "Jewish question" would become just a memory.

Antoni Sobański

For travelogue writer Antoni Sobański too, there was no "Jewish question," only a "collective psychosis" (August 29, 1937). Polish-Jewish relations had been chronically bad but rarely catastrophic. Not until a recent and sudden turn for the worse, when the "long-standing quarrel" between Poles and Jews reached an "unexpected and urgent crisis, deeper than any before." Sobański was hard-pressed to explain why. If economics were the only issue, this sudden upsurge of antisemitism should have occurred when the depression was at its height, not in 1937 when conditions were improving. Perhaps, Sobański suggested, it was because the nazis had proven the omnipotent solidarity of world Jewry to be a myth. If so, Poland's nationalists only demonstrated that they lacked any sense of "fair play." In any case, the sudden escalation of anti-Jewish violence was certainly connected with the death of Piłsudski. Under Marshal Piłsudski anything like a semi-official antisemitism would never have been tolerated.

There was no question for Sobański but that Jews would remain in Poland. They had no place else to go. Even if stripped of their civil rights and locked in ghettos, they would remain. And because they were patient, intelligent, and industrious, they would eventually regain their equality before the law. To even contemplate a Poland without Jews was distressing to Sobański. Without Jews and the vital link they provided to the west, Poland would be inclined to totalitarianism and autarky, many times more underdeveloped than it already was.

Wanda Wasilewska

Wanda Wasilewska was an active member of the Socialist Party and a leader of the Polish Teachers Association. In her contribution to the series (August 26, 1937), she recounted a trip to Poland's eastern provinces (Polesie), where she looked for antisemitism among the peasants. Instead she found Jews, Poles, and Byelorussians living together harmoniously. There were Jewish farmers, blacksmiths, millers and mechanics, who were known and respected for their hard work. A popular Jewish village administrator (*sołtys*) was elected by Jews and non-Jews alike. Whatever anti-Jewish feelings existed were superficial. There was no deep instinctual antisemitism among peasants, only the dirty dealings and politics by Endecja. So-called "spontaneous reactions" against Jews were artificially created by Endek agitators from outside. Indeed, the Byelorussians felt closer to Jews than to the Poles, with the Jews constituting a bridge between the two groups. Endecja's antisemitic agitation was not only callous, Wasilewska concluded, but also, to use their own jargon, detrimental to the nation and the state.

Manfred Kridl

Literary historian and critic Manfred Kridl explored the distinction some Poles were making between "brutal" antisemitism and so-called "ethical" or "cultured" antisemitism (October 31, 1937). The "brutal" antisemites were encouraging Jews to leave Poland with primitive tactics like beating and looting. Not only liberals but the government and the moderate right wing press condemned such activity. So-called "ethical antisemites" did not attack Jews physically or break their windows but found mitigating circumstances to justify those who did. These "cultured" antisemites knew how to be ardent Catholics and hate Jews at the same time, although they would use the word "dislike" instead of "hate." But like the "brutal" antisemites, they too dreamed of a Poland without Jews and believed that the "Jewish question" was the most important that Poland faced, the remedy for all its other problems. Such "cultured," "ethical" antisemites, according to Kridl, were to be found among the intelligentsia, students and professors, and on all levels of government. Often unwittingly, they were creating an atmosphere conducive to violence against Jews, preparing the ground for others to sow the seeds of pogroms.

"Ethical" antisemites spoke of the boycott as an "economic war." But every farmer knew that quite often he could get the same goods cheaper at a Jewish store. Jews in general had better organization and more experience at business. Christian Poles were making headway but still lagged behind western Europe. The marketplace was no place for patriotic phrases, just honest competition. As for those who would defend Polish culture from the "poison" of the Jewish spirit, they assumed either that Polish culture was so weak spiritually that it could not withstand Jewish influence, or else that it was so perfect that it needed nothing from outside and should be kept pure. Only demagogues and ignoramuses could speak of a pure national spirit.

"Ethical antisemites" neglected considerations of justice and honor and preferred to go along with the "spirit of the times." But should they do so, Kridl asked, even when the times were barbaric? The connection between antisemitism and an oversimplified patriotism was obvious. Such oversimple patriotism was much more difficult for people who could see their nation's needs and failings, who knew its history and could compare its culture.

Kridl deplored the fact that universities had become playing fields for "racist-political contests." Significant numbers of students were going to classes only in order to sit on the right side of the lecture halls. The Endeks had begun with segregating Jews, but their intention was to limit and then halt their admission altogether. But why stop there? Why not close the universities to Masons, liberals, and atheists as well, to those with some Jewish background and those who believed differently? The potential for such a state already existed, Kridl feared. The Vice-Minister of Education had stated in the Sejm that segregation at the universities was out of the question, yet before the semester was out some rectors had introduced it. Organized terror groups had transformed the moral autonomy of universities into a right to commit crimes on university property. Kridl was open to breaking with academic tradition. The moral authority of university administrators was no longer enough to maintain order. Antisemitic agitators on the streets were arrested, tried, and punished, and the same should be true within the universities.

In Kridl's opinion there was no reason why Jewish workers and intellectuals could not assimilate into Polish society and culture. It might take time, but no more than it had to create a national consciousness among the peasantry. Whether they wished to emigrate or stay, it was for the individual Jew, as for every Polish citizen, to decide. Not long before, Kridl concluded, remarks such as these would have been dismissed as banal. But no longer was that the case. Antisemitism and nationalism had become rampant. More threatening than any so-called "Jewish danger," they were "diseases" that required resistance on every field.

Józef Łobodowski

Poet and essayist Józef Łobodowski agreed (February 27, 1938). Although antisemitism was hardly the most critical issue facing Poland, for the average Pole it had become a litmus test of one's ideology: tell me what you think about Jews, and I will tell you who you are. Antisemitism, in Łobodowski's opinion, had become the "daily bread of the majority of the people." The years of National Democratic propaganda had taken its toll: good, kind people sincerely believed that any injury to Poland was the work of Jews. But it was oversimple to lay the blame solely on Endecja's demagoguery, Łobodowski believed. Even more superficial in his opinion, was the "nonsensical" Marxist view that antisemitism was created by capitalism to distract the masses. Rather, the seeds sown by Endecja had fallen upon quite fertile soil. Rarely was that soil a reasoned-out hostility; even less was it hate. Mostly it was a matter of contempt and dislike, caused by differences in customs, dress, speech, and psyche.

As Łobodowski saw it, even determined philosemites—Poles who on the basis of moral principle or party affiliation fought against antisemitism—deep down in their hearts did not especially like Jews. He blamed the Jewish affinity for commercial enterprise and urban life. Poles were an agrarian people with a certain disdain for the merchant class. It was not an attitude peculiar to Poles but comparable to the aversion to Armenians one found in Ukraine and the Middle East. Poland's social structure was the problem. If Jews were ten percent of the population in an industrialized country like England or Belgium, the social impact would be quite different. But Poland was economically underdeveloped. Its three million Jews constituted eighty percent of the small towns and almost half of the cities. Łobodowski was certain that antisemitism would lose its "epidemic character" if a large number of Jews would settle in the country. But for a variety of reasons, in Łobodowski's opinion, the assimilation of three million Jews into Polish society was impossible.

Theoretically the ideal solution would be complete equality not only at universities but in all areas of life. But the outcome, Łobodowski was sure, would be a profusion of Jewish intellectuals that would at least retard, if not altogether arrest, the social advancement of the peasant class. Complete integration of Jews into Polish society would lead to their numbers in the professions and arts being proportionate not to their percentage of the population at large, but to Poland's urban population. Although those who demanded an immediate, massive exodus of Jews from Poland were "simpletons" in Łobodowski's opinion, he could see no "humane" alternative but gradual emigration.

The harsh reality was that Poland was one of the poorest countries in all of Europe. Poland labored under an atrocious social structure that left it outdistanced by its neighbors in almost every way. Łobodowski did not spare his readers their pride: Poland's economy was plagued by insufficient railroads and minimal electricity. Its industry was underdeveloped, its rivers silted. A shortage of schools resulted in a high rate of illiteracy among Poles, their piety marked by a "pseudo-religiosity," which had "nothing in common with the practical realization of Christian principles." Within this bleak situation, chauvinists appealed to racial and national pride, and antisemitism became amplified to the absurd point of justifying and absolving anything. It had become the line of least resistance, elevated to being the "foremost idea" in the nation.

The "Jewish question," Łobodowski concluded, required much good will from both sides. Poles must consider the tragic fate of Jews in diaspora, while Jews must try to appreciate Polish arguments and postulates. Both sides needed to understand the other. Violent antisemitism and agitation were suicidal. The time had come for mutual cooperation. Sooner or later, avenues for immigration would open up and allow for a gradual correction of the imbalance in Poland's population. While this would not totally resolve the "Jewish question" in Poland, it would at least mitigate the more intense irritation.

The Polish Catholic Press

These Polish opponents of antisemitic nationalism, though generally of Roman Catholic background, hardly represented official Roman Catholic thinking. Their opinions may have been situated at various degrees of the political spectrum, but they were all left of center, and it did not matter whether they were liberals, socialists, or communists. For the leadership of the Roman Catholic church, they were the enemy. They were Poland's intellectual elite, educators, cultural leaders and writers of varying degrees of renown, some with no mean influence. But neither individually nor collectively could they command anything comparable to the moral authority exercised by the Roman Catholic church in Poland.

Thus far, the only Catholic churchman cited here as a critic of antisemitic nationalism has been Bishop Chomyszyn, himself a member of Poland's Ukrainian minority. For the leaders of the Roman Catholic church, antisemitic violence was unethical but so too was a liberal secularism that relegated the Catholic church to the merely private sphere of Polish life as one group among others. Being truly Polish meant being Catholic and nationalist, and Catholic nationalism usually meant explaining antisemitism rather than opposing it. When antisemitic violence was criticized, the tone of the censure was more than likely to be laced with stereotypes like the celebrated remarks of Cardinal Hlond.

Illustrative of this kind of thinking was an unsigned article published in the influential journal for priests, *Głos Kapłański*.[7] The church, it claimed, had never opposed Jews simply because they were a different race or religion. Catholic ethics rejected an antisemitism characterized by "pogroms, moral or material injury, or the desire to abolish the legal and political rights of Jews." There was no doubt but that there were "some good citizens" among Poland's Jews, and that they had rendered service to both the arts and sciences. But that was beside the point. There were good reasons why the church had enacted strict laws enjoining Catholics from living together with Jews, from sharing the same table, using the same public baths, or employing Jewish physicians.

The anonymous author granted that "here and there" the nationalist movement had become aggressive. But more typically it was a defense against the "overwhelming influence of Jews in political, economic, and

---

[7] *Głos Kapłański*, 11 (1937): 62–65.

cultural life," an influence which was offensive and corruptive of Catholic Poles who had a right to a "sovereign position" in the nation. Jews could be found in every group of enemies waging war against the church, against Christian social order and Christian family life. They were the chief culprits of capitalism and the most fanatical Marxists. They were a disruptive element in the schools, especially when it came to sexual ethics. Although one could not generalize and accuse all Jews, the "greater part" of them were guilty of these moral deficiencies. Moreover, the worldwide solidarity of Jews was not an illusion but a reality. As a result, "certain antisemitic transgressions" in Poland had united Jews on all continents into a "solid anti-Polish front."

As one would expect from a publication aimed at Catholic clergy, the "Jewish question" had to be resolved "within the strict confines of law and justice." Jews were equal before the law and enjoyed equal access to the professions, offices, and honors. But such access could not be unlimited. There was a need to de-judaize Polish culture. The policy at universities to set quotas for Jewish students should not be called *"numerus clausus,"* but *"numerus proportionatus."*

In contrast to the foregoing, one could find condemnations of antisemitic violence in the Catholic press without mitigating excuses. But, as exceptions quite revealing of the rule, they often made no mention of either Jews or antisemitism. Instead they attacked the violence and hatred provoked by "extreme nationalism" and generically propounded the Christian obligation to love one's neighbor. In this vein Witold Paweł attacked the "very many adherents" of totalitarianism in the radical nationalist camp (ONR).[8] Christian faith required helping and supporting all who were in need, treating every person as unique, regardless of their value to the state or society. Nazism was primitive and neo-pagan barbarism, incompatible with the religion of Jesus.

Similarly, the *Głos Misji Wewnętrznej* published an article asserting that it was precisely the command to love one's neighbor that made Christianity superior to other religious traditions. Other religions might speak of tolerating outsiders, but for Christianity every human being was a brother or sister, a child of God. Unfortunately, there were "many people" who counted as their neighbor only persons of their own nationality and religion. But in the parable of the Good Samaritan, Jesus

---

[8] *Ruch Charytatywny,* 2 (1938): 180–83.

taught that every stranger, even one's enemy, was a neighbor. Human beings constituted one great family, in which we are all called to salvation. Loving your neighbor meant more than empty words or not harming others. It meant demonstrating goodwill with good deeds. It meant rejoicing in their successes and sympathizing in their misfortunes. It meant offering them a friendly greeting, since, as the saying goes, "kind-heartedness is the sister of love." There could be no doubt that the intent of this article was to appeal for wider parameters to Christian charity. The title was a quotation from Saint Paul: "There is neither Jew nor Greek..." But most striking about this collection of truisms was not only that they were regarded as worth repeating but that they were signed with a pseudonym.

Writing from Wilno, Henryk Dembiński also appealed to the commandment that Christians love all people as the children of God.[9] The laws of love must guide all social relations, including those between peoples. Dembiński was no liberal. He agreed with Pope Pius XI that liberalism prepared the way for communism. Liberalism's "exaggerated" view of human rights justified the brutality of unmitigated capitalism and provoked communism as a reaction. Both communists and extreme nationalists, like the Nazis, put the interests of a nation or a class above the love of neighbor. To make one's nation or class an object of ultimate allegiance, as Nazis and communists did, was a moral disorder and defiance of God. According to the teaching of the Church, the nation may not be regarded as an end in itself.

Dembiński saw the Papal condemnations of communism and nazism as addressing moral defects in Poland as well as in Germany and Russia. Without mentioning the National Democrats by name, he accused the political parties on both the Left and the Right of perpetrating errors. Poland was overwhelmingly Catholic, but where, he asked, was there a true Christian to be found? It was time for a collective examination of conscience. Poland, like Germany, would have to deal with its extreme nationalist movements or else prepare for an "hour of great punishment."

As a bare minimum, wrote Kazimierz Sołtysik, love of neighbor required treating people as equals.[10] This was the basic principle of democracy and a strict obligation for Catholics, not to treat the dignity

---

[9] *Verbum*, 2 (1937): 247–65.

[10] *Kultura*, August 8, 1937.

of other persons as less than your own. The Catholic camp in Poland was not exclusively right wing, Sołtysik insisted. Not all Catholics were socially conservative. There were also Catholic democrats. It was not true that only a small number of Polish Catholics seriously wanted basic social change. Despite the widespread opinion to the contrary, there was no lack of democratic leanings even among the Polish clergy.

But Sołtysik felt the need to explain that democracy did not impinge upon the Catholic church's claims to a divinely established hierarchy. A democratic society meant abolition of class divisions but not hierarchy. Class divisions were responsible for the worst social injustices. But hierarchy, as Sołtysik defined it, was based on the social creativity of individuals. If, as the Catholic church taught, people were equal before God, they were equal before each other. That meant that Catholic Poles should be creating a democratic Poland in which the equal dignity of every human being would be recognized.

In January of 1939, Jerzy Turowicz joined the staff of *Głos Narodu,* edited at that time by Father Józef Piwowarczyk. Almost immediately a different tone could be discerned in the Kraków Catholic daily. Turowicz would win an international reputation for his courageous moral stance as editor of a Catholic weekly in postwar communist Poland. In the months before the invasion by Germany, he took a similar stand against antisemitic nationalism.

Turowicz was outraged when *Prosto z Mostu,* which regarded itself as a nationalist Catholic periodical, accorded Adolf Nowaczyński an award for excellence as a Catholic writer. A "supposedly Catholic" periodical, fumed Turowicz, should know that for someone to be called a Catholic writer takes more than a baptismal certificate. A Catholic world view was also necessary. Turowicz excoriated Nowaczyński as an "extreme nationalist" and advocate for racist antisemitism, an apologist for nazism without any trace of love of neighbor.[11] In the same vein, *Głos Narodu* in the last months before the war became more outspoken in its opposition to "racist and neo-pagan" ideologies in Poland. The Vatican's condemnation of racism pertained to more than just Nazi Germany. There were racist ideologues to be found among Italian fascists, in the Baltic

---

[11] *Głos Narodu,* March 19, 1939.

states, especially Lithuania, and in Poland as well. The "degenerate" nationalism represented by Nazi Germany could only lead to war.[12]

Odrodzenie

The young Turowicz, Dembiński, and Sołtysik all represented the thinking of the one Catholic organization that could be regarded as actively opposing the antisemitic nationalism of Endecja. All three were associated with *Odrodzenie* (Renaissance), an organization of Catholic college and university students founded in 1919 as a social action movement.[13] On the basis of papal social teaching, Odrodzenie opposed what it called the "materialistic liberalism" which was so "widely accepted" by the Polish intelligentsia. It opposed the concept of religion as a purely private affair of the individual. But it also opposed Roman Dmowski and the National Democrats for trying to separate individual from social ethics on behalf of a some sort of nationalist ethics. By its opposition to a nationalist double standard, Odrodzienie was at odds not only with Endecja but, more immediately and directly, with *Młodzież Wszechpolska* (All Polish Youth), a sizable right wing organization wedded to Endek principles.

With its avowed purpose to "restore the nation to Christ," Odrodzenie could hardly be called a liberal organization. Its program was to base Polish life on the law of God as interpreted by the Catholic church. Its goal was a resolute and energetic Catholic Poland, to be achieved by promoting social justice. It held that the right to private property was limited, not absolute, and that Catholic social teaching opposed both capitalist exploitation on one side and class hatred and warfare on the other. Odrodzenie rejected internationalism in favor of what it called "healthy national thinking." At the same time its 1923 statement of principles declared: "We are children of one Father. On this fact we base our democratism."[14] This was also to be the basis for Polish-Catholic

---

[12] *Głos Narodu,* July 8, 1939.

[13] For a history of Odrodzenie, see Stefan Kaczorowski, *Historia, działalność, i tradycje "Odrodzenia"* (London: Odnowa, 1980).

[14] Kaczorowski, *Historia,* 33.

relationships with Poland's minorities. Such relationships according to Odrodzenie ought to be characterized not only by Christian ethics but renunciation of personal or political exclusivity.

Virtually alone among Catholic organizations, Odrodzenie actively opposed the antisemitic activity of Endecja and Młodzież Wszech-polska.[15] The nationalist reaction was to resort to the familiar right wing tactic of accusing Odrodzenie of communist tendencies. According to one nationalist writer for the *Gazeta Warszawska*, the "once influential" Odrodzenie was "originally Catholic" but had since come under the influence of Masons and Jews.[16]

Although its members tended to be identified with the Christian Democratic party, Odrodzenie itself was constitutionally independent of any political affiliation. One of its sharpest criticisms of Polish academic life was the politicization of the student body. As early as 1932, long before the worst of the disturbances at Polish universities, Jerzy Sadownik, speaking for Odrodzenie, complained of the animosity dividing individuals and groups along party lines.[17] Universities had become battle grounds where politics separated students into enemy camps. Student political organization were hindering serious scholarship by creating an atmosphere of a *"bellum omnium contra omnes"* (a war of everyone against everyone). A consistent Catholicism meant surmounting political hatreds by assuming a world view that was Catholic in the sense of being universalist and impartial. Odrodzenie opposed liberal secularism just as it did racism but it made an important distinction: "We fight against ideas," wrote Sadownik, "not against people."

At its height, Odrodzenie numbered several thousand members, not only university students throughout Poland but as of 1927 young workers as well. Affiliated with young Catholic student and worker organizations in Belgium, France, and Holland, Odrodzenie had as its primary activity the sponsorship of "social awareness weeks." These conferences would draw together not only the students but *"seniores,"* intellectuals and activists, clerical and lay, who would serve as mentors to the young people. Among these mentors were Father Stefan Wyszyński, who after

---

[15] Personal interview with Jerzy Turowicz, May 15, 1987.

[16] See *Prąd*, 23 (1932): 95.

[17] *Prąd*, 22 (1932): 288–95.

the war would become the Cardinal Primate of Poland, and Monsignor Władysław Korniłłowicz, the editor of *Verbum,* a quarterly devoted to cultural and literary issues.

The most influential mentor of Odrodzenie, however, and its primary theoretician was Father Antoni Szymański. A professor of Catholic social ethics and eventually rector at the Catholic University of Lublin, Szymański was also the editor of *Prąd* (Current), a Catholic monthly he transformed into the voice for Odrodzenie. While other Catholic periodicals encouraged the boycott of Jewish merchants, *Prąd* under Szymański was singular in encouraging cooperation between Catholics and Jews. Despite "strong antagonisms" in areas like politics and religion, wrote Professor Leopold Caro in *Prąd,* there were mutual benefits to people working together. Poland was failing economically not for want of natural or human resources but for want of peaceful coexistence among its various communities. "Influential individuals" were sowing seeds of distrust, dividing people who, though they lived in proximity to each other, really did not know one another. Collaboration was the only way Poland's economic situation could be improved. Without social solidarity the economic situation was hopeless. What was needed was seeing the whole picture, respecting your opponent, and entering into a mutual give-and-take for the common good.[18]

Long before Hitler's rise to power and throughout the 1930s, *Prąd* under Szymański's editorial direction consistently denounced racism and antisemitic brutality as unchristian.[19] Though *Prąd* necessarily adhered to the Catholic position calling for state support of Catholic schools, Jews were not incarnate evil, nor were Jewish teachers consciously demoralizing Christian children. Jewish teachers could hardly be expected to represent a Christian culture, however, and religiously neutral schools represented a secular world view that was essentially atheistic.[20] The position of Odrodzenie and its leaders was that the liberal agenda of introducing civil marriage and religiously neutral schools into Poland was anti-Catholic. Masonic thinking had made an impact on Polish

---

[18] *Prąd,* 7–8 (1926): 360–67.

[19] *Prąd,* 19 (1930): 268–71; 24 (1933): 272–75; 35 (1938): 339–45.

[20] *Prąd,* March, 22 (1929): 144–51; 28 (1935): 3–6.

intellectuals. The fact that most of them were indifferent regarding religion provided a fertile field for anti-Catholic activity.[21]

Szymański was no liberal. The popes had made liberal and Catholic antithetical concepts. Like the Vatican and Polish bishops, Szymański favored a Catholic Poland. He expressed the conviction that a religious state was more tolerant than one confessionally neutral. He rejected the arguments for introducing civil marriage into Poland. But he also criticized right wing Catholics and those supposedly Catholic political organizations which were based on "liberal-radical, nationalist, or socialist principles," organizations based on "faith in the human person."[22] Here was an implicit reproach of Endecja as well as Sanacja and the socialists.

Szymański viewed it as dangerous that in "wide circles" Jews were being held liable for the Bolshevik revolution. Such thinking ignored the destructive work of non-Jews. Szymański did not deny that Jews were among the creators and propagators of communism. And he was sure that Jews were implicated in the French Revolution. But the Bolshevik revolution was fomented not by Jews but by Germans, who did it for military purposes. One could not identify Judaism and communism. Most socialists were Poles. To equate Christianity with aryanism was mistaken, since Christian civilization itself was a product in part of Judaism.

In 1932 Szymański expressed indignation at anti-Jewish rampages by college students.[23] Poland should be a Christian country with a Christian culture, but one could never use immoral means to attain that goal. Szymański granted that there was a "Jewish problem" consisting in the fact that Jews and Christians each had what he regarded as divergent "civilizations," based in part at least on differences in their ethical systems. There were conflicts between the two systems that could not be resolved. The state had to choose one set of moral principles as its basis. Poland was, and by right ought to be, a Catholic country. But exercising this right, Szymański conceded, inevitably led to difficulties that were almost insurmountable.

---

[21] *Prąd,* (1929): 99–105.

[22] Antoni Szymański, *Wpływy rewolucji bolszewickiej* (Warszawa: 1926. Reprinted from *Prąd).*

[23] *Prąd,* 23 (1932): 239–45.

The law of Sunday rest, for example, posed a distinct disadvantage for religious Jews observant of the Sabbath rest. But exempting them from the Sunday law would give them an advantage over their Christian competitors, since Sunday was the day when farmers from the country came to town. Such an exemption would also detract from Poland's character as a Christian country. It would defeat the whole purpose of a day of rest. From a religious, social and governmental point of view, Szymański argued, the good of the majority had to take precedence over that of the minority.

Szymański was openly sympathetic to the Jewish predicament, but sympathy did not entail openness to secularism. Certainly it was reasonable for Poles to want to strengthen their economy, since economic deficiencies were among the causes for Poland's historic decline and the partitions. Equally defensible was the desire of Catholic Poles to preserve a Christian culture. But this, Szymański argued, meant more than simply preferring Poles in schools and universities, in journalism and government. There were Polish intellectuals endeavoring to make Polish culture secular. To preserve a Christian culture in Poland required favoring people with Christian convictions for leadership and influence. Szymański viewed it as superficial and mistaken for those on the right to impute all guilt for Poland's problems on Jews and Masons. But he did grant the nationalists the truth of at least one point. Even if Jews did not attack Christian culture, they certainly could not be expected to build it up. Jewish intellectuals were harmful to Christian culture, not as agents of Jewish culture, but as exponents of an anti-religious secularism.

A Catholic Poland was a praiseworthy end, but it did not justify immoral means. Szymański roundly denounced the Polish students who assaulted Jews, smashed their store windows, and evicted Jewish students from lecture halls. In response to those who claimed these were reprisals for Jewish transgressions, he answered that Christian ethics did not permit revenge by vigilantes. Christ the Good Shepherd promised to care for sheep, not wolves. Szymański was especially incensed that nationalist students had used religious services as occasions for political demonstrations, leaving church to go on anti-Jewish rampages. It did not matter that only a handful of students were responsible for these outbreaks nor that the police had put them down. It was a profanation of religion attributable to the students' thoughtlessness but also to the "perversity and bad will" of their ringleaders.

Szymański believed that *Prąd's* readers should know more about Jews, whom he saw as racially distinctive on the basis of certain demonstrable attributes, psychological as well as physical.[24] Polish Jews not only had a different religion and culture from the rest of the population, they were a distinct race, joined in solidarity with other Jews throughout the world. Szymański's thinking in this vein was not without stereotypes, but neither were they all negative. He saw Jews as characterized by extremely speculative intellects, an attachment to tradition, and a hunger for knowledge. Jews had great imitative abilities, allowing them to assimilate and profit from the thought of others. They were gifted with initiative and enterprise. Other Jewish traits were perseverance in achieving their goals, candidness and depth of feeling, quick temper, and sensitivity.

It was not a belief that Jews were a "chosen people" that made Judaism a distinctive religion. Other religions made the same claim to superiority. Rather it was Judaism's strict monotheism and absolutely abstract conception of God, its emphasis upon divine omnipotence and justice. Other hallmarks of Judaism were an unfulfilled messianism, an identification of religion with knowledge, an ossified system of absolute prohibitions and commands, and an immensely developed casuistry.

From these racial and religious differences ensued the distinctiveness of Jewish culture. The Talmud affected Jews totally by regulating every aspect of their lives and relationships. The ghetto walls set up by civil law to separate Jews from Gentiles may have fallen, but those created by the Talmud still existed. There were, however, both individuals and groups who had broken with traditional Jewish attitudes toward non-Jews. Jews were not a monolith, and Szymański went to some length to describe the religious, political and social diversity within the Jewish community. They were orthodox and progressive, small merchants and property owners, adherents of Poale Zion and the Bund, right wing Zionists and left wing socialists. Szymański thought it important, too, for *Prąd's* readers to know about the inner workings of the some seven hundred Jewish communities in all of Poland. He described them as "all Polish citizens of the Mosaic religion."

Szymański responded harshly when a right wing student organization published a pamphlet advocating that citizenship be limited only to Poles and such minorities as could be "polonized." Others, according to this

---

[24] *Prąd*, 24 (1933): 68–75.

nationalist publication, could only be affiliates, not citizens. Even baptism should not qualify a Jew for citizenship, and the state should have the right to confiscate Jewish property without compensation. Szymański rebutted this blatant racism with a defense of Jewish rights.[25] He pointed out that there was no such thing as a pure race. Poles had Lithuanian, Tartar, German, Dutch, and French blood in their veins. Polish culture had been influenced by the east, not least by Jesus and the apostles, all of whom were Jews. Baptized Jews could certainly contribute toward creating a Christian civilization in Poland. And whether they were citizens or not, Christian ethics did not permit Jews or anyone else to be expropriated without compensation.

Szymański continued to oppose racist antisemitism by underscoring the close ties between Christianity and Judaism. In a 1937 book on ethics, he contrasted Christianity with the doctrines of Nietzsche and Maurras.[26] Christianity regarded mercy as among the highest of virtues, because Christianity was "descended from Judaism." Christianity was indeed a "morality of slaves and the disinherited," because Jesus and his apostles were what antisemites regarded as "dirty Jews." Szymański faulted Judaism for being "almost exclusively ritualistic," and he saw European culture as based on Catholic Christian principles at variance with those of Judaism. But race had little significance when it came to creating culture. If Jews had not produced great painters and sculptors, it was because of the commandment prohibiting idolatry. If Jews had a particular psyche, it was not because of race but their diaspora and alienation from the soil. All races had contributed to religion, art, and science.

To my knowledge, Szymański did not evaluate Judaism as a religion nor offer any concrete solutions for resolving Poland's "Jewish question." Under his editorship, however, *Prąd* published the opinions of his clerical colleagues at the Catholic university of Lublin, and there is no reason to believe that his opinions were substantially different. For Father J. Kruszyński writing in *Prąd*, Judaism as a religion had been superseded by Christianity. Before the time of Jesus, the "Mosaic religion" had been superior to all others, but since that time its exclusivism, based on the

---

[25] *Prąd*, (1933): 34–37.

[26] *Etyka, wiadomości wstępne* (Lublin: Uniwesytet, 1937), 124–27.

Talmud, rendered Judaism inferior to Christian universalism.[27] Father Tomasz Wilczyński writing in *Prąd* described much anti-Jewish writing (like that of Monsignor Charszewski) as not only ignorant but contrary to Catholic dogma (denials of Jesus' Jewishness or the capacity of Jews to become good Christians). Catholic Poles must not lose their sense of Christian chivalry and begin imitating the Germans. A sincere convert to Christianity could become a Pole, but otherwise, the only solution was for Jews to emigrate to wherever they wanted to go.[28]

Clearly there were outspoken liberal opponents to antisemitism in interwar Poland, but the leaders of the Roman Catholic church were not among them. Father Antoni Szymański, Odrodzenie, and *Prąd* are the closest one can come to finding active, representative Catholics truly outraged at antisemitic violence, not merely explaining it. But even they held fast to the ideal of a Catholic Poland. They adhered to the teachings of the popes who throughout the nineteenth and twentieth centuries had rejected the concept of a modern secular state in which all citizens and all religious bodies were treated as equal. The church after long years had been compelled to make peace with a secular France. It had made peace with a reunited secular Italy. But it did not have to accept disestablishment in a secular Poland. On this front the Catholic church continued its struggle against liberal, secular culture, a struggle which included Polish Masons but even more so, secular Jews.

---

[27] *Prąd*, 31 (1936): 263–85.

[28] *Prąd*, 37 (1939): 104–17.

Epilogue

The moral issues raised in this study of antisemitism and the Catholic church in interwar Poland are plainly of more than merely historical interest. The collapse of the Soviet Union and its bloc has provoked the reemergence of nationalism and antisemitism in Eastern Europe, xenophobic violence in Germany, and even genocidal efforts of "ethnic cleansing" in the Balkans. Living in pluralistic societies remains problematic all over the globe as once again, and not only in Europe, one hears the rhetoric of "host" and "guest," reminiscent of Poland in the 1930s. Even while making the proper distinctions and bearing in mind the uniqueness of historical situations and events, anyone reading this material from 1930s Poland cannot help but be struck by analogies to more contemporary situations in the United States, Eastern Europe, India, South Africa, and the Middle East.

How a society treats the minorities in its midst is arguably the single most telling criterion of that society's morality and civilization. Treating the "outsider" with fairness and dignity is a perennial challenge to any society, one recognized for thousands of years and certainly more clear-cut than some of the other complex, more modern moral questions raised here and related to it: is a secular state necessarily fairer or more tolerant than one which favors a particular religious system? Is it inherently unjust to practice discrimination to alleviate an inequitable socio-economic situation ("affirmative action")? What are the rights of a majority to impart its moral code or standards on the entire body politic of a nation? One encounters here the difficulties facing traditional (e.g., Islamic) societies. But the questions obtrude upon Western democracies as well with regard to race relations, women's rights, abortion, state support of religious institutions, hiring quotas, medical and health care ethics, and the civil rights of sexual minorities. The complexity of these issues obviously precludes the kind of reflection here which they deserve.

Poland in the period between the wars was, even more than the rest of Europe, in a welter of political, social, and spiritual upheaval. In the twenty years prior to the period brought into focus here, Poles went through the end of the partitions, World War I, the February and October Revolutions, the Polish-Bolshevik War, an error-ridden initiation into parliamentary democracy, the birth-pangs of urbanization, and the onset of the world depression. The traditionalist Polish church found itself competing with socialism, communism, fascism, feminism, anti-clericalism and atheism—with all the perils attendant upon modern secularity and the religiously neutral state.

The moral perplexities that confronted Polish church leaders between the wars were formidable, the circumstances daunting. Without ignoring the complexity of either the issues or the situation, I believe the following personal reflections and, in some instances perhaps contro-versial, conclusions are warranted.

1. The Catholic clergy, as represented by the Catholic press and the pronouncements of bishops, were not innocent bystanders or passive observers of the wave of antisemitism that encompassed Poland in the later half of the 1930s. Along with the National Democrats, they were very much integral to it, as their liberal opponents testified and the sheer volume of the material I have surveyed here confirms. Even when nation-alistic youth translated antisemitic attitudes into violence, one did not hear ringing denunciations from Catholic church leaders or the Catholic press. Instead of subjecting the violence to unambiguous criticism, church leaders rather gave explanations for antisemitism that ultimately served to justify it.

2. Even at its worst, however, Polish antisemitism was not comparable to the antisemitism rampant at the time in Germany and Austria. Vatican condemnations of racism and of antisemitism understood as "hate" clearly had an impact on Polish Catholics. But this simply indicates the inadequacy of understanding antisemitism merely as anti-Jewish hatred or violence as the Vatican and the influential Rome-based journal, *La Civiltà Cattolica,* did in the 1930s. By restricting its meaning to hatred or violence, virtually all the writers surveyed here could acquit themselves of antisemitism, even though they themselves would not necessarily have rejected the term at the time. Antisemite in the 1930s

was more of a political description than the pejorative label that it is today.

If one defines antisemitism as hostility manifested toward all Jews as a group for whatever reasons (cultural, theological, or political), Monsignors Trzeciak and Charszewski were unquestionably antisemites. They were among the three million ethnic Poles murdered under German occupation along with six million Jews. But by this same definition so too was Zofia Kossak an antisemite. Not because of their religion but their cultural differences (their "Eastern excitability"), Kossak found Jews irritating, unpleasant, and "so terribly foreign." She did not want Jews to convert en masse to Polish Catholicism, lest they impose their traits on the Polish psyche and produce a new nationality and culture. She granted that the resulting nationality and culture might very well be valuable, but to her mind they would not be Polish.

Kossak wanted what she called an "honest" solution to Poland's Jewish question. No issue facing Poland was in her judgment more urgent. But when Nazi Germany began imposing its own "final solution" to that question, she risked her life to resist it. With Henryk Woliński and Władysław Bartoszewski, Kossak helped to organize a unit of the Polish underground (under the cryptonym *Żegota*) devoted solely to rescuing Jews from death during the German occupation. She wrote and published appeals in the underground press, describing Nazi atrocities and urging Poles to help save Jews, even though, it meant endangering their lives. But even in her published appeals to rescue Jews, Kossak still expressed her conviction that Jews were alien and generally hostile to Polish interests. She still wanted Jews to leave Poland–but without harm. *Żegota,* the group she helped organize, was able to save some four thousand Jewish children and adults, and is honored today on the Avenue of the Righteous at the Holocaust Memorial in Jerusalem, Yad Vashem. Implicitly, therefore, Kossak is honored too. The idea of a "righteous" antisemitic rescuer of Jews certainly appears oxymoronic, but Zofia Kossak epitomizes superbly some of the profound inner contradictions of Polish Catholic antisemitism.

3. The concept of whether one can be a "righteous" antisemite raises the question of Father Maximilian Kolbe, canonized by the Catholic church as a saint. Kolbe gave his life for a fellow Polish prisoner at Auschwitz and is honored for that heroic act as a martyr of charity. But he founded and oversaw the largest Catholic publishing center in Poland from which

there flowed some of the most vicious antisemitic material published in interwar Poland. The fact that the *Mały Dziennik* was a daily newspaper does not of itself explain or excuse the fact that, for sheer volume and intensity, no other Polish Catholic periodical even approximated it in its antisemitism.

Kolbe himself wrote little about Jews. On one occasion he advised against stirring up hostility against Jews, Freemasons, or heretics; love was the only way to convert them. On the issue of the boycott of Jewish merchants, Kolbe suggested that it was better not to speak of excluding Jews but rather of developing Polish enterprises. The *Mały Dziennik,* however, made no such distinctions.

If antisemitism is defined as hostility toward Jews as Jews, Kolbe himself was not antisemitic. He did not exhibit animosity toward religious or traditional Jews. But he was anti-liberal, anti-Masonic, and anti-secular. He was hostile to any proponent—Jew or Gentile—of modern, secular culture. He believed that secularists, Polish or Jewish, must be resisted militantly, as a danger to the church and to Poland. Militancy was an essential part of Kolbe's Catholicism, quite in keeping with the policies of the Holy See and Catholic Action. His attitude toward Jews was very much like that of Pope Pius XI and the Catholic orthodoxy of his day: anti-racist but conversionary, anti-Nazi but laboring under several of the stereotypes that Nazis and others were touting about supposed Jewish economic and cultural influence. As head of the monastery at Niepokalanów, Kolbe had the responsibility *ex officio* of overseeing the material it published. There is no question but that, in tolerating the antisemitism published at his monastery, he was negligent in that responsibility. His negligence was shared, however, by the Polish bishops, the papal nuncio to Poland, and the Holy See.

4. In his anti-liberal, anti-Masonic, anti-secularist stance, Maximilian Kolbe typified not only the church in Poland but interwar Catholicism altogether. The church in Poland was not out of step with the Catholic church elsewhere in Europe. It was rather quite in congruity with such leading Catholic thinkers and scholars as Hilaire Belloc in Great Britain, France's Père Lagrange, and such preeminent German theologians as Joseph Lortz, Karl Adam, and Michael Schmaus. The Polish church was hardly at odds with Father Charles Coughlin and the bishops, clergy and thousands of American lay Catholics who supported him. Certainly it was not out of step with the Holy See.

For over a century the popes had waged an unremitting campaign against the political liberalism that advocated a secular state separated from the direct influence of the church. In France and Italy and then in Eastern Europe, they struggled against such fallout from the French Revolution as civil marriage and divorce and confessionally neutral public schools. Catholic church leaders had come to regard the privileges once accorded them by the Roman emperors as their possessions by divine right. In interwar Poland as wherever else Catholics constituted a majority, the Vatican, the bishops, Catholic Action and the Catholic press simply carried on an old war on a new front.

Since the late nineteenth century, the leadership of the Catholic church saw Freemasons and assimilated Jews as the principal agents of liberalism, secularity, and what the Jesuit journal *La Civiltà Cattolica* called "semitism," the impact which assimilated Jews were having on the economy and culture of Christian nations. Published in the shadow of Saint Peter's and utterly committed to Vatican orthodoxy, *La Civiltà Cattolica* served as a bellwether for other Catholic periodicals in interpreting the mind of the Holy See. Throughout the 1930s, until virtually the end of the decade, the Jesuit journal saw non-traditional Jews and Freemasons as committed to the common enterprise of secularizing Christian, especially Catholic nations and cultures. The theme was common to bishops, theologians, and priests throughout Europe. In the United States it was not Father Charles Coughlin but his critics who were out of step with Catholic thinking on liberalism and Jews. It is in this context that one must interpret the words of August Cardinal Hlond, when he wrote that Polish Catholics may not hate anyone, "not even Jews." His well-intended meaning was that Christians must love even their enemies. Polish Catholics may not hate even the secularists who were hostile to Christian culture and the concept of a "Catholic Poland."

5. Not all Catholic leaders were unsympathetic to the situation of Jews in interwar Poland. The Catholic youth movement *Odrodzenie* (Renaissance) actively opposed right wing student organizations responsible for anti-Jewish violence at universities. Its principal mentor, Father Antoni Szymański, denounced racism and the violent antisemitic rampages by university students. He opposed the widespread identification of Jews with communism. He criticized the idea that Jewish teachers were consciously demoralizing Christian children. But he acknowledged, too,

that no Jewish teacher or any other Jew could be expected to represent or reinforce a Christian culture in Poland. And that for him constituted the Jewish question.

As Father Szymański perceived it, the Jewish question consisted in the fact that Jews and Poles had differing cultures based on differing ethical systems, and those differences necessarily led to insurmountable difficulties. Szymański could sympathize with orthodox Jews, who had to refrain from business on Sundays as well as the Sabbath. But he had no doubt that Poland was and by right ought to be a Christian nation with a Catholic culture. Religiously neutral schools in his opinion could not help but represent a secular world view that was essentially atheistic. He saw civil marriage and divorce as anti-Catholic. Szymański was no liberal. He could not be. The popes had made liberal and Catholic polar concepts.

6. In a March 22, 1984 address to the Anti-Defamation League of B'nai B'rith, Pope John Paul II spoke of the Catholic church condemning antisemitism "even before the Second Vatican Council." The printed version of his address made reference to the 1928 Vatican declaration that had condemned both antisemitism and *Amici Israel,* and the 1938 statement of Pope Pius XI that Christians were "spiritual Semites" for whom antisemitism was inadmissible. Vatican speech writers would be well advised, in my opinion, not to make too much of these declarations.

The 1928 condemnation of antisemitism defined it simply as "hate" for Jews. That was hardly a momentous step forward in human relations or in the history of Christian-Jewish encounter. And the same Vatican decree also condemned *Amici Israel,* a Catholic organization that in truth did represent at least some of the positive attitudes later adopted by the Second Vatican Council toward Jews. But in 1928 it was too progressive for the times, and the Holy See condemned it as "acting and thinking contrary to the opinion and spirit of the church, to the thinking of the Holy Fathers, and to the very liturgy." The 1928 Vatican declaration condemning *Amici Israel* did not anticipate the Second Vatican Council but only proves just how much of a revolution the Council really was.

Even less do Vatican apologists have reason to make much of Pope Pius XI's celebrated 1938 statement that Christians were "spiritual Semites" for whom antisemitism was disallowed. There is no doubting that the pope's words erupted spontaneously from feelings of deep compassion for the plight of Jews in Germany and Austria. There is no question but that they made an impact on the popular consciousness of the Christian world. They are, I believe, the most remembered words Pius XI ever spoke or wrote. But they are also simply a reconstruction of a private conversation. They were not recorded in the official *Acta Apostolicae Sedis* or even reported in the semi-official Vatican newspaper. For Vatican diplomats and administrators trained in the principles of Roman jurisprudence, what was not in the official records might as well not exist.

7. In that same reconstructed conversation, Pius XI was also quoted as acknowledging people's right to protect their "legitimate interests." That is precisely what the Polish Catholic bishops, clergy, and press saw themselves as doing in their support of the nationalist boycott against Jewish merchants. They were defending their people's legitimate interests. Catholic leaders right up to Cardinal Hlond generally supported the concept of favoring Polish merchants at the expense of their Jewish competitors. They saw the boycott as a peaceful and ethically appropriate means to offset the advantages Jews enjoyed in virtue of their centuries of commercial experience. Polish Catholics, in their view, had the same right as Jews to "prefer" their own kind.

There is no doubt that there were inequities in Poland's economy which needed to be addressed, and that the bishops and clergy had a right to be concerned about the poverty, joblessness, and major population shifts that were taking place from agriculture to the urban industrial work force. They had a right to encourage and support the development of professional, managerial, and commercial skills among their Catholic faithful. But, despite the best efforts of National Democrats and the clergy to "nationalize" Poland's economy, as they put it, the boycott against Jewish merchants was a failure. It was a slogan in interwar Poland that Jews sold for less, and most Poles, putting economic self-interest ahead of prejudice, preferred to do business with Jews.

As I hope to have shown here, for the Catholic clergy at least, there was much more to the Jewish question than economics. The issue for church leaders was rather political liberalism, secular culture, and the struggle for a "Catholic Poland." Ironically, it was precisely that struggle which served to deter Poland's economic recovery. Clerics may be excused for not fathoming the complexities of economic theory, and the 1930s were not yet the era of ecumenism. But it hardly required economic expertise or prescience to recognize that Poland required precisely the kinds of human and material resources that Jews were singularly capable of providing.

The church's liberal critics recognized that Jewish capital investment and entrepreneurial skills were necessary for Poland to make any economic headway. They argued that the National Democrats' antisemitic campaign was deterring economic development. Poles needed to learn precisely the kind of managerial, commercial, and entrepreneurial skills that Jews could teach them. Social stability and solidarity were required to induce foreign investment. Jews in the West could hardly be expected to invest in a Poland bent on discriminating against their co-religionists. Yet, in all my research into the Catholic press in interwar Poland, I found only one article that encouraged collaboration among Catholics and Jews, a striking exception that proved the rule.

But for leaders in the Catholic church, whatever economic benefits might accrue to Poles from cooperating with Jews was far outweighed by other considerations. Jewish influence in the economy meant Jewish influence in education, the professions, literature, and the arts. Cooperating with Jews meant allowing the secularizing trends at work in the west to undermine Poland's allegedly traditional Catholic culture. From all appearances the economic advantages of Catholic and Jewish cooperation did not even occur to most writers for the Polish Catholic press. Even if they did, the idea would have been dismissed. For the clerical mind set of the 1930s, poverty in a culture that was Catholic was preferable to prosperity in a secular one.

8. Throughout Europe but particularly in Poland, the stereotype of Jewish solidarity provided the basis for the virulent identification of Jews with communism. When a delegation of rabbis asked Cardinal Kakowski of Warsaw to speak out against anti-Jewish violence, he blamed the antisemitic incidents on provocations and blasphemies by Jewish communists and atheists. The Cardinal expressed his confidence that the Jewish community was able to guarantee respect for the faith and traditions of Christians, since it was able to unite in solidarity to guarantee its own interests. Similarly Cardinal Hlond acknowledged that there were "very many Jews" who were believing, honest, upright, and just. But when he wrote of waging war against the Catholic church, bolshevism, atheism, and corruption of morals, he simply referred to "Jews." With a blind spot to their inconsistency, these churchmen held the Jewish community accountable for the activities of apostate Jewish

communists, but they did not hold the Vatican or German bishops similarly accountable for apostate Catholic Nazis.

The fear which communism generated in church leaders throughout Europe could only be compounded in Poland. Its proximity to the Soviet Union made anyone left of center open to suspicion of Soviet sympathies, no one more so than non-traditional Jews. The Catholic press generally ignored the afflictions which the Soviets (including apostate Jews) visited upon traditional Jews, the restriction of Jewish religious life. Rather, the high profile of these apostate Jews in the Soviet Union and the various communist parties throughout Europe made "Judeo-communism" (*Żydokomuna*) a cliché that was only intensified by the propaganda of the Third Reich.

In Poland, Jews made up only about one quarter of the communist party. Out of over three million Jews in prewar Poland, a meager five thousand were communists. The irony is that there might have been even fewer Jewish communists in Poland had it not been for the nationalist identification of Polish with Catholic. Polish Jews who were dissatisfied with traditional orthodox religious lifestyles, convinced by Catholic nationalists that they were excluded from participating in a secular Polish culture, were left with the alternatives of either Zionism or internationalism.

Throughout Europe but especially in Poland, the identification of Jews with communism yielded disastrous consequences. When the Soviet Union invaded Poland two weeks after Nazi Germany did, every Polish communist was an enemy behind the lines, every assimilated Jew a potential suspect. In the absence of any substantial help from other sources, Jewish partisans turned for aid to the Soviets. Under the threat of Nazi annihilation, Polish Jews saw the Soviet army as the only real and proximate hope of rescue. Fighting on two fronts, the Poles saw their future quite differently. The specter of Soviet rule was just as abhorrent to them as domination by German Nazis. Once again, especially to those already inclined to see them that way, Polish and Jewish interests appeared to divide into mutual exclusivity.

9. Helping Jews was exceedingly more difficult and dangerous in Poland than in other occupied countries. Unlike the situation in the west, in Poland under the Nazis, the death penalty was automatic for helping Jews, and the German occupation made sure that there was no doubt as

to the seriousness of their resolve. Entire families were killed and their property burned when it was discovered that they had hidden Jews.

Most of the Polish Jews who survived Nazi annihilation plans did so behind the lines of the Soviet army. It is estimated that somewhere between one and two percent (forty to sixty thousand) survived by hiding successfully in the Polish ethnic area. Given the penalties that their actions would incur if discovered, it is, I believe, altogether remarkable that so many thousands, arguably tens of thousands, of Poles risked their lives to save people whom their church's leaders for years had marked as alien and hostile to Polish interests.

Those Poles who risked their lives to help Jews ran the whole range of Polish society. They were working class people, peasants, and professionals; freethinking liberals, socialists and Catholics. Illustrative of the Catholics who acted out of religious motivation were the Ursuline sisters and other orders of religious sisters who hid Jewish children; the Catholic Scouts who helped their Jewish comrades in the scouting movement; Archbishop Andreas Szeptycki of Lwów who ordered his clergy to hide Jews. At the opposite end of the moral spectrum were the Poles who blackmailed Jews or pointed them out to the Germans. But both groups, rescuers and extortionists, were exceptions. By and large most Poles were simply acquiescent. Frightened and threatened themselves, they were more concerned about their own survival and that of their loved ones than to be overly concerned about what Germans were doing to Jews. Some even expressed satisfaction that the Germans were solving Poland's Jewish problem.

Polish writers looking back at the nightmare of Nazi German occupation tended until recent years to focus almost exclusively on the sufferings endured by ethnic Poles, an aspect of the war too often neglected in the literature ("the Forgotten Holocaust"). Ethnic Poles, they point out, were slated for what can aptly be described as selective genocide; three million Poles died–intellectuals, Catholic priests, ordinary farmers, even children. These authors highlight the common martyrdom of Jews and Poles ("Bloodshed Unites Us") and the heroism of Poles who helped rescue Jews ("the Samaritans"; "He Who Saves One Life"). They protest that there was no more blackmail or extortion in Poland than elsewhere in occupied Europe and that the acquiescence of the majority of Poles was no different from that which prevailed in Western Europe and the United States (including that in the American Jewish community).

More recently, at least since 1987, a number of prominent Polish writers have been much more self-critical. Jan Błoński, Jerzy Turowicz, and others (see Antony Polonsky, *My Brother's Keeper?*) have begun to address the neuralgic issue of the Polish response to the mass murder that the Third Reich carried out largely on Polish soil. Though Poles certainly could have done more to rescue Jews, it is generally recognized that they could not have done much. But these authors still acknowledge that they feel a certain amount of shame and guilt—not that Poles participated in the murder or withheld reasonable assistance, but that they were widely indifferent to the crime perpetrated before their eyes. Their criticism of the Polish response to the Shoah is that Poles held back. Despite the long cherished and cultivated Polish tradition of resistance to tyranny, the Poles, they say, did not rise up en masse and resist what the Nazis were doing. They thus condemned the Jews to much lonelier and more solitary deaths than they would have suffered otherwise.

These self-critical opinions have understandably sparked a defensive reaction and debate within Poland. It is a debate in my opinion best left to Poles and Polish Jews. As an American who has always lived comfortably in the West, I have never felt competent to pass moral judgment on what people—Poles or Jews—did to survive under the horrific circumstances of the Nazi German occupation. As a Roman Catholic theologian, however, I do feel qualified to pass appropriate judgment on the teaching and leadership of my church.

There was not a direct link between Catholic (including Polish) anti-semitism and the Holocaust. The antisemitism of the Nazis was racist and pagan in inspiration, and they despised Christianity for its links to Judaism. But there was an indirect connection between Christian, including Catholic, antisemitism and the Holocaust, the linkage of a *conditio sine qua non*. The Holocaust would have been inconceivable without the prior history of alienation and hostility which divided Christians and Jews. It was an alienation for which the church was not wholly but greatly responsible, and a hostility for which church leaders have yet to acknowledge accountability.

10. The Polish Bishops in 1990 issued a pastoral letter on Jewish-Catholic Relations. In it, after noting the heroic example of Poles who risked their lives to rescue Jews, the bishops acknowledged the culpability of the Polish Catholics who cooperated with the "final solution" or were indifferent to it. The bishops asked for forgiveness if

only one Polish Christian caused a death or could have helped and did not. The bishops' letter was historic. It described antisemitism as contrary to the gospel. After it was issued, priests reported incidents of Catholics confessing antisemitism as a sin. There is no telling what difference such a letter would have made in the mid-1930s. As the foregoing pages amply demonstrate, the popular Catholic attitude during the Shoah was not substantially different from what it had been in the years prior to it: Jews were regarded as excluded from what has been called the "universe of obligation" (Helen Fein), that circle of persons to whom rules apply and obligations are owed. The conviction that Jews were hostile to Catholic interests constituted a major reason for that exclusion.

While asking for forgiveness for the failures of Polish Catholics during the German occupation, the Polish bishops justifiably insisted, "Not by our wish, and not by our hands.... Murderers did this on our land." The bishops' letter addressed the Holocaust, but not the years prior to it. There was no acknowledgement of the fact that for years the church's hierarchy and clergy had fostered antisemitic attitudes that would only naturally view a Jewish calamity with something less than outrage. The Polish bishops wrote of failures of the Poles but not of the church. They did not acknowledge the culpability of their forebears in the hierarchy, clergy, Catholic Action, and Catholic press. More likely than not, the Polish bishops did not admit guilt at the highest levels of the church, because the Holy See has not done so either.

I find it altogether remarkable that there are Catholic Poles who were never antisemitic, who actively fought against antisemitism, yet feel they cannot totally absolve themselves of collective moral responsibility for the antisemitism that swept their country on the eve of the Holocaust. I regret that I do not perceive a similar acknowledgement of responsibility from the Holy See for the failures of the institutional church. I hope that the foregoing study will encourage the Vatican and European bishops to do so. For institutions as well as for individuals, confession is good for the soul. But confession, of course, to be efficacious, requires a firm purpose of amendment.

The Second Vatican Council, in its decree on non-Christian religions (*Nostra Aetate*) marked a watershed in the way Catholics and subsequently other Christians view Jews and Judaism. The Council rejected the unofficial albeit popular tradition of blaming Jews for the death of Jesus. It repudiated the idea that Jews have been rejected by God and are now superseded by the Christian church. But, as this study shows, these were hardly the issues that preoccupied Catholic leaders and writers in Poland or anywhere else. Jewish guilt for Jesus' death may have been assumed and the idea of rejection may have been below the surface, but the main reasons for Catholic antagonism against Jews were much more contemporary, this worldly, and self-interested.

Just as much as the statement on Jews, the Second Vatican Council's declaration on religious liberty (*Dignitatis Humanae*) constituted a revolution in Catholic thinking. The prevailing Catholic teaching prior to the Council was that governments were not justified in treating all religions as equal. Only one faith could be true, and error had no rights. Breaking with that essentially illiberal stance, the Second Vatican Council taught that neither truth nor error but only people have rights. And they have those rights in virtue of their human dignity, whether they are in error or not.

Obviously this teaching has implications, which the Vatican unfortunately has yet to develop: implications for the nature of just governments; implications for defining the appropriate role of the church in modern pluralistic society. Governments committed to separation of church and state are not the same as governments committed to secularity as an ideology. Not all religiously neutral governments respect integrity of conscience. And not all governments with established churches or religions necessarily persecute religious minorities or dissenters. But experience teaches that separation of church and state makes for better government and better religion. The new climate of respect, dialogue, and cooperation among Christians and between Christians and Jews would have been unthinkable without what we in the United States call "Jeffersonian democracy"—and what conservative European Catholics once called "Masonic democracy."

If one takes the gospels as a standard for Christianity and the Second Vatican Council as a criterion for catholicity, one must conclude that, at least with respect to the Jewish question, the Polish Socialist Party, Freemasons and other Polish liberals were much more Christian and catholic than the leadership of the Roman Catholic church. The Polish Socialist Party was the only important organization in prewar Poland opposed to antisemitism. In Poland, unlike the rest of Europe, a political organization of considerable and even growing strength set its face squarely against the antisemitic campaign that engulfed Europe in the mid-1930s. Unlike other European nations, Gentile opposition to antisemitism was not restricted to isolated individuals. That opposition came, however, from groups and individuals, including lay Catholics, who criticized and opposed the church's anti-liberal policies. Opposition to antisemitism came from those whom the church's leaders considered to be their enemies.

The destruction of so much of European Jewry on Polish soil was a crucial event not only for Jews and Poles but for western civilization and the Christian churches altogether. The events that led up to it, the attitudes that made it possible, deserve the closest scrutiny. It has not been pleasant for me, reckoning with these less than admirable aspects of my church's past. I have tried to be accurate and fair in my exposition and analysis. If I have been critical of the Catholic church, it has been out of loyalty to some of its best traditions.

The leadership of the Catholic church has never taken criticism well. The belligerence it once reserved for liberal Jews and Freemasons, it now directs toward its own liberal theologians. For me personally, however, one of the more gratifying corollaries of this study is the confirmation it affords a longstanding conviction of mine. No one serves the church so well as its critics.

Index